FIELD GUIDE TO
WILD FLOWERS
OF SOUTHERN EUROPE

Paul Davies
Bob Gibbons

D1642866

The Crowood Press

First published in 1993 by
The Crowood Press Ltd
Ramsbury, Marlborough
Wiltshire SN8 2HR

www.crowood.com

This impression 2013

British Library Cataloguing-in-Publication Data
A catalogue record for this book is available from the British
Library.

ISBN 9780 1 85223 659 5

All photographs by the authors with the exception of the
following: Bernd-Hansen R, 275 (bottom right), 291 (bottom
centre), 305 (top left); Martin S, 43 (top left); Wilson P. 21
(bottom left), 23 (bottom right), 99 (centre right), 185 (centre
left), 231 (bottom right), 257 (bottom centre).

Line drawings by Chris D Orr.

Phototypeset by FIDO Imagesetting, Witney, Oxon

Edited and designed by D&N Publishing, Hungerford, Berkshire

Printed and bound in Malaysia by Times Offset (M) Sdn. Bhd.

Contents

The Scope of this Book

This book is a pocketable guide to the flowers of southern Europe, covering the area defined below. The total flora of the area that we cover probably approaches 10,000 species, so it is clearly impossible to cover more than a modest proportion of these in a single-volume field guide. To make the number of species more manageable, we have excluded high-mountain specialist plants, which are generally well covered by Alpine flower guides, and we have limited coverage of those species that are also prevalent in northern Europe (which is covered by a wealth of more complete field guides), unless they are obvious features of the flora of the area.

Of the remaining species, we have selected those that we believe most people are likely to notice. We have therefore concentrated on the conspicuous and common species, but with appropriate reference to similar less widespread species where relevant. We have also included a number of naturalized species that are not native, and a few obvious and interesting crop species; it is by no means always obvious whether a plant is native or not, and it seems unnecessary to introduce a rigorous division, when the intention of the book is to help the user to identify all plants that are likely to be noticed. Overall, we cover some plants in more detail than others. For some families, which are inconspicuous or notoriously difficult to identify, only a low proportion of the species in the family are covered; for more obvious or easier families, we have included a much higher percentage, and for orchids we have included every species that regularly occurs in the area.

The geographical coverage of this book is shown on the map on page 6. Essentially, we cover the whole of Spain, Portugal and Italy, together with the southern part of France, thus juxtaposing roughly with the area covered by most guides to northern European and Alpine floras. The areas further east, notably the former Yugoslavia, Greece and the islands, have a very different flora, and warrant a separate guide of their own. In practice, although we give good coverage only to the area defined, users will find the book relevant in many peripheral areas such as south-east Europe and the warmer parts of adjacent central Europe, where many of the same species occur.

How to Use this Book

This book is intended primarily as a visual field guide, based around the photographs, most of which were taken specifically for the purpose. The reader's initial approach will therefore normally be to scan through the pictures to find something that looks similar to the species to be identified. When doing this, bear in mind that colour variations are frequent, and some species habitually occur in two or three colour forms that cannot all be shown in the pictures: *Bellardia trixago* (see page 186), for example, occurs normally as a pink and white plant, but is not infrequently wholly yellow.

If the species cannot readily be matched with a picture, find the plant that seems to be most similar in structure, and check the text for descriptions of similar or related

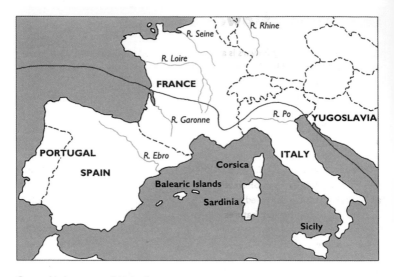

Geographical coverage of this book.

species to see if any of these fit better. Inevitably, there will be occasions when no good match is found, but even in these cases the book should help in identifying the correct plant family.

Generally, we have avoided the use of keys, partly because they demand a level of detail that is finer than most people will want, but also because they are more useful when complete coverage of a group of species is given, and this is rarely the case here.

The descriptions give more details about the plant, especially of features not shown in the photograph. It pays to check the details described in the text to see if they match the plant to be identified. Flowering times may vary from those given, especially on the boundaries of the area covered by this book, or in unusual years. In some cases, we have used line-drawings to clarify a feature that is important but not visible in the photograph. For example, some species may have highly distinctive fruits.

Each description follows the same pattern, with details of the size and type of plant, the leaf shape, the flowers, and the fruits, though not all aspects are necessarily covered. Then, there follows a brief description of the most likely habitats within the distribution area. The average flowering time is denoted by '**Fl**' followed by the numbers of the months: for example, '**Fl** 3–5' means 'flowering time March–May'.

After the description of the main species, there may be a description of subsidiary species, which are less common or conspicuous, but worth mentioning. The salient differences from the main species are given. If no additional information on flowering time, distribution and habitats is given, these will be similar to those of the main species.

Identifying Flowers

The process of identifying flowers is a skill that can be acquired and used anywhere in the world. Whilst good books are essential to the identification process, it also helps greatly to set about it in the right way. Some general guidelines to identifying flowers, with this or any other book, are:

1. Take the book to the flower where possible. This is very important. Apart from obviating the need to pick the flower and risk it being damaged by the time you get to the book, there are also other factors: for example, you may pick a piece of a plant, then discover later that you needed to know the shape of the basal leaves, whether it was spreading by rhizomes, or whether it was annual or perennial. These questions are much more easily answered on the spot.

2. Look carefully at the key features of the plant, and especially details such as number of petals; this rapidly improves one's understanding of the relationships and differences between plants. Two plants that may look superficially similar can turn out to be very different on closer examination: for example the attractive blue-flowered *Aphyllanthes monspeliensis* (see page 246) can look very like a bushy blue flax *Linum* species; however, closer examination will reveal that *Aphyllanthes* has six petals and narrow linear leaves (indicating its relationship with the Lily family), in contrast to the five-petalled flax flowers and their broader net-veined leaves. If possible, carry a small hand-lens (preferably × 8 or × 10) to look more closely at features of the plant, some of which may be useful for identification. When using the lens, maximum magnification and detail is obtained by holding the lens to the eye, then bringing the plant up until it comes into focus, while keeping it in as bright a light as possible.

Areas of Botanical Interest

Although most of this part of southern Europe is of some botanical interest, and most of the species in the book are reasonably widespread, there are nevertheless some areas that are of especial interest, where the visitor can expect to see many more flowers, both common and rare. We have made a selection of over 50 of these, from areas that we have visited. No attempt has been made to give detailed species descriptions, but enough information is given to provide the flavour of the area, together with suggested times to visit it.

PORTUGAL
Portugal forms most of the western boundary of the region, and it is strongly affected by the Atlantic weather systems. In general, the climate is warm and moist, though the Algarve has a climate similar to the Mediterranean areas. For its size, Portugal boasts a rich flora with over 3,000 species, of which around 65 are endemic.

1. The Northern Mountains

Much of northern Portugal consists of mountain areas. In general, these are well-wooded and unspoilt by major developments, though many areas are cultivated. Places of particular interest to the botanist include Portugal's only national park, at Peneda-Geres, where granite mountains reach a maximum height of 1,545m. The flora is rich, with a mixture of northern, western, southern and endemic species. The Serra de Estrela, in north-central Portugal, consists of acid, well-rounded mountains reaching 1,991m (the highest peak in Portugal); there is a varied flora, though not as intensively rich as that of limestone areas. The whole area of the northern Portugal mountains is good for *Narcissus* species, heathers and leguminous shrubs, amongst other things. It is best visited between April and July.

2. Serra de Arabida

The Serra de Arabida, part of which has been declared a nature park, lies south of Lisbon and west of Setubal. The mountains are limestone and largely covered with garrigue and maquis. The herbaceous flora is very rich, with a fine mixture comprising elements of both Mediterranean and Lusitanian plants, with over 1,000 species recorded. Bulbous plants such as tulips and fritillaries are not uncommon, and there are many species of orchid. April to June is the best time for a visit.

3. The Algarve

This is a superbly varied area which, though increasingly developed for tourism, retains much of interest. It has very mild winters and warm springs, which means that plant-hunting can begin early in the year. Areas of particular interest include: the windswept western limestone headlands of St Vincent and Sagres, which have many endemics and rarities; the acidic Monchique mountains just inland from Lagos, which are well-wooded, though increasingly planted with Eucalyptus trees; and the limestone *Barrocal* area which runs roughly parallel with the coast, a little inland, where orchids and bulbous plants occur in reasonable numbers in the less-cultivated areas. The coast has numerous habitats, including sand-dunes and saltmarshes, and in many areas, such as around Faro, there are impressive displays of the uncommon parasite *Cistanche phelypeae* (see page 188). The best time to visit the Algarve is from February to May.

SPAIN

Spain is a large country with an extremely rich flora and numerous areas or habitats of interest. It is impossible to do justice to such variety and wealth in a brief description, and many good areas will be found elsewhere. Climatically, Spain is extremely varied: the driest parts of Europe are to be found in the south around Almería and the Cabo de Gata, while there are some very wet areas in the northern mountains.

1. The Coto Doñana Area

This area lies in south-west Spain, south of Seville, with the famous national park of Coto Doñana at its centre. The park itself is better known for its fauna than for its flora, and it is difficult to gain adequate access for a study of flowers, except along the extensive coastal dunes that front the park. However, to the west there are further dunes and large areas of heathland and open woodland. The climate is mild in winter and hot in summer, and the additional Atlantic influence brings in occasional extra rain. There are numerous widespread Mediterranean species to be seen, plus specialities like the impressive thrift *Armeria gaditensis*, and the attractive little snowflake *Leucojum trichophyllum*. An early visit is required, from late February through to late May.

2. The Ronda–Grazalema Area

This superb area of limestone mountains lies inland from Marbella, in south-west Spain. The mountains are not high enough to have many mountain specialities, but they are high enough to remain greener and cooler than the adjacent coastal areas, and they are wonderfully unspoilt. The flora is a rich combination of widespread Mediterranean/south European species, pan-European species, and specialities of the area. The area around Grazalema and Ubrique is especially rich in endemics such as the poppy *Papaver rupifragum*, and the lovely shrubby crucifer *Biscutella frutescens*. The best time for a visit is between April and June.

A mass of cornfield-edge weeds in the Sierra de Grazalema, southern Spain, with *Galactites tomentosa*, *Echium plantigeneum* and other plants.

3. The Almería Badlands

Around Almería and the Cabo de Gata lies an extremely arid region, the closest European equivalent to a desert. Inland, around the area known as mini-Hollywood, there is an eroded hilly area reminiscent of Arizona. Although many widespread species are rare here, it is the home of many other rare, local or endemic specialities that thrive on warmth and drought. The strange *Cynomorium coccineum* (see page 32) is not uncommon, while many salt-steppe species occur. Best from March to May.

4. Southern Spain Mountains

Although some of the plants of the higher sierras are outside the scope of this book, there are nevertheless many species of interest in these mountain ranges. Sierras such as the Sierra Nevada and Sierra de Cazorla are especially rich in endemic species, including the beautiful *Viola cazorlensis* in the Cazorla mountains. There are huge areas of unspoilt country to explore in these mountains, and the limestone peaks, cliffs and woods of Cazorla are especially rich. May and June are best.

5. The Sierra de Montserrat

The extraordinary conglomerate peaks of the Sierra de Montserrat to the north of Barcelona are well known for their fantastic shapes and their ancient monastery. They are also a largely unspoilt, well-wooded area, rich in flowers. There is a good mixture of Mediterranean, montane and more widespread species, depending on the aspect and shade cover. May and June are the best months for a visit.

6. The Picos de Europa

This is a superb area for plant-hunting, with a very rich flora amidst wonderful and largely unspoilt scenery, lying just south-west of Santander. Although the peaks are high enough to support plants that are beyond the scope of this book, the lower areas have a marvellous mixture of hay meadows, pastures, woods and wet areas that collectively support many species of interest. The hay meadows alone have had over 600 species recorded from them, and they are some of the finest in Europe. The area is especially rich in *Narcissus* species, and is also good for orchids. The best time for a visit is in May and June, though the high peaks are good later than this.

The Cantabrian Mountains continue westwards, and have much of interest, though the mountains are generally more acidic and less jagged than the Picos de Europa, with a less spectacular flora.

7. The Spanish Pyrenees

The Pyrenees are one of Europe's finest mountain ranges, and form the boundary between France and Spain. On the Spanish side they fall gradually, with many secondary mountain ranges, towards the plains. Apart from their western end, the Spanish Pyrenees are relatively dry and warm at lower altitudes, which allows a wonderful mixture of habitats and species to thrive, from Mediterranean, through temperate forest, to high Alpine. There are also many endemic and local species. Good centres for plant-hunting include Ordesa, Val de Pineta, Val d'Aran, the higher parts of Andorra, and the national park of Aigües-Tortes y lago de St Mauricio. The best time for a visit is from May to July.

8. The Balearic Islands

The Balearic Islands (Mallorca, Minorca and Ibiza) are sometimes dismissed simply as a busy tourist destination, but to the botanist they are of great interest and are easily and cheaply accessible. The total flora of the islands is not large (about 1,300, plus introduced species), but it is an easy area in which to see plants, and one never has to travel far to see something new. In general, the mountain areas are least spoilt, though there are also protected coastal areas such as at S'Albufeira on the east coast of Mallorca. In addition to widespread Mediterranean species, there are also a number of Balearic endemic species and subspecies to be seen. The best time for a visit is from late February to early May, or a little later for the higher mountains.

FRANCE

1. Les Landes
South of Bordeaux, there is a vast area of low-lying land known as Les Landes. The character of the area is due to windblown sand from the Atlantic invading former coastal marshes. This was once a vast, wild, uninhabited area. Now, it is heavily planted with pines, partly drained, and with an increasingly built-up coast. However, it is still an excellent place to go to see a wide range of plants that thrive on sand-dunes, heaths, open acid woods, and neutral to acidic waters and wetlands. The climate is mild in winter and hot in summer. The best times for a visit are from early April to early July.

2. The French Pyrenees
The north side of the Pyrenees, which lies almost entirely in France, is rather different in character to the Spanish side, with higher rainfall, and steeper slopes falling quickly to the plains. The flora is different, too: there are more northern species and fewer Mediterranean species, except at the eastern end. There are many superb unspoiled habitats, especially deciduous and coniferous woodlands, pastures, meadows, lakes and wetlands. Good centres for botanical exploration include Gedre or Gavarnie and Bagnères de Luchon. The season is relatively long, thanks to the higher rainfall and the advantage of a wide altitude range. April is good for crocuses, *Narcissus Erythronium,* and other early flowers, though access can be difficult. May to August is good for a continuing range of species, and even September can be quite rewarding.

3. Les Corbières
This is a little-known hilly limestone area in south-west France, centred around Carcassone and merging southwards into the Pyrenees. The area has a rich mixture of Mediterranean and Pyrenean plants, together with many from further north. The limestone soils support a good range of orchids, together with bulbous plants such as *Fritillaria pyrenaica.* The best time to visit is between late March and early June, though higher or damper areas continue to have plants of interest after this.

4. The Auvergne
The southern central part of France is dominated by the Massif Central. At the heart of this lies the volcanic region known as the Auvergne, of which a huge area is designated as a natural regional park. Although there are a few montane plants, much of the interest for the botanist lies in the wealth of flowers in the lower habitats. It is a

region of cold winters and relatively damp summers, so there are numerous wetland habitats, together with extensive woodlands, pastures and meadows, and even the roadsides are excellent. Such plants as do occur tend to be abundant, and fields can be white or yellow with *Narcissus* species, while roadsides can be covered with orchids. It is worth visiting at any time from late April throughout the summer months.

5. The Causses
Occupying the south-western part of the Massif Central, around the town of Millau, the Causses form a huge area of lightly populated limestone hills. The whole area is very unspoilt, and rich in limestone-loving flowers in grassland, woods, bare rock habitats, and scrub. Orchids are an especially notable feature, with over 40 species recorded, many of them in considerable abundance. There is an intriguing blend of species, with increasing numbers of Mediterranean plants towards the south, and a number of local specialities which include two endemic species of *Ophrys* orchids. The best time for a visit is between late April and late June, though there are still flowers to be seen after this.

6. The Cévennes
The south-eastern part of the Massif Central is composed of moderately high and rather acidic granite or schist mountains. It has a markedly different flora from the adjacent Causses, though there are areas of limestone, too. The plant life is rich, and combines elements of Alpine, lowland limestone, Mediterranean and northern flora, all in an attractive and varied landscape. The best time to visit is mid-May to mid-July.

7. The Lubéron
The Lubéron Natural Regional Park lies to the north of Aix-en-Provence. It consists of limestone hills with deep valleys, and has extensive areas of scrub, grassland and rough woodland. The flora is a rich mixture of species, with many Mediterranean plants and numerous species that are rare in northern Europe but abundant here. It is another excellent area for orchids. It is best visited from April (in the warmer, drier areas) through to late June.

8. The Massif des Maures
This is an area of dry hills on rather acid schistose rock, north of Cannes and St Tropez. The hills are well-wooded, with areas of scrub and more open grassland, and extensive heaths and open woodland to the north. Although it lacks many of the lime-loving species, there is an excellent variety of general Mediterranean species, especially plants of maquis, such as *Cistus* species and their parasites. Late March to early June is the best time for a visit.

9. Port-Cros Island
The whole of Port-Cros and its adjacent sea has been declared a national park. It lies just off the coast near Le Lavandou, and is an excellent place to see relatively

Coastal flowers and scrub on Port-Cros Island National Park, with Gladiolus and Hare's-tail Grass visible amongst other plants.

undisturbed Mediterranean forest, together with areas of maquis and garrigue, and some more open habitats. The flora is not spectacular, but there are numerous species of interest, such as the sea-ball grass *Posidonia oceanica*, of which there are extensive beds just offshore. The best time for a visit is between late March and early June.

10. The Camargue
The Camargue is the delta of the Rhône, west of Marseilles. Although the region is better known for its birds, the protection of large areas of habitat has allowed a good range of flowers to survive. It is a particularly good area for sand-dune, saltmarsh and wetland plants. Sand-dunes are rare in Mediterranean France, and those along the coast of the Camargue are easily the best examples. Any time between April and July is suitable for a visit.

11. Corsica
Corsica is a large and varied island, with a considerable range of unspoilt habitats remaining. Its rocks are primarily acidic in character, though there are some significant limestone areas, most notably around Bonifacio in the south of the island. There are huge areas of maquis and garrigue, extensive ancient beechwoods, and some good wetlands on the west coast; pastures and hay meadows are rare. Particularly good areas include the Desert des Agriates in the north for scrub plants; the Asco valley and Forest of Aitone in the centre for woodland and mountain plants, including endemics; and the area around and to the south of Bonifacio for orchids, coastal plants and limestone specialities. However, virtually the whole island is of interest to the botanist, and most of it is remarkably unspoilt by development or agriculture.

ITALY

1. The Portofino Peninsula
Situated south-east of Genoa, the Portofino peninsula juts out into the Mediterranean. It is protected from development by its natural regional park status and still retains extensive scrub and woodland habitats with some open grassland and rocky cliffs. The flora is a rich mixture of Mediterranean and more northern or western elements, which can occur because of the high humidity in the wooded valleys. Access is possible only on foot. The best time for a visit is somewhere between late March and early June.

2. The Maremma Regional Park
Maremma comprises a substantial area of coastal and hilly habitats lying roughly south of Siena. The main habitats are damp pasture, sand-dunes, stone-pine forest, and scrub on the limestone hills just inland. The flora is varied and rich, though lacking much in the way of rarities. Access into the area is possible only on foot. The best period for a visit is between March and June, or a little later for the Sea Daffodils *Pancratium maritimum*.

3. The Circeo National Park
This small national park lies on the Mediterranean coast south-east of Rome. Considerable development has taken place recently, though it still possesses a reasonable mixture of sand-dunes, lagoons, woodland, and limestone habitats. It is a good place to see a range of widespread plants, coastal species, and plants of limestone scrub. It is best visited between March and June.

4. The Gargano Peninsula
The Gargano peninsula is a large limestone headland jutting out into the Adriatic, due east of Rome. Despite the popularity of the coastal zone as a holiday resort, it remains one of the finest places in Europe to see flowers. The main habitats are scrub, grassland and bare rock on limestone, and extensive mixed deciduous forest. Altogether, over 2,000 species of flowering plant have been recorded, including over 60 species of orchid. All parts that are away from the main towns are of some interest. The best period to go is from March to June, though some woodland areas will remain of interest later than this.

5. Vesuvius
The volcanic cone of Vesuvius, near Naples, has a remarkably rich flora, comprising over 1,000 species. These are a mixture of montane, Mediterranean, and endemic or local specialities, and there are some fine deciduous woodlands on the southern slopes. The mountain is best visited from April to June.

6. The Lattari Peninsula

This limestone peninsula lies west of Salerno, jutting out into the Mediterranean towards Capri. The flora and mixture of habitats is rather similar to that of Gargano, though slightly less rich mainly because the woods are less extensive. Orchids, bulbous plants and endemics are all well represented. The best time to visit is between March and early June.

7. Sicily

Sicily is a substantial island, with numerous mountains (including the vast Mount Etna) and many unspoiled habitats. Among the many good areas for plants are the following: Mount Etna proposed national park, which has a spectacular and interesting flora that includes endemics; the Zingaro Nature Reserve on the north coast west of Palermo, which has numerous garrigue flowers including orchids; and the natural park in the Nebrodi mountains, close to the north coast. The whole of Sicily is good for orchids. Despite its extreme southern locality, Sicily is not such an early flowering island as Sardinia, perhaps because there is little low-lying undeveloped land. It is best visited between April and early June, or later for high altitudes.

8. Sardinia

Sardinia is a very large island lying immediately south of Corsica, but it belongs to Italy rather than France. It is remarkably undeveloped, similar to Corsica, but even larger and more varied. Almost everywhere on the island is of interest to the botanist, but there are several areas of particular interest. There is the Gennargentu area on the east coast and adjacent mountains; and north and west of Arbatax, there is an extensive hilly wilderness area with numerous habitats on both acid and limestone rock. The Giara di Gesturi is an extensive plateau on acidic to neutral rock, east of Oristano, which is dominated mainly by pasture and cork oaks, with scattered open water and wetlands. The flora is rich and includes most of Sardinia's orchids. The north-eastern tip of Sardinia, closest to Corsica, has a good range of habitats. The island is worth a visit from mid-March through to early June, or later in the mountains and forests.

THE MALTESE ARCHIPELAGO

Malta and Gozo are the two main islands of this small country that lies south of Sicily, almost as close to Africa as it is to Europe. The position and limestone geology of the islands mean that they have an inherently rich flora, but this has been severely affected by agriculture, tourism and general wanton destruction. The best areas are on the north-western end of Malta, and over much of Gozo – especially at the western end – and on the dunes at Ir-ramla. One big advantage of Malta is that its southerly position allows a reasonable range of species to flower at any time of year, but in other respects it is a depressing place for the naturalist. Peak time to visit is March to May.

Conifers, Gymnosperms

PINE FAMILY, PINACEAE

Cone-bearing trees, usually evergreen (except larches). Leaves needle-like. Male and female flowers separate, on the same tree.

Silver Fir *Abies alba* A large tree, reaching 50m, with greyish, scaly bark. Leaves narrow, 2–3cm long, flexible, deep green above, whitish below, and slightly notched at the tip, spread out into 2 ranks. Cones erect, up to 20cm long, cylindrical-ovoid, with conspicuous bracts between the scales. Frequent as a woodland tree in mountain areas from E Spain westwards; also widely planted. Fl 4–5.
Spanish Fir *A. pinsapo* similar to above, but has stiffly pointed leaves, 1–1.5cm long, arranged evenly around the shoots. Buds resinous (not so in Silver Fir); cone bracts not visible. Very local in the mountains of SW Spain.

European Larch *Larix decidua* A deciduous tree, to 35m (or more), with greyish-brown scaly bark. The needle-like leaves are borne in clusters of 30–40, green above but with 2 paler bands below, 1.5–3cm long. Female cones have conspicuous red bracts when young, ripening to woody ovoid cones 3–4cm long; male cones small, yellowish. Common on the slopes of mountains in France and Italy, also widely planted and naturalized. Fl 3–5.

PINES *Pinus*

(a) Mature cones normally at least 7cm long.

Maritime Pine *Pinus pinaster* A large pyramidal tree, to 40m, with dark red-brown fissured bark; the lower trunks of older trees are often bare of branches; twigs reddish-brown. Needles 10–25cm long, stiff and spine-tipped, greyish-green. The female cones (illus.) are ovoid, symmetrical, 8–22cm long, in clusters of 2–8; the cone scales are usually spiny. Occurs throughout the area, both in coastal habitats and in the lower montane zone; also widely planted. Fl 4–5.

Aleppo Pine *Pinus halepensis* A medium-sized slender tree, to 20m, with distinctly twisted branches; the bark and twigs are greyish. Leaves mid-green, flexible, 6–15cm long, twisted and curved. Female cones (illus.) 6–12cm long, roughly ovate, reddish at first, solitary or 2–3 together, on thick stalks 1–2cm long; cone scales shiny, not spiny. Widespread and common throughout the area in a range of dry habitats; often forms woodland. Fl 3–5.

Stone, or **Umbrella, Pine** *Pinus pinea* A distinctive tree, normally with an umbrella-shaped crown, up to 30m. Bark greyish-brown, peeling to reddish. Leaves stiff, pointed, 10–20cm long, with tiny forward-facing teeth on the margins. Cones heavy, almost spherical when open, 8–15cm long, shiny red-brown, with large seeds (illus.). Native and common throughout the warmer parts of the area, especially near the coast; also planted. Fl 4–5. *The seeds are eaten as a delicacy.*

(b) Mature cones normally less than 7cm long.

Black, or **Corsican, Pine** *Pinus nigra* Very variable, up to 50m. Bark greyish-brown, dark, rough; young shoots yellowish. Needles dark green on both sides, stiff, pointed, minutely toothed, 10–15cm long, densely clothing branches. Cones solitary or in small clusters, ovoid, 3–8cm long, unstalked (illus.). Ssp *salzmannii* occurs in the mountainous parts of the area; ssp *nigra* reaches southwards into Italy; ssp *laricio* (**Corsican Pine**) is native in Corsica and parts of S Italy. Fl 4–5. **Scots Pine** *P. sylvestris* is similar to above, but has reddish bark on the upper trunks of old trees; needles blue-green, less than 8cm long, cones (illus.) distinctly stalked. Almost throughout area, especially in the hills; absent from Corsica. Widely planted. Fl 4–6.

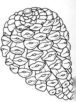

Maritime Pine

Aleppo Pine

Stone Pine
Umbrella Pine (left)

Black Pine

Scots Pine

CYPRESS FAMILY, CUPRESSACEAE

Evergreen coniferous trees with small scale-like leaves and globular cones.

Italian, or **Funeral, Cypress** *Cupressus sempervirens f. sempervirens*   A distinctive narrowly columnar tree, described as the 'vegetable minarets of the Mediterranean landscape', up to 30m. Leaves dark green, scale-like, only 5–10mm long, closely overlapping. Female cones roughly spherical, 2.5–4cm across, yellowish-brown when mature. The native form, *f. horizontalis*, which has more spreading branches, does not occur in this area; the common form in this area is the columnar form, which is very widely planted in gardens and cemeteries throughout. Fl 3–5.

Prickly Juniper *Juniperus oxycedrus*   A shrub or small tree, up to 8m (rarely more), with separate male and female plants. Leaves needle-like, sharply pointed, 1–2.5cm long, in whorls of 3, with 2 whitish bands along the upper surface. The female cones are globose, 8–15mm in diameter, ripening to red-brown. Three subspecies occur: ssp *oxycedrus* has cones 8–10mm in diameter, and occurs in dry rocky places throughout the area; ssp *macrocarpa* has cones 12–15mm in diameter, and occurs mainly in coastal areas, especially on sand-dunes; ssp *transtagna* has very narrow leaves, less than 1mm wide, and occurs only on sand in SW Portugal. Fl 4–5. **Common Juniper** *J. communis* is rather similar to above, but has only 1 broad pale band on the upper surface of the leaf, and the fruits are bluish-black when ripe. Widespread in dry places throughout.

Phoenician Juniper *Juniperus phoenicea*   A shrub to 8m, spreading or erect. Distinguished from the above 2 species by the tiny scale-like leaves with membranous margins closely pressed to the shoots. Female cones spherical, 8–14mm across, dark red when ripe. In maquis, garrigue and sandy areas throughout. Fl 2–4.

YEW FAMILY, TAXACEAE

Evergreen trees or shrubs, with spirally arranged flattened leaves. Single seed surrounded by a fleshy aril.

Yew *Taxus baccata*   A broadly conical, dark-green evergreen tree to 25m, with reddish-brown flaking bark. Leaves dark green above, paler with 2 yellowish bands below, linear, flattened, 2–4cm long, abruptly pointed. Male and female flowers both minute; fruits conspicuous, ovoid, fleshy, 6–10mm long, ripening to scarlet. Local throughout, usually in dry, rocky or lime-rich areas. Fl 2–4.

JOINT-PINE FAMILY, EPHEDRACEAE

A small family of conifers, unusual in not being trees or large shrubs. Shoots green, appearing leafless.

Joint-pine *Ephedra distachya*   A low subshrub, to 1m, with erect stems from creeping rhizomes. Stems green, leafless except for tiny scale-leaves at joints, branched with upwardly slanting branches. Male and female flowers separate; small, greenish-yellow, the males in clusters, the females in pairs. Fruit globose, fleshy and reddish, with the seed protruding. In dry places, sandy and rocky coasts, and river banks, throughout. Fl 3–6. *E. fragilis* is similar to above, but is climbing or prostrate, to 4m, and has fragile stems that break easily at the nodes; the seeds are completely enclosed by the fleshy fruit, not protruding. In dry, sandy or calcareous places in the W Mediterranean area. Fl 4–6.

Seed Plants, Angiosperms

WILLOW AND POPLAR FAMILY, SALICACEAE

Deciduous trees or shrubs, with alternate leaves having stipules. Flowers in catkins, males and females separate.

White Poplar *Populus alba* A medium-sized tree, to 20m, with a broad crown, and greyish-white bark becoming darker and more fissured with age; there are usually numerous suckers around the base. Leaves ovate-triangular, but deeply lobed (illus.), green above and greyish-white below, with a 3–4cm long white stalk. Catkins cylindrical, 4–8cm long in flower, longer in fruit, drooping; males have bright-red stamens. Local in damp and sandy places, and frequently planted as a roadside tree or for coastal shelter, throughout. Fl 3–4. **Grey Poplar** *P. canescens* is similar to above, but differs in being larger, to 30m or more, with leaves much less lobed (illus.). The catkin scales are more deeply cut in Grey Poplar. Occurs in similar places; also often planted. Fl 2–4.

Black Poplar *Populus nigra* A medium-sized tree to 30m, with a broad uneven crown, and a short dark-brown trunk that has numerous bosses and pro-truberances, but rarely suckers. Leaves ovate to diamond-shaped, toothed but not lobed (illus.), mid-green above, shiny, 5–10cm long, with a green, flattened petiole. Male catkins reddish, about 5cm long; female catkins longer. In wet places, river valleys, fields and roadsides, almost throughout; often naturalized. Fl 3–4. **Lombardy Poplar** *P. nigra* var. *italica* has erect branches, giving it a narrow columnar habit; it is invariably male. Widely planted for ornament and shelter.

WALNUT FAMILY, JUGLANDACEAE

Deciduous trees, with alternate leaves and single-seeded fruits.

Common Walnut *Juglans regia* A medium-height spreading tree, to 30m, usually less, with greyish bark becoming cracked and fissured with age. Leaves alternate, pinnate, with 7–9 elliptical untoothed leaflets 6–15cm long. Male catkins 5–15cm long, pendent, yellowish-green; female flowers in short erect spikes. The fruit is shiny green, ovoid and hairless, 4–5cm long; the single seed is the walnut. Native to SE Europe, but widely planted and often naturalized throughout. Fl 4–6. **Black Walnut** *J. nigra* has 15–23 narrower toothed leaflets, and the fruit is hairy. Native to N America, planted in a few places in the east of the area.

BIRCH FAMILY, BETULACEAE

Deciduous trees or shrubs with alternate leaves. Male flowers in hanging catkins, female flowers erect.

Common Alder *Alnus glutinosa* A small to medium tree, reaching 20m, with dark grey-brown bark, fissuring with age. Twigs are hairless, sticky when young. Leaves rounded, blunt, 4–10cm long, widest above the middle, toothed or wavy-edged, mid-green. Male catkins thinly cylindrical, pendent, 3–5cm long, purplish becoming yellower; female catkins ovoid, 8–15mm long, stalked, reddish when young, becoming green then eventually woody; all catkins appear before the leaves. Common by water or in wet places, virtually throughout. Fl 2–3. **Italian Alder** *A. cordata* differs from above in having only 1–3 female catkins in a cluster (cf. 3–5 in Common Alder), and leaves that are usually heart-shaped at the base. Occurs as a native plant in Corsica and Italy, but often planted elsewhere. Fl 2–4.

Grey Poplar catkins (left)

Black Poplar catkins (right)

White Poplar

Walnut (right)

Grey Poplar

Black Poplar

Black Walnut (left)

Common Alder male catkins (right)

HAZEL FAMILY, CORYLACEAE

Deciduous trees or shrubs. Male flowers in pendent catkins, female flowers paired in bracts. Fruit a nut.

Hornbeam *Carpinus betulus* A deciduous tree, to 30m, with a short, often twisted trunk, and silvery-grey bark with darker bands, becoming fissured with age; often pollarded. Leaves oval, pointed, 5–10cm long, distinctly pleated, double-toothed (illus.). The male catkins are pendulous, up to 5cm long, greenish tinged red; female flowers smaller, but becoming conspicuous as the fruit ripens by enlargement of a group of paired, deeply lobed bracts (illus.). Frequent in woods and hedgerows from the Pyrenees eastwards; also often planted. **Fl** 4–5. **Oriental Hornbeam** *C. orientalis* is rather similar to above, but has smaller leaves, to 6cm long, more wedge-shaped at base (illus.), and the bracts enclosing the fruit are toothed, not lobed (illus.). Mainly eastern, reaching Italy and Sicily.

Hop Hornbeam *Ostrya carpinifolia* A deciduous shrub or small tree, to 10m, occasionally more. Very similar in form to Hornbeam, but the fruiting clusters have whitish-green, swollen bladder-like bracts, not toothed or lobed, somewhat resembling a large hop. Locally frequent in deciduous woods, from SE France eastwards. **Fl** 4–5.

Hazel *Corylus avellana* A deciduous shrub, to 6m, occasionally more, with a broad spreading crown and virtually no trunk; very frequently coppiced. Leaves circular to heart-shaped, 5–10cm long, with stiff glandular hairs. Male flowers are familiar pendulous narrow catkins, up to 8cm long; female flowers are an inconspicuous cluster of red stigmas. Fruit is a nut surrounded by toothed bracts, in small clusters. A common woodland undershrub; also in scrub, hedgerows and gardens throughout the area. **Fl** 1–4.

BEECH FAMILY, FAGACEAE

A large family of deciduous and evergreen trees, with male and female flowers separate on the same plant.

Common Beech *Fagus sylvatica* A large, broadly domed tree, to 40m, with a smooth silvery-grey bark; twigs have long, narrow cylindrical pointed reddish-brown buds. Leaves ovate, 5–8cm long, short-pointed, with a wavy but normally untoothed margin, fringed with short hairs when young. Male flowers in dense rounded drooping stalked clusters; female flowers 1–2 together and erect. Fruit consists of 1–2 red-brown nuts enclosed by a woody spiky cup of 4 bracts. In woods and as solitary trees; throughout but mainly in hill areas. **Fl** 4–5.

Sweet Chestnut *Castanea sativa* A large spreading tree, to 30m, with distinctive brownish-grey bark with markedly twisted fissures. Leaves oblong, 10–25cm long, pointed, spiny-toothed, with prominent veins. Male flowers in long narrow pendulous or spreading catkins up to 18cm long, with a few female flowers next to the stalk. Fruit familiar: clusters of red-brown chestnuts enclosed in green cup-like structures, with masses of radiating spines. Common throughout the area, where it has been frequently planted for nuts, often naturalizing. **Fl** 5–7.

Hornbeam
catkins (left)

Hop Hornbeam
catkins (right)

Hornbeam leaf and fruit

Hazel
catkins (left)

Sweet Chestnut (right)

Oriental Hornbeam
leaf and fruit

Beech
male flowers (left)

Turkey Oak

(a) Leaves evergreen, leathery.

Holm, or **Evergreen, Oak** *Quercus ilex*   A medium to large, broad spreading tree, to 25m, with brownish-black bark cracking into square plates. Leaves very variable, oblong to lanceolate, 3–7cm long, usually untoothed (but sometimes toothed on young shoots), dark green above, but whitish and downy below, with prominent veins; stalk 6–20mm long. Male flowers in clusters of greenish-yellow catkins; female flowers tiny. Acorns small, in softly hairy cup 12mm wide. In woods and scrub throughout, except in higher mountain areas; often taken as indicating the extent of the Mediterranean climate zone. **Fl** 3–5. *Q. rotundifolia* is very similar to above, and is now normally considered to be a variant of *Q. ilex*. It differs in having more rounded leaves, with fewer veins, and acorns that are not bitter.

Kermes Oak *Quercus coccifera*   An evergreen shrub or small tree, to 5m. Similar in form to small Holm, Oak, but differs in the leaves, which are always toothed, green below, with veins prominent only on upper surface, and leaf stalks that are less than 4mm long; also differs in the acorn cups, which are covered with spreading prickly scales. In woods and scrub, throughout the lowlands. **Fl** 3–5. *Formerly used as the food plant for coccid insects, source of a red dye.*

Cork Oak *Quercus suber*   Similar in general form to Holm Oak, but differing particularly in the thick corky greyish bark, which is stripped to reveal a reddish trunk below. Leaves very similar to Holm Oak, equally variable, but with 5–8 (not 7–11) pairs of veins, and a rather wavy (not straight) midrib. The acorn cups have loosely spreading scales. Common throughout the area, both in woods and scrub and as a planted tree. **Fl** 3–5. *The cork is harvested commercially, with the first crop taken at 25–30 years, and regularly after that.*

Downy Oak

(b) Leaves deciduous, or semi-evergreen (remaining on tree over winter, then falling), not very leathery.

Turkey Oak *Quercus cerris*   Tree, up to 35m, with grey-brown fissured bark. Leaves roughly oblong, divided with 4–10 lobes on each side (illus.). The acorn cups have long outward-curving downy scales. Native to SE Europe, extending west to SE France, but widely planted and naturalized elsewhere. **Fl** 4–6.

Downy Oak *Quercus pubescens*   A tree, to 25m, with dark grey-brown fissured bark. Twigs and buds densely downy. Leaves roughly oblong, 5–12cm long, wedge-shaped at base, but pinnately lobed to less than half-way to the midrib (illus.), densely downy below (when young), and on the stalk, which is 5–12mm long. Acorns almost unstalked, with downy cup that has closely appressed scales. Widespread and common through most of the area, forming extensive open woods. **Fl** 4–5. **Sessile Oak** *Q. petraea* is similar to above, but not downy (except for leaf undersurface when very young). Mainly northern, but extending into higher parts of this area. **Pyrenean Oak** *Q. pyrenaica* is similar to Downy Oak, but has larger leaves (up to 20cm), which are deeply cut, more than half-way to the midrib, into 4–8 pairs of narrow lobes (illus.); leaves are distinctively pink when emerging in spring. Throughout the area, eastwards to N Italy, mainly in mountain areas. **Fl** 4–5.

Pyrenean Oak

Lusitanian, or **Portuguese, Oak** *Quercus faginea* (including *Q. lusitanica*)   A semi-evergreen tree or large shrub, to 20m. Leaves mid- to dark-green, 4–10cm long somewhat leathery, roughly elliptical, sinuately toothed, hairless above, felted below, short-stalked (illus.). Acorns virtually stalkless, in downy cups with appressed scales. Usually in hilly areas, in the S Iberian Peninsula and Balearic Islands. **Fl** 3–4.

Lusitanian Oak

ELM FAMILY, ULMACEAE

Deciduous trees, with alternate leaves, and unisexual or hermaphrodite flowers in small clusters. The classification and identification of elms *Ulmus* species in S Europe is difficult, and there have been many name changes. Our treatment is very simplified.

Smooth-leaved Elm *Ulmus minor*   A medium to large tree, to 30m, with an open crown; bark grey-brown, with deep ridges and furrows; suckers produced from the base of the plant. Leaves roughly ovate, 6–10cm long, with 7–12 pairs of veins, shiny dark green above, paler below with tufts of hairs in the vein axils; base of leaf unequal. Flowers hermaphrodite, with white stigmas and reddish stamens; fruit elliptical, 1–2cm long, with a single seed above the centre of the wing. Native and frequent throughout, in various forms, and also planted as a street tree. Fl 2–4, before leaves. **Wych Elm** *U. glabra* is similar, but leaves often larger (12–18cm long), with 12–18 pairs of lateral veins and a very uneven base; leaf stalk only 2–5mm long (about 5mm in *U. minor*). The seed is placed centrally in the wing of the fruit. Scattered throughout.

Nettle Tree *Celtis australis*   A medium-sized deciduous tree, to 25m, with smooth grey bark, marked brown. Leaves oval to lanceolate, to 15cm long, narrow and pointed, with sharp teeth, rather downy below. Flowers are in the axils of the leaves, producing globose fruits, 9–12mm in diameter and fleshy, turning blackish when ripe. Occurs as a native plant in woods and scrub throughout the Mediterranean zone; planted as a street tree more widely. Fl 3–5. *The small fleshy fruits are edible and sweet.*

MULBERRY FAMILY, MORACEAE

Small deciduous trees with very variable compound flowers.

Common, or **Black, Mulberry** *Morus nigra*   A small irregular deciduous tree, up to 12m, often with a thick gnarled trunk, with greyish-brown bark. Leaves ovate to heart-shaped, up to 20cm long, glossy green and rough above, paler and downy below. Flowers in ovoid-cylindrical spikes, males 2–3cm long, females shorter. Fruit rounded 2–2.5cm long, cylindrical and knobbly, becoming deep red-purple when ripe. Cultivated and occasionally naturalized throughout most of the area. Fl 4–5. **White Mulberry** *M. alba* is very similar, but leaves are usually narrower and smoother above. Fruit similar, but more commonly pink, with a stalk about 2cm long (common mulberries are almost stalkless). Cultivated and naturalized locally; mainly eastern. *The foliage is used as the food for silkworms.*

Fig *Ficus carica*   A small, spreading, deciduous tree, with separate male and female plants. Leaves alternate, deeply 3- or 5-lobed palmately, up to 20cm long. The flowers are produced inside fleshy pear-shaped structures, which have a small hole at the top to allow pollination; these develop into figs, eventually becoming brownish-purple. Extensively cultivated and naturalized, and locally native, throughout the warmer parts. Fl 6–9.

HEMP FAMILY, CANNABACEAE

Aromatic herbs, usually dioecious flowers 5-parted.

Hemp or **Cannabis** *Cannabis sativa*   A slender erect strong-smelling leafy annual, to 2.5m, usually less. Leaves alternate, palmately lobed to the base into 3–9 narrow, toothed segments 8–15cm long. Male flowers in branched clusters; female flowers in whorls on longer spikes. Native to Asia, but a frequent weed of waste places throughout. Fl 6–9. *Formerly cultivated for fibres and medicinal purposes; now used to produce marijuana.*

NETTLE FAMILY, URTICACEAE

Herbs with simple opposite or alternate leaves, with stipules. Flowers unisexual, on the same or different plants.

Urtica dubia An annual plant, to 80cm, with stinging hairs. It resembles Common Nettle, but leaves are long-stalked, almost as long as blade. The flowers are produced in long cylindrical spreading reddish catkins 4–10cm long; upper male catkins longer than leaf stalks, lower female ones shorter. Widespread throughout as a weed of nutrient-rich places, especially near houses. **Fl** all year. *U. atrovirens* is similar, but perennial, and has 4 stipules (not 2) at each node. Only in Corsica, Sardinia, Balearics and N Italy.

Roman Nettle *Urtica pilulifera* An annual plant with stinging hairs, similar in form to the above species, but leaves are more deeply and sharply toothed. Readily distinguished from other nettles in flower by the branched male inflorescences and the stalked globular female flower heads. Widespread throughout in damp nutrient-rich waste places. **Fl** 2–11. **Common Nettle** *U. dioica* and **Small Nettle** *U. urens* are both frequent in the area. Small Nettle is a small, spreading plant, with short ascending branched flower spikes.

Pellitory-of-the-wall *Parietaria diffusa* A branched perennial herb with spreading reddish stems and erect flower spikes, to 40cm. Leaves alternate, ovate to elliptical, 2–5cm long. Flowers small, in reddish clusters in leaf axils, 4-parted, with bracts joined at the base; shorter than the perianth at fruiting time. On walls, banks and in shady places throughout. **Fl** 4–10. *P. officinalis* is very similar to above, though often taller, to 1m, with stems much less branched; leaves longer, up to 12cm. Widespread in similar habitats. **Fl** 4–10. *P. lusitanica* is much smaller and more delicate, annual, with leaves less than 4cm. Widespread and frequent.

Mind-your-own-business *Soleirolia soleirolii* A low, creeping, hairy, evergreen perennial, forming mats with slender stems that root at the nodes. Leaves stalked, rounded, only 2–6mm across. Flowers tiny and pinkish, produced at the base of leaves, with males above and females below. Native to the islands of the area, but widely naturalized elsewhere on walls and in shady places. **Fl** 2–4.

SANDALWOOD FAMILY, SANTALACEAE

Herbs or small shrubs, with linear leaves, all semi-parasitic on other plants.

Osyris alba A small broom-like shrub, with erect green stems to 1.5m. Leaves small, 1–2cm long, lanceolate, leathery and veinless apart from the midrib. Flowers inconspicuous, yellowish-green, with 3-lobed perianth; male and female flowers on separate plants, males in small clusters, females solitary. Fruits red, fleshy and globular, 5–7mm across. In woodland, maquis and dry rocky places, extending up into mountain zones; throughout. **Fl** 4–7. *O. quadripartita* is rather similar, though larger, to 2.5m, with larger leaves, up to 4cm long, that have more visible pinnate veins. Flower bracts papery (green in *O. alba*). In S Spain and the Balearics.

MISTLETOE FAMILY, LORANTHACEAE

Parasitic shrubs with opposite leaves. Flowers 3- or 4-parted.

Mistletoe *Viscum album* A familiar, branched, parasitic shrub, occurring commonly on the trunks and branches of various trees including conifers. Leaves oblong, leathery, 2–6cm. Flowers inconspicuous, 4-parted, in stalkless clusters, with males and females on separate plants. Berries globular, fleshy, white or yellowish, 6–10mm across. Widespread and common wherever suitable host plants occur; throughout. **Fl** 1–4. *V. cruciatum* has stalked flower clusters and red berries. Parasitic on olive and other trees. S Iberian Peninsula only.

Arceuthobium oxycedri   A curious tiny shrubby plant, 5–20cm, growing parasitically on the branches of juniper, particularly Prickly Juniper. Leaves scale-like and paired. Flowers tiny and yellowish. Fruits tiny, 2–3mm, green and explosive, with sticky seeds. Unlikely to be confused with anything else, but easily overlooked. Very local, from S France westwards. **Fl** 7–9.

BIRTHWORT FAMILY, ARISTOLOCHIACEAE

Herbs with alternate untoothed leaves. Flowers 3-parted, with a distinct perianth tube.

Asarabacca *Asarum europaeum*   A creeping, hairy, evergreen perennial. Leaves kidney-shaped, 2–5cm across, dark green and stalked. Flowers solitary, and hidden beneath leaves, reddish-brown, with a tubular corolla and 3 lobes. In woods, especially of beech, mainly in damper hill and mountain areas; absent from S Spain. **Fl** 3–6.

BIRTHWORTS *Aristolochia*   Curious erect or scrambling plants with heart-shaped leaves, and flowers that have a long corolla tube and asymmetrical lip.

(a) Flowers pale yellow, not solitary.

Birthwort *Aristolochia clematitis*   An erect or ascending, hairless, strong-smelling perennial, to 80cm. Leaves oval, 3–15cm long, usually heart-shaped at base and stalked (1.5–5cm long). Flowers dull yellow, tubular, 2–3cm long, in clusters of up to 8 at the nodes. In grassy and rocky places, scattered throughout the area. **Fl** 5–9.

(b) Flowers solitary, not pale yellow, stems woody.

Aristolochia baetica   An evergreen climber with woody stems reaching 2–3m with support. Leaves grey-green, to 10cm long, hairless and rather leathery, with basal lobes about a quarter the length of blade. Flowers 2–5cm long, brownish to blackish purple, strongly curved, on long hairless stalks. In dry habitats; S Iberian Peninsula. **Fl** 4–6. *A. sempervirens* is very similar, but flowers are on hairy stalks.

(c) Flowers solitary, not pale yellow, stems not woody.

Aristolochia pistolochia   Herbaceous perennial with creeping rhizomes giving rise to erect hairy stems up to 50cm. Leaves alternate, ovate but heart-shaped at the base (illus.), shiny on upper surface but glaucous and rough below and on the margins, with a short stalk less than 5mm long. Flowers 2–4cm long, pale brownish, with an almost straight tube and enlarged purplish lip. In dry rocky places or cultivated ground; eastwards to Corsica. **Fl** 3–6. *Aristolochia longa* Similar in form to above, but leaves distinctly stalked (about as long as flower stalks), not glaucous. Flowers brownish or yellowish-green, 3–6cm long, with a brownish-purple unstriped lip. On cultivated ground and roadsides throughout. **Fl** 4–6.

Round-leaved Birthwort *Aristolochia rotunda*   An erect or spreading plant, branched or unbranched, to 60cm, with a bulb-like rhizome. Leaves rounded heart-shaped, 2–7cm long, virtually stalkless, with rounded bases clasping the stem (illus.). Flowers 3–5cm long, with an almost straight yellowish-green tube, and a dark-purplish lip with dark stripes running into the tube. In damp or shady places, occasionally in cultivated land, throughout most of the southern part of the area. **Fl** 4–6.

Asarabacca (le

Birthwort (rig

Aristolochia pistoloch
(le

Aristolochia pistoloch

Round-leaved Birthwo

Aristoloch
sempervirens (lef

**Round-leave
Birthwort** (righ

RAFFLESIA FAMILY, RAFFLESIACEAE

Cytinus hypocistus (left

Cytinus ruber (right

Parasitic plants with scale-like leaves lacking chlorophyll. Flowers variable: solitary or in clusters. The family includes *Rafflesia*, the flowering plant with the largest flower in the world.

Cytinus hypocistis   Strange and distinctive parasite, growing on the roots of *Cistus* (mainly white-flowered species) and *Halimium*. The main visible part of the plant is the cluster of yellow flowers with scarlet bracts, on very short stems only a few centimetres high. Flowers 4-lobed with 2 bracts. Frequent throughout the warmer parts of the area, though easily overlooked, especially when out of flower. Fl 3–6. *C. ruber* is very similar to above, and sometimes treated as a subspecies. It has white to pale-pink flowers, and occurs on pink-flowered species of *Cistus*. Throughout southern parts of the area, but rarer than *C. hypocistis*.

BALANOPHORACEAE

Wholly parasitic herbs, lacking chlorophyll. Flowers unisexual in dense inflorescences.

Cynomorium coccineum (left

Cynomorium coccineum   An extraordinary parasitic plant, unlikely to be confused with anything else (except, perhaps, a fungus). The visible part consists of a reddish-brown club-shaped cylindrical structure, up to 30cm, densely covered with tiny flowers, with a cluster of scale leaves at the base. It is parasitic on the roots of salt-tolerant species, especially members of the Goosefoot family (see page 34); uncommon and strongly southern in distribution. Fl 4–5.

DOCK FAMILY, POLYGONACEAE

Herbs or small shrubs, with alternate leaves, usually with stipules in the form of a membranous sheath around the stem. Flowers usually inconspicuous.

Sea Knotgrass *Polygonum maritimum*   A prostrate or ascending, branched perennial, with a woody base. Leaves narrowly oval, unstalked, 1–2.5cm long, grey-green, usually with curled margins; stipule sheaths silvery, reddish at the base. Flowers pink or white, 2–4mm across, 5-lobed, solitary or in small groups at the nodes. A distinctive plant of sandy and shingly beaches, often in places washed by the highest tides; throughout, wholly coastal. Fl 3–10.

Polygonum equisetiforme   A distinctive plant, rather horsetail-like in appearance, with bare stems up to 1m. Stems have toothed stipular sheaths at intervals and small unstalked narrow leaves, which soon fall off. Flowers small, about 4mm across, pink or white, produced at the nodes, collectively forming a long narrow spike. In cultivated and waste ground, mainly southern. Fl 4–6.

Horned Dock (left

Sea Knotgrass (right

Tangier Dock *Rumex tingitanus*   Perennial plant, to 50cm, often branched from the base. Leaves spear-shaped and greyish-green, gradually tapering to the apex. The inflorescence has large persistent sheaths. Widespread and frequent on maritime sands throughout the mainland coast; more common in the west. Fl 4–6.

Horned Dock *Rumex bucephalophorus*   A variable annual plant, up to 40cm, branched or not, erect or ascending. Leaves greyish-green, ovate or spoon-shaped, stalked, 1–2cm long. Flowers small, reddish, and in clusters of 2–3 in the leaf axils, forming a spike. The most distinctive feature of this species is the fruit: 3 of the perianth segments become enlarged and have straight or hooked teeth on each side. Often abundant in cultivated and waste ground throughout. Fl 3–9.

Shore Dock *Rumex rupestris* An erect perennial, to 80cm with straight stems and bluish-green, oblong-lanceolate leaves up to 15cm long. Flowers reddish, small, in whorled clusters up the stem, with a single leaf at the base of the inflorescence. Ripe fruit has 3 equal-sized warts. On shingle and sand dunes, mainly N Spain and France. **Fl** 6–8.

GOOSEFOOT FAMILY, CHENOPODIACEAE

Herbs and small shrubs with alternate fleshy leaves. Flowers very small. Many species are adapted to saline conditions, and Spain is especially rich in species from this family. Identification is often difficult, and only the more distinctive and wide-spread species are covered here.

Sea Beet *Beta vulgaris* A variable hairless biennial, to 1.5m, though often prostrate. Basal leaves dark green, shiny, leathery and fleshy, roughly ovate to lanceolate to 20cm long, and untoothed. Flowers small, green, in a long series of clusters forming a leafless spike. Common almost throughout in many coastal habitats. **Fl** 5–8.

Shrubby Orache *Atriplex halimus* A silvery-white branched, shrubby perennial, to 3m. Leaves variable, up to 6cm long, ovoid to triangular, sometimes with pointed lobes at the base, grey-green. Flowers inconspicuous, in a long inflorescence with numerous short branches, all yellowish-grey. In saline and coastal habitats around all the coasts, rarely inland. **Fl** 6–9.

Sea Purslane *Halimione portulacoides* A greyish-green subshrub, spreading to form clumps, with ascending stems to 80cm. Leaves mostly opposite, grey-green, fleshy, oval, untoothed, and wedge-shaped at base. Flowers yellowish, tiny, in clusters on short branches, collectively forming a conspicuous inflorescence. Common, and often dominant, in saltmarshes and other damp saline areas; mainly coastal, throughout. **Fl** 7–10.

Arthrocnemum glaucum A perennial hairless fleshy shrub, with jointed stems up to 1m. Leaves scale-like and tiny. Whole plant is greyish-green at first, becoming yellowish or red. Flowers tiny, barely visible, in groups of 3. Rather similar to the glassworts *Salicornia*, but differing in being perennial. Saltmarshes, and occasionally inland on saline soils, throughout. **Fl** 5–9. **Perennial Glasswort** *A. perenne* is similar but more creeping, forming mats. Greenish-brown seeds with hooked hairs, in contrast to the warty black seeds of *A. glaucum*. Mediterranean and Atlantic coasts of the area.

Prickly Saltwort *Salsola kali* A very variable hairy annual, spreading or erect to 1m. Leaves narrowly linear, 1–4cm long, bluish-green, spine-tipped, broadest at their base, and opposite in the lower parts of the plant. Flowers small, 5-lobed, usually solitary in the leaf axils, with 2 stiff spiny bracts, which are longer than the flowers. Common in sandy coastal areas, often close to the tideline and occasionally inland; throughout. **Fl** 7–10. *S. soda* is rather similar, but hairless, with half-cylindrical clasping leaves. Flower bracts about the same length as the flowers. Widespread in sandy and muddy coastal habitats.

AMARANTH FAMILY, AMARANTHACEAE

Herbs or small shrubs. Leaves without stipules. Perianth dry and scaly, in spike-like inflorescences. Several species are naturalised, mainly from the tropics.

Common Amaranth or **Pigweed** *Amaranthus retroflexus* A robust hairy rather greyish-green erect annual, to 80cm. Leaves oval to lanceolate, stalked, up to 15cm long. Flowers tiny, greenish-white, in short dense spikes, leafless towards the top; flower bracts stiff, slightly prickly, about twice as long as the 5 sepals. A N American alien, now widely established throughout S Europe in waste ground, cultivated ground, and disturbed areas. **Fl** 7–10.

NYCTAGINACEAE

Usually shrubs or woody climbers. Flowers solitary or in small clusters, with large bracts.

Bougainvillea *Bougainvillea glabra* A vigorous woody hairless climber, reaching 10m with support. Leaves ovate, up to 6cm long, stalked, and alternate. Flowers creamy-white inside, greenish-white outside, tubular, in groups of 3, but the conspicuous part is the ruff of 3 ovate, purplish or reddish, bracts, much longer than the flowers, and persisting after the flowers have gone. Native of Brazil, but very widely cultivated on and around habitations. Fl 2–10. *B. spectabilis* is very similar, and easily confused with Bougainvillea. It differs in the densely hairy under-surface to the leaves, and the flowers that are purplish, not greenish, outside. Similar situations and distribution.

POKEWEED FAMILY, PHYTOLACCACEAE

Herbs or shrubs, with alternate leaves and flowers in racemes.

Pokeweed or **Virginian Poke** *Phytolacca americana* A shrubby perennial plant, woody at the base, with forked, leafy stems up to 3m. Leaves oval to lance-olate, 10–40cm long, and stalked. Flowers white, 5-lobed, 2–4cm across, in ter-minal cylindrical erect spikes 10–15cm long; fruits globular 4–7mm diameter, becoming purplish-black, on curving-back stems. Cultivated, and widely natural-ized. Fl 7–10. *The berries yield a dye, used, among other things, for colouring red wine.*

MESEMBRYANTHEMUM FAMILY, AIZOACEAE

A family consisting mainly of succulent plants adapted to semi-desert life. Leaves fleshy, undivided and opposite. Flowers solitary, often with numerous petals and stamens, appearing like a member of the Daisy family.

Aizoon hispanicum A spreading annual plant, to 15cm, with alternate, oblong, blunt, fleshy, and stalkless leaves, up to 8mm long. Flowers solitary, virtually stalk-less, with 5 yellowish sepals (no petals), about 5–8mm across, and 20 stamens in bundles of 4. In sandy and rocky places, usually saline. Mainly in Spain, naturalized locally in Italy. Fl 4–6.

Ice Plant *Mesembryanthemum crystallinum* A spreading annual plant, with stems up to 80cm long. Leaves fleshy, oval, 6–12cm, flat, covered with shiny crys-talline swellings like frost. Flowers 2–3cm across, virtually stalkless, with numer-ous whitish, yellow or very pale-pink narrow petals, longer than the 5 sepals. In sandy, rocky and saline situations, usually coastal; throughout the Mediterranean region and Portugal. Fl 3–6. *Occasionally eaten as a salad. M. nodiflorum is similar to above, but differs in having more cylindrical leaves, often tinged red, and smaller flowers to 1.5cm across, with petals shorter than sepals. Similar habitats and dis-tribution. Fl 3–6.*

Hottentot Fig *Carpobrotus edulis* A vigorous creeping perennial, often forming extensive mats. Leaves 8–12cm long, paired, fleshy, triangular in section, finely toothed along the upper edge, and narrowing towards tip. Flowers solitary on swollen stalks, with numerous narrow petals and masses of yellow stamens; they are 6–10cm across, yellow, pink or orange in colour. Fruit fleshy and edible. Native of S Africa, but very widely naturalized in coastal habitats throughout the area. Fl 3–7. **Red Hottentot Fig** *C. acinaciformis* is similar to above, but has leaves broadest above the middle, narrowing abruptly to a sharp point; and larger flow-ers, 10–12cm across, that are bright red-carmine with purple stamens. Similar habitats and distribution, though less frequent. Fl 3–7.

PINK FAMILY, CARYOPHYLLACEAE

Annual or perennial herbs, with pairs of opposite undivided leaves that are often fused together at the base. Petals 4–5, unfused and often deeply divided.

Paronychia argentea   A branched spreading mat-forming perennial, up to 30cm long. Leaves ovate to lanceolate, 4–10mm long, greyish-green, in opposite pairs, with membranous stipules that are shorter than the leaves. Flowers in rounded heads in the axils towards the ends of branches; the flowers are tiny, with 5 equal sepals, dwarfed by the membranous, pointed, silvery bracts, 4–6mm long. Common in sandy and grassy areas, especially coastal, throughout the lowland areas. Fl 3–6. *P. capitata* is similar, but has hairier leaves that are equal in length to the stipules, and larger denser flower heads. The bracts are longer, 6–10mm long, and the orange sepals have recurved points and are unequal in length, the 3 outer ones being longer. In dry, rocky places, especially in hilly areas, throughout. Fl 3–6.

Purple Spurrey *Spergularia purpurea*   A slender annual or biennial, up to 25cm high, often growing in large masses. Leaves narrow, linear, with narrow, pointed, silvery stipules. Flowers red-purple, about 8mm across, in branched inflorescences; petals longer than sepals; 10 stamens. Locally abundant in dry and sandy waste ground, often on roadsides, throughout most of the Iberian Peninsula, rarely elsewhere. Fl 3–5.

Corncockle *Agrostemma githago*   A greyish, hairy, erect annual, up to 1m. Leaves opposite, 6–13cm long, narrow, long-pointed, and hairy. Flowers dull reddish-purple, 3–5cm across, usually solitary on long stalks, with long narrow calyx lobes protruding beyond the slightly notched petals. In cornfields and waste places; throughout but rarest in the extreme south. Fl 4–7.

CAMPIONS AND CATCHFLIES *Silene*   This genus has numerous representatives in S Europe. Flowers are showy, with 5 petals, a fused calyx.

(a) Flowers pinkish, opening only at night.

Night-flowering Catchfly *Silene noctiflora*   An erect annual, to 40cm, with simple or branched stems, hairy below and sticky-hairy above. Leaves narrowly ovate, unstalked except at the plant's base. Flowers 1.7–2cm across, pinkish above, yellow below, rolling up inwards (exposing the yellow) during the day, opening fully at night, when they are fragrant. A weed of cultivated ground, throughout except the far west and south of the area. Fl 5–7.

(b) Day-flowering, with flowers normally pink or red.

Silene colorata   A finely hairy annual, usually branched, erect, up to 50cm. Leaves linear to spoon-shaped, and opposite. Flowers usually deep to pale pink, rarely white, 1–2cm across, in lax clusters; styles 3; calyx cylindrical, 1.1–1.3cm long (occasionally longer), 10-veined, with blunt hairy teeth broadening to club-shaped as the fruit ripens. Seeds winged. Sandy beaches and cultivated ground, mainly near the coast; in Portugal and the Mediterranean region. Fl 4–6. *S. sericea* is very similar to the above, except that flowers are usually solitary (occasionally 2–3 together); calyx teeth are usually pointed, and seeds are grooved, not winged. Coastal sands; France, Italy and the W Mediterranean islands.

Sweet-William Catchfly *Silene armeria*   An erect hairless grey-green annual or biennial, with unbranched stems to 40cm. Leaves spoon-shaped at base, withering early; ovate to lanceolate, clasping stem, all grey-green. Flowers bright reddish-pink, in terminal clusters; calyx reddish, cylindrical and 10-veined, 10–15mm long. In dry rocky places, often semi-shaded; throughout, though local. Fl 5–8.

Sand Catchfly *Silene conica*   An erect or ascending annual, greyish-green, hairy all over, with stems to 40cm. Leaves lanceolate, stalkless above. Flowers in clusters of up to 30, pink, rarely white, 8–14mm across; calyx flask-shaped, 10–15mm long with 30 clear veins, becoming swollen in fruit. Common in sandy places, especially near the coast, throughout. Fl 3–6.

Sand Catchfly (left)

Sea Campion (right)

(c) Day-flowering, flowers normally white or pale pink.

Bladder Campion *Silene vulgaris*   A very variable species. Perennial, with grey-green hairless or downy stems, frequently branched, up to 60cm. Leaves ovate to lanceolate, to 12cm long, unstalked on the stems. Flowers 1.6–1.8cm across, usually in small clusters, rarely solitary, with white deeply notched petals; calyx inflated and bladder-like, persisting in fruit, with 6 teeth, 20-veined. Common and widespread in waste ground and grassy places throughout the area. Fl 4–9.
Sea Campion *S. maritima* is sometimes treated as a subspecies of Bladder Campion, ssp *maritima*. It differs in being a mat-forming plant, and having larger flowers (to 2.5cm across) with overlapping petals. In coastal habitats on the Atlantic coasts only. Fl 4–7.

Silene nicaeensis   An annual plant, up to 40cm, usually branched, covered with sticky glandular hairs. Leaves linear to spoon-shaped at the plant's base, narrower up the stem. Flowers individually stalked in whorl-like clusters up the stem, forming a long branched or simple inflorescence; petals white or pink, deeply bifid, often inrolled; calyx tubular, 10-veined, 10–13mm long, with 5 short pointed teeth. On coastal sands throughout the area. Fl 4–6.

Small-flowered Catchfly (left)

Italian Catchfly *Silene italica*   A perennial erect plant, with a woody base, and branched stems up to 80cm, sticky-hairy above, downy below. Leaves lanceolate to spoon-shaped at the plant's base, narrower and unstalked higher up. Flowers 1.5–2.2cm across, with 5 deeply bifid petals, white above, pinkish or greenish below; calyx cylindrical and sticky-hairy. In dry grassy places throughout the area. Fl 5–7.

Nottingham Catchfly *Silene nutans*   A very variable species. Erect perennial, usually unbranched, sticky above, downy below. Leaves roughly spoon-shaped at the plant's base, to 10cm long, becoming narrower and unstalked higher up. Flowers white above, greenish or reddish below, with petals deeply bifid, the lobes rolling inwards, in a loose 1-sided drooping inflorescence; calyx 9–12mm long, sticky-hairy. In dry grassy or disturbed habitats; throughout. Fl 4–8.

Small-flowered Catchfly *Silene gallica*   A downy annual, with simple or branched stems up to 45cm, sticky above. Leaves roughly ovate below, becoming narrower up the stem. Flowers small, 6–12mm across, white or pink, in rather 1-sided inflorescences; calyx 7–10mm long, cylindrical to ovoid, with teeth about a quarter the length of the tube, sticky hairy, and 10-veined. In waste places, arable land and roadsides throughout. Fl 4–9. Var. *quinquevulnera* is a highly distinctive variant, with a deep-red spot on each petal. Similar habitats. Fl 4–9.

Nottingham Catchfly (left)

Bladder Campion (right)

(d) Day-flowering, flowers greenish-yellow.

Spanish Catchfly *Silene otites*   An erect biennial or short-lived perennial, to 60cm (rarely to 1m), sticky-hairy below but hairless in the inflorescence. Leaves ovate-elliptical, stalked at plant's base in loose rosettes, unstalked above. Flowers small, 3–4mm across, greenish-yellow, and numerous in loose branched terminal clusters. In grassy and rocky places, especially on calcareous or sandy soils; throughout except for the islands. Fl 5–8.

Berry Catchfly *Cucubalus baccifer*   A weak-stemmed hairy perennial plant, up to 1.2m, with widely diverging branches. Leaves oval, pointed, untoothed, short-stalked. Flowers greenish-white, 1.6–2.0cm across, drooping, in loose clusters, with petals divided into 2 pointed lobes. The fruit is black, globose, 6–8mm across, and berry-like (the main difference from *Silene*, which has a dry capsule). In shady places and river banks throughout. **Fl** 6–9.

Rock Soapwort *Saponaria ocymoides*   A spreading, much-branched hairy perennial, with reddish stems, sometimes forming large mats. Lower leaves oval-lanceolate, blunt; upper ones narrower and more pointed. Flowers pink or purplish, 6–10mm across, in loose branched clusters, sometimes almost covering the plant; calyx reddish and glandular-hairy. In dry rocky places, occasionally in woods, throughout; most common in mountain areas, rarest in the east. **Fl** 3–9. **Soapwort** *Saponaria officinalis* is very different from above, being erect, up to 90cm, hairless, with large pale-pink flowers, 3–4cm across, in dense terminal clusters. Frequent in grassy places, roadsides and near habitations; throughout. **Fl** 5–9.

Cow Basil *Vaccaria pyramidata*   An erect, branched, hairless annual plant, up to 60cm. Leaves oval to lanceolate, grey-green, to 5cm long. Flowers pink or purplish, 1–1.5cm across, with inflated calyx that has 5 green wings (illus.); styles 2. A frequent weed of cultivated land, hedges and waste places, throughout. **Fl** 5–7.

Tunic Flower *Petrorhagia saxifraga*   An erect or ascending, hairless or rough, perennial plant, up to 45cm. Leaves greyish-green, narrowly linear, normally 1-veined, in opposite pairs. Flowers pink or white, 5–6mm across, with 4 bracts at the base, which are shorter than the calyx, in loose inflorescences; calyx 3–6mm long, with 1-veined teeth. In dry places; throughout but local. **Fl** 5–10. *P. prolifera* is rather similar, but perennial, to 50cm; the flowers are in small dense heads, with wide papery-brown bracts below that completely enclose the calyx. Leaves 3-veined. From E Spain eastwards, in dry hilly areas. **Fl** 3–5. *P. velutina* is very similar to above, but has the middle part of the stem densely glandular-hairy, with leaf sheaths at least twice as long as wide (cf. about as long as wide in *P. prolifera*). Throughout the area in grassy and stony places.

Fringed Pink *Dianthus monspessulanus*   A loosely tufted perennial plant, up to 50cm, with slender sparsely-branched stems. Leaves narrow, linear, pointed, and grey-green. Flowers large, 2.5–3.5cm across, pink or white, with petals divided to about half-way into numerous narrow lobes forming a fringe. In grassy and rocky places, especially the lower parts of mountains, throughout the mainland part of the area. **Fl** 5–8.

Deptford Pink *Dianthus armeria*   An erect stiffly branched downy annual or biennial to 60cm. Basal leaves oblong, blunt, stem leaves linear, all dark green and rather thin; stem leaves have sheaths that are not as long as twice the diameter of the stem. Flowers small, 8–12mm across, reddish-pink, in dense terminal clusters surrounded by long, thin, pointed bracts. In grassy and scrubby places throughout. **Fl** 5–9. **Carthusian Pink** *Dianthus carthusianorum* is rather similar, but hairless. Length of leaf sheaths at least 3 times the diameter of stem. Flowers larger, 1.8–2.0cm across, surrounded by darker brownish bracts. In grassy and rocky places; throughout except Portugal and most islands.

Cow Basil

BUTTERCUP FAMILY, RANUNCULACEAE

Herbs or woody climbers, normally with alternate leaves without stipules. Flowers usually hermaphrodite with masses of stamens; flower structure very variable.

Stinking Hellebore *Helleborus foetidus*   An erect strong-smelling perennial herb, up to 80cm, with leafy overwintering stems. Lower stem leaves dark green, deeply palmately divided; uppermost leaves and bracts small and undivided (illus.). Flowers bell-shaped, nodding, 1–3cm across, green with reddish-purple rim, in large clusters. Widespread throughout, in grassy, bushy and shady places. Fl 1–4. *Helleborus lividus* is rather similar to above, but has leaves with only 3 distinctly separated oval-lanceolate segments. Flowers greenish or pink flushed. 2 geographically separate subspecies occur: ssp *corsicus* has leaf segments closely spine-toothed (illus.). In Corsica and Sardinia. Fl 12–4. Ssp *lividus* has distantly toothed or untoothed leaf margins. In scrub, grassland and open woodland; in the Balearic islands. Fl 12–4.

Winter Aconite *Eranthis hyemalis*   A hairless perennial with tuberous rhizomes, producing stems up to 15cm. Basal leaves stalked, deeply palmately divided; stem leaves similar but unstalked; all shiny. Flowers solitary, yellow, 2–3cm across, surrounded by a ruff of leaf-like divided bracts. In woods and scrub, native from SE France eastwards, but often naturalized in parks and gardens. Fl 1–3.

Love-in-a-mist *Nigella damascena*   An erect hairless annual, simple or branched, to 50cm. Leaves finely divided 2–3 pinnately, with very narrow segments. Flowers solitary, pale to mid-blue, 2–4cm across, with 5 petals and 5 small greenish honey-leaves, and an erect cluster of stamens and carpels in the centre; the flower is surrounded by a ruff of pinnate feathery bracts; the carpels are joined for most of their length, forming an inflated fruit. On cultivated land, and naturalized from cultivation, throughout the lowland areas. Fl 5–7. *N. arvensis* is similar, but has paler smaller flowers, 2–3cm across, without the ring of bracts immediately below, and with the carpels joined for only half their length. On arable land, throughout; rarer in the west. Fl 5–9.

Stavesacre or **Licebane** *Delphinium staphisagria*   An erect hairy annual or biennial, up to 1m. Leaves basal or alternate on stem, palmately divided into 5–7 pointed lobes, which are sometimes 3-lobed themselves. Flowers deep blue, 2–3cm across, with all perianth segments the same colour, and spur very short; carpels become swollen in fruit. In maquis and scrub throughout the Mediterranean area. Fl 5–7. *Delphinium halteratum* is an annual, with stems to 40cm (rarely more); upper leaves often undivided. Flowers bright blue, with spur longer than blue sepals; perianth segments finely downy all over. In France and Italy. Fl 5–8. *D. gracile* has paler flowers, with spur 2–2½ times as long as the perianth segments. In Spain and Portugal only. Fl 5–8. *D. peregrinum* grows to 80cm, and has dull bluish-violet flowers, with honey-leaves longer than perianth segments. Dry scrubby places, from Italy eastwards.

Larkspur *Consolida ambigua*   *Consolida* differs from *Delphinium* in having only 2 inner perianth segments (honey-leaves), which form a spur themselves. Annual, to 1m. Leaves finely divided and feathery. Flowers stalked, deep blue, in long spike-like inflorescence, with up to 16 flowers; spur 1.3–1.8cm long; fruit a single hairy carpel. In fields and dry slopes, throughout the Mediterranean area; naturalized elsewhere. Fl 4–7. *C. regalis* is smaller, up to 50cm, with a branched inflorescence of violet-blue flowers; spur up to 25mm long. Fruit hairless. In cultivated and waste ground; throughout except in the extreme south and west. Fl 4–8.

Stinking Hellebore

Winter Aconite

Corsican Hellebore

Delphinium peregrinum (left)

Larkspur (right)

Crown Anemone *Anemone coronaria* Perennial herb, with flowering stems up to 45cm. Basal leaves ternate, with each segment divided again. Flowers solitary, reddish, blue or white, 3.5–6.5cm across, with 5–8 elliptical segments, hairy underneath; below the flowers, there is a whorl of unstalked deeply lobed bracts. In pastures, rough ground and on roadsides, and naturalized from cultivation; throughout. Fl 2–4. *Anemone hortensis* is similar in form to above, but lower leaves less divided, with broader segments; stem leaves linear-lanceolate, usually undivided. Flower solitary, pale purple-blue, with 12–19 (most commonly 15) narrowly elliptical perianth segments; anthers blue. Locally frequent in pastures, cultivated ground and garrigue; from France and Corsica eastwards. Fl 2–4. *A. pavonina* is similar, but with fewer perianth segments (7–12), individually broader, usually scarlet, pink or purple, sometimes yellowish towards centre. Local from SW France eastwards in Mediterranean area.

Hepatica *Hepatica nobilis* A short hairy evergreen perennial, with flowering stems up to 15cm. Leaves distinctive: basal, 3-lobed, 3–5cm across, deep green and often mottled, with a red-purple edge and undersurface. Flowers solitary, bluish-purple, pink or white, 1.5–2.5cm across with white anthers and 3 ovate leafy bracts below each flower. In woods and shady places; throughout except the far west, and absent from the islands except Corsica. Fl 2–4.

Fragrant Clematis *Clematis flammula* A climbing perennial, with a woody-based stem up to 5m. Leaves opposite, 2-pinnate, with stalked, entire or lobed oval to circular leaflets. Flowers white, about 2cm across, fragrant, with 4 narrow perianth segments, hairy only on margins and undersurface, in dense branched inflorescence. In maquis, and scrub throughout Mediterranean region. Fl 5–8. **Traveller's-Joy** *C. vitalba* (the widespread species in N Europe) differs from above in the once-pinnate leaves and the duller greenish-white flowers, with segments hairy on both sides. In scrubby places throughout. Fl 5–9. *C. recta* is an erect herb to 1.5m, with white flowers; perianth segments downy only on the margin. Widespread in scrubby and rocky places, except the far west. Fl 4–6.

Virgin's Bower *Clematis cirrhosa* An evergreen climber, up to 4m. Leaves very variable, from simple to twice-ternate, 2.5–5cm long. Flowers large, 4–7cm across, nodding, greenish-yellow sometimes tinged with red, with a distinctive 2-lipped cup-shaped involucre below the flowers. In maquis, scrub and rocky places; throughout, but predominantly southern. Fl 12–4.

Pheasant's-eye *Adonis annua* An erect annual herb, up to 50cm, branched or simple. Leaves ferny, 3-pinnate with very narrow segments. Flowers solitary, 1.5–2.5cm across, scarlet with dark centres, with 5–8 petals, and 5 spreading hairless sepals that are shorter than petals. In cultivated ground; throughout except the far west. Fl 4–6. *A. microcarpa* is similar, but flowers often yellowish, smaller (about 1cm across); achenes have a distinct tooth on their inner margin (flat in Pheasant's-eye). In similar habitats throughout the Mediterranean area. Fl 4–6.

BUTTERCUPS *Ranunculus* Annual or perennial plants, with simple yellow or white flowers; fruits consist of clusters of single-seeded achenes.

(a) Sepals reflexed.

Spiny-fruited Buttercup *Ranunculus muricatus* A virtually hairless annual plant, up to 50cm. Leaves roughly circular to kidney-shaped in outline, usually divided into 3 lobes and coarsely toothed, becoming less divided and more short-stalked up the stem. Flowers yellow, 1–1.5cm across, with 5 well-separated petals and 5 recurved sepals. Fruits individually compressed-ovoid, warty, with a 2–3mm long spiny beak and a smooth broad margin (illus.). In cultivated ground or disturbed damp places; throughout except the far west. Fl 4–5.

Clematis recta (lef

Virgin's Bower (righ

Pheasant's-eye (lef

Spiny-fruite
Buttercup (righ

Ranunculus muricatus fru

Small-flowered Buttercup *Ranunculus parviflorus* A spreading hairy annual plant, up to 40cm. Lower leaves have 3–5 toothed lobes; upper leaves simple or less lobed. Flowers small, 3–6mm across, yellow, with 5 petals and reflexed sepals. Achenes about 3mm long, with a spine at the tip. In cultivated land and grassy places; throughout. Fl 4–7. **Bulbous Buttercup** *R. bulbosus* and **Hairy Buttercup** *R. sardous* both have yellow flowers and reflexed sepals, though their flowers are larger, 1.5–3cm across. Bulbous Buttercup is perennial, with a bulbous base, and spreading hairs only in lower part of plant; Hairy Buttercup is annual, with spreading hairs all over. Both are common in grassy places.

(b) Flowers with sepals erect, not reflexed.

Corn Buttercup *Ranunculus arvensis* Rather similar to Spiny-fruited Buttercup, though generally more erect, and downy all over. Lowest leaves simple, upper leaves deeply 3-lobed. Flowers bright yellow, 4–12mm across, with sepals spreading, not reflexed. Achenes 6–8mm long, spiny or warty (illus.). In cultivated and waste land throughout. Fl 4–5.

Ranunculus bullatus A distinctive downy perennial plant, up to 20cm. Leaves all basal, spreading horizontally, broadly ovate, 3–5cm long, toothed, bristly below and distinctly embossed. Flowers large (2–2.5cm across), yellow, scented, 1 or 2 together on leafless hairy stems; fruit hairless, beaked but not spiny. In grassy and rocky places throughout the Mediterranean area. Fl 9–2.

Grass-leaved Buttercup *Ranunculus gramineus* An erect downy or hairless, grey-green perennial, up to 50cm. Basal leaves long, narrow, flat and grass-like; stem leaves fewer and shorter. Flowers deep yellow, 2–3cm across, with 5 petals. In dry rocky places, especially in hills; widespread but local, and absent from most of the islands. Fl 5–7. **Lesser Celandine** *R. ficaria* is a familiar plant in N Europe, with small heart-shaped fleshy leaves, and flowers with 8–12 narrow yellow petals. Widespread in shady places. Fl 2–5.

Mousetail *Myosurus minimus* A distinctive buttercup-like annual, to 12cm. Leaves narrowly linear, untoothed, in a basal rosette. Flowers solitary on leafless stalks, petals absent, sepals pale greenish-yellow, 3–4mm long; but the distinctive feature is the conical central receptacle bearing ovaries, becoming greatly elongated in fruit into a 'mouse tail'. In cultivated ground and bare places; widespread, but absent from the far west and south. Fl 2–4. **Beakwort** *Ceratocephalus falcatus* is rather similar to Mousetail, but has divided basal leaves, yellow flowers, and a cylindrical receptacle covered with beaked achenes. In cultivated fields and waste places; mainly in mainland Spain and Italy.

Columbine *Aquilegia vulgaris* An attractive erect hairy perennial, often branched, up to 60cm, very variable in form. Leaves stalked, 2-ternate, toothed or lobed. Flowers large (3–5cm long), usually blue-purple, occasionally pink or white, with 5 similar petals and sepals except that each petal is prolonged into an erect curving spur. In grassy and shady places, occasionally in wetlands, throughout. Fl 4–7.

Small-flowered Buttercup (left)

Bulbous Buttercup (right)

Corn Buttercup

Ranunculus bullatus (left)

Columbine (right)

Mousetail (left)

PEONY FAMILY, PAEONIACEAE

A small family of low-growing shrubs or herbs, with large divided leaves. Flowers large, solitary and showy, with numerous stamens.

Peony *Paeonia mascula*   An erect bushy herb, to 90cm. Leaves large, simply biternate (illus.), or with a few leaflets further divided; lower leaves have 9–16 elliptical to ovate leaflets, 5–10cm wide, with untoothed margins. Flowers solitary, red, 8–14cm across, with 5–8 petals. Fruits (follicles) in clusters of 3–5, 2–4cm long, usually downy. Two subspecies occur in this area: ssp *mascula* has hairless leaves below; ssp *russii* has downy leaves below. Widespread throughout in scrub, grassland and open woods, especially in mountains. ssp *russii* is only on W Mediterranean islands. Fl 3–6. *P. coriacea* is very similar, but has rounder leaflets with wavy margins, and only 2 hairless follicles. In S Spain and possibly some islands. *Paeonia officinalis* is similar in form to above, but has most leaflets divided again so that lower leaves have 17–30 segments; leaflets brownish and downy below (illus.); leaf stalk deeply channelled on upper surface. Flowers red, 7–13cm across, with filaments of stamens red. Fruit consists of 2–3 follicles. Several subspecies occur in the area. Throughout the southern part of the area in similar habitats. Fl 3–6. *P. broteroi* is very similar to *P. officinalis* but its leaflets are hairless and grey-green below; filaments of stamens yellow. In similar habitats in SW Spain and Portugal only. Fl 3–6.

BARBERRY FAMILY, BERBERIDACEAE

A variable family. Shrubs or herbs, flowers hermaphrodite, 3-parted. Stamens 4–6.

Barberry *Berberis vulgaris*   A much-branched deciduous spiny shrub, up to 3m, with ridged, yellowish twigs. Leaves oval, 25–55mm long, with fine spiny teeth around the margin. Flowers small (6–8mm across), yellow, with up to 30 in hanging racemes; fruit an oblong berry, reddish when ripe. Widespread in scrub, hedges, and dry rough places, but rare in the south of the area. Fl 4–6.

LAUREL FAMILY, LAURACEAE

Evergreen glandular trees or shrubs. Flowers small, usually hermaphrodite. Fruit a berry.

Laurel or **Sweet Bay** *Laurus nobilis*   An evergreen shrub or small tree, up to 20m, usually less. Leaves narrowly ovate to oblong, up to 10cm long, pointed, shiny dark green, hairless, with wavy margins. Male and female flowers on separate plants, yellowish, small, in clusters of 4–6 in the leaf axils; fruit ovoid, 10–15mm long, black when ripe. Widespread in shady places throughout the Mediterranean area; naturalized further north. Fl 3–4. *L. azorica* is very similar to above, but has densely downy young twigs (hairless in Laurel), and rounder leaves that are hairy below. Forms extensive forests in Madeira and the Canary Isles.

Paeonia brotera

Peony

Paeonia officinalis

Peony (left)

Laurel (right)

Barberry (left)

POPPY FAMILY PAPAVERACEAE

Herbs, with latex usually present. Flowers usually solitary, with undivided petals and sepals, and numerous stamens.

Opium Poppy *Papaver somniferum*   An erect grey-green herb, with pinnately lobed oval leaves 7–12cm long; the upper leaves have clasping bases. Flowers large (10–18cm across), solitary, variable in colour from white to purple, with a dark spot at the base of each petal; filaments white, anthers pale yellow. Two subspecies occur in the area: ssp *somniferum* is the cultivated form, which is hairless, with rounded leaf lobes. Widely cultivated as a crop and in gardens, and also naturalized. Ssp *setigerum* has finely bristly, more pointed leaves. Widespread and probably native in the south of the area. Fl 5–8.

Common Poppy capsule

Common Poppy *Papaver rhoeas*   A familiar erect bristly annual, up to 90cm, usually less. Leaves pinnately lobed, to 15cm long, with pointed segments, often further divided. Flowers solitary, on long stalks with bristly hairs spreading out at right angles to the stem; petals red, 30–45cm long, overlapping; anthers bluish; capsule ovoid-rounded and hairless, 1–2cm long (illus.). Common throughout in cultivated fields and waste places. Fl 4–9. **Long-headed Poppy** *P. dubium* is very similar to above, but has appressed hairs on the upper parts of the stem; leaf segments blunt, not pointed; flowers more orangey-red; and capsule narrower, oblong, widening somewhat towards the tip (illus.). Common throughout in similar habitats. Fl 4–9.

Long-headed Poppy

Papaver argemone   An erect bristly annual, up to 50cm. Leaves pinnately lobed and bristly. Flowers pale scarlet, 2–6cm across, with petals not overlapping, usually dark-blotched at the base; anthers bluish. Capsule oblong-cylindrical, 1.5–2cm long ribbed, with a few erect bristles. Common in cultivated and disturbed ground throughout. Fl 3–7. **Rough Poppy** *P. hybridum* is similar to above, but has darker crimson-red flowers; capsule ovoid to globose with many stiff erect bristles (illus.). Similar distribution and habitats. Fl 3–7.

Long-headed Poppy capsule

Prickly Poppy *Argemone mexicana*   A spiny grey-green annual, up to 90cm. Leaves ternately lobed and spiny. Flowers solitary, yellow-orange, petals 2–3cm long, with 2–3 bracts below each; capsule spiny (illus.). Native of the SW USA; widely naturalized in waste places in the south of the area. Fl 5–8.

Rough Poppy capsule

Violet Horned-poppy *Roemeria hybrida*   A poppy-like annual, to 40cm. Leaves thrice-pinnate, with narrow bristle-pointed terminal segments. Flowers solitary, 1.5–3cm across, deep violet, with petals soon falling; capsule up to 10cm long. On cultivated and waste land, from France westwards. Fl 4–6.

Yellow Horned-poppy *Glaucium flavum*   A grey-green branched biennial or perennial, up to 90cm, slightly downy; whole plant has yellow latex. Leaves pinnately lobed, wavy, 15–35cm long, with smaller upper leaves clasping the stem. Flowers solitary, terminal or in leaf axils, with 4 yellow petals each 3–4cm long; stamens yellow; sepals 2, downy. Fruit distinctive: narrowly cylindrical and up to 30cm long often curved, hairless. Frequent on sand, gravel and shingle around the coasts, occasionally inland. Fl 4–9. **Red Horned-Poppy** *Glaucium corniculatum* is rather similar to above, with flatter leaves; flowers usually orange-red; capsule usually straight, up to 20cm long, downy. In waste places and cultivated ground; throughout though rarer in the north of the area. Fl 4–6.

Californian Poppy *Eschscholzia californica*   A grey-green annual, occasionally perennial, up to 60cm. Leaves ternately divided, with narrow terminal segments. Flowers solitary, on long stalks, with orange-yellow petals, and yellow stamens; fruit a straight hairless cylindrical capsule up to 10cm long. Originally from the SW USA; widely naturalized, but local, throughout. Fl 3–6.

Prickly Poppy capsule

Hypecoum procumbens   A hairless grey-green annual, with wide-spreading grooved stems up to 15cm. Leaves twice-pinnate, grey-green, with narrow lobes. Flowers in small branched clusters, each 1–1.5cm across, with 4 yellow petals; the 2 larger outer petals have lateral lobes smaller than the central one; fruit 4–6cm long, thin, curved and jointed. In sandy and gravelly places, mainly coastal, through-out the Mediterranean region. Fl 3–6. *H. imberbe* is similar, but more erect; the lateral lobes of the outer petals are as large as, or larger than, the central one and the fruits are scarcely jointed. In waste places and cultivated ground throughout the south of the area. *H. pendulum* has an ungrooved stem and the outer petals are twice as long as wide, without lobes. In similar habitats to above; in the south of the area only.

White Ramping-fumitory *Fumaria capreolata*   A hairless blue-green scram-bling annual, without tendrils. Leaves bipinnate. Flowers in a cylindrical raceme of up to 20 flowers; each flower narrow, 1–1.4cm long, creamy-white with red-tipped petals; sepals 2, falling early; fruit spherical, about 2mm across, with stalk curved back when ripe. Common and widespread throughout, in disturbed ground, walls and hedges. Fl 4–9.

Spiked Fumitory *Platycapnos spicata*   A grey-green annual, up to 30cm, with twice-pinnately lobed leaves. Flowers tiny in dense rounded heads, almost like a clover; petals creamy to pink, tipped with dark red, fruit ovate. In cultivated and disturbed ground; widespread in the southern part of the area, eastwards to Italy. Fl 4–6.

CAPER FAMILY, CAPPARIDACEAE

A small family, with only 4 European representatives. Herbs or shrubs; flowers variable, but with 4 petals, 4 sepals and numerous stamens.

Caper *Capparis spinosa*   A low-growing, spreading shrub, often hanging over walls or banks. Leaves alternate, fleshy, grey-green, ovate to circular, blunt or slightly notched at the tip, with curved spines at the base of the leaf stalks. Flow-ers showy, 5–7cm across, with white petals and numerous violet stamens. Fruit is a large fleshy berry with pink flesh. Throughout the Mediterranean region in dry rocky and waste places. Fl 4–8. *C. ovata*, also known as Caper, is very similar to above. It differs in having narrower leaves, with a distinct spine at the tip where the midrib is prolonged; flowers smaller (4–5cm across), and more irregular in shape. The 2 species are not always clearly distinguishable. *The buds of either species, especially C. spinosa, are eaten pickled as capers.*

Cleome violacea   An erect, branched, sticky annual, up to 60cm. Lower leaves ternate, upper ones simple. Flowers in long racemes, each consisting of 2 larger erect petals; fruit long, narrow, pendulous. Local in dry disturbed places; in Por-tugal, and S and W Spain. Fl 4–6.

CRESS FAMILY, CRUCIFERAE

Woad fruit

A large and important family, with well over 300 species in the area. Although it is easy to recognize members of the family by the symmetrical flowers with 4 clawed petals, and 4 sepals in a cross, it can be difficult to identify individual species. Most of the yellow-flowered species require ripe fruit for identification. This account gives prominence to the most conspicuous and easily identified species.

Woad *Isatis tinctoria*   One of the more distinctive yellow-flowered crucifers: an erect biennial, to 1.2m. Leaves grey-green, upper ones clasping the stem. Flowers small (3–4mm across), yellow, in dense branched inflorescences; fruit oblong-elliptical, pendent, 2–3cm long, becoming dark brown (illus.). Widespread throughout in waste ground, cliff-tops, roadsides and other disturbed habitats. **Fl** 4–7. *Formerly used as the source of a blue dye made from the crushed fermented leaves.*

Southern Warty-cabbage *Bunias erucago*   A roughly hairy annual or biennial, to 60cm. Lower leaves pinnately lobed or wavy-edged, upper leaves usually toothed. Flowers yellow, 8–10mm across, with notched petals; fruit 10–12mm long, distinctively square in section, with irregularly toothed wings on the angles. Widespread throughout in waste ground. **Fl** 4–7.

Dame's-violet *Hesperis matronalis*   An erect biennial or perennial, up to 1m, with branched hairs that are often glandular. Leaves lanceolate, toothed and short-stalked. Flowers white or purple, to 2cm across, in branched, often dense, inflorescences, sweetly scented; fruit long and thin, up to 10cm long. Widespread in damp or shady places, or naturalized on waste ground; throughout. **Fl** 4–7. *H laciniata* is rather similar, but has pinnately lobed leaves, and yellow flowers, variably suffused with purple. On cliffs and rocks, mainly in mountains; throughout the south of the area.

Malcolmia littorea   A perennial herb, up to 40cm, woody towards the base, and with numerous non-flowering shoots, all grey-green with short, branched hairs. Basal leaves variable, lobed or not, virtually stalkless. Flowers purple, 1.5–2cm across; some sepals strongly pouched at base; fruit up to 6.5cm long, narrow, not constricted between the seeds. In sandy places, mainly coastal, in the south of the area. **Fl** 4–6. Two other species occur, with sepals not distinctly pouched at base: *M. ramosissima* has a downy fruit, up to 3.5cm long, smoothly rounded, but constricted between the seeds; *M. africana* has longer fruit (to 6.5cm), hairy, 4-angled, not constricted between the seeds. Both occur throughout the Mediterranean part of the area.

STOCKS *Matthiola*   These are very similar to *Malcolmia*, although *Malcolmia* has a 2-lobed stigma with the lobes pressed together, while *Matthiola* has a 2-lobed stigma with erect lobes that are always thickened with horns; sometimes these become enlarged in fruit.

Hoary Stock *Matthiola incana*   A stout perennial plant, up to 80cm, densely white-downy, woody at the base. Leaves lanceolate, usually unlobed. Flowers conspicuous and fragrant, 2–3cm across, white, purple or pink, in loose racemes. Fruit long and thin, up to 16cm, laterally compressed, with small glandular hairs and a small pair of horns at the tip. In coastal habitats throughout. **Fl** 4–6. **Sea Stock** *M. sinuata* is rather similar to above, but often less bushy and smaller (to 60cm). Lower leaves wavy-lobed. Flowers usually pale purple. Fruit similar to above, but sticky with conspicuous yellow or black glands; apical horns not conspicuous. Similar habitats and distribution, especially common on sand-dunes. **Fl** 4–7.

Sad Stock *Matthiola fruticulosa*   A variably downy perennial, up to 60cm, with a woody base. Leaves linear, very narrow, variably wavy, lobed or unlobed, with a basal rosette. Flowers very variable in colour from yellowish to red-purple or rust, with narrow wavy petals 15–28cm long. Fruit narrowly cylindrical, up to 12cm long, with or without 2 horns. In stony places, garrigue and coastal habitats; throughout the Mediterranean part of the area. Fl 4–7. **Three-horned Stock** *M. tricuspidata* is an annual, to 40cm, with lobed leaves and purple flowers. Fruit narrowly cylindrical, up to 10cm long, with equal apical horns. Throughout the Mediterranean area. Fl 4–6.

Arabis verna   A small annual, with basal rosettes of oval, toothed leaves and erect stems up to 40cm. Flowers few or solitary, with pale-violet petals 5–8cm long, yellowish at the base. Fruit up to 6cm long, very narrow. In stony places, bare ground and open grassland; in lowlands or mountains throughout the Mediterranean region. Fl 3–5.

Sweet Alison *Lobularia maritima*   A downy spreading woody-based perennial, with stems up to 40cm, but more commonly prostrate. Leaves narrow, linear-lanceolate, usually pointed. Flowers small (3–4mm across), but clustered into dense racemes that lengthen in fruit; fruit ovate, 3–3.5mm long. Common in dry sunny places; throughout but mainly coastal. Fl virtually all year, but mainly 3–8. *L. libyca* is similar to above, but annual, with blunt leaves; fruit 3–7mm long, with 4–5 seeds (not 1) in each compartment. Coastal sands; S Spain.

Disk Cress *Clypeola jonthlaspi*   A small erect annual, up to 20cm. Leaves linear to ovate, grey-downy. Flowers small (about 2mm across), yellow becoming white, in elongating racemes; fruit a distinctive pendulous winged disc, 2–5mm across. In dry sandy or stony places in the Mediterranean region. Fl 4–6. *C. eriocarpa* is very similar to above, but has slightly larger flowers, with downy (not hairless) petals; fruit scarcely winged, but densely white-hairy. Central and S Spain only.

Burnt Candytuft *Aethionema saxatile*   A low-growing annual or perennial, spreading, ascending or erect, up to 30cm. Leaves ovate and blunt below, narrower and more pointed higher up the stem. Flowers small (5mm across), white or lilac, in dense terminal cluster which elongates in fruit. Fruit ovate to almost circular, notched at tip 5–9mm long. In hilly or mountain areas throughout. Fl 4–7.

Iberis saxatilis   A small, branched, spreading, evergreen shrublet to 40cm, usually less. Leaves almost cylindrical on non-flowering stems, but narrow flat and pointed on flowering shoots up to 20mm long. Flowers white, in a flat-topped terminal clusters that elongate in fruit; fruit ovate, winged, up to 8mm long. On calcareous rocks and mountains, throughout the area. Fl 5–8. *I. pinnata* is an annual species, erect, to 30cm high, with most leaves divided pinnately into 1–3 pairs of segments. Flowers white or lilac, fruit squarish. A cornfield weed; widespread but absent from Portugal and adjacent Spain. Fl 4–6.

Buckler Mustard *Biscutella laevigata*   A highly variable tufted perennial, with erect branched stems to 50cm. Leaves usually forming a basal rosette, ovate to spoon-shaped, toothed, lobed or entire. Flowers yellow, 6–10mm across, in branched racemes; fruit distinctive, consisting of 2 discs attached to each other at 1 edge, either side of their stalk. Split into numerous subspecies. Widespread on roadsides, rough ground and rocky places, especially in mountains, throughout. Fl 5–8. *B. didyma* is an annual, up to 40cm. Flowers very small, with petals gradually narrowing towards the base, not clawed or eared. In dry places, from Italy and Sardinia eastwards.

Three-horned Stock (left)

Arabis verna (right)

Sweet Alison (left)

Iberis pinnata (right)

Buckler Mustard (left)

Biscutella didyma (right)

Dittander *Lepidium latifolium*   A stout, erect, hairless perennial, up to 1m or more, branched above. Leaves leathery, oval, toothed; lower ones stalked, up to 30cm long, upper ones stalkless. Flowers white, 2–3mm across, in broad branched panicles; fruit almost round, 2mm diameter, usually not notched, but with a short style protruding. In saltmarshes and damp sandy places; throughout though largely coastal. Fl 5–7.

Hoary Cress *Cardaria draba*   An erect hairless or slightly downy perennial, up to 90cm. Leaves roughly ovate, toothed or wavy-edged; lower ones stalked, upper ones clasping. Flowers white, 5–6mm across, in dense flat-topped clusters. Fruit heart-shaped, to 5mm across, with protruding style. Throughout, in waste places and roadsides; often abundant. Fl 4–7.

Violet Cabbage *Moricandia arvensis*   An annual or short-lived perennial, with woody-based branched stems. Leaves grey-green and hairless, the lower ones ovate with curved teeth, the upper ones entire and clasping the stem, all rather fleshy. Flowers conspicuous, violet-purple, 2–2.5cm across, in long racemes. Fruit up to 8cm long, narrow, 4-angled. Local in disturbed and rocky places in the south of the area; absent from mainland France. Fl 3–6. *M. moricandioides* is rather similar to above, but a larger more sprawling plant. Inflorescences have 20–40 flowers (cf. 10–20 in Violet Cabbage); the outer sepals are markedly hooded, and the fruit is rounded in section. In dry hilly places in the southern half of Spain. *M. foetida* has only 5–12 whitish flowers per inflorescence; upper stem leaves minute, and fruit compressed. Local in S Spain only.

White Rocket *Diplotaxis erucoides*   An ascending or erect annual plant, occasionally overwintering, with many leafy stems to 50cm. Basal leaves variable, 5–15cm long, but usually pinnately lobed in a lax rosette; upper leaves stalkless, clasping the stem. Flowers white, petals 7–13mm long, veined with violet, sometimes turning violet on ageing, in loose racemes; fruit long and thin, up to 4cm, almost erect. In waste places, rough ground and cultivated land throughout; often an abundant weed. Fl 3–6, mainly.

Eruca vesicaria   A roughly hairy annual or biennial, up to 1m. Leaves pinnately divided, with a large end-lobe and 2–5 pairs of lateral lobes. Flowers white to yellowish, 2–3cm across, with violet veins and erect reddish sepals, in terminal clusters. Fruit erect, narrow, up to 2.5cm long, with a sword-shaped beak. Widespread as a weed of cultivated land in the Mediterranean, and as a casual further north. Fl 4–6.

Vella spinosa   A distinctive much-branched low rounded shrub, to 60cm, with numerous rigid spines among the upper branches. Leaves narrowly linear to lanceolate, with finely spiny margins. Flowers yellow or creamy, with violet veins, 1cm across. On calcareous mountains, in the 'hedgehog plant' zone in the southern part of Spain. Fl 5–6. *V. pseudocytisus* is a taller spineless shrub, with broader leaves and flowers in denser inflorescences. Local in S Spain.

Sea Rocket *Cakile maritima*   A fleshy grey-green hairless branched annual up to 60cm. Leaves variable, from deeply lobed to undivided. Flowers lilac to white, petals 4–14mm long, in bractless racemes, lengthening in fruit; fruit variable, to 2.5cm long, held out horizontally, divided into 2 sections (illus.). In ssp *aegyptiaca*, the lower section has 2 conspicuous projections, while in ssp *maritima* the projections are very small. Common all around the coasts, most commonly on sand. Ssp *aegyptiaca* is the common Mediterranean form; ssp *maritima* occurs from central Portugal northwards up the Atlantic coasts. Fl 3–10.

Morisia monanthos   A distinctive and attractive little perennial, rarely reaching more than 8cm, with a deep rosette of pinnately cut leaves and bearing solitary flowers. Flowers yellow, on stalks up to 2.5cm long, elongating and curving as the fruit ripens. Local in sandy places and on limestone; in Corsica and Sardinia only. Fl 3–5.

Violet Cabbage (le

White Rocket (righ

Vella spinosa (le

Sea Rocket (righ

Morisia monanthe

Sea Rocket fr

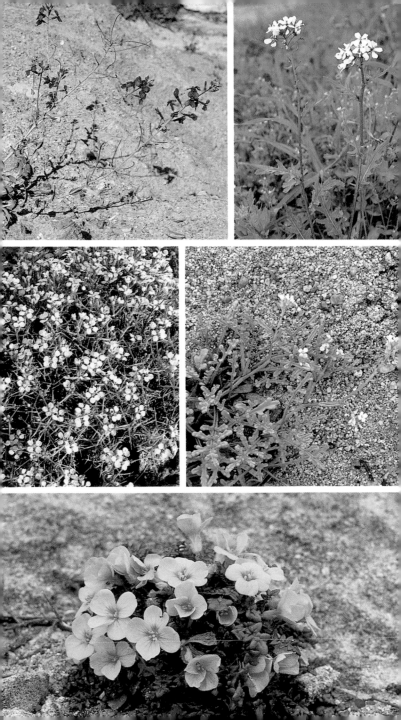

MIGNONETTE FAMILY, RESEDACEAE

Annual or perennial herbs, with flowers in long spikes. Flowers have 4–8 free petals and sepals.

Weld or Dyer's Rocket *Reseda luteola*　An erect hairless biennial, to 1.3m. Leaves lanceolate, unlobed but wavy-edged to 12cm long. Flowers yellow, with 4 petals, of which the uppermost has a 4–8 lobed limb, in long narrow spikes. Fruit rounded, with 3 pointed lobes. Widespread and common almost throughout in stony and disturbed places. **Fl** 5–9. **Corn Mignonette** R. *phyteuma* is a shorter annual, to 50cm, with undivided or slightly lobed leaves. Flowers white, with 6 petals and sepals, and nodding oblong fruit. In cultivated ground throughout.

White Mignonette *Reseda alba*　An erect annual or perennial, to 80cm, often branched above. Leaves pinnately cut, with 5–15 untoothed lobes on each side. Flowers white, with 5 or 6 petals (4–6mm long) and sepals, in long erect or ascending spikes. Fruit elliptical, constricted at the top, 4-angled, erect when ripe. Widespread and common in rough ground, waste land and disturbed areas; throughout. **Fl** 3–9. **Wild Mignonette** R. *lutea* also has pinnately cut leaves, with 1–4 pairs of leaflets. Flowers yellow with 6 petals; capsule oblong, usually erect. In disturbed ground and grassland throughout.

STONECROP FAMILY, CRASSULACEAE

Annuals or perennials with undivided, usually fleshy, leaves. Flowers variable, with 3–20 fused or free sepals and petals.

Navelwort *Umbilicus rupestris*　An erect or ascending hairless fleshy perennial 20–50cm high. Basal leaves almost circular, 2–5cm across, with a central hollow above, and a long stalk from the centre below; upper leaves more kidney-shaped, with rounded teeth. Flowers whitish-green or yellowish, sometimes tinged with pink, 7–10mm long, pendent, in a raceme that occupies more than half of the stem. On walls and rocks throughout. **Fl** 4–7. U. *horizontalis* is similar to above, but differs in that the inflorescence occupies less than half of the stem, usually with many more stem leaves; the flowers are held out horizontally, and are usually narrower and shorter (up to 7mm long). In similar habitats in Spain and Italy.

Aeonium arboreum　A branched perennial plant to 80cm high with woody stems and succulent leaves. Leaves broadly strap-shaped, to 6cm long, alternate and in terminal rosettes, fleshy and shiny. Flowers yellow, 8–10cm across, in dense conical terminal inflorescences. Native of Morocco; widely planted and naturalized on rocks and walls in the Mediterranean region. **Fl** 12–4.

Sedum sediforme　A strong-growing perennial, with spreading to ascending non-flowering shoots, and erect flowering stems to 60cm. Leaves roughly oblong, thick but flattened on the upper surface, 1–2cm long, with a fine apical point. Flowers greenish-white to pale yellow, with 5–8 petals, each 4–7mm long; sepals 2.5mm long, hairless, ovate; inflorescences almost spherical at first, spreading as the flowers open. In dry and stony places throughout the Mediterranean zone. **Fl** 5–8. S. *ochroleucum* is very similar to above, but shorter, to 30cm, and more slender. Leaves rounded, distinctly spurred at the base; sepals 5–7mm long, narrowly triangular, glandular-hairy; petals 7–10mm long. Similar habitats and distribution, though rare in the south-west.

Thick-leaved Stonecrop *Sedum dasyphyllum*   A fleshy perennial, usually tinged greyish-pink, with glandular-hairy stems up to 10cm long. Leaves ovoid or almost spherical c.1cm long, slightly flattened on the upper surface, mostly opposite. Flowers pinkish-white, 5–6mm across, with 5–6 petals, in small branched inflorescences. On walls and rocks; throughout except in the far west. **Fl** 4–7. *S. brevifolium* is very similar to above, but completely hairless, with globose leaves. Local, from S France westwards.

Meadow Saxifrage (lef

Thick-leave

Stonecrop (righ

SAXIFRAGE FAMILY, SAXIFRAGACEAE

Perennial, rarely annual, herbs. Flowers 4- or 5- parted, in branched inflorescences.

Meadow Saxifrage *Saxifraga granulata*   A perennial plant, with most leaves in a basal rosette, and erect flowering stems to 60cm. Leaves stalked, kidney-shaped, 2–4cm long, hairy, with bulbils at the base. Flowers white, 2–3cm across, in a loose branched inflorescence. Local throughout, especially in cooler areas, in grasslands and rocky places. **Fl** 4–6. *S. corsica* is very similar to above, and replaces Meadow Saxifrage in Corsica. It differs in having basal leaves that are 3-lobed, and an inflorescence that is branched from near the ground, with spreading branches. In Corsica, Sardinia and E Spain.

London Plane (righ

PITTOSPORUM FAMILY, PITTOSPORACEAE

Trees or shrubs, with simple alternate leaves. Flowers 5-parted.

Pittosporum tobira   An evergreen shrub, up to 3m. Leaves ovate, 2–5cm long, narrowing into a stalk, shiny dark green and hairless, clustered towards the tips of the branches. Flowers greenish-white to yellow, fragrant, about 1cm across, with 5 blunt petals. Fruit a brownish-yellow globose capsule, splitting to reveal the seeds in a sticky liquid. Native of E Asia, but very widely planted in the Mediterranean region. **Fl** 3–8.

PLANE FAMILY, PLATANACEAE

Trees, with peeling bark. Male and female flowers separate.

London Plane *Platanus × hybrida*   A large deciduous tree, up to 35m, with bark peeling away in flakes, giving the trunk a mottled appearance. Leaves alternate, 10–20cm long, palmately 5- to 7-lobed, cut to the middle at most, with the central lobe barely longer than its width across the base (illus.). Flowers in dense globular heads, usually 2 together; fruit globular, 2–3cm across, pendent. Origins uncertain, but very widely planted as a street and garden tree throughout the area. **Fl** 4–6. **Oriental Plane** *P. orientalis* is very similar to above, but its leaf lobes are more deeply cut, with central lobe much longer than its basal width (illus.); fruit normally 3–6 together. Native to SE Europe, but widely planted in S Europe.

Pittosporum tobira (lef

London Plane

Oriental Plane

ROSE FAMILY, ROSACEAE

A large and varied family of herbs, shrubs and trees, with alternate leaves with stipules. Flowers usually have 5 petals and sepals, but numerous stamens and carpels.

Rosa sempervirens   A climbing or scrambling evergreen rose, reaching 10m with support. Prickles rather few, curved, running down from the base. Leaves pinnate, with 5–7 leaflets, leathery, shiny dark green, with narrow stipules. Flowers white, 4–5cm across, in clusters of 3–7; styles united into a central column; sepals unlobed, long-pointed, glandular. Hips globose to ovoid, red, about 1cm long. In scrub, hedges and open woods throughout the area. **Fl** 5–6.

Service-tree *Sorbus domestica*   A medium-sized tree, to 20m, with spreading branches, and shredding bark. Leaves pinnate, with 6–8 pairs of toothed leaflets 3–4.5cm long (illus.). Flowers white, 1.6–1.8cm across, with 5 styles; fruit roughly ovoid to pear-shaped, about 2cm long, greenish-brown. In woods and rocky places; local throughout except Portugal. **Fl** 4–5. **Wild Service-tree** *S. torminalis* has oval-triangular leaves, with 3–4 pairs of triangular leaflets; flowers similar to above, but smaller (1–1.5cm across), with 2 styles; fruit smaller (1.2–1.8cm long), brownish. Local in woods and scrub throughout. **Fl** 4–5.

Loquat *Eriobotrya japonica*   Evergreen shrub or small tree, up to 10m. Leaves oblong-lanceolate to 25cm long, toothed, dark green above with strongly marked veins, and felted reddish-brown below. Flowers dirty-white, about 1cm across, in pyramidal inflorescences; fruit yellow, ovoid to pear-shaped, 3–6cm long, edible. Chinese in origin, but widely planted for ornament or the fruit; occasionally naturalizing. **Fl** 10–2.

Snowy Mespilus *Amelanchier ovalis*   An erect or spreading deciduous shrub, up to 3m, with blackish bark. Leaves oval to 5cm, blunt, downy when young, toothed. Flowers creamy-white, about 2cm across, slightly bell-shaped, with 3–8 together in erect clusters. Fruit a globose black berry. In rocky places and open woods throughout; commonest in mountains, especially on base-rich soils. **Fl** 4–6.

Fire Thorn *Pyracantha coccinea*   An evergreen, densely branched spiny shrub, up to 2m. Leaves elliptical to 4cm, dark green and shiny above, paler below, with rounded teeth. Flowers creamy-white, 5–10mm across, in flat-topped clusters. Fruit ovoid-globular, 5–7mm long, bright red. In scrub and hedgerows from NE Spain eastwards through France and Italy; also grown in gardens. **Fl** 4–6.

Almond *Prunus dulcis*   A shrub or small tree, up to 8m, densely branched and spiny in the wild, but with fewer, straighter, spineless branches in cultivation. Leaves oblong-lanceolate to 12cm long, hairless, with rounded teeth. Flowers appear before the leaves, usually in pairs, and have 5 pink petals about 2cm long, that gradually fade to white. Fruit ovoid-oblong, grey-downy, to 6cm long. Very widely cultivated in S Europe as a food crop, and elsewhere for ornament; often naturalized. **Fl** 2–4. **Peach** *P. persica* is similar to above, but has narrower leaves on shorter stalks (less than 1.5cm), with solitary flowers remaining pink, not fading. Commonly cultivated in warmer areas. **Apricot** *P. armeniaca* has broader to almost round leaves on stalks 2–4cm long; flowers white or very pale pink throughout flowering time. Widely cultivated throughout; occasionally naturalized.

St Lucie's Cherry *Prunus mahaleb*   A deciduous shrub or small tree, to 10m, usually less, without spines. Leaves broadly ovate, to 7cm, rounded to heart-shaped at the base, and toothed. Flowers white, fragrant, 8–12mm across, in short racemes of 3–10. Fruit ovoid c.1cm long, red becoming black, fleshy but bitter. In woods and scrub, especially on calcareous soils, throughout. **Fl** 4–5. **Portugal Laurel** *P. lusitanica* is rather similar to above, but has evergreen leathery elliptical-ovate leaves, and numerous flowers in long erect racemes that considerably exceed the length of the adjacent leaf. Native from SW France westwards; planted elsewhere.

Rosa sempervirens (left)

Wild Service-tree (right)

Service-tree leaf and leaflet

Loquat (left)

Snowy Mespilus (right)

Wild Service-tree

Almond (left)

St Lucie's Cherry (right)

LEGUME FAMILY, LEGUMINOSAE

A very large family, divided into 3 subfamilies, often treated as distinct families.

CAESALPINIOIDEAE (CAESALPINIACEAE)

Flowers are more or less pea-like, with overlapping petals and free stamens.

Judas Tree *Cercis siliquastrum* A deciduous shrub or small tree to 10m. Leaves heart-shaped, to 12cm long, blunt, long-stalked, hairless. Flowers pink-purple, 1.5–2cm long, produced abundantly in clusters arising from the older wood, and usually appearing before the leaves. In scrub and woodland as a native plant, from S France eastwards, but also very widely planted as an ornamental. **Fl** 3–4.

Carob or **Locust Tree** *Ceratonia siliqua* A dark, evergreen shrub or tree, to 10m. Leaves pinnately divided into 2–5 pairs of rounded, leathery, untoothed leaflets each up to 5cm long. Male and female plants separate: both types of flowers arise directly from the trunk in short racemes and are greenish-yellow, small, without petals. Fruits are large dark bluish-brown pendent pods, up to 20cm long. Widespread both as a native plant, and in cultivation; throughout the Mediterranean zone and Portugal. **Fl** mainly 9–1. *Used for cattle food, and as a substitute for chocolate, and various other uses; the seeds were the original 'carat', owing to their even weight.*

MIMOSOIDEAE (MIMOSACEAE)

Flowers are regular, not pea-like; the stamens are numerous, free, and much longer than the corolla.

Silver Wattle *Acacia dealbata* A shrub or tree, to 30m, with smooth grey bark, and white-downy young twigs. Leaves grey-green, twice-pinnate, with 8–20 pairs of primary leaflets 3–4mm long. Flower clusters globular, 5–6mm across, pale yellow, in dense inflorescences that are longer than the leaves. Widely planted for ornament, soil-stabilization and timber; often naturalizing. **Fl** 2–4. *The 'Mimosa' of florists.*

Acacia retinodes A shrub or small tree, up to 10m. Leaves (strictly speaking, phyllodes) are lanceolate, straight or slightly curved, 6–15cm long, leathery, and light green, with a single vein. Flower heads pale yellow, 4–6mm across, in racemes of 5–12 from the leaf axils. Widely planted in S Europe, mainly for ornament, and frequently naturalized. **Fl** mainly 2–4, but also at other times.

LOTOIDEAE (PAPILIONACEAE)

Flowers are typically pea-like and easily recognized. They are divided into an upper standard, 2 lateral wings, and the lower 2 petals are partially fused into a keel; stamens are usually joined by their filaments. This is an important group in S Europe, with hundreds of species.

Bean Trefoil *Anagyris foetida* A deciduous shrub, with green stems, up to 4m, unpleasant-smelling. Leaves trifoliate, with narrowly elliptical leaflets, silvery-hairy below, and 5mm long papery stipules. Flowers yellow, 2–2.5cm long, in short clusters; calyx bell-shaped, often bluish. Pod 10–20cm long. In rocky and dry places throughout the Mediterranean region. **Fl** 1–4.

Spiny Broom *Calicotome spinosa* A spiny, densely branched shrub, up to 3m, with stout spines on the branches. Leaves trifoliate, each 5–15mm long, silvery-hairy below. Flowers yellow, 12–18mm long, usually solitary, occasionally clustered; calyx tubular with 5 short teeth, but the upper part breaks away as the flower opens, leaving a cup-like structure – diagnostic for this genus; pod 3cm long, hairless. In scrub, open woodland and rocky ground, throughout the Mediterranean part of the area. **Fl** 2–5. *C. villosa* is similar to above, but is less spiny, and more densely silky-hairy. Throughout the southern part of the area. **Fl** 2–6.

Broom *Cytisus scoparius* Rather similar to Spanish Broom (see page 72), but has angled stems, many more leaves, at least some of which are trifoliate, and smaller flowers. Widespread throughout; locally abundant. Fl 4–8.

(see page 72)

Cytisus sessilifolius An erect, hairless, spineless shrub, up to 2m, with numerous rounded green leafy branches. Leaves trifoliate unstalked on flowering branches, sometimes stalked elsewhere, with broadly ovate leaflets to 2cm long. Flowers yellow, in leafless racemes of 3–12; calyx 2-lipped; pod roughly oblong, 2–4cm long, curved. In hilly scrub and woodland, from E Spain to Italy. Fl 4–6.

Cytisus villosus An erect, leafy, hairy, spineless shrub, to 2m, with 5-angled ascending branches. Leaves trifoliate, with central lobe largest, to 3cm long, all with appressed hairs below. Flowers yellow, streaked with red at the base, in clusters of 1–3 that collectively form a loose leafy raceme. Pod 2–4.5cm long, very hairy at first, though becoming hairless when ripe. In maquis and woodland, generally avoiding calcareous soils throughout except Portugal. Fl 3–5. **White Spanish Broom** *C. multiflorus* is rather similar to above, but has undivided leaves on the upper branches and white flowers; similar habitats in the northern half of the Iberian Peninsula. *C. purgans* is vegetatively very similar to *C. multiflorus*, but has yellow flowers, and pods that ripen to black. Widespread in similar habitats from SW France westwards.

Teline monspessulana An erect, much-branched, leafy shrub, to 3m. Leaves trifoliate, stalked, with ovate hairy leaflets to 2cm long. Flowers dark yellow, in axillary clusters; calyx silvery-hairy, 2-lipped. Pod roughly oblong, about 2cm long, densely hairy. In maquis and open woodland throughout the Mediterranean area and Portugal. Fl 3–4. *T. linifolia* is similar to above, but has almost stalkless leaves, with long thin leaflets that are densely hairy below and dark green above; flowers yellow, with a silky-hairy standard (glabrous in above species). Similar habitats in France, Spain and the Balearics. Fl 3–5.

Genista cinerea An erect spineless shrub, to 1m, with numerous flexuous branches. Leaves simple, narrowly ovate to 1cm long. Flowers yellow, mainly in pairs, and borne directly on the main branches, with clusters of bracts; standard of flower hairless, or with a central line of hairs. In woods and maquis, throughout the warmer parts of the area. Fl 4–6. **Hairy Greenweed** *G. pilosa* is similar to above, but usually more prostrate; flowers often borne singly; calyx, keel and standard all densely silvery-hairy.

Genista scorpius An erect or spreading densely branched shrub, very spiny, gorse-like. Leaves simple, less than 1cm long. Spines stout, spreading, with flowers borne directly on them, or on short branches arising from them. Flowers golden yellow, 7–12mm long; calyx virtually hairless, with teeth shorter than tube. Pod 2–4cm long, hairless, constricted between seeds. In scrub and open hillsides; in Spain and S France. Fl 3–5. *G. corsica* is similar to above, but flowers are never borne directly on the spines; calyx teeth as long as tube, and pod less than 2cm long. In similar habitats, in Corsica and Sardinia only.

Genista hirsuta A domed, much-branched, very spiny shrub, to 1m, closely resembling a dwarf Gorse, with straight spines up to 5cm long. Leaves narrowly lance-shaped, about 1cm long, hairy below and on the margins. Flowers yellow, 1.2–1.5cm long, in dense tapering clusters; calyx woolly-hairy, petals often hairy. In scrub, open woods and dry hillsides; in S Spain and Portugal, and the Balearics. Fl 4–6. *G. tournefortii* is very similar, but has branched spines. Similar habitats and distribution, but absent from the Balearics.

Genista umbellata A distinctive rounded tufted shrub, with numerous erect almost leafless rush-like branches, bearing tight dense rounded heads of yellow flowers, 4–16 in a cluster; calyx conspicuously silvery-hairy, 5mm long. Leaves simple, hairy, narrowly elliptical. Locally common on dry stony hillsides and roadsides in S Spain. Fl 3–5.

Broom (left)

Cytisus villosus (right)

Genista cinerea (left)

Genista corsica (right)

Genista hirsuta (left)

Genista umbellata (right)

Winged Broom *Chamaespartium sagittale* A distinctive mat-forming sub-shrub, with flattened winged green stems. Leaves elliptical, 1–2cm long. Flowering stems erect or ascending, to 50cm, with rounded terminal clusters of yellow flowers, each about 1cm long; calyx 2-lipped, silvery-hairy. In woods, scrub and rocky places almost throughout; absent from most islands. **Fl** 5–8. *C. tridentatum* is similar, but usually more erect, to 70cm. Wholly leafless; stem wings are elongated at each node into 3 prickly teeth or lobes. Heathy places and maquis; Portugal and W Spain.

White Broom (left)

Spanish Broom (right)

White Broom or **Retama** *Lygos monosperma* A slender, erect, almost leaf-less much-branched shrub, to 3m. Leaves narrowly lanceolate, silky-hairy. Flowers small, 1–1.2cm long, white, fragrant, produced abundantly in long racemes. Calyx 2-lipped, bell-shaped, reddish and hairless; pod wrinkled. In coastal habitats, in the S Iberian Peninsula. **Fl** 2–5. *L. sphaerocarpa* is similar to above, but yellow-flowered, with smooth pods. In dry habitats in the S and W Iberian Peninsula.

Spanish Broom *Spartium junceum* An easily recognized shrub, with numer-ous erect cylindrical green spineless stems, to 3m. Leaves few, simple, narrowly oblong to 3cm long. Flowers large, 2.5cm long, yellow, conspicuous, sweet-scented; calyx spathe-like, split above; pod flattened, 5–8cm long. Throughout the area in scrub, dry hillsides, and hedges, but also very widely planted. **Fl** 4–8.

Hedgehog Broom *Erinacea anthyllis* A very distinctive hummock-forming, extremely spiny shrub, up to 40cm. Leaves small with numerous spines. Flowers blue-violet, calyx inflated and silvery-hairy. Locally abundant on dry, usually cal-careous, hillsides in S central Spain, and just into SW France. **Fl** 4–6.

Hedgehog Broom
(left)

Ulex parviflorus (right)

Ulex parviflorus A rounded very spiny shrub, to 1.5 m tall. Stems greyish-green, hairless or very shortly hairy. Spines stiff, very sharp, curved or straight, up to 3cm long, much longer than the flowers. Flowers small (6–8mm long), yellow, with petals no longer than calyx. A variable species, occurring in scrub and dry places from S France westwards; absent from the islands. **Fl** 3–6

Adenocarpus complicatus An erect spineless shrub, up to 4m, with variably silvery-hairy twigs and leaves. Leaves trifoliate with narrow leaflets to 2.5cm long. Flowers orange-yellow, 1–1.5cm long, in dense leafless racemes; standard silvery-hairy; calyx sometimes with glandular warts. Fruit distinctive: oblong, silky-hairy, with glandular warts. In woods and scrub throughout the area. **Fl** 5–9. *A. telonen-sis* is similar to above, but smaller, to 1m, with larger flowers in terminal umbel-like clusters of 2–7. In similar habitats from S France westwards.

Yellow Lupin *Lupinus luteus* An erect hairy annual plant, to 80cm. Leaves palmately divided, with 6–8 narrow, pointed leaflets each 4–6cm long, with appressed hairs on both surfaces. Flowers bright yellow, scented, in whorls that form a long raceme up to 16cm long; pods 4–5cm long, black and hairy. In sandy grassy places, and frequently cultivated, throughout the Mediterranean. **Fl** 3–6. *L. hispanicus* is similar to above, but leaflets are hairless above, not bristle-pointed; flowers cream, becoming pinkish, unscented. W Iberian Peninsula only.

Yellow Lupin (left)

Narrow-leaved Lupin
(right)

Narrow-leaved Lupin *Lupinus angustifolius* An erect, hairy annual, to 80cm. Leaves palmate, leaflets only 2–5mm wide, hairless above and slightly hairy below. Flowers blue, 1.1–1.3cm long, alternate (not whorled) in racemes 10–20cm long. Pod slightly hairy, yellow to black. In grassland, cultivated ground and waste places; throughout area. **Fl** 4–6. Ssp *reticulatus*, a small form found on coastal sands. *L. micran-thus* is similar to above, but shorter, to 40cm, brown-hairy; the leaflets wider, 5–15mm across. Flowers in the racemes are alternate below, but slightly whorled higher up. Pod 3–5cm long, hairy, red-brown. Widespread throughout. *L. varius* is similar to Narrow-leaved Lupin, but has oblong to ovate leaflets, 6–9mm wide; all flowers irregularly whorled, blue but with a white and yellow blotch on the standard; larger than above 2 species (1.5–1.7cm long). Throughout the Mediterranean area.

False Acacia *Robinia pseudacacia*   A deciduous tree, up to 25m. Leaves pinnate, with 3–10 pairs of ovate leaflets to 4.5cm long, sometimes with spines at the base. Flowers white to 2cm long, with yellow at the base of the standard, in many-flowered racemes 10–20cm long. Native of N America; widely planted and often naturalized, throughout S Europe. Fl 4–6.

Bladder Senna *Colutea arborescens*   A much-branched deciduous shrub, to 6m, usually less. Leaves pinnate, with 3–6 pairs of ovate to elliptical leaflets to 3cm long. Flowers yellow, 1.6–2cm long, in lax axillary racemes of 3–8 flowers. Pods very distinctive when ripe: 5–7cm long, strongly inflated, papery, pinkish to light brown. In woodland and maquis throughout the Mediterranean zone; planted elsewhere. Fl 4–7. *C. atlantica* is very similar, but has persistently downy young shoots, and a downy ovary. S Spain only.

Astragalus echinatus   A spreading or ascending annual plant, up to 60cm long. Leaves pinnate, 4–8cm long, with 6–9 pairs of roughly oblong leaflets. Flowers purplish, in dense globular heads of 10–15 on stalks that are usually longer than the leaves. Fruit covered with twisted scales and hairs. Common in disturbed ground, especially roadsides, throughout the Mediterranean part of the area. Fl 4–6.

Astragalus alopecuroides   A robust erect herbaceous perennial, up to 75cm. Leaves unevenly pinnate, with 12–15 pairs of oblong leaflets with hairy stipules. Flowers pale yellow, large, with the standard up to 2.7cm long, in rounded heads in the upper leaf axils; calyx shaggy-hairy. A striking plant. In dry grassy and disturbed places, from S France westwards. Fl 4–6.

Astragalus massiliensis   A very spiny perennial, forming low rounded tussocks up to 40cm. Leaves silvery, small, 2–7cm long, pinnate, with 6–12 pairs of leaflets and a spiny central stem, which persists as a spine after the leaflets fall. Flowers white, c.1.5cm long, in terminal clusters; fruit hairy, about 1cm long. In garrigue and bare rocky places, often near the coast; frequent from S France westwards, rare or absent in Italy. Fl 3–6.

Montpellier Milk-vetch *Astragalus monspessulanus*   A spreading plant, with flower clusters arising directly from the rootstock. Leaves pinnate 10–20cm long,, with 10–20 pairs of oblong or rounded leaflets. Flowers purplish, occasionally almost white, in ovoid clusters of 7–30 flowers; pods cylindrical, to 4.5cm long, slightly curved. In dry rocky ground and on roadsides, especially in hilly areas, throughout the Mediterranean region. Fl 4–8.

Biserrula pelecinus   A spreading downy annual, to 40cm. Leaves unevenly pinnate, with 7–15 pairs of notched leaflets to 1cm long. Flowers in short-stalked axillary clusters of 3–10; corolla 4–6mm long, blue, or pale yellow with a blue tip. The distinctive feature is the fruit, which is up to 4cm long and shaped like a straight double-edged saw, ripening to brown. In dry open places, throughout the Mediterranean region. Fl 4–6.

Liquorice *Glycyrrhiza glabra*   A strong-growing erect perennial, up to 1m, hairless or downy. Leaves pinnate, with 4–8 pairs of blunt ovate-oblong leaflets, each 2–4cm long, often sticky. Flowers bluish-white, 8–12mm long, in racemes that are shorter than their subtending leaves. Pods oblong, flattened, hairless. Native or naturalized in dry open habitats throughout the Mediterranean region. Fl 5–7.

Pitch Trefoil *Psoralea bituminosa*   An erect branched perennial, to 30–100cm, smelling strongly of tar when crushed. Leaves long-stalked, trifoliate, with narrow or broad untoothed leaflets to 6cm long. Flowers blue-violet, in dense clover-like heads on long stalks. Pod ovoid, flattened, with a sickle-shaped beak. In grassy places, roadsides, and dry waste ground, throughout; frequent. Fl 4–7. *P. americana* has toothed leaflets; the flowers are in longer racemes, on stalks about equalling the leaves; corolla white, often violet-tipped. In southern parts of Italy and Iberian Peninsula.

False Sainfoin *Vicia onobrychioides*   A hairless or downy perennial, to about 1m. Leaves pinnate, with 5–9 pairs of linear to oblong untoothed leaflets to 3cm long, with untoothed or slightly toothed stipules. Flowers large, 1.7–2.4cm, bluish-violet with a paler keel, in rather 1-sided long-stalked racemes of 4–12 flowers. Legume reddish-brown, hairless, up to 4cm long. In dry grassy and rocky places, especially in mountains; throughout except the north. Fl 5–7.

Fodder Vetch *Vicia villosa*   A very variable species. An annual herb, reaching 2m with support. Leaves pinnate, with 4–12 pairs of narrowly elliptical leaflets, with untoothed, usually hairy, stipules. Flowers violet to purple, 1–2cm long, often with creamy-yellow wings, in narrow racemes that exceed the leaves, with flowers mostly opening at the same time; calyx swollen at the base. Pod brown, hairless, 2–4cm long. Widespread throughout in disturbed and grassy places. Fl 4–6. *V. benghalensis* is very similar, but usually smaller. Flowers reddish-purple, darker at tip, without creamy wings, in racemes that are no longer than the leaves; pod usually downy. In similar habitats throughout the Mediterranean region. Fl 3–6.

Yellow-vetch *Vicia lutea*   A variably hairy or almost hairless annual, up to 60cm. Leaves pinnate, with 3–10 pairs of narrowly oblong leaflets, and branched or unbranched tendrils. Flowers solitary or 2–3 together in the leaf axils, 2–3.5cm long, pale yellow, often tinged or veined with purple. Pod 2–4cm long, usually hairy with swollen-based hairs. Widespread throughout in dry, usually grassy, places. Fl 4–6. **Hairy Yellow-vetch** *V. hybrida* is very similar to above, but generally has fewer (3–8) pairs of broader leaflets; flowers solitary, standard downy on the back (hairless in Yellow-vetch). In similar habitats throughout; rarer in the north.

Broad-leaved Everlasting-pea *Lathyrus latifolius*   A variable scrambling perennial herb, downy or hairless, with winged stems up to 3m long. Leaves consist of a single pair of large linear to ovate leaflets, 4–15cm long; stipules at base of leaf stalk large, arrow-shaped at base, more than half the width of the stem. Flowers large, 2–3cm long, purplish-pink, in long-stalked racemes of 5–15 flowers; pods hairless. Widespread throughout in rough grassy and bushy habitats; also cultivated and naturalized. Fl 4–7. **Narrow-leaved Everlasting-pea** *L. sylvestris* is rather similar to above, but has smaller flowers, and the stipules are less than half the width of the stem. In similar habitats; widespread, but absent from the far south. *L. heterophyllus* differs from Broad-leaved Everlasting-pea in having 2–3 pairs of leaflets on the upper leaves, and smaller flowers (1.2–2.2cm). Widespread on mainland S Europe.

Tangier Pea *Lathyrus tingitanus*   An annual herb, with winged stems, to 1.2m long. Leaves have a single pair of lanceolate to ovate leaflets; stipules 3–12mm wide, half-arrow-shaped at base. Flowers large, 2–3cm long, bright purple, in racemes of only 1–3 flowers. In grassy and bushy places; in the southern half of the Iberian Peninsula, and Sardinia. Fl 3–6.

Lathyrus cicera   A slender hairless annual, up to 80cm, with narrowly winged stems. Leaves with usually 1 (occasionally 2) pair of lanceolate leaflets 1–10cm long, with simple or branched tendrils on the upper leaves. Flowers solitary, on stalks 1–3cm long, with reddish-purple petals that are 1–1.5cm long; calyx teeth narrowly triangular, all equal; pod hairless, 2–4cm long, with 2 keels. Widespread throughout the Mediterranean area in grassy or cultivated ground. Fl 3–6.

Annual Yellow Vetchling *Lathyrus annuus*   A hairless annual, with winged stems up to 1.5m (usually less). Leaves with 1 pair of narrowly lanceolate leaflets, 5–15cm long, with half-arrow-shaped stipules and branched tendrils. Flowers in erect racemes of 1–3, corolla yellow to orange, 1.2–1.8cm long; calyx teeth equal; pod pale brown, glandular-hairy when young, 3–8cm long. In rough and cultivated ground throughout the Mediterranean area. Fl 4–6.

Lathyrus clymenum A hairless scrambling annual with winged stems up to 1m. Leaves have a broad leaf-like stalk, the lower ones with no leaflets, the upper ones with 2–4 pairs of linear to elliptical leaflets (2–6cm long) that are broader than the winged stem. Flowers in erect racemes of 1–5, corolla crimson with lilac wings, 1.5–2cm long; pod 3–7cm long, hairless, channelled along the back edge. Widespread and common throughout the Mediterranean region, in grassy and disturbed places. **Fl** 3–6. *L. articulatus* is similar to above, but its leaflets are less than 5mm wide (more than 5mm wide in *L. clymenum*); corolla has white or pink wings; the style is blunt, not bristle-tipped, and the pod is not channelled. Similar habitats and distribution.

Winged Vetchling *Lathyrus ochrus* A hairless grey-green annual, to 70cm, with broadly winged stems and leaf stalks. Lower leaves consist of broad stalk ending in 3 tendrils, while the upper leaves have 1–2 pairs of leaflets 2–4cm long, and branched tendrils. Flowers pale yellow, 1.5–1.8cm long, solitary or paired; pods 4–6cm long, hairless, with 2 wings on the back. Throughout the Mediterranean area in dry grassy and cultivated places. **Fl** 3–6.

Yellow Vetchling *Lathyrus aphaca* A distinctive hairless grey-green scrambling annual, with angled stems up to 1m long. Mature leaves consist only of a tendril, but are dwarfed by the enlarged spearhead-shaped stipules 1–5cm long. Flowers yellow, usually solitary, 6–18mm long, on stalks up to 5cm long; pod brown, hairless, 2–3.5cm long. Widespread and common in dry grassy and disturbed places throughout. **Fl** 3–6.

Large Yellow Restharrow *Ononis natrix* An erect or spreading branched subshrub, rather variable, up to 70cm, densely glandular-hairy all over. Leaves trifoliate, rarely simple or pinnate. Flowers solitary, but forming loose leafy inflorescences; corolla yellow, often red-veined, 6–20mm across. Pods pendulous, hairy, 1–2.5cm long. Widespread throughout in various habitats, especially coastal or hilly sites. **Fl** 4–7 (or almost throughout in extreme south). **Fl** 4–6. *O. viscosa* is similar to *O. pubescens*, but taller (up to 80cm), with calyx teeth 3-veined (not 5-veined), and seeds markedly warty, not smooth. In similar habitats throughout the Mediterranean region. **Fl** 3–6

Ononis variegata A spreading or ascending hairy annual, up to 30cm, branched from the base. Leaves all with 1 short-stalked, strongly-veined, ovate leaflet. Flowers solitary, yellow, 1.2–1.4cm, aggregated into a loose, often branched, inflorescence. Frequent on coastal sands throughout the Mediterranean region, except France and the Balearics. **Fl** 4–6.

Spiny Restharrow *Ononis spinosa* A variable dwarf shrub, up to 80cm, erect or ascending, always spiny, usually with 2 opposite rows of hairs on young stems. Leaves usually trifoliate, or simple above. Flowers pink, 1–2cm, singly or in pairs at each node, forming a loose inflorescence. Pod hairy, 6–10mm long, usually with 1 warty seed. Common in dry grassy places throughout the area. **Fl** 4–7. **Small Restharrow** *O. reclinata* is a slender spreading annual plant, with shaggy-hairy stems, not exceeding 15cm. Flowers small, 5–10mm, pink-purple, solitary, forming loose leafy inflorescences. In dry, grassy and sandy places, especially near the coast; scattered throughout. **Fl** 4–6.

Small-flowered Melilot *Melilotus indica* An erect or ascending branched or simple annual, up to 50cm. Leaves trifoliate, with toothed leaflets, but stipules virtually untoothed. Flowers small (2–3mm), pale yellow, in dense many-flowered racemes; wings and keel equal, shorter than standard; pod virtually spherical (illus.), 2–3mm long, net-veined. In waste places or saline areas throughout the Mediterranean region. **Fl** 4–6. *M. messanensis* has stipules that are toothed, at least in part; flowers yellow, 4–5mm, in few-flowered racemes that do not exceed their subtending leaves. Pod ovoid, striped (illus.). Similar habitats and distribution. **Fl** 4–6.

Lathyrus clymenum (left)

Yellow Vetchling (right)

Large Yellow Restharrow (left)

Small-flowered Melilot (right)

Spiny Restharrow

Small-flowered Melilot

Melilotus messanensis

Furrowed Melilot *Melilotus sulcata*   An erect branched or simple annual, up to 40cm. Leaves trifoliate, with stalked, oblong, toothed leaflets; stipules of at least the middle leaves toothed. Flowers yellow, 3–4mm, 8–25 together in clusters as long as or longer than their leaves. Pods globose, 3–4mm across, concentrically striped. In cultivated ground and open habitats throughout the Mediterranean region. Fl 3–6.

Tree Medick *Medicago arborea*   A densely leafy shrub, up to 4m, with silky-hairy young branches. Leaves trifoliate, with young leaflets silky-hairy below. Flowers yellow, 1.2–1.5cm, in short 4- to 8-flowered racemes; pod coiled 1–1½ times (illus.), flattened, 12–15mm across, smooth, with a hole through the centre. In rocky places, often coastal, in the southern parts of the Mediterranean region; absent as a native from France, though planted and occasionally naturalized. Fl 4–8.

Large Disk Medick *Medicago orbicularis*   A spreading hairless or slightly hairy annual, 20–90cm long. Leaves trifoliate. Flowers small, 2–5mm long, yellow, in racemes of 1–5; the plant becomes distinctive in fruit: the fruits are spiralled 4–6 times, producing a 'Chinese lantern' effect (illus.); smooth, weakly veined, light green at first, light brown later 1–2cm across. In grassy and cultivated ground throughout the Mediterranean area. Fl 4–7.

Sea Medick *Medicago marina*   A distinctive spreading or ascending perennial, densely covered with white-woolly hairs. Leaves trifoliate, with obovate pointed leaflets. Flowers pale yellow, 6–8mm long, 5–12 together in a short dense inflorescence, with leaves just below it. Pods woolly-white, spiralled 2–3 times (illus.), 5–7mm across, often spiny. Frequent on coastal dunes and sandy beaches, throughout the Mediterranean and Atlantic coasts. Fl 3–6. *M. rigidula* is annual, glandular-hairy but not woolly-white; the pods are densely glandular-hairy, with 4–7 coils and numerous spines (illus.). Throughout the Mediterranean region.

Toothed Medick *Medicago polymorpha*   A downy or hairless, erect or spreading annual, up to 40cm. Leaves trifoliate, with broadly obovate to almost heart-shaped unblotched leaflets. Flowers yellow, 3–4.5mm long, in racemes of 1–5. Fruit 4–10mm across, with 1½–6 loose coils, somewhat flattened, with 2 rows of spines (illus.), and a hairless net-veined surface. Common in waste ground, and cultivated areas in the Mediterranean area. Fl 3–6. **Spotted Medick** *M. arabica* is very similar to above, but the leaflets are nearly always dark-blotched, and the fruits (illus.) have 3 grooves on the margin (cf. 2 in *M. polymorpha*). Common throughout.

Woolly Trefoil *Trifolium tomentosum*   A variable but distinctive spreading annual plant, with stems up to 15cm. Leaves trifoliate with obovate leaflets. Flower heads woolly-white, with small pink flowers, globular, becoming 7–12mm across in fruit, almost stalkless; calyx woolly-white, becoming inflated. In dry grassy places throughout the Mediterranean region. Fl 4–6. **Reversed Clover** *T. resupinatum* is similar in form to above, but is often more erect, with a less woolly calyx; heads up to 2cm across in fruit. Native or naturalized throughout, often in damper places.

Starry Clover *Trifolium stellatum*   A distinctive softly hairy annual plant, creeping or erect to 20cm high. Flower heads globose to ovoid with small white flowers, become distinctive and conspicuous in fruit as the silky-haired calyx enlarges to become star-like. Throughout the Mediterranean area, and locally further north. Fl 3–6.

Crimson Clover *Trifolium incarnatum*   An erect or ascending, annual to 50cm. Leaflets ovate or almost round. Flower heads solitary, on long stalks, ovoid to cylindrical, up to 4cm long; corolla 1–1.2cm long, exceeding the sepals, usually blood-red, less commonly yellowish-white. Two subspecies occur: ssp *incarnatum* is more robust, often cultivated, with blood-red flowers; ssp *molineri* (Long-headed Clover) is hairier, less robust, with yellowish-white flowers, whose petals considerably exceed the sepals. Both occur in grassy places throughout the area, but ssp *molineri* is much more local, and usually coastal. Fl 4–7.

Furrowed Melilot (left

Large Disk Medick
(right

Tree Medick po

Large Disk Medick po
Sea Medick (left

Toothed Medick (right

Sea Medick po

Medicago rigidula po

Woolly Trefoil (left

Starry Clover (right

Toothed Medick frui

Spotted Medick frui

Narrow-leaved Crimson Clover *Trifolium angustifolium*   An erect or ascending hairy annual, to 50cm. Leaves trifoliate, with linear-lanceolate long narrow pointed leaflets. Flower heads long, up to 8cm, conical to cylindrical; flowers pink, 1–1.2cm long, no longer than the bristle-like calyx teeth, and not particularly conspicuous, all opening at about the same time. In grassy and disturbed places, generally on more acid soils, throughout the Mediterranean region. Fl 4–7. *T. purpureum* is similar to above, but has broader leaflets, and larger red-purple flowers that greatly exceed the calyx teeth, in conical heads with flowers opening progressively from the base upwards. In dry disturbed and grassy places; from France eastwards.

Sulphur Clover *Trifolium ochroleucon*   An erect or ascending tufted softly hairy perennial plant, up to 50cm. Leaflets obovate to oblong. Flower heads large (2–4cm), globose to oblong, tending to become ovoid in fruit; corolla 1.5–2cm long, creamy-yellow (rarely pink), greatly exceeding the sepals. In damp or semi-shady grassy places throughout. Fl 4–7.

Hairy Clover *Trifolium hirtum*   A spreading or ascending hairy annual, up to 35cm. Leaves trifoliate, with obovate leaflets; stipules narrow lanceolate, abruptly contracted into a long hairy point. Flowers purple, with corolla 1.2–1.5cm, exceeding calyx teeth; heads 1.5–2cm across, spherical, hairy, solitary, unstalked, with a distinct ruff of enlarged stipules and leaves below it. In dry places throughout the Mediterranean region. Fl 4–6.

Dorycnium hirsutum   An erect or ascending perennial hairy herb or subshrub to 50cm, rather clover-like but with 5-foliate leaves. Flowers in axillary heads of 4–10, with a white or pinkish corolla 1–2cm long, and a darker-tipped keel; calyx teeth unequal, shaggy-hairy; pods small, up to 1.2cm long. In rocky, grassy or sandy places throughout the Mediterranean region. Fl 4–7. Two other species occur in the region, both of which have smaller flowers (less than 7mm long): *D. rectum* has the middle and lower leaves with an axis of at least 5mm long; heads have 20–40 flowers, with equal calyx teeth. *D. pentaphyllum* has leaves without a distinct axis and unequal calyx teeth. Both occur locally throughout the Mediterranean region.

Lotus edulis   A distinctive prostrate or ascending downy annual herb, to 50cm. Leaves (as in all the genus *Lotus*) have 5 leaflets, but the lowest 2 are situated at the base of the leaf stalk, appearing more like stipules. Flowers yellow, solitary or paired, 1–1.6cm long, on stalks much longer than the leaves; pod distinctive when ripe, 2–4cm long, strongly inflated, grooved on the back, and slightly curved. In grassy and cultivated places throughout the Mediterranean region. Fl 2–6.

Southern Bird's-foot-trefoil *Lotus creticus*   A perennial, up to 50cm, usually with dense silvery hairs. Flowers yellow, in clusters of 2–6, corolla 1.2–1.8cm long, and the keel has a long straight purple beak; calyx strongly 2-lipped, with upper 2 teeth curved upwards, and lateral 2 teeth pointed and almost as long as upper. In sandy coastal sites; throughout much of the Mediterranean, but absent from France and the islands except Sicily. Fl 3–5. *L. cytisoides* is very similar to above, but usually less silky-hairy. The lateral calyx teeth are blunt, and much shorter than the upper ones, while the keel petal has a short curved purple-tipped beak. In rocky and sandy coastal sites; more widespread than above. Fl 3–6.

Lotus ornithopodioides   A downy branched ascending or erect annual plant, up to 50cm. Leaves stalked, with all leaflets ovate to rhombic, wedge- or heart-shaped at the base. Flowers in heads of 2–5, with 3 stalkless bracts below, on stalks about as long as the leaves. Corolla yellow, small, 7–10mm long, with very short and blunt lateral calyx teeth. Pods pendent, long and cylindrical, 2–5cm long, slightly curved, and constricted between the seeds. Common in grassy and sandy places throughout the southern part of the area. Fl 3–6.

Dorycnium hirsutum
(left)

Lotus edulis (left)

Lotus ornithopodioides
(right)

Dragon's-teeth *Tetragonolobus maritimus* A grey-green spreading mat-forming hairless or downy perennial, to 40cm. Leaves trifoliate, up to 3cm long, with ovate leafy stipules. Flowers solitary, pale yellow, 2.5–3cm, on stalks much longer than leaves, with a trifoliate bract below the flower. Fruit 3–6cm long with 4 narrow wings. In dry or slightly damp grassy places throughout. Fl 4–7.

Asparagus Pea *Tetragonolobus purpureus* A softly hairy spreading or ascending annual, to 40cm. Leaves as for Dragon's-teeth. Flowers solitary or paired, 1.5–2.2cm long, deep red, on stalks no longer than leaves. Pod 3–9cm long, with 4 broad wings, each 2–4mm wide. In disturbed, cultivated and grassy places throughout, though only native in the south; also widely cultivated. Fl 3–6. *The fruits are edible, with a taste of asparagus, when young. T. requienii* is rather similar to above, with slightly smaller, more orange-red flowers; pods with 2 narrow wings, on the upper side only. In grassy places throughout the Mediterranean region, excluding France and most of the islands. Fl 4–6.

Anthyllis cytisoides A small spineless shrub, with white-downy stems and young leaves. Lower leaves simple, upper leaves trifoliate with the terminal leaflet much the largest. Flowers pale yellow, collectively forming a long narrow spike-like inflorescence; calyx woolly, 4–7mm long, with 5 equal teeth. In rocky and scrubby places, mainly coastal; from S France westwards; also in the Balearics. Fl 3–6. A. *hermanniae* is a densely branched spiny shrub, to 50cm, with simple or trifoliate leaves and interrupted spikes of deeper yellow flowers. In rocky places and garrigue, from Corsica eastwards. Fl 5–8.

Jupiter's Beard *Anthyllis barba-jovis* A striking shrub, up to 2m (usually less), with woody branches and silvery-white foliage. Leaves unevenly pinnate, with 6–9 or more pairs of narrow equal leaflets. Flowers yellow, in terminal heads of 10 or more, with silvery deeply cut bracts below; calyx white-hairy 4–6mm long – altogether an unmistakable combination. In rocky coastal areas, and in cultivation, along the Mediterranean from E Spain eastwards. Fl 4–6.

Bladder Vetch *Anthyllis tetraphylla* A spreading or ascending hairy annual. Leaves pinnate, usually with 2 pairs of small leaflets and a large terminal leaflet, all hairy. Flowers in axillary clusters of 1–7; corolla pale yellow, about 1.5cm, with keel often red-tipped; calyx is distinctive, silky-hairy in flower, strongly inflated in fruit, often reddish-tinged. Cultivated and grassy places in Mediterranean region. Fl 3–7.

Orange Bird's-foot *Ornithopus pinnatus* A hairless or slightly downy annual, up to 50cm. Leaves pinnate, with 3–7 pairs of narrow leaflets. Flowers orange-yellow, 6–8mm long, solitary or in heads of 2–5, on long stalks. Fruit cylindrical, narrow, 2–3.5cm long, curved like an uncoiling spring, not contracted between the seeds. In grassy and disturbed ground throughout, eastwards to Italy. Fl 3–6. O. *compressus* is similar to above, but differs in normally being more downy; leaves have 7–18 pairs of leaflets; and flower heads have a pinnate leafy bract below them (absent in above). Similar habitats; widespread throughout. Fl 2–5.

Scorpion Senna *Coronilla emerus* A small leafy shrub, to 2m (usually less), with slender, green, ribbed twigs. Leaves pinnate, with 2–4 pairs of obovate rather grey-green leaflets. Flowers pale yellow, 1.4–2cm long, in long-stalked clusters of 2–8; pods pendent, 5–11cm long, only slightly constricted between seeds. The subspecies throughout most of the region are ssp *emerus*, which has only 1–5 flowers per head; and ssp *emeroides*, which has up to 8 flowers, and occurs from Italy eastwards. In rocky and grassy places, mainly calcareous, throughout. Fl 4–6. C. *valentina* is rather similar to Scorpion Senna, but is usually a more compact shrub, to 1m, with more blue-green foliage. Flowers yellow, 7–12mm long, in clusters of 4–12 on stalks up to 7cm long. In rocky places and garrigue, throughout the Mediterranean coastal zone; also grown in gardens, often as C. *glauca*. Fl 3–7.

Rush-like Scorpion Vetch *Coronilla juncea* A hairless shrub, with slender almost leafless rush-like stems, to 1m, with long internodes. Leaves pinnate, with 1–3 pairs of fleshy leaflets, falling early. Flowers yellow, 6–12mm long, in dense rounded heads of 5–12 on long stalks. Pods 1–5cm long, bluntly 4-angled. Local in dry sunny places throughout the Mediterranean region. Fl 4–6.

Crown Vetch *Coronilla varia* A spreading or ascending leafy perennial herb, up to about 1m. Leaves pinnate with 7–12 pairs of oblong or elliptical leaflets, with narrow membranous margins. Flowers pink, white, or multi-coloured, 1–1.5cm long, in dense clusters of 10–20. Pod 2–6cm long, erect and 4-angled. Widespread and frequent in grassy and bushy places throughout; also often cultivated as a fodder plant. Fl 4–8.

Annual Scorpion Vetch *Coronilla scorpioides* An ascending or erect hairless annual, up to 40cm. Leaves distinctive: trifoliate with a large almost circular terminal leaflet, and 2 smaller lateral leaflets; lower leaves often simple. Flowers yellow, 4–8mm, in small long-stalked clusters of 2–5; pod 2–6cm long, slender, pendent, strongly curved. In dry disturbed and grassy places; throughout the Mediterranean region, and further inland in places. Fl 3–6. *C. repanda* differs from above in having unevenly pinnate leaves with 2–4 pairs of leaflets. In similar habitats in southern parts of the area only.

Hippocrepis unisiliquosa A slender spreading annual, up to 20cm. Leaves pinnate, with 3–7 pairs of oblong notched leaflets. Flowers yellow, small (4–7mm long), solitary or paired in the axils of the upper leaves, with very short stalks. Fruit distinctive: 2–4cm long, laterally compressed, slightly curved, and divided into 7–11 segments by deep keyhole-shaped constrictions (illus.). In cultivated land and dry stony places throughout the Mediterranean region. Fl 3–6. *H. multisiliquosa* is similar to above, but has slightly larger flowers in stalked clusters of 2–6; fruit similar, but strongly curved. In similar habitats; Iberian Peninsula and the larger islands only.

Scorpiurus muricatus A spreading or ascending annual plant, up to 60cm. Leaves simple, spathulate, narrowing gradually into the stalk, with 3–5 parallel veins. Flowers yellow, 5–7mm long, 2–5 together in stalked axillary heads. Fruits distinctive, narrowly cylindrical, but coiled irregularly and covered with warts and spines (or rarely smooth). In grassy, disturbed and cultivated places, throughout except in the north of the region. Fl 4–6. *S. vermiculatus* is very similar to above, but has solitary or paired flowers; fruit covered with club-shaped swellings on the outer ridges. Similar habitats and distribution.

Italian Sainfoin or **French Honeysuckle** *Hedysarum coronarium* A robust leafy sparsely hairy branched perennial, up to 1m. Leaves pinnate, with 3–5 pairs of broadly ovate leaflets. Flowers bright carmine-red, each 1.2–1.5cm long, in conspicuous ovoid-cylindrical clusters with 10–35 flowers. Fruit straight, but constricted into 2–4 disc-shaped segments, covered with spiny warts. In grassy places and cultivated ground throughout the Mediterranean region; also widely cultivated. Fl 3–6. *H. spinosissimum* is a smaller annual, to 35cm. Flowers pale pinkish-purple or white, 8–11mm long, in clusters of 2–10 on long stalks. Fruit divided into 2–4 hairy segments, with hooked spines. Throughout the Mediterranean region, east to Italy. *H. glomeratum* (illus.) is similar to *H. spinosissimum*, but has larger darker flowers, 14–20mm long, with corolla 2–5 times as long as the calyx (1½–2 times as long in *H. spinosissimum*); leaflets broad ovate, not narrow. Similar habitats and distribution.

Cockscomb Sainfoin *Onobrychis caput-galli* A hairless or slightly downy erect annual, up to 90cm. Leaves pinnate, with 4–7 pairs of linear to obovate leaflets. Flowers in tight heads of 4–8 on stalks about as long as the leaves; corolla reddish-purple, 4–7mm long; fruit 6–10mm long, in a semicircle, with deep pits and numerous spines – the 'cockscomb' of the name. In stony and dry places, throughout the Mediterranean region. Fl 4–6.

Crown Vetch (left)

Annual Scorpion Vetch (right)

Hippocrepis unisiliquosa fruit

Hippocrepis unisiliquosa (left)

Scorpiurus muricatus (right)

Italian Sainfoin

Hedysarum glomeratum fruit

WOOD-SORREL FAMILY, OXALIDACEAE

Shining Crane's-bill
(left)

Bermuda-buttercup
(right)

Herbs, with compound leaves and simple, regular 5-merous flowers. Most species now found in Europe are naturalized from tropical America or S Africa.

Bermuda-buttercup *Oxalis pes-caprae* A vigorous bulbous perennial herb to 30cm. Leaves all basal, long-stalked to 20cm, trifoliate, with heart-shaped leaflets. Flowers bright yellow, with petals 2–2.5cm, much longer than sepals, in terminal umbels of 6–12. Neither a buttercup nor from Bermuda; originally from S Africa, but now widespread and often very abundant, in cultivated and disturbed ground throughout the Mediterranean; increasingly invading uncultivated areas. Fl 12–5.

CRANE'S-BILL FAMILY, GERANIACEAE

Herbs, with lobed or divided leaves, with stipules at the base. Flowers 5-merous, more or less regularly symmetrical; petals and sepals all unfused.

Shining Crane's-bill *Geranium lucidum* An annual herb, sparsely hairy and often tinged red, up to 40cm. Leaves distinctively shiny above, rounded but divided beyond half-way to the centre into 5 lobes. Flowers bright pink, with petals 8–10mm long, divided into a marked claw and unnotched limb. Widespread throughout the area in shady rocky places. Fl 3–7.

Mallow-leaved
Stork's-bill (left)

Mallow-leaved, or **Soft, Stork's-bill** *Erodium malacoides* A softly hairy, spreading or ascending annual or biennial herb. Leaves variable, from ovate-heart-shaped to 3-lobed or pinnately divided. Flowers in umbels of 3–8, longer than the leaves, on a glandular-hairy common stalk, petals purplish, 5–9mm long; bracts oval, 3–6 together; fruit has a beak 2–4cm long. Common in dry grassy and disturbed places throughout. Fl 2–6. **Common Stork's-bill** *E. cicutarium* is similar to above, except that the leaves are deeply pinnately divided, with lobed lobes. Common in dry, often sandy places. Fl 3–7.

Corsican Stork's-bill *Erodium corsicum* A beautiful greyish-hairy perennial, in low spreading mounds up to 25cm. Leaves ovate-oblong, grey-green, toothed or pinnately lobed. Flowers showy, pinkish-white, veined deeper purple, 1.5–2cm across, solitary or in umbels of 2–3. In grassy or rocky places close to the sea, in Corsica and Sardinia only. Fl 3–9.

Rock Stork's-bill *Erodium petraeum* A low perennial plant, with stalked flowers arising directly from the stemless rosette of leaves. Leaves 1–7cm long, pinnately divided, (with additional smaller leaflets present between the main leaflets); leaflets divided again similarly, to produce a ferny effect. Flowers large, about 2cm across, pink to white, usually veined with deeper purple; petals even or uneven, sometimes the 2 upper petals are dark-blotched. A very variable species, with 5 subspecies distinguished in this area. The photograph shows ssp *petraeum*. Scattered throughout, especially in hilly or mountain areas, though absent east of SE France. Fl 4–7. *E. acaule* is also a stemless rosette perennial, but the leaves lack the intermediate leaflets and the flowers occur in umbels of 3–10; petals pink, equal, without dark patches. Widespread throughout the Mediterranean region. Fl 3–6.

Corsican Stork's-bill
(left)

Erodium acaule (right)

CALTROP FAMILY, ZYGOPHYLLACEAE

A mainly tropical family of herbs and shrubs, with leaves usually pinnate, and stipules present. Flowers usually regularly 5-merous.

Peganum harmala An erect, fleshy, hairless, greyish-green, much-branched herb, to 60cm. Leaves alternate, irregularly pinnate, fleshy, with narrow, pointed lobes. Flowers greenish-white, 1–2cm across, solitary, terminal; fruit globose, 7–10mm across. In dry waste places and salt-rich steppe areas; in S Spain, Italy and Sardinia. Fl 5–8.

Fagonia cretica A prostrate or ascending hairless, much-branched perennial herb up to 40cm. Leaves opposite, stalked, 3-lobed, up to 1.5cm with spiny stipules. Flowers conspicuous, purplish-red, 1–2cm across, with 5 distinctly clawed petals; fruit has 5 sharp wings. In dry stony places in the southern parts of the region only: S Spain, Sicily and the Balearics. Fl 4–6.

Maltese Cross or **Small Caltrops** *Tribulus terrestris* A downy spreading annual plant, with branched or simple stems up to 60cm long. Leaves opposite, often uneven in size, pinnately divided into oblong leaflets. Flowers yellow, 4–5mm across, solitary on short stalks from the leaf axils. Fruit distinctive, with 5 lobes arranged in a star, each with keels, warts and spines. In dry, open and disturbed habitats throughout the area. Fl 4–9.

FLAX FAMILY, LINACEAE

Herbs or small shrubs, with simple, usually alternate, undivided leaves without stipules. Flowers regularly 5-parted (occasionally 4-parted); petals contorted in bud.

Linum campanulatum A woody-based perennial, usually branched, often with non-flowering rosettes; flowering stems erect or ascending, up to 25cm. Lower leaves narrowly spoon-shaped, upper leaves lanceolate, usually 1-veined. Flowers rich yellow, in inflorescences of 3–5, with petals 2.5–3.5cm long, appearing to be partially tubular; sepals narrow and pointed. In dry and rocky places, especially on serpentine, from E Spain to Italy. Fl 6–8. *L. maritimum* also has yellow flowers, but they are smaller (8–15mm long), and have ovate sepals. Leaves 3-veined below. In saltmarshes and inland saline areas throughout the Mediterranean region. Fl 5–8.

Beautiful Flax or **Blue Flax** *Linum narbonense* A grey-green, hairless, erect or ascending perennial, up to 50cm. Leaves long and narrow, pointed, 1- to 3-veined. Flowers distinctively large, with bright-blue petals up to 3cm long, 2½–3 times as long as the sepals, which are lanceolate with papery margins. On dry hillsides and rocky areas throughout Spain and the Mediterranean region. Fl 5–8.

White Flax *Linum suffruticosum* A stiffly branched, woody-based, hairless, small shrub, up to 50cm. Leaves very narrow, bristle-like, with strongly inrolled margins. Flowers white, violet or pink towards the base, sometimes pink-veined, in lax, branched clusters; petals 1.5–3cm, 3–4 times as long as the sepals, yellowish in bud. In dry rocky places; in France, N Italy, and southern half of Spain. Fl 6–8.

SPURGE FAMILY, EUPHORBIACEAE

Herbs, or rarely shrubs, usually with white latex. Leaves simple, usually alternate. Flowers commonly without petals; female flowers with a 3-cavitied ovary and 3 styles.

Turn-sole *Chrozophora tinctoria* A greyish-hairy branched annual, up to 50cm, lacking milky latex. Leaves ovate to rhombic, stalked, toothed or not, wedge-shaped at the base. Male and female flowers separate on the same plant: male flowers small, yellowish, in erect clusters, with a few long-stalked drooping female flowers at the base of each cluster. Fruit 3-lobed, covered with warts. In bare and cultivated ground, especially near the coast, throughout the Mediterranean region. Fl 5–10. *C. obliqua* is similar to above, but much more densely white-hairy; leaves truncate or almost heart-shaped at base, and male flowers each have 4–5 (not 9–11) stamens. In similar habitats, in the south of the region only.

Fagonia cretica (le

Beautiful Flax (rig

Linum campanulatur
(lef

White Fla

Hairy Mercury *Mercurialis tomentosa*   A much-branched densely downy perennial up to 60cm. Leaves roughly oblong, to 5cm long, pointed or blunt, untoothed or slightly toothed. Male flowers in rounded clusters, collectively forming a rounded spike; female flowers 1 or few; fruit densely woolly, 4–6mm across. In dry pastures, hillsides and rough ground; from Portugal to S France, and the Balearics. Fl 4–6.

Castor Oil Plant *Ricinus communis*   A fast-growing plant, variable from being annual up to a shrub to 4m high. Leaves large, up to 60cm long, palmately divided into 5–9 lobes. Flowers reddish, in erect terminal branched clusters; female flowers in the upper part, each with 3 bilobed reddish styles, with the male flowers below, each with branched filaments. Fruit globular, 1–2.5cm across, spiny. Native to the tropics, but very widely planted and naturalized in S Europe. Fl 2–12. *Source of the widely used castor oil, but highly poisonous in the natural state.*

Purple Spurge *Euphorbia peplis*   A spreading slightly fleshy hairless annual, with (usually) 4 reddish branches from the base, each up to 40cm long. Leaves small, oblong but slightly curved, blunt, untoothed, greyish-green. Flowers tiny, in the leaf axils; glands semicircular. A distinctive plant of sandy shores (or occasionally inland) throughout the region. Fl 5–10.

Tree Spurge *Euphorbia dendroides*   A stout, regularly branched shrubby perennial, up to 2m, occasionally more. Leaves oblong-lanceolate, 2–6cm long, blunt with a tiny point, mainly present during the wetter periods of the year. Flowers in yellowish umbel-like terminal clusters, with 5–8 rays; glands in flowers almost round, irregularly lobed. Whole plant becomes reddish as the leaves age. Widespread and often common in rocky coastal areas around the Mediterranean. Fl 3–6.

Whorled Spurge *Euphorbia biumbellata*   An erect hairless perennial, occasionally branched from the base, up to 65cm. Leaves linear, 2–5cm long, untoothed. Inflorescences distinctive, with 2 or 3 umbels, each with 8–21 rays, standing above each other and separated by a leafless part of the stem. Flowers yellowish-green with horned glands. In rocky and sandy coastal habitats, or more rarely inland, throughout the W Mediterranean region as far east as Italy. Fl 4–6.

Euphorbia pithyusa   An erect or ascending, grey-green, minutely warty perennial to 55cm, often much-branched at the base, and with axillary branches occasionally forming whorls. Leaves narrowly ovate, 1–4cm long, pointed, numerous, overlapping and curved back near the base of the stem. Rays of inflorescence, 5–8, often branching several times; nectar glands either hornless or with divided horns. On sandy and rocky shores, or inland on garrigue in Corsica and the Balearics (as a subspecies). Throughout the Mediterranean region, as far east as Italy. Fl 4–8.

Cypress Spurge *Euphorbia cyparissias*   A hairless perennial, with rhizomes producing erect shoots to 50cm; these are usually unbranched at the base, but may branch higher up to produce numerous leafy non-flowering shoots. Leaves long and narrow, less than 3mm wide, dull green at first but turning yellowish then red as they age. Umbels with 9–18 rays; glands horned. In grassy places and waste ground throughout; common. Fl 4–6.

Large Mediterranean Spurge *Euphorbia characias*   An impressive downy grey-green erect perennial, up to 1.8m, usually branched from the base. Leaves untoothed, linear to lanceolate, 3–13cm long, clustered towards the top of the stem. Uppermost bracts (raylet-leaves) almost round, often joined at the base in pairs. Flowers in umbels with 10–20 rays, usually branched again several times, forming a substantial inflorescence; glands usually dark reddish-brown with short horns; this describes ssp *characias*, which is the western subspecies. Widespread in garrigue, scrub and rocky ground throughout the Mediterranean region. Fl 2–7.

Purple Spurge (le
Castor Oil Plant (rig
Tree Spurge (le
Cypress Spurge (lef
Large Mediterranea
Spurge (righ

RUE FAMILY, RUTACEAE

Herbs, shrubs or trees, usually with evergreen, simple or compound, alternate or opposite leaves. Flowers regular, 4- to 5-merous, usually with twice as many stamens as petals. The European species tend to be strongly aromatic.

Common Rue *Ruta graveolens* A hairless, greyish-green, woody-based perennial, up to 70cm, and strongly aromatic. Leaves pinnately divided 2–3 times, with narrowly oblong to obovate segments. Flowers yellow, 1.5–2cm across, in a loose branched cluster; petals widely separated, with untoothed or very finely toothed margins; fruit a capsule, with blunt spreading lobes. Native to SE Europe, but very widely planted and often naturalized through lowland areas of SW Europe. Fl 4–7. *A very poisonous plant, which can burn the skin on contact; widely used medicinally.* Three other similar species occur widely through the area: *R. montana* is rather similar to the above, but its ultimate leaf segments are linear, and the petals are never toothed or fringed. Widespread. The other 2 species have markedly fringed petals: *R. angustifolia* has bracts no wider than the branches they subtend; the plant is glandular-hairy in the upper parts, and the fringes on the petals are usually as long as the width of the petal. *R. chalepensis* has lower bracts much wider than their branches; hairless throughout, and the petal fringes are shorter than the width of the petal. Both are widespread.

Burning Bush *Dictamnus albus* A distinctive bushy, erect, glandular, aromatic perennial, up to 1m, woody at the base. Leaves alternate, pinnate, with 3–6 pairs of rather leathery leaflets. Flowers white or pink, veined and dotted with purple, in long lax terminal spikes, each flower about 4–5cm across. In open woods and garrigue; widespread though local, and absent from large areas including the islands. Fl 4–6. *The volatile oils emitted strongly from the bush are said to burst into flames occasionally in hot weather – hence the name.*

CITRUS FRUITS *Citrus* A number of closely related citrus fruits are grown in the region, and very occasionally naturalized. All are small evergreen rounded shrubs or small trees. They can be found in flower or fruit at almost any time. **Lemon** *Citrus limon* has more than 4 times as many stamens as petals, with flowers of 2 sorts – male and hermaphrodite; petals often streaked purple. Fruit yellow, with a terminal nipple-like swelling. The remainder have about 4 times as many stamens as petals, flowers all hermaphrodite. **Tangerine** *C. deliciosa* has narrowly elliptical leaves and smaller slightly flattened fruits. **Orange** *C. sinensis* has broadly ovate leaves, globular orange fruit, and narrowly winged flattened leaf stalks. **Seville Orange** *C. aurantium* is very similar to above, with more bitter fruit and rounder, and more broadly winged leaf stalks. **Grapefruit** *C. paradisi* is similar in form to Orange, but readily distinguished by the large globular yellow fruit, the spines, and the very broadly winged leaf stalks.

CNEORUM FAMILY, CNEORACEAE

There is only one species in Europe.

Cneorum tricoccon A small hairless dense evergreen perennial shrub, to 1m. Leaves thick, leathery, oblong, blunt, narrowed to the stalkless base. Flowers small, yellow, in axillary clusters of 1–3, with petals about 5mm long. The fruit are more conspicuous: bright red, strongly 3-lobed, eventually turning black and splitting. In woods and maquis throughout the Mediterranean part of the area. Fl 3–6.

MAHOGANY FAMILY, MELIACEAE

Trees or shrubs, with pinnate leaves. Flowers 5-parted, hermaphrodite.

Indian Bead Tree or **Persian Lilac** *Melia azederach*   A distinctive deciduous tree, up to 15m. Leaves large, up to 90cm long, 2-pinnate. Flowers bluish-lilac, fragrant, 1.2–1.5cm across, in loose branched clusters up to 20cm across. Fruit almost spherical, about 1–1.5cm across, yellowish, remaining on the tree through the winter. Native of China, but very widely planted for ornament and occasionally naturalized, throughout the Mediterranean region. Fl 4–5.

CORIARIA FAMILY, CORIARIACEAE

Shrubs with opposite or whorled leaves, lacking stipules. Flowers 5-parted.

Mediterranean Coriaria *Coriaria myrtifolia*   An erect hairless shrub, with numerous 4-angled branches to 3m, forming dense thickets. Leaves oval-lanceolate, to 6cm long, opposite, leathery, unstalked. Flowers small, greenish, 5-petalled, in short axillary racemes up to 5cm long; anthers large and reddish. Fruit berry-like, 4mm long, ridged, becoming black and shiny. In scrub, woodland and rocky hillsides throughout most of the Mediterranean region, though absent from Corsica and Sardinia. Fl 3–6. *The fruits are highly poisonous.*

CASHEW FAMILY, ANACARDIACEAE

A mainly tropical family of trees and shrubs, with alternate, usually divided, leaves. Flowers 5-merous, with 5 or 10 stamens.

Sumach *Rhus coriaria*   A softly hairy shrub or small tree, up to 3m, with almost evergreen leaves, and densely downy young shoots. Leaves unevenly pinnate, with 7–21 roughly oblong, toothed leaflets; stalk between leaflets distinctly winged, at least towards the tip. Flowers small, whitish, in dense erect hairy panicles, up to 10cm long. Fruit globular, woolly, becoming brownish-purple. In dry rocky and scrubby places; throughout most of the Mediterranean region, though absent from some islands. Fl 5–7. **Stag's-horn Sumach** *R. typhina* is very similar to above, but differs in having round leaf stalks, not winged at all; leaflets are usually more numerous (up to 31), and fruit crimson. Native of N America, widely cultivated and locally naturalized.

Turpentine Tree or **Terebinth** *Pistacia terebinthus*   A deciduous, aromatic shrub or small tree, up to 5m. Leaves unevenly pinnate, with 3–9 ovate, bristle-tipped leathery leaflets on an unwinged axis. Flowers small, without petals, brownish, in long, branched, axillary inflorescences; male and female flowers on separate trees; fruit ovoid, compressed, reddish-brown. In dry woodland, scrub and rocky places, usually calcareous, throughout the Mediterranean. Fl 4–7. The **Mastic Tree** *P. lentiscus* is similar to above, but has evenly pinnate narrower leaflets on a broadly winged stalk; flowers in tighter spike-like inflorescences. Similar habitats and distribution.

Californian Pepper-tree or **Peruvian Mastic-tree** *Schinus molle*   A small evergreen tree, up to about 10m, with graceful hanging branches. Leaves pinnate, with 7–13 pairs of narrow pointed leaflets on an unwinged axis. Flowers yellowish-white, very small, in much-branched hanging inflorescences; fruits globose, 6–7mm across, pinkish. Native of Central and S America; widely planted for ornament, and occasionally naturalized, throughout the southern part of the area. Fl 4–8. *S. terebinthifolia* is similar to above, but branches are not hanging, leaflets are much wider, leaf axis is winged in upper part, and inflorescence is dense, producing bright-red fruits. Planted, and rarely naturalized, in the Iberian Peninsula.

Turpentine Tree (lef

Turpentine Tr

Mastic Tree (lef

Californi
Pepper-tree (righ

Mastic Tr

MAPLE FAMILY, ACERACEAE

Deciduous, or occasionally evergreen, trees or shrubs with opposite leaves lacking stipules. Flowers simple, 5-merous, in clusters; there are usually 8 stamens inserted on a disc.

Italian Maple *Acer opalus* A shrub or small tree, rarely up to 15m. Leaves up to 8cm long, palmately divided into 5 wide, short, pointed lobes. Flowers yellowish, rather few in a short-stalked cluster and opening before the leaves appear. Fruit a 2-lobed winged structure, as in most maples, with wings diverging at an acute angle. In hilly areas and mountains from S Spain to Italy. **Fl** 4–5. *A. granatense* is very similar to above, but the leaves have 3 deeper-cut parallel-sided lobes, and 2 smaller basal lobes, all hairy on undersurfaces. In S Spain and Mallorca only.

Montpelier Maple *Acer monspessulanum* A shrub or small tree, up to 12m. Leaves 3-lobed, 3–8cm long with each lobe untoothed, diverging roughly at right angles from the next. Flowers greenish-yellow, in erect then drooping inflorescences. Fruit almost hairless, with wings nearly parallel to each other. In dry hilly places and woods, especially on limestone; widespread throughout. **Fl** 4–5.

BOX FAMILY, BUXACEAE

Shrubs with simple leaves, lacking stipules. Flowers unisexual.

Box *Buxus sempervirens* An evergreen shrub or small tree, up to 5m, with downy 4-angled young shoots. Leaves ovate to oblong, 1.5–3cm long, dark glossy green above, paler and sometimes hairy below. Male and female flowers separate on the same plant, clustered together in small axillary inflorescences, about 5mm in diameter, greenish. Fruit an ovoid, 3-horned capsule. Widespread and often common, especially on lime-rich soils, though absent from the Balearics and Sicily. **Fl** 3–4. *B. balearica* is very similar to above, but whole plant is virtually hairless; shoots more erect; leaves larger (2.5–4cm long), less dark above, with larger inflorescences up to 1cm across. Confined to the Balearics, Sardinia, and very locally in S Spain.

BUCKTHORN FAMILY, RHAMNACEAE

Trees or shrubs, often spiny, with simple leaves, usually without stipules. Flowers small, inconspicuous, 4- to 5-merous, usually greenish, in axillary clusters. Fruit usually fleshy.

Christ's Thorn *Paliurus spina-christi* A virtually hairless much-branched shrub, to 3m, with long flexible zigzagging branches. Leaves alternate, ovate, 2–4cm long, 3-veined and finely toothed, with stipules that are modified into spines. Flowers yellowish-green, in small short-stalked branched axillary inflorescences; fruit distinctive: hemispherical, 2–3cm across, surrounded by a membranous wavy wing. In dry places throughout the region except for the islands. **Fl** 5–9.

Mediterranean Buckthorn *Rhamnus alaternus* An erect, evergreen unspiny shrub, up to 5m, variable in habit. Leaves on short petioles, lanceolate to ovate, 2–6cm long, blunt or pointed, untoothed or distantly toothed, but always rather leathery. Flowers yellowish, in small axillary clusters, lacking petals, with male and female flowers separate. Fruit roughly ovoid, 4–6mm long, red then black, and hard. In garrigue, scrub, open woods and hedges, throughout the Mediterranean region; also often planted for ornament. **Fl** 3–4. *R. ludovici-salvatoris* is very similar to above, but has broader leaves with strongly spiny margins. In Balearic Islands and SE Spain only. *R. lycioides* is similar in form to *R. alaternus* but has spines present, and the flowers are usually 4- (not 5-) parted. In similar habitats throughout.

Italian Maple (left)

Montpelier Maple (right)

Italian Maple

Box (left)

Christ's Thorn (right)

Montpelier Maple

Acer granatense

Mediterranean Buckthorn

VINE FAMILY, VITACEAE

Climbing shrubs, by means of tendrils. Leaves alternate. Flowers small, clustered, 5-parted.

Grape-vine *Vitis vinifera*   A woody climber, reaching 35m with support. Leaves long-stalked, palmately lobed with 5-7 lobes, and branched tendrils opposite some of the leaves. Flowers small, 5mm, pale green, in dense branched axillary inflorescences. Fruit ovoid, fleshy, bluish-black in the wild form. Ssp *sylvestris* which has small, acid, bluish-black fruits, c.6mm long, and male and female flowers on different plants, occurs wild from France and Corsica eastwards in rough rocky places. Ssp *vinifera* is the cultivated form, found throughout the region in many varieties. **Fl** 4–6.

MALLOW FAMILY, MALVACEAE

Herbs or shrubs with simple (though often deeply lobed) alternate leaves, with stipules. Flowers regular, hermaphrodite, 5-merous, with numerous stamens. Epicalyx of bracts present just below the sepals.

Malope malacoides   An erect or ascending hairy perennial, to 50cm. Leaves ovate, toothed or slightly lobed, sometimes upper ones distinctly 3-lobed. Flowers solitary, long-stalked, produced from the axils of the upper leaves; petals 2–4cm, deep pink to purple, 2–3 times as long as the calyx, which is twice as long as the epicalyx. Fruit resembles a green strawberry (illus.), and is surrounded by the epicalyx lobes. In waste places and cultivated ground throughout the Mediterranean region except Portugal. **Fl** 6–7. *M. trifida* is similar to above, but annual, with leaves broader than long, petals 3.5–6cm. Local in SW Spain and adjacent Portugal.

Malope malacoides calyx

Tree Mallow

Malva cretica   An erect or spreading hairy annual, up to 40cm. Lower leaves nearly round, shallowly lobed; upper leaves more deeply divided into 3 or 5 oblong, toothed leaves. Flowers long-stalked, pink, produced from the leaf axils, about 1.5cm across; epicalyx and calyx segments both linear or narrowly triangular, hairy. Fruit hairless, ridged. In cultivated and waste ground in the Mediterranean region excluding Portugal. **Fl** 4–6.

Malva calyx

Smaller Tree-mallow *Lavatera cretica*   An erect or ascending annual or biennial plant, up to 1.5m, densely or lightly covered with star-shaped hairs. Lower leaves rounded heart-shaped, shallowly 3- to 7-lobed, upper leaves deeply 5-lobed. Flowers pink, in axillary clusters of 2–8, shorter than the leaves; petals 1–2cm long, epicalyx segments 6mm long, free almost to the base, shorter than the triangular-oval long-pointed calyx (illus.). In waste ground, tracksides and bare areas throughout. **Fl** 3–6. *Malva sylvestris* is very similar to above in general appearance, differing in having both simple and star-shaped hairs, and narrow epicalyx segments that are free completely to the base (illus.). Widespread.

Lavatera calyx

Tree Mallow *Lavatera arborea*   A robust biennial or perennial, up to 3m with a woody stock. Leaves large, rounded, with 5–7 shallow lobes. Flowers large (3–4cm across), rosy-purple with darker veins, in clusters of 2–7; epicalyx segments 8–10mm long, rounded to ovate, longer than sepals, fused at the base, becoming considerably enlarged in fruit. In rocky places and shingle, usually coastal, throughout. **Fl** 3–9. *L. maritima* is rather similar to above, but has white-felted leaves, and pale bluish-pink flowers that are solitary or in pairs; there are distinct gaps between the petal bases, where the sepals show through. In dry rocky, mainly coastal sites throughout the Mediterranean area. **Fl** 2–5.

Lavatera olbia   A robust erect shrub, to 2m, with young parts of stem covered with starry hairs. Lower leaves 3- to 5-lobed, upper leaves oblong-ovate to lanceolate, only shallowly lobed. Flowers solitary in leaf axils, collectively forming a Hollyhock-like spike; petals purple, 1.5–3cm long, sepals and epicalyx segments both ovate, pointed. Fruit downy but not ridged. In hedges, scrub and damp waste ground throughout the Mediterranean area. **Fl** 3–6. *L. trimestris* is an erect or ascending annual, to 1.2m. Flowers solitary in leaf axils, bright pink, 5–7cm across, with epicalyx slightly inflated, and fused for most of its length. Widespread throughout the Mediterranean region, and cultivated elsewhere. *L. triloba* is a woody-based greyish, musk-scented perennial, up to 1m, with simple glandular as well as stellate hairs. Leaves slightly 3-lobed, and stipules up to 2.5cm. Flowers purplish, suffused with yellow, or entirely yellow (in Italy and Sicily). In damp, usually sandy or saline places in S Iberian Peninsula, and most islands.

Lavatera olbia (left)

Lavatera trimestris (right)

Hibiscus rosa-sinensis   A deciduous shrub or small tree, up to 5m. Leaves broadly ovate and coarsely toothed, shiny dark green above. Flowers scarlet, 10–15cm across, produced singly on stalks from the leaf axils, with a distinctive long central protruding column consisting of 5 stigmas and numerous stamens. Widely grown in the Mediterranean region as an ornamental plant; occasionally naturalized. **Fl** 3–10.

Hibiscus rosa-sinensis (left)

DAPHNE FAMILY, THYMELAEACEAE

Small shrubs, rarely herbs, with simple, entire, usually alternate leaves, without stipules. Flowers 4-merous, but petals usually absent; sepals often coloured.

Mediterranean Mezereon *Daphne gnidium*   An erect, sparsely-branched evergreen shrub, up to 2m, with straight, slender leafy shoots. Leaves linear to oblong, pointed, leathery, hairless. Flowers whitish (browner outside), 4-lobed, fragrant, small, in clusters amongst the leaves at the end of the stem. Fruit fleshy, ovoid and red. In maquis and woodland throughout the area, though local. **Fl** 4–8. *The berries and foliage are highly poisonous.* **Spurge-laurel** *D. laureola* has shinier obovate to spoon-shaped leaves, and yellowish-green flowers. In scrub and woods throughout, except Portugal.

Thymelaea hirsuta   A small shrub, to 1m, erect or spreading, usually with drooping branches that are densely clothed with overlapping scale-like leaves. Leaves rather fleshy or leathery, ovate to lanceolate, only 3–8mm long. Flowers small, yellowish-green, in clusters of 2–5 from the leaf axils, especially towards the tips of the branches. In dry rocky and sandy places, mainly coastal, throughout the Mediterranean area. **Fl** 10–5. *T. tartonraira* is smaller than above, to 50cm, with larger (1–1.8cm), flatter, spreading, oblong leaves. Similar habitats and distribution to above species. **Fl** 3–5.

Thymelaea hirsuta (left)

Oleaster (right)

OLEASTER FAMILY, ELAEAGNACEAE

Trees or shrubs with scale-like hairs. Flowers lacking true petals.

Oleaster *Elaeagnus angustifolia*   A variably spiny small tree or shrub, to 10m, with dark-brown older branches and silvery twigs that are covered in scales. Leaves oblong-lanceolate; green above but silvery-scaly below. Flowers yellow, silvery-hairy outside, very fragrant, about 1cm across, in axillary clusters. Fruit olive-shaped, 1–2cm long fleshy, yellowish-brown and scaly. Frequently planted for ornament or hedging, and occasionally naturalized; native of Asia. **Fl** 4–6. *The dried fruits are edible, and known as 'Trebizond grapes'.*

ST JOHN'S WORT FAMILY, GUTTIFERAE

Stinking Tutsan (left

Cistus crispus (right)

Herbs or shrubs, with translucent glands. Leaves simple, flowers regular.

Stinking Tutsan *Hypericum hircinum*   An erect semi-evergreen shrub, to 1m, with 4-angled or 2-lined stems, smelling of goats when crushed. Leaves narrowly lanceolate to broadly ovate, unstalked. Flowers yellow, in few-flowered branched terminal inflorescences, with petals 1.1–1.8cm long; fruit ellipsoid, 8–13mm long. In damp and shady places, often near rivers; native from Corsica and Sardinia eastwards, naturalized further west. Fl 5–9. *H. balearicum* is a small shrub, with oval, crinkly-edged, very glandular leaves. Flowers solitary, terminal, with yellow petals 1–1.5cm long. In open woodland in the Balearic Islands only, but naturalized elsewhere locally. Fl 6–10.

ROCKROSE FAMILY, CISTACEAE

Shrubs or herbs, with simple, usually opposite leaves. Flowers with 5 petals and 3 or 5 sepals, stamens numerous. Fruit a capsule.

(a) Flowers pink or purplish.

Grey-leaved Cistus *Cistus albidus*   A compact bush, up to about 1m. Leaves oblong to elliptical, 2–5cm long, unstalked, flat, and densely greyish-white with down. Flowers large and attractive, 4–6cm across, rose-pink, with crumpled petals, in clusters of 1–7, with each flower stalk 5–20mm long. In maquis, open areas and light woodland throughout the Mediterranean part of the area. Fl 3–6. *C. crispus* is similar to above, but usually smaller, to 50cm. Leaves oblong to elliptical, markedly wavy. Flowers smaller (3–4cm across), on very short stalks that are less than 5mm. Similar habitats and distribution, though less common.

Narrow-leaved Cistus (left)

Cistus incanus   A densely branched erect shrub, to 1m or more. Leaves ovate to elliptical, usually flat (the SE European subspecies has wavy leaves), downy, with strongly embossed veins, on stalks 3–15mm long (cf. above species, which has stalkless leaves). Flowers large, purplish-pink, 4–6cm across, in clusters of 1–7. Fl 3–6. Two subspecies occur in the area in dry places: ssp *corsicus* has numerous starry, but few long, hairs on the sepals and flower stems. In Italy and the islands. Ssp *incanus* has numerous long white hairs on the sepals and stems, hiding the starry hairs. In Corsica and Italy only. Fl 3–6.

(b) Flowers white.

Narrow-leaved Cistus *Cistus monspeliensis*   An erect or spreading bush, up to 1m. Leaves narrow, linear-lanceolate, unstalked, sticky, dark-green above, greyish-hairy below, with inrolled margins. Flowers white, sometimes marked with yellow, 2–3cm across, in 1-sided inflorescences of 2–8. In garrigue, woods and rocky slopes throughout the Mediterranean area. Fl 4–6. *C. psilosepalus* is very similar to above, but has oblong leaves, 1–5 flowers in more symmetrical inflorescences, and the outer sepals are heart-shaped (not wedge-shaped) at base. In Portugal and W Spain only.

Narrow-leaved Cistus (left)

Sage-leaved Cistus (right)

Sage-leaved Cistus *Cistus salvifolius*   A spreading or ascending shrub, to 1m, aromatic but not sticky. Leaves sage-like, ovate to elliptical, and stalked; wrinkled above with starry hairs on both surfaces. Flowers white, 2–4cm across, solitary, or up to 4 together, stalked. In dry stony places, garrigue and open woods throughout. Fl 4–6. *C. populifolius* is rather similar to above, but has large broad, oval to heart-shaped leaves, which are hairless, green and smooth above. Flowers large, 4–7cm across, white, usually yellow in the centre. In dry rocky places from S France westwards.

Gum Cistus *Cistus ladanifer*   A tall erect shrub, to 3m, with branched very sticky twigs. Leaves linear to lanceolate, almost stalkless, green and hairless above, very sticky and grey-hairy below. Flowers solitary, very large (6–9cm across), sometimes with a crimson spot at the base of each petal; sepals 3. In open woods or dry rocky slopes from S France westwards. Fl 4–6. *The medicinal gum laudanum is obtained from the leaves.*

Laurel-leaved Cistus *Cistus laurifolius*   An erect, branched shrub, up to 3m, with sticky twigs. Leaves oval to lanceolate, dark green, and stalked, hairless but sticky above, grey-hairy below. Flowers in terminal almost umbel-like inflorescences, with 4–8 white flowers, 5–6cm across. In dry rocky places, garrigue and open woodlands throughout the Mediterranean area. Fl 5–7. *C. clusii* is rather similar to above, but has virtually stalkless, very narrow leaves (less than 2mm wide), with turned-back margins. Flowers white, only 2–3cm across. Throughout the mainland Mediterranean region.

Halimium atriplicifolium   An attractive tall shrubby erect plant, to 1m. Leaves elliptical-ovate, 3-veined on non-flowering shoots; oblong to heart-shaped, pinnate-veined, unstalked on flowering branches. Flowers large, 4–5cm across, golden yellow, in rigid, leafless, branched inflorescences, with spreading purplish sticky hairs; sepals 3. In open pine-forests and maquis in the southern half of Spain only. Fl 4–6. *H.alyssoides* is more compact, leaves dark green above; flowers in short terminal inflorescences, shaggy-hairy but without the purple hairs. In N Iberian Peninsula and W-central France.

Halimium halimifolium   A silvery-grey, much-branched small erect shrub, up to 1m. Leaves elliptical-oblong, short-stalked except for uppermost ones, greyish-white on both surfaces when young, with silvery scales and starry hairs. Flowers yellow, spotted or unspotted, 2–3cm across, in numerous branched inflorescences; sepals 5, scaly. On sand-dunes, beaches, and dry sunny places inland, throughout the S Mediterranean region; absent from France. Fl 4–6.

Halimium umbellatum   A low shrublet, to 30cm, with ascending tortuous white-felted twigs. Leaves dark green above, downy below, linear with recurved margins, crowded towards the tips of shoots. Flowers white, 2–3cm across, in terminal umbel-like inflorescences of 3–6 flowers. In scrub and pinewoods, in SW France and N Iberian Peninsula. Fl 3–5.

Tuberaria lignosa   The *Tuberaria* species differ from *Halimium* and *Helianthemum* in having a basal rosette of leaves. An erect perennial up to 40cm, with basal plantain-like rosettes of leaves, roughly oval, with 3 distinct veins. Flowers yellow, about 3cm across, in branched inflorescences, with bracts, of 3–7 flowers; sepals lanceolate and pointed. In grassy, bushy and lightly wooded sites throughout the area. Fl 3–7. *T. globularifolia* is similar to above, but has leaves that narrow abruptly into a stalk as long as the blade, and larger flowers (3–5cm across), usually with a purplish-brown blotch at the base of each petal. NW Iberian Peninsula only, in heathy areas.

Spotted Rockrose *Tuberaria guttata*   A hairy annual plant, up to 30cm, with a rosette of leaves that withers at about flowering time. Basal and lower stem leaves broadly elliptical, upper leaves narrower and 1-veined. Flowers variable in size, 1–2cm across, yellow or almost white with dark spots at the base of each petal, on slender stalks in loose leafless terminal inflorescences. In sandy places, heaths and open woodland throughout. Fl 4–6.

Gum Cistus (left)

Cistus clusii (right)

Halimium atriplicifolium (left)

Halimium halimifolium (right)

Halimium umbellatum (left)

Tuberaria lignosa (right)

Helianthemum lavandulifolium   A distinctive low shrub, up to 50cm, densely grey-felted. Leaves lanceolate or linear-lanceolate, greyish-green, with recurved margins, white-downy below. Flowers numerous in characteristic forked inflorescences that are coiled at first, then spreading, producing numerous drooping fruits; petals yellow, 5–10mm long. On rocky slopes, scrub and open pinewoods, usually on limestone, throughout the Mediterranean area. Fl 4–6. *H. squamatum* is densely covered with silvery scales; the leaves have flat margins, and inflorescences are not markedly coiled in bud. In southern half of Spain only. *H. caput-felis* is distinctive by virtue of the dense white felt on the branches and both surfaces of the leaves. Flowers in compact few-flowered inflorescences; sepals in bud are densely hairy, like a cat's head. In Balearic Islands and SE Spain only.

Helianthemum hirtum   A small tufted shrub, to 30cm with erect or ascending branches. Lower leaves ovate-rounded, narrower further up the stem, all rather fleshy; green above but densely downy with starry hairs below. Flowers yellow or white, about 1.5cm across, in unbranched inflorescences of 5–17. In scrub, open woodland and dry grassland, usually calcareous, throughout the southern mainland area and Corsica. Fl 4–6. **White Rockrose** *H. apenninum* A loose spreading shrub, with linear-oblong grey-downy leaves. Flowers white (occasionally pink) with a yellow claw to each petal, in clusters of 3–10. In grassy and rocky places, often calcareous, throughout.

Fumana thymifolia   A small heath-like little shrub, erect or ascending, to 20cm. Leaves very narrow (less than 1mm wide), glandular-hairy, with strongly rolled-under margins, lower ones opposite, usually alternate higher up the stem. Flowers yellow, about 1cm across, in loose terminal clusters of 3–9; flower stalks much longer than their bracts. In stony and rocky places throughout the Mediterranean region. Fl 3–6.

Fumana arabica   Similar in form to above, up to 25cm high, but with broader ovate to lanceolate leaves, up to 5mm wide by 12mm long, alternate, and not reducing significantly in size up the stem. Flowers yellow, in a distinctly separate cluster of up to 7 flowers. In dry open habitats, S Europe from Sardinia and mainland Italy eastwards. Fl 4–6. *F. ericoides* is rather similar to above, but has leaves evenly spaced up the stem, not reducing in size; flowers rather scattered and not in a distinct inflorescence. Throughout the Mediterranean region.

TAMARISK FAMILY, TAMARICACEAE

Shrubs or small trees with scale-like or much-reduced leaves. Flowers 4- or 5-merous, usually in spike-like inflorescences.

Tamarix africana   A shrub or small tree, to about 5m, with blackish bark. Leaves scale-like, under 4mm long, pointed. Flowers white or pale pink, 5-merous, with petals 2–3mm long, mostly persisting; flowers in cylindrical spike-like inflorescences; appearing before or with the leaves; anthers blunt. In coastal marshes and river banks, occasionally planted elsewhere, throughout. Fl 3–6, occasionally later. Two other species with pink flowers occur frequently; both have petals less than 2mm long: *T. canariensis* has linear to triangular bracts, equalling or exceeding the toothed calyx; petals less than 1.5mm long. *T. gallica* has bracts not exceeding the untoothed calyx; petals 1.5–2mm long. Both occur throughout in similar habitats to *T. africana*.

SEA-HEATH FAMILY, FRANKENIACEAE

Herbs or dwarf shrubs, with opposite leaves, lacking stipules. Flowers 4–6-parted.

Sea-heath *Frankenia laevis*   A prostrate, much-branched, finely hairy perennial, with stems up to 40cm. Leaves linear-lanceolate, 2–5mm long, with the margins rolled under, sometimes covered with a white crust. Flowers pinkish-purple
or paler, 9–11mm across, with 5 petals; scattered singly or in clusters through the
upper parts of the branches. In various soft coastal habitats throughout. Fl 5–8.
F. hirsuta is very similar to above, but the flowers are in conspicuous terminal flat-
topped clusters. In similar habitats from SW France eastwards. *F. thymifolia* has
erect or ascending stems, with flowers in long terminal 1-sided spikes. In saline
habitats in the southern parts of Spain.

GOURD FAMILY, CUCURBITACEAE

Mainly climbing herbs with tendrils. Flowers single-sexed, 5- or 6-merous. Fruit
usually fleshy.

Squirting Cucumber *Ecballium elaterium*   A distinctive spreading bristly
rather fleshy perennial herb, with thick stems 15–60cm long. Leaves triangular to
heart-shaped, wavy, long-stalked. Flowers yellow, c.2cm 5-lobed, with male flowers in clusters, female flowers solitary in leaf axils. Fruit cylindrical-ovoid, green,
very bristly, 4–5cm long. Seeds are ejected explosively from the fruit when it is
ripe, and the whole structure takes off like a rocket. In waste ground and coastal
habitats throughout the Mediterranean area. Fl 3–9, or all year in the far south.

Bryonia alba   A spreading or scrambling perennial herb, with rough warty
stems, up to 4m, with unbranched tendrils. Male and female flowers separate on
the same plant. Leaves usually palmately 5-lobed, with acute segments, though variable. Flowers greenish-white, 5-lobed, in axillary clusters. Fruit fleshy, 7–8mm
across, black when ripe. In waste and rough ground native or naturalized throughout. Fl 4–8.

Bitter Cucumber *Citrullus colocynthis*   A prostrate or scrambling perennial
herb, with rough slender stems, and tendrils. Leaves once- or twice-pinnately cut,
with wavy-edged segments. Flowers greenish-yellow, with 5 pointed lobes. Fruit
spherical, roughly hairy, 4–8cm in diameter, green and yellow, with bitter flesh. In
dry and sandy places, especially near coast, only in S Spain and Sicily. Fl 6–8.

CACTUS FAMILY, CACTACEAE

Perennial succulent often spiny plants. Leaves absent or tiny.

Prickly Pear *Opuntia ficus-barbarus*   One or more species of prickly pear are
widely naturalized in the Mediterranean region, though there is much controversy
over the correct name. The commonest species, referred to here, has been hith-
erto referred to as *O. ficus-indica*, but is probably correctly referred to as *O. ficus-
barbarus*. In any event, it is readily recognizable, as a much-branched shrub or small
tree, whose stems consist of large flat fleshy ovate-oblong plates, with constrictions between, covered with tufts of yellowish spines. The flowers are yellow, with
numerous petals and stamens, producing fleshy fig-shaped spiny fruits, that usually
turn red. Widespread and common in the Mediterranean region, especially near
cultivation. Fl 3–7. *Grown both for its edible fruits and as an impenetrable hedge.*

LOOSESTRIFE FAMILY, LYTHRACEAE

Herbs with simple leaves. Flowers regular, 4–6-parted.

Lythrum junceum A slender, straggling or ascending, hairless perennial, to 75cm, often branched from the base. Leaves roughly linear-oblong, alternate, unstalked, regularly spaced. Flowers pink-purple, with 6 petals, each 5–6mm long, solitary in upper leaf axils. In wet places throughout the area. Fl 5–9. *L. acutangulum* is similar to above but annual, erect or ascending to 30cm. Flowers pink-purple, with a distinct white centre. In wet places, including seasonally wet areas, in the southern half of Spain and S France.

MYRTLE FAMILY, MYRTACEAE

Evergreen trees or shrubs, with simple, opposite aromatic leaves. Flowers 4- or 5- merous, with numerous stamens. Only 1 European native, but numerous introduced species.

Myrtle *Myrtus communis* A dense evergreen shrub, up to 3m, hairless except for the glandular-hairy young twigs. Leaves ovate-lanceolate, pointed, untoothed, leathery, dotted with glands, and very aromatic when crushed. Flowers white, fragrant, 2–3cm across, solitary on long stalks from the leaf axils. Fruit ovoid, 7–10mm long, to almost spherical and blue-black. In scrub, maquis and open woodland, most commonly on acid soils; throughout most of the area, mainly near the Mediterranean. Fl 5–7. *The volatile oils are used medicinally and in perfumery.*

Blue Gum *Eucalyptus globulus* A tall, fast-growing, graceful tree, up to 40m, with peeling bark. Two leaf types occur, as in most gums: juvenile leaves are opposite and ovate, grey-green; mature leaves are alternate, narrow and curving, bright glossy green. Flowers solitary creamy-white; the petals and sepals united into a cap (which is hemispherical with a central point in this species), that falls early to free the numerous stamens. Widely planted for timber and ornament through much of the region. Fl 3–5. *One of the sources of oil of eucalyptus, widely used medicinally.* Various other Australasian species of *Eucalyptus* are planted and occasionally naturalized in S Europe.

POMEGRANATE FAMILY, PUNICACEAE

Shrubs and small trees. Fruit berry-like, fleshy.

Pomegranate *Punica granatum* A deciduous spiny shrub, or sometimes a spineless tree, up to 5m, with 4-angled stems. Leaves oblong-lanceolate, untoothed. Flowers 3–4cm across with red crumpled petals and a red fleshy enlarged calyx (the hypanthium), in clusters of 1–3 towards the ends of the branches. Fruit globular, up to 9cm in diameter, with brownish rind surrounding the fleshy seeds. Cultivated throughout S Europe, and often naturalized. Fl 5–8.

MALVACEAE

CARROT FAMILY, UMBELLIFERAE

A very distinctive family characterized by its flowers, which are arranged in inflorescences like the spokes of an umbrella, known as umbels; these may have few or many rays, and the primary rays may give rise to secondary umbels. The rays of any one umbel all arise from a single point. Many species are aromatic, and many others (such as carrot, parsnip) are the forerunners of vegetables.

Sea-holly *Eryngium maritimum*   A stiff bluish erect bushy hairless perennial, up to 60cm. Leaves basically rounded-triangular, but lobed and with long spiny teeth; blades leathery, bluish, with whiter veins and margins. Flowers electric blue, in dense oval heads up to 3cm long, subtended by lobed bluish-green spiny bracts (illus.). Frequent on coastal sands throughout the region, including on the islands. Fl 5–9.

Field Eryngo *Eryngium campestre*   A bushy spiny perennial, up to 70cm, rather similar in form to above, but pale yellowish-green. Leaves deeply lobed with spiny teeth. Flowers greenish-white, in dense round to oval heads, to 1.5cm long, subtended by long, narrow bracts (illus.), usually with a pair of teeth. Widespread and common in dry grassy places throughout the area. Fl 6–8. *E. dilatatum* is a smaller perennial, to 40cm, with small bluish stalked flower heads, up to 1.5cm long, and 5–10 narrow spiny bracts. In dry places on the Iberian Peninsula.

Echinophora spinosa   A much-branched stiff spiny perennial, hairy or not, up to 80cm. Leaves twice-pinnately divided, with thick leathery spiny lobes, keeled below and furrowed above. Flowers white, in tight umbels with 4–8 rays, and narrow spiny bracts and bracteoles. There is a central bisexual flower, surrounded by male flowers whose stalks are fused together to form a covering for the fruit. Frequent on dunes and coastal sands throughout. Fl 6–10 (–12). *E. tenuifolia* has yellow petals, and flat (not keeled or furrowed) leaves. In dry places, from Italy and Sicily eastwards.

Shepherd's-needle *Scandix pecten-veneris*   A variable, more or less hairless perennial, creeping or erect, up to 50cm. Leaves 2- to 3-pinnate, with narrow linear lobes. Flowers white, in umbels with 1–3 rays; divided or simple bracteoles, bracts usually absent. The distinctive feature is the fruit, which is cylindrical, up to 8cm long, with a tapering beak that is at least as long again – hence the name. Common and widespread throughout in grassy places and arable land. Fl 3–8. *S. australis* is very similar to above, but has smaller fruits, to 4cm, with the beak less strongly differentiated from the fruit itself. In similar habitats, throughout most of the area. *S. stellata* is smaller and more slender, and has pinnate bracts. Only in the extreme south of the area.

Alexanders *Smyrnium olusatrum*   An erect strong-smelling biennial, up to 1.5m, with solid stems, becoming hollow as they age. Leaves dark green, shiny, with basal ones triangular in outline, ternate, with the segments pinnately divided; stem leaves less divided. Flowers greenish-yellow in large compound umbels with 7–15 rays; fruit egg-shaped, 7–8mm long, ridged, becoming black when ripe. On hedgebanks, waste ground, cliffs and other rough habitats, especially near the sea, throughout. Fl 3–5. **Perfoliate Alexanders** *S. perfoliatum* has undivided upper leaves (illus.), clasping the stem (divided and not clasping in Alexanders), and finely toothed. In open and grassy places throughout. *S. rotundifolium* differs from Perfoliate Alexanders in having upper leaves that are usually untoothed, and main stem angled not winged. In similar habitats, but only from Corsica and Sardinia eastwards.

Rock Samphire *Crithmum maritimum*   A hairless much-branched woody-based perennial, to 50cm. Leaves 1- or 2-pinnate, roughly triangular in outline, but with narrow fleshy pointed segments. Flowers greenish-yellow, in umbels with up to 36 stout rays; bracts and bracteoles triangular, becoming deflexed. On coastal cliffs and rocks, throughout in suitable habitats. Fl 6–9. *Edible, with a tangy salty taste.*

Sea-holly (left)

Field Eryngo (right)

Sea Holly flower and bract

Echinophora spinosa (left)

Shepherd's-needle (right)

Field Eryngo flower and bract

Rock Samphire (left)

Alexanders (right)

Perfoliate Alexanders

Fennel *Foeniculum vulgare*   A tall greyish tufted aromatic perennial, up to 2.5m; stems hairless, slender, ridged and solid, becoming slightly hollow. Leaves roughly triangular in outline, but finely pinnately divided 3 or 4 times, with narrow fleshy lobes. Flowers yellow, in umbels with up to 30 rays, usually lacking bracts or bracteoles. There are 2 subspecies: ssp *piperitum* has leaf lobes that are less than 10mm, rather rigid, and the terminal umbel is usually overtopped by the lateral ones. Grows wild in rocky and dry places throughout the Mediterranean region. Ssp *vulgare* is the cultivated form, with leaf lobes usually longer than 10mm, and the terminal umbels not overtopped by lateral ones; there are usually 12–25 rays in this subspecies (4–10 in ssp *piperitum*). Widely naturalized in waste and rough places. **Fl** 6–9. **Florence Fennel** is a variety of ssp *vulgare*, with a much-enlarged stock.

Thorow-wax *Bupleurum rotundifolium*   An erect greyish-green annual, to 75cm, sometimes purple-tinged. Leaves ovate to almost round (illus.), encircling the stem. Flowers yellowish-green, in small umbels with 5–10 rays, surrounded by a conspicuous ruff of yellowish-green bracts that become white as they age. On arable land and dry open places; widespread except for the extreme west and north of the area, but declining. **Fl** 5–7. **False Thorow-wax** *B. lancifolium* is very similar to above, but has more markedly ovate leaves (illus.), only 2–3 rays per umbel, and warty, not smooth, fruit. In similar habitats throughout the area. **Fl** 5–9.

Bupleurum spinosum   A distinctive much-branched greyish-green spiny perennial, up to 30cm, with lower parts of stems woody; the upper parts of the stems bear previous year's umbels, which become hard and spiny. Leaves narrowly linear. Flowers yellow in small open umbels with 2–7 rays; bracts and bracteoles short and bristly. In stony and bare places in hilly parts of S and E Spain. **Fl** 7–8.

Shrubby Hare's-ear *Bupleurum fruticosum*   An aromatic, branched, evergreen perennial shrub, up to 2.5m, with reddish stems. Leaves oblong to narrowly elliptical, unstalked, pale bluish-green below. Flowers deep yellow, in umbels with 5–25 stout rays, and 5 or 6 bracts and bracteoles, which bend back and fall early. Local in scrub and sunny dry places in warmer southern part of the region. **Fl** 4–9.

Giant Fennel *Ferula communis*   A striking tall erect perennial to 2.5m. Leaves several times pinnate, with narrow linear segments up to 5cm long, and margins not markedly inrolled; all leaves have conspicuous sheathing bases, and the upper leaves are reduced simply to these. Flowers yellow, in numerous umbels forming a large conspicuous inflorescence; bracts and bracteoles usually absent. In dry rocky and grassy places throughout the warmer parts of the region. **Fl** 4–6. *F. tingitana* is very similar to above, but the leaf segments are less than 1cm long, and they have distinctly inrolled margins. In similar habitats in S Iberia only.

Thapsia villosa   A robust, downy, greyish-green perennial, up to 2m, slightly reminiscent of Giant Fennel. Leaves woolly-hairy, pinnately divided several times into toothed leaflets with spiny points; upper leaves consist solely of an inflated stalk. Flowers yellow, in large open umbels with 10–24 rays, usually lacking bracts or bracteoles. Widespread and locally common in dry grassy places, on the Iberian Peninsula and in S France. **Fl** 4–6. *T. maxima* is similar to above but has leaves simply pinnate only. On S Iberian Peninsula only. *T. garganica* resembles *T. villosa*, but the ultimate segments of its leaves are untoothed or slightly toothed (cf. regularly toothed in *T. villosa*). Throughout the southern part of the area.

Orlaya *Orlaya grandiflora*   A branched or simple erect annual, up to 40cm, usually hairy towards the base. Leaves 2- to 3-pinnate, with oval-oblong toothed segments. Flowers white or pink, with the outermost petals up to 8 times as long as the remainder; umbels long-stalked, with 5–12 rays; fruit egg-shaped, c.8mm long, with rows of hooked bristles. In dry grassy places, often on limestone, throughout the lowlands, except for Portugal and the islands. **Fl** 6–8. *O. kochii* is similar to above, but the umbels have only 2–4 rays. Widespread in similar habitats throughout.

Fennel (left)

Giant Fennel (right)

Thorow-wax

Thapsia villosa (left)

False Thorow-wax

Thorow-wax (left)

Orlaya (right)

WINTERGREEN FAMILY, PYROLACEAE

A small family of low-growing perennial hairless herbs with 5-petalled flowers.

Green Wintergreen *Pyrola chlorantha*   A small, creeping herb, to 30cm, with loose rosettes of oblong to oval, toothed leaves. Flowers yellowish-green, bell-shaped, about 1cm in diameter, in loose nodding racemes; style 6–7mm long, curved, protruding beyond petals. Widespread, but local, in damp coniferous woods, especially in mountain areas; absent from Portugal, and most islands except Corsica. Fl 6–7. Two similar wintergreens with white flowers occasionally reach southwards into the area: **Common Wintergreen** *P. minor* has a short style (1–2mm), that does not protrude beyond the petals (illus.), while **Intermediate Wintergreen** *P. media* has a straight style, 4–6mm long, protruding beyond the petals (illus.).

One-flowered Wintergreen *Moneses uniflora*   Similar in form to the wintergreens above, reaching 15cm, but the leaves are opposite, not alternate. Flowers distinctive: solitary, white, 1.3–2cm across. An attractive little plant. Local, though occasionally common, in shady woods, especially coniferous; most frequent in mountain areas; absent from the far west, and all islands except Corsica. Fl 6–8.

HEATHER FAMILY, ERICACEAE

Dwarf shrubby plants or small trees, usually evergreen, frequently with very small scale-like leaves. Flowers often bell-shaped, with 4–5 free or joined petals.

ERICA *Heathers*

(a) Anthers not protruding beyond petals.

Dorset Heath *Erica ciliaris*   A dwarf shrub, to 80cm, with erect branches from a spreading base. Leaves 2–4mm long, narrowly ovate, in whorls of 3; glandular-hairy, whitish below. Flowers large, 8–12mm long, bright reddish-pink, urn-shaped but slightly curved, in distinct terminal racemes. In bogs, heaths, scrub and open woods, often damp; westwards from central France, absent from the islands. Fl 5–10.

Corsican Heath *Erica terminalis*   A taller shrub, up to 2.5m. Leaves about 5mm long, narrow, in whorls of 4, green below. Flowers 5–7mm long, bright pink, in terminal umbel-like clusters of 3–8. Local in shady woods, scrub and ravines in Spain, S Italy, Corsica and Sardinia; introduced elsewhere. Fl 7–9.

Tree Heath *Erica arborea*   A shrub or small tree, up to 4m, occasionally more. Leaves usually in whorls of 4, dark green, 3–5mm long, with margins rolled under, completely hiding lower surface. Flowers small, 2–4mm long, white (rarely pink), with bell-shaped corolla and 4 lobes, in long dense inflorescences; sepals ovate, 1.5mm long, hairless, and pouched at the base; stigma white. In woods, maquis, and shady habitats throughout the region; often abundant. Fl 3–8. *E. lusitanica* is very similar to above, but is usually smaller, with light-green longer leaves (up to 8mm). Flowers larger, 4–5mm long, pinkish. On damp heaths, woodland clearings and scrub, from SW France westwards. Fl 3–6.

Green Heather *Erica scoparia*   A slender erect shrub, to 6m, though usually less. Leaves narrow, hairless, 4–7mm long, with rolled-under margins, in whorls of 3 or 4. Flowers small (only 1.5–3mm long), greenish-white, sometimes reddish-tinged, in narrow racemes; stigma reddish, distinctly club-shaped. In woods, maquis and heaths, on acid soils; throughout the lowland parts of the region, east to central Italy. Fl 2–6.

Green Wintergreen (left)

Common Wintergreen (right)

Common Wintergreen

Intermediate Wintergreen

One-flowered Wintergreen (left)

Tree Heath (right)

Dorset Heath (left)

(b) Anthers protruding distinctly beyond petals.

Irish Heath *Erica erigena* An erect shrub to 2m, usually less. Leaves narrow, in whorls of 4 or 5, with margins rolled under leaving a line of white underside showing. Flowers pale pink or white, 4–7mm long, with conspicuous dark-brown anthers at least partly protruding, aggregated into large, branched inflorescences. In damp heathy places throughout most of the Iberian Peninsula, into SW France. **Fl** 2–5.

Cornish Heath *Erica vagans* A low shrub, with spreading or ascending branches, up to 60cm, rarely more. Leaves narrowly linear, 6–11mm long, with margins rolled under, totally concealing undersurface. Flowers bell-shaped, pink or white, 2.5–3.5mm long, in dense leafy racemes, often ending in a tuft of leaves; anthers dark brown, conspicuously protruding. In acid woods and heaths throughout N Spain, the Pyrenees, and W and central France. **Fl** 6–9. *E. multiflora* is similar to above, but is usually a more erect plant. Flowers longer, 4–7mm long, with sepals about 2mm long (about 1mm long in Cornish Heath), usually in more distinctly terminal clusters. In rocky and dry places, often shady, usually on neutral to basic soils; throughout except Portugal. **Fl** 8–12.

St Dabeoc's Heath *Daboecia cantabrica* A straggling heath-like evergreen dwarf shrub, reaching 50–70cm if supported, lower otherwise. Leaves alternate, distinctly broader and more ovate than most heathers, 1–1.4cm long, dark green and shiny above, whitish and downy below. Flowers large, 1–1.4cm long, flask-shaped, in a loose terminal cluster of 3–10 nodding reddish-purple flowers. In rocky and heathy places, or open woods, on acid soils; in mainland Spain, Portugal and SW France. **Fl** 5–10.

Strawberry-tree *Arbutus unedo* An evergreen shrub or small tree, reaching 12m, though usually less. Bark reddish-brown, flaking. Leaves dark green, 4–11cm long, roughly elliptical, toothed, leathery and virtually hairless. Flowers white or very pale pink, globular to bell-shaped, 8–10mm long, in drooping branched inflorescences. Fruit globular, warty, yellowish ripening to red, about 2cm in diameter; the fruit from the previous year ripens as the current year's flowers are open – a highly attractive and distinctive combination. Locally common in maquis, woodland and rocky places throughout; also in gardens. **Fl** 9–3.

THE PRIMROSE FAMILY, PRIMULACEAE

Herbs with simple leaves and 5-petalled flowers.

Cyclamen A highly distinctive genus, with simple leaves and solitary flowers on leafless stalks, and strongly reflexed petal lobes.

(a) Autumn-flowering.

Cyclamen *Cyclamen hederifolium* A perennial tuberous herb, producing lobed, somewhat toothed, pointed, marbled leaves, up to 14cm long, in the autumn after flowering. Flowers pale pink or white, with purplish blotches in the throat; corolla lobes about 2cm long, with ear-like appendages where they join the corolla tube (illus.); style barely protruding. In deciduous woods from S France eastwards. **Fl** 8–11. **Sowbread** *C. purpurascens* is similar to above, but has rounded leaves, slightly toothed but not angled; petals deeper reddish-pink, without ear-like appendages; style protrudes by about 1mm. In similar habitats, but a more northerly species, extending into S France and Italy.

Cyclamen

(b) Spring-flowering.

Cyclamen repandum   Similar in form to Sowbread, with heart-shaped some-what angled leaves, which are produced in early spring before the flowers. Flowers evenly purplish-pink, without ear-like appendages or purplish blotches, though occasionally pale pink or white with darker areas; petal lobes 1.5–3cm long; style protrudes by 2–3mm. In woods and shady maquis from Corsica and S France eastwards. Fl 3–5. *C. balearicum* has white flowers, veined pink but without darker areas, no auricles, and style not protruding at all. In similar habitats, only in the Balearics and very locally in S France. Fl 3–5.

Scarlet Pimpernel *Anagallis arvensis*   A spreading or ascending annual or biennial, with square stems up to 50cm. Leaves ovate to lanceolate, 1.2cm long (illus.). Flowers orange-red, pink or blue, 4–8mm across, with 5 petals that have distinctly hairy margins. Very common in disturbed ground and waste places throughout the area. The blue-flowered form is frequent in S Europe. Fl 4–10. **Blue Pimpernel** *A. foemina* is very similar to above, and frequently confused with blue forms of Scarlet Pimpernel. It differs in having narrower upper leaves (illus.), flower stalks shorter than leaves at flowering time (longer in Scarlet Pimpernel), flowers always blue; petals wholly concealed by the sepals in bud and barely hairy on the margins; gaps between petals allow the sepals to be seen from above. In similar habitats throughout, though rarer on the southernmost islands. Fl 4–10.

Shrubby Pimpernel *Anagallis monelli*   An ascending or erect perennial, with round stems, woody at the base, up to 50cm. Leaves narrowly lanceolate, 1–1.5cm long. Flowers solitary, up to 12mm across, on stalks 2–5cm long, always longer than their leaves; petals bright blue (rarely red), with reddish bases; the stamens have masses of purple or yellow hairs at the base. Usually a more conspicuous densely flowered plant than the preceding two. In dry open habitats in the Iberian Peninsula, Sardinia and Sicily. Fl 3–6.

Coris monspeliensis   A distinctive plant, more like a thyme than a member of the Primrose family. Annual or biennial, with ascending or erect round stems, woody at the base, to 30cm. Leaves narrowly linear, c.2cm long, unstalked, alternate, spread evenly up the stem. Flowers in a dense terminal head, with a 2-lipped pinkish-blue corolla divided into 5 unequal lobes; stamens 5. In dry rocky or sandy places, almost throughout; commonest near the coast, but locally abundant on some inland hills. Fl 4–7.

SEA-LAVENDER FAMILY, PLUMBAGINACEAE

Herbs or shrubs, often with basal rosettes. Flowers with 5 parts, usually in branched inflorescences. Sepals wholly or partly membranous.

European Plumbago *Plumbago europaea*   An erect perennial herb to 1m, with numerous stiffly ascending branches. Leaves alternate, 4–8cm long, simple, stalked and ovate near the plant's base, becoming clasping further up. Flowers violet-purple to pinkish, about 1cm across, with 5 spreading petal lobes, in dense inflorescences; calyx conspicuously bristly and glandular-hairy. On dry rocky hillsides, sandy places and roadsides throughout the area. Fl 7–10.

Thrift *Armeria maritima*   A densely tufted hairy perennial, often forming cushions. Familiar as a coastal plant in N Europe. Leaves only a few millimetres wide, but up to 12cm long, 1-veined. Flowers pale to deep pink, in dense globular heads, 1.5–3cm across, borne on leafless stalks up to 30cm tall, with papery bracts below the head. Rather variable, with different forms and subspecies. Common throughout, except on the islands; mainly coastal, but more widespread inland in Spain. Fl 3–7. A number of other *Armeria* species occur in the area, especially in Spain.

Cyclamen repandum (left)

Scarlet Pimpernel (right)

Scarlet Pimpernel

Shrubby Pimpernel (left)

Thrift (right)

Blue Pimpernel

Coris monspeliensis (left)

Winged Sea-lavender *Limonium sinuatum* A distinctive roughly hairy perennial, with a rosette of deeply lobed leaves and flowering stems to 40cm. The flowering stems have 3–4 marked wings, up to 3mm wide. The flowers are borne in a dense branched rather flat-topped inflorescence; individual flowers have a conspicuous mauve-blue calyx with a smaller yellowish corolla. In dry, sandy mainly coastal sites; locally abundant, throughout the area. Fl 4–9.

Limonium ferulaceum A distinctive much-branched perennial subshrub, to 40cm, with numerous non-flowering shoots. Leaves either scale-like and brownish on brush-like branches, or green, in a basal rosette that is absent by flowering time. Flowers pink, 5–6mm across, with 5 petal lobes, borne in terminal clusters; calyx cylindrical, enclosed by pointed bracts. In saltmarshes and damp saline places, usually coastal; widespread, though absent from many parts including mainland Italy and Corsica. Fl 6–8.

Limonium insigne A beautiful plant, with much-branched narrow silvery-grey stems, and long, branched clusters of bright-pink flowers, each 7–8mm across. Only occurs in SE Spain, in arid areas.

Common Sea-lavender *Limonium vulgare* ssp *serotinum* A hairless perennial with a rosette of leaves and flowering stems to 70cm. Leaves roughly spoonshaped (illus.), 10–15cm long, pinnately veined, held erect. Inflorescence stalk branched from about half-way up, producing long curving branches bearing numerous small reddish-lilac flowers; sterile branches absent. In coastal saltmarshes, frequent throughout the area. Fl 7–10. **Matted Sea-lavender** *Limonium bellidifolium* is similar to above, but smaller and less erect, to 30cm. Leaves 3-veined, withering by flowering time. Inflorescence much-branched, often from below the middle, in zigzag fashion, with numerous non-flowering branches present. In saltmarshes, from E Spain eastwards. Fl 6–9. *Limoniumastrum monopetalum* is similar to the Sealavenders, but a dwarf shrub. A distinctive branched leafy shrub to 1.2m. Leaves narrow, fleshy, blue-green, 2–3cm long, with a clasping sheath at the base. Flowers pink, 1–2cm across, with 5 rounded lobes, borne in a series of 1- to 2-flowered spikelets up the stem. Occurs locally in saltmarshes and sandy places throughout the area, though absent from Corsica. Fl 6–8.

STORAX FAMILY, STYRACACEAE

Shrubs or trees with alternate, simple leaves. Stamens twice as many as petals.

Storax *Styrax officinalis* A deciduous shrub or small tree, up to 7m, with starshaped hairs on stems. Leaves roughly ovate, untoothed, up to 7cm long, midgreen above, paler below. Flowers white, 2cm across, bell-shaped with a short tube and 5–7 overlapping lobes, in drooping clusters of 3–6; calyx cup-shaped, untoothed or with 5 tiny teeth. In open woods and scrub; primarily eastern but extending naturally into Italy, and naturalized further west; occasionally planted for ornament. Fl 4–5. *The aromatic gum storax is obtained from the trunk.*

Common Sea-lavende

OLIVE FAMILY, OLEACEAE

Usually trees or shrubs with leaves opposite. Flowers hermaphrodite, rarely uni-sexual, 4- to 6-merous, calyx bell-shaped, often small; corolla with fused or free petals; stamens 2, often inserted on the corolla tube. Ovary superior, style usually short or absent.

Manna Ash *Fraxinus ornus*   A deciduous tree, 6–15m, with smooth, grey bark and twigs flattened at the nodes. Leaves opposite, each pair at right angles to the next on a stalk about 30cm long, with 5 leaflets. On mature trees, leaflets distinctly stalked, 3–8cm long and irregularly toothed. Flowers scented, appearing with the leaves in panicles which are initially erect, later arching. Calyx small, deeply lobed; corolla: white with 4 petals united in pairs at the base, linear 6–9mm long (other long ash species have no petals). Stamens with long filaments; fruit winged, 2–4cm long, dark brown and tongue-shaped. In warm, mixed deciduous woods into mountain zone; S Europe into Asia Minor. Fl 4–6. *Planted in Sicily as a source of 'manna'; the dried juice obtained from incisions in the bark has laxative properties; leaves used for fodder.*

Narrow-leaved Ash *Fraxinus angustifolia*   A tree, to 25m, with grey, finely grooved and fissured bark; twigs and petioles smooth, buds dark brown. Leaves 3–8cm long, comprising oblong to linear-lanceolate, pointed, almost sessile leaflets; leaves serrated, smooth beneath. Fruit a samara with oblong-lanceolate wing. On river banks, flood plains and in deciduous woods in S and E-central Europe. Ssp *oxycarpa* has leaves that are hairy along underside midrib. In S Europe from NE Spain eastwards.

Shrubby Jasmine *Jasminum fruticans*   An evergreen or semi-evergreen shrub, to 3m, with slender, erect or patent 4-angled branches. Leaves alternately arranged with 3 oblong to ovate-oblong leaflets 7–20mm long. Flowers yellow, highly fra-grant; inflorescence a cyme with 1–5 flowers on short, lateral branches. Corolla limb 1.2–1.5cm in diameter with 5 lobes each slightly shorter than the tube. Berry globose, 7–9mm. In scrub and wood-margins throughout southern Europe. *Several species are cultivated in S France for the perfume industry. J. odoratissima*, from Madeira, has larger flowers and fruit. *J. grandiflora*, from SE Asia, possesses calyx lobes twice the length of the tube. *J. officinale* is a climbing shrub up to 10m, from SW Asia, with white flowers, purplish outside, largely grown for ornamental purposes. *J. humile*, from W China, has alternate leaves and yellow flowers in cymes of 2–6. The corolla limb is 1cm long; calyx lobes about half as along as the tube.

Phillyrea angustifolia   An evergreen shrub, up to 2.5m, with hairless or finely hairy young stems. Leaves all similar, linear to lanceolate, 3–8cm × up to 1.5cm, oppositely arranged. Leaf surfaces leathery, dark green, with margins entire or finely toothed with wide-spaced teeth. Veins in 4–6 pairs, inconspicuous, making a small angle with the midrib. Flowers in short racemes in the leaf axils, scented, with a 4-lobed greenish-white corolla (lobes about 2mm). Calyx thick, brownish, lobed for about a quarter of its length. Fruit a blue-black drupe, 6–8mm in diam-eter, appearing in September and October; styles persistent. In evergreen scrub, mainly on chalk; W and central Mediterranean, Portugal through to the former Yugoslavia, Albania and the Canary Islands. Fl 3–5. *P. latifolia* is an evergreen shrub, up to 5m; young stems covered with a downy felt. Leaves dark green, leathery, oppositely arranged with a shape varying from ovate to cordate or ovate-lanceolate; 2–7cm long, 1–4cm broad, with toothed margins. Each leaf has 7–11 pairs of conspicuous lateral veins making a wide angle with the midrib. Flowers similar to above, but with a thin, yellowish 4-lobed calyx which has triangular lobes for three-quarters of its length. Fruits blue-black, 7–10mm, styles not persistent. In open woods and maquis, mainly on chalk throughout the Mediterranean and Canary Islands. Fl 3–5. *P. media* is identical to *P. latifolia* in the adult leaf stages.

Olive *Olea europaea*   An evergreen tree (or shrub), up to 15m, with a broad crown and grey, deeply fissured bark; old specimens have a gnarled and divided trunk. Leaves leathery, short-stalked, oblong-lanceolate, 2–8cm long: upper surface dark green, lower shining silver-grey. Flowers scented, small, yellowish-white arranged in a panicle. Fruits fleshy, 1–3.5cm, with a hard stone, initially green, ripening to brownish or blue-black. Throughout the Mediterranean – often taken as an indicator of the limits of the Mediterranean region; most widely cultivated tree in the region. Fl 5–6. Harvested 11–12. *Cultivated for fruits and olive oil.* **Wild Olive** *O. europaea* var. *sylvestris* has spiny lower stems, smaller leaves, and small, bitter fruits with little oil. In woods and maquis.

GENTIAN FAMILY, GENTIANACEAE

Hairless, bitter-tasting herbs usually with undivided, opposite, stalkless leaves connate at the base, no stipules. Flowers 4- to 5-merous in a branched cluster with joined petals, often opening only in bright sunshine: calyx more or less deeply lobed and stamens inserted on the corolla tube. Fruit a dry capsule.

Yellow-wort *Blackstonia perfoliata*   An erect, hairless plant, 10–60cm, with stems branching from the base or middle. Basal rosette of broadly ovate leaves soon falling; numerous stem leaves, opposite, ovate-triangular, narrowed at the base, pointed, and more or less joined in pairs to encircle the stem. Flowers yellow, 8–20mm in diameter, with a short corolla tube and 6–8 (–10) spreading lobes. Calyx deeply divided into 12 segments. In damp places in woods, roadsides and maquis, especially on sand. Around the Mediterranean, W and central Europe, and the Canary Islands. Fl 5–7. Several subspecies known including: ssp *perfoliata*, which has leaves ringing stem, not narrowing to base; widespread. Fl 5–7. Ssp *imperfoliata* has upper leaves not or scarcely connected at base. In S Italy and Sicily, near the sea. Fl 5–7. Ssp *grandiflora* has numerous flowers 2–3.5cm across. In Sicily, Sardinia, the Balearics and SE Spain. Fl 5–7.

Common Centaury *Centaurium erythraea*   A biennial with solitary stems, 10–50cm, branched in the upper part. Basal leaves in rosette, ovate to elliptical, 1–5cm long, stem leaves much smaller, narrower, pointed. Inflorescence corymb-like, flowers variable in size, pink to pinkish-purple. Calyx half to three-quarters as long as the corolla tube. In dry grassland throughout S Europe and further north. Fl 6–9. Ssp *grandiflorum* has stems sometimes branched from the base, stem leaves elliptical. Corolla lobes usually 6–8mm, equalling tube; calyx half as long as tube. In SW Europe. Fl 5–9.

Spiked Centaury *Centaurium spicatum*   Hairless plant with erect stems 10–55cm, branched from base or middle. Basal rosette consists of broadly ovate leaves, 1–4cm long; numerous stem leaves, stalkless, opposite, elliptical-oblong to ovate-lanceolate. Inflorescence erect, spike-like, with stalkless pink flowers 1.2–1.4cm in diameter. Corolla tube 4–5mm long with 5 spreading lobes. Calyx with linear teeth, about as long as the corolla tube. In dune-slacks, saltmarshes and cultivated land in the Mediterranean and Canary Islands. Fl 6–10.

Lesser Centaury *Centaurium pulchellum*   A small, slender annual, 2–20cm, with stems well branched to unbranched, lacking a basal leaf rosette. Leaves elliptical, pointed, with 3–7 veins branched from below the leaf middle. Flowers stalked, in lax, wide-spreading clusters, occasionally solitary; corolla pinkish-purple, 5–9mm rarely wider, petals narrow. In open places and damp grassy meadows near the sea; widespread in S Europe. Fl 6–10.

Perennial Century *Centaurium scilloides*   A low to short spreading perennial with relatively large pink flowers, 1.5–2cm across, solitary or in a cluster of few, stalked, 5-petalled. An Atlantic seaboard species; in Portugal and NW Spain. Fl 6–8.

PERIWINKLE FAMILY, APOCYNACEAE

Small trees or shrubs with poisonous latex. Leaves simple, with glands in or above the axils. Flowers solitary or in cymes, 5-merous; corolla with lobes cut obliquely at the free ends, stamens 5, anthers closely surrounding the stigma. Fruit of 2 cigar-shaped follicles.

Oleander *Nerium oleander*   A robust, evergreen shrub, 1–4m, with leathery leaves mostly in whorls of 3. Leaves lanceolate, narrowing into the stalk, up to 15cm long. Flowers in terminal inflorescences with a rose-pink (occasionally white) corolla, 3–4cm in diameter. Corolla tube funnel-shaped with 5 spreading lobes cut obliquely at their ends. Calyx densely glandular inside with 5 united sepals. Fruits conspicuous, reddish-brown, 8–18mm long, seeds have a tuft of brown hairs. On river banks, in dry stream beds, hedges and roadsides; often planted for decoration. Throughout the Mediterranean region. Fl 6–10. *The milky juice is highly toxic, containing glycosides which have an effect on the heart.*

Intermediate Periwinkle *Vinca difformis*   A creeping perennial, up to 2m, with erect or ascending flowering stems, 30cm high. Leaves opposite, ovate to lanceolate 2.5–7cm long with short evergreen stalks, hairless on the margins. Flowers solitary in leaf axils, flower stalk shorter than accompanying leaf. Corolla pale blue spreading flat to 3–4.5cm in diameter with 5 obliquely cut lobes, corolla tube funnel-shaped, 1.2–1.8cm long. Calyx lobes very narrow, triangular, 5–14cm long, hairless. In shady and damp hedges, ditches and thickets, throughout W Mediterranean region to Italy. Fl 2–5. Ssp *sardoa* has flowers 6–7cm in diameter, leaf margins and calyx lobes have minute hairs. In Sardinia.

Greater Periwinkle *Vinca major*   An evergreen perennial with stems up to 1m. Leaves shiny bright green, mostly ovate 2.5–9cm long, margins and calyx with hairs 0.1–1mm long. Flowering stems up to 30cm, corolla blue-purple with tube 1.2–1.5cm long and spreading flattened lobes 3–5cm across. Calyx lobes 7–17mm, very narrow triangular. In hedges and woodland edges in W and central Mediterranean region, but widely naturalized elsewhere. Fl 3–5. **Lesser Periwinkle** *V. minor* is similar to above, but has flowering stems up to 20cm, and smaller lanceolate or elliptical leaves 1.5–4.5mm long. Flowers blue; corolla limb 2.5–3cm in diameter, with tube 9–11mm. Calyx lobes hairless, 3–4mm, narrowly ovate-triangular. In S, W and central Europe. Fl 2–5. *Latex in stems is poisonous.*

MILKWEED FAMILY, ASCLEPIADACEAE

Shrubs or perennial herbs, sometimes with twining stems, and leaves usually opposite, simple and sometimes scale-like. Flowers in axillary or terminal cymes or
umbels, 5-numerous, anthers united in a ring. Fruit a pair of follicles often with only
1 developing.

Bristly-fruited Silkweed *Gomphocarpus fruticosus* An erect shrub, with
stems 1–2m, branched, woody at the base and containing a milky sap. Leaves in
whorls of 3, opposite, with short stalks, linear-lanceolate, 2–10cm long, curled up
at the margins, green on both sides. Inflorescence umbel-like with stalked hanging
flowers. Corolla white, 5-lobed with ovate-oblong lobes: margins with fine hairs.
Fruit capsule inflated, pointed-ovate with a softly spiny surface (illus.). Seeds have
silky hairs. On river banks, damp places near the coast, also grown ornamentally;
throughout the Mediterranean region, naturalized in many places. Fl 5–10. *Stem
sap poisonous.*

Bristly-fruited Silkweed
fru

Strangle-wort *Cynanchum acutum* A climbing plant, 1–3m, with blue-green
leaves and stems. Leaves opposite, thin, heart-shaped and deeply notched at the
base, with stalks 1–5cm long. Flowers scented, in stalked cluster in the leaf axils.
Corolla 8–12mm in diameter, white, with 5 spreading lobes. Calyx 5-lobed, finely
hairy. Fruit smooth, 8 × 1cm (illus.); seeds have long silky hairs. On saline soils, also
river banks and hedges near the sea, in the Mediterranean region and Canary
Islands, but absent from Corsica and Sardinia. Fl 6–9. *Poisonous.*

Strangle-wort fru

Swallow-wort *Vincetoxicum hirundinaria* A plant with erect or slightly twining stems up to 1.2m. Leaves broadly ovate to ovate-lanceolate, sometimes heart-
shaped at base, with stalks 5–10mm long; more or less hairy, especially in veins
and margins. Flowers in small clusters of 6–8 formed in the leaf axils; corolla white
or yellowish, 5-lobed, 3–10mm in diameter. Fruit a pair of follicles about 5–6cm,
smooth, split along 1 side to release seeds, which have a tuft of whitish hairs. A
variable species with many subspecies; usually yellow forms in the Mediterranean
region. In grassy pastures, waste ground, woodland edges, generally on calcareous
soils, from S Europe to Asia Minor. Fl 6–9. *Poisonous.*

MADDER FAMILY, RUBIACEAE

Herbs or dwarf shrubs with square stems, often scrambling over other vegetation.
Leaves usually elliptical or lanceolate, unstalked, in whorls, with often leaf-like stip-
ules. Flowers in clusters or loose heads, small, usually open, with 4 corolla lobes.
Calyx frequently absent. Fruit fleshy or dry, dividing into 2 lobes.

Blue Woodruff *Asperula arvensis* A short, slender, hairless annual with stems
10–55cm. Leaves lanceolate to linear-lanceolate, 1-veined in whorls of 6–8. Flowers 4mm across, bright blue or bluish-violet, 4-parted, in clusters surrounded by
a collar of leaf-like bracts. Fruit brown, smooth, 2–3cm long. In fields and waste
places to 1,500m. A casual in France and Germany as a weed of cultivation; a widely
naturalized alien. Fl 4–7.

Sand Woodruff *Galium arenarium* A low to short, 10–50cm, hairless or
sometimes slightly hairy perennial with 4-angled stems. Rootstock has very long
underground stolons and numerous non-flowering shoots. Leaves broadly
lanceolate, 3–8mm, long with a short translucent apex, rather fleshy and shiny,
slightly roughened at edges. Flowers yellow, 3–4mm across in a rather narrow
inflorescence. Fruit 3mm, hairless and smooth, roughened when dry. In coastal
habitats, maritime sands; locally distributed in France and also N coast of Spain.
Fl (5–) 6–7.

Putoria calabrica   A much-branched trailing subshrub with a fetid smell, forming mats up to 1m in diameter. Leaves are opposite, short-stalked, lanceolate, 1–2cm long, curled under at the margins; surface leathery turning blackish on
drying. Inflorescence with pink flowers in terminal clusters; corolla a narrow-
funnel shape, 1–1.5cm long, with spreading linear-lanceolate lobes 3–6mm long,
stamens protruding. Fruit about 5mm (illus.), red to red-black. In rocky crevices,
mainly on limestone, in the Mediterranean region but absent from France and the
W Mediterranean islands. **Fl** 4–9.

Putoria calabrica

Putoria calabrica fruit

Crucianella maritima   A prostrate or ascending woody perennial with smooth,
whitish, hairless stems 10–50cm high. Leaves leathery, blue-green with white margins, ovate-lanceolate and sharply pointed, 4–10mm long in whorls of 4, often
closely overlapping on young stems. Inflorescence a spike 2–4cm long with narrow, funnel-shaped yellow flowers, 1–1.3cm long with 5 short converging lobes.
Flowers arise singly in the axils of separate, oval, fringed bracts and just protrude
beyond them. On rocks and established dunes in the W Mediterranean region and
Iberian Peninsula. **Fl** 5–9. *C. angustifolia* has leaves in whorls of 6–8 and an inflorescence 2–8cm long; corolla pale yellow, 4-lobed but not protruding beyond the
bract. Throughout the Mediterranean region and S Europe. *C. latifolia* has leaves in
whorls of 4–6. Inflorescence about 15cm long, corolla 4-lobed and slightly longer
than the bracts. Throughout the Mediterranean region and S Europe.

Valantia hispida   A delicate, slightly fleshy annual, with erect or ascending
stems, 6–20cm, branched from the base and carrying rough, spreading hairs in the
upper part. Leaves in whorls of 4, narrowly oblong-ovate to lanceolate, and more
or less pointed, 2–10mm long. Inflorescence spike-like, arising from the axils with
flowers in threes, 1.5–2mm across, the central one hermaphrodite but the laterals both male, 3-lobed, with stalks that bend down at fruiting time; stalks are thickened to enclose the fruit (illus.) and have 15–25 straight bristles on the back. In flat
stony or sandy places and walls in the Mediterranean region and Canary Islands.
Fl 6–9. *V. muralis* has upper part of stem more or less softly hairy, leaves usually
smaller, blunt; bristles hooked, stalks with a prominent horn. In the Mediterranean
region.

Valantia hispida fruit

Wild Madder *Rubia peregrina*   A climbing perennial with 4-angled stems,
woody at the base; stems, leaf margins and midribs are rough to the touch because
of small, recurved spines. Leaves are dark green, firm, leathery in whorls of 4–8,
narrowly or broadly ovate, 1.5–6cm long; lateral veins inconspicuous. Infores-
cence many-flowered: flowers in terminal cymes 4–10cm long and in the leaf axils
distinctly larger than the leaves. Corolla yellowish-green, 4–6mm in diameter with
5 lobes 2–3mm long, bristle-tipped. Fruit a black berry 4–6mm in diameter (illus.).
In hedges and thickets and rocky ground in S and W Europe. **Fl** 4–8. **Madder**
R. tinctorum is similar to above, but has softer leaves, distinctly net-veined beneath.
Flowers bright yellow with less-pointed lobes. Fruit reddish-brown. In scrub and
woodland in the Mediterranean region. **Fl** 6–8. *Formerly grown for the red dye,
madder, which can be extracted from the roots.*

Wild Madder fruit

Valantia hispida (left)

Wild Madder (right)

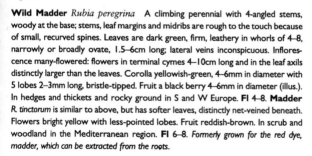

BINDWEED FAMILY, CONVOLVULACEAE

Herbs or shrubs, stems often climbing, with alternate leaves lacking stipules. Corolla tubular or bell-shaped, usually 5-lobed or 5-angled; stamens 5, alternating with corolla lobes. Fruit a capsule.

Greater Dodder *Cuscuta europaea* A herbaceous, parasitic annual with short, twining stems from which suckers (haustoria) grow; leaves, minute scales. The plant forms a dense, reddish tangle, often, but not exclusively, on Stinging Nettle or Hop. Flowers are usually 4-pointed, pinkish, 2mm in diameter, in dense rounded heads; flower stalks very short, stamens not protruding. Mainly in mountains in the south; otherwise widespread throughout Europe. Fl 7–10.

Sea Bindweed

Sea Bindweed *Calystegia soldanella* A hairless, creeping perennial, with stems up to 1m, not twining. Leaves dark green, rather fleshy and distinctly kidney-shaped (illus.), 1–2 times as wide as long, with long stalks (superficially similar to Alpine Snowbell – *Soldanella* – hence specific name). A pair of broad bracts immediately below the sepals distinguishes *Calystegia* from *Convolvulus* species. Flowers large, pink, solitary and funnel-shaped, 3.2–5.2cm across. On maritime sands and dunes on Mediterranean and Atlantic coasts. Fl 4–10.

Pink Convolvulus *Convolvulus cantabrica* An ascending or erect perennial 10–50cm tall with several stems, woody at the base; spreading hairs obvious in the lower part. Basal leaves broadened but narrowing to a stalk at the base; stem leaves linear to lanceolate-oblong, stalkless and narrowing at the base (illus.). Inflorescence stalks longer than the accompanying leaf, 1–2 flowers formed on short stalks bearing 2 bracts. Corolla funnel-shaped, pink, 1.5–2.5cm long, with silky hairs on the outer surface of the folds; calyx lobes have long woolly hairs. In garrigue, maquis, grassy pasture and on waysides in SE Europe and the Mediterranean region. Fl 5–7.

Convolvulus lineatus A dense silky-hairy perennial, with a woody stock and spreading or ascending stems up to 25cm. Leaves narrowly oblong (illus.). Flower stalks shorter than the accompanying leaf stalks; flowers 1.2–2.5cm, pink. Ovary and capsule downy. On dry, open ground in S Europe. Fl 5–7.

Pink Convolvulus

Convolvulus cneorum A dense silky-hairy species, with woody stems 10–50cm. Flowers white, 1.5–2.5cm across, in crowded terminal heads. Seed capsule downy-haired. On calcareous rocks near the sea in the W and central Mediterranean. Fl 4–7.

Convolvulus lanuginosus A down-covered perennial, 10–30cm, with a branched, woody stock. Leaves narrow, linear, silvery. Flowers pink, 1.5–2.5cm across, in a crowded head surrounded by lanceolate, leafy bracts, which are longer than the hairy calyx. Ovary and capsule hairless. On dry calcareous rocks in SE Spain and S France. Fl 3–7.

Convolvulus tricolor A plant with hairy, erect or ascending stems 20–60cm. Leaves oblong, gradually narrowing towards base; lower leaves stalked, upper ones stalkless. Flowers 2–5cm across, 3-coloured, yellow, white and blue from the base upwards, veins hairy. Minute bracteoles some way below the densely hairy calyx. Fruit hairy. In hedges and fields in W Mediterranean eastwards to Greece. Fl 4–6.

Small Blue Convolvulus *Convolvulus siculus* A delicate plant with stems 10–40cm (see photograph on page 139), prostrate at first becoming erect, branched at the base. Leaves thin-stalked, ovate, pointed, with heart-shaped or rounded base. Flowers blue with yellow tube usually solitary on stalks shorter than the accompanying leaves; corolla distinctly 5-lobed, funnel-shaped, 7–12mm long. Calyx hairy with paired, lanceolate bracteoles immediately beneath. Ssp *agrestis* from Sardinia has linear bracteoles well below the calyx. On open stony ground and fallow land, in the Mediterranean region. Fl 3–5.

Mallow-leaved Bindweed *Convolvulus althaeoides* A plant with prostrate or twining stems up to 1m. Leaves stalked and very variable, but upper leaves usually deeply lobed becoming heart-shaped or arrow-shaped towards the base (illus.). Flowers pink, funnel-shaped, 2.5–4cm long; 1–(3) arising in the leaf axils on stalks longer than the accompanying leaves. Ssp *althaeoides* has spreading hairs, lower leaves crenately lobed, upper leaves irregularly lobed not as far as the midrib. Calyx segments 8–10mm. Ssp *tenuissimus* has appressed hairs, upper leaves lobed to midrib, calyx segments 4–7mm. On waysides, cultivated land and fallow fields. In the Mediterranean region and Canary Islands, with ssp *tenuissimus* predominating in the east. Fl 4–6.

Morning Glory *Ipomoea purpurea* A plant, usually annual, with long trailing or climbing stems to 5m. Leaves entire, ovate to broadly ovate, 4–16cm, often heart-shaped; petioles long and distinct. Flowers usually solitary with deep-purple trumpet-shaped corolla 4–6cm long; sepals 1–1.6cm, finely hairy and with conspicuous bristles below. A native of tropical America, but naturalized in hedges and on roadsides in S France, Spain, Italy; widely grown for ornament and found as a casual. Fl 6–9. *I. acuminata* is similar to above, but is usually perennial, with leaves entire to deeply 3-lobed. Inflorescences few- to many-flowered, with flowers white, blue, pink or multi-coloured, usually fading to pink; sepals 1.3–2.2cm, lanceolate and finely hairy. Naturalized on roadsides.

Sweet Potato *Ipomoea batatas* Leaves broadly ovate, entire to deeply 3-lobed, 4–14cm long. Inflorescences 1- to several-flowered; flowers white or violet to purple, corolla 3–5cm long, sepals 7–12mm, hairless to hairy. Cultivated for its edible tubers in parts of S Europe; native of tropical America. Fl 7–9. *I. stolonifera* has creeping stems rooting at the nodes, leaves more or less fleshy 1–5cm long, usually oblong, entire to deeply 3- or 5-lobed. Flowers solitary with white or pale-yellow corolla 3.5–5cm long, sometimes with a purple centre; sepals 8–15mm. In sandy places near the sea in S Italy; a very local native in S Europe. Fl 5–8.

BORAGE FAMILY, BORAGINACEAE

Plants usually roughly hairy with leaves alternate, undivided. Flowers with 5 joined petals usually in 1-sided, stalked inflorescences, which are tightly coiled in bud; plants with blue flowers are often pink in bud. Stamens 5, alternating with the lobes, inserted on the corolla.

Heliotrope *Heliotropium europaeum* A softly hairy plant, 5–40cm, with erect or unbranched ascending stems. Leaves entire, ovate to elliptical, up to 5.5cm × 2.8cm. Inflorescences many-flowered, simple or forked, coiled at first but unrolling as flowers open; flowers stalkless, scentless. Flowers white, 2–4mm across, with 5 spreading lobes. Calyx with spreading lobes almost divided to base; nutlets 4, persistent, separate, wrinkled, hairless or hairy. On cultivated land, waste ground and roadsides throughout the Mediterranean and SE Europe, and the Canary Islands. Fl 5–10. *H. suaveolens* is similar to above, but has scented flowers 4–8mm across. In SE Europe. *H. supinum* has a prostrate stem, leaves white-hairy beneath with stalk about 1.5cm. Corolla only 1mm across; calyx divided for a quarter of its length and enclosing the single nutlet at fruiting time. In the Mediterranean region and Canary Islands.

Neatostema apulum A stiffly erect plant, 3–30cm, with 1 (sometimes 2) stems branched from about the same point. Basal leaves more or less linear, narrowing to the stalk; stem leaves stalkless, numerous, linear, up to 7cm long with spreading bristly hairs especially at the margins. Inflorescence leafy and dense with almost stalkless flowers. Corolla yellow, about 6mm long, with 5 hairy lobes. Calyx about 4mm with 5 pointed lobes, slightly shorter than the tube, bristly outside, soft white-hairy inside. In open grassland and garrigue throughout Mediterranean. Fl 3–6.

Purple Gromwell *Buglossoides purpurocaerulea*   An erect perennial, stems 15–60cm tall with spreading hairs arising unbranched from a rhizome together with several prostrate, rooting non-flowering shoots. Leaves bright shiny green, lanceolate, 3.5–8cm long the lower ones narrow into a short stalk, the upper ones are stalkess with rough, flattened hairs. Inflorescence usually consists of 3 terminal clusters surrounded by leaf-like bracts. Corolla red-purple at first becoming bright blue, funnel-shaped, with 5 lobes 1.4–1.9cm long; hairy on the outer surface and 5 bands of hairs inside on the throat. Calyx bristly, 6–8.5mm long, with pointed lobes; nutlets smooth, shiny white, 3.5–5cm. In deciduous oakwoods and thickets in mountain areas; widespread in S Europe. **Fl** 4–6.

Scrambling Gromwell *Lithodora diffusum*   A low, prostrate or erect, spreading shrub. 10–40cm high. Leaves alternate, narrow and blunt, 1.5–2cm long, 2–4mm wide, rough-hairy on the upper surface, paler beneath with margins rolled under. Inflorescence consists of terminal clusters of bright-blue, funnel-shaped flowers, corolla tube 1–2cm opening out to 5 rounded lobes outside, and throat with dense, silky hairs. In stony places, scrub, hedges and pinewoods, in N Portugal, SW, central and N Spain, and W France. **Fl** 4–7. Ssp *lusitanica* is in clumps formed by erect, unbranched stems. Leaves linear, with unrolled margins, pressed against stems. In S and central Portugal, and S Spain. *L. rosmarinifolia* has linear leaves 1–6cm long, rolled under at the margins; corolla hairy on the outside. In S Italy and Sicily.

Shrubby Gromwell *Lithodora fruticosum*   A dwarf shrub, up to 50cm, with erect, interwoven branches. Leaves linear, whitish with flattened bristly hairs and inrolled margins. Flowers blue, about 1cm across (smaller than Scrambling Gromwell). Corolla tube hairless outside and only sparsely bristle-haired on the outside of the lobes. On stony hillsides, mainly on limestone, in S, central and E Spain, and SW France. **Fl** 4–7. *L. oleifolium* has broader leaves, dull green above and silvery-white below. Flowers in small clusters, initially pale purplish turning blue, 6–7mm long. Endemic to rocky areas of E Spanish Pyrenees.

Golden Drop *Onosma echioides*   A stiff, erect, bristly-haired perennial with several flowering stems 15–40cm, with woody bases and a number of non-flowering shoots with tufts of leaves. The bristles arise from small tubercules surrounded by about 10–20 bristles about a fifth as long. Basal leaves linear-lanceolate, 2–7cm long and 2–7mm broad, narrowed towards the base, green or grey-green with simple hairs. Inflorescence slightly branched with terminal clusters of tubular, pendulous, almost sessile, pale-yellow flowers, 1.2–2.5cm long, with 5 short lobes. Each calyx divided almost to base; lobes 6–12mm in flower, expanding to 1.8cm in fruit; bracts about as long as calyces. In stony and grassy pastures, on chalk and serpentine, in Italy, Sicily and W Balkans. **Fl** 5–7. *O. fastigiata* is a similar species, biennial with hairy branched stems, 10–30cm high. Lower leaves 50–100mm long with setae 1.5–2mm long. Inflorescence branched, corolla pale yellow sparsely haired 1.6–2.2cm long. Central and S France, and NW Italy.

Onosma arenaria   A perennial or biennial, with a single flowering stem 15–70cm, and a basal rosette of oblong spoon-shaped leaves. Leaves pale green or greyish, covered mostly with straight hairs but also star-shaped hairs, especially on lower leaves. Flowers pale yellow, 1.2–1.9cm in branched terminal clusters; calyx 6–12mm in flower, up to 1.8cm in fruit. In rocky, grassy and stony places to 1,700m, from N Italy eastwards into the Balkans.

Pyrenean Golden Drop *Onosma bubanii*   A short grey-green perennial, with unbranched flowering stems and narrow-oblong leaves 4–5cm long, covered in straight bristles. Flowers pale yellow with corolla 1.6–2cm long, hairless. In dry stony places, mainly on limestone, to 1,700m, in Spanish Pyrenees. *O. vaudensis* is similar to above but has more robust appearance with several branched flowering stems; lower leaves broadest about the middle. In the Rhone Valley.

*Lithodora
rosmarinifolia*

Honeywort *Cerinthe major*   An erect, blue-green, almost hairless perennial, with stems 15–60cm. The lower leaves are short-stalked, spoon-shaped, with white-dotted surfaces and fringed at the margins; upper leaves are ovate, heart-shaped at the base, and stem-clasping. Flowers in clusters with reddish-purple-tinged bracts (illus.). Corolla yellow, often tinged purplish near the base, tubular, straight, about 3cm long and 8mm broad, lobes very small, recurved at their tips. Calyx half the length of the corolla; bracts as long as or longer than calyx. On cultivated and fallow land and roadsides throughout the Mediterranean region. Fl 3–6.

Lesser Honeywort *Cerinthe minor*   A low to medium annual (also biennial or perennial) 15–60cm high. Leaves oblong to oval, greyish-green, rough and frequently with white spots; upper leaves stalkless, lower ones short-stalked. Flowers pale yellow, often with 5 violet spots in the throat; corolla bell-shaped, 1–1.2cm with pointed lobes. In meadows, waste places and fields, on limestone, in mountain regions to 2,600m in French Alps and Apennines. Fl 5–9.

Smooth Honeywort *Cerinthe glabra*   A biennial or perennial, with smooth, unspotted, oblong to oval leaves; upper leaves heart-shaped at base, unstalked. Flowers yellow with 5 dark reddish-purple spots in the throat; corolla 8–13mm, a tubular-bell shape, with rounded lobes. In meadows and damp woods in mountain regions: Pyrenees, Alps and Apennines. Fl 5–7.

Dyer's Alkanet *Alkanna tinctoria*   A prostrate or ascending perennial, 10–30cm, with grey hairs but no glands. Lower leaves stalked, linear-lanceolate, 6–15cm long and up to 2.5cm broad; upper leaves stalkless with a heart-shaped base. Flowers in clusters, which are initially dense but elongate later; corolla bright blue, hairless outside, tubular, with ends opening to a funnel shape 6–8mm in diameter. Calyx 5-parted almost to base, slightly shorter than corolla; bracts as long as calyx. In stony pasture, fallow fields and sandy places in the Mediterranean region and into E Europe. Fl 4–6. *Outer layers of root when dried are a source of a red dye, Alkannin. A. lutea is a glandular-hairy annual with yellow corolla 5–7mm in diameter. Bracts at least twice as long as the calyx. In the W Mediterranean region.*

BUGLOSSES *Echium*   Corolla funnel-shaped with an oblique throat and 5 irregular teeth: plants with stiff rough hairs, stems often speckled.

Pale Bugloss *Echium italicum*   An erect plant, 30–100cm, with a dense covering of spreading, whitish to yellowish bristles. Basal leaves lanceolate, 2–35cm long and 1.5–4cm broad, narrowed to a stalk at the base; stem leaves stalkless. The inflorescence is spike-like or branched to form a pyramidal shape. Corolla whitish to flesh-coloured or pale blue, 1–1.2cm long, a narrow funnel shape cut obliquely at the end and finely haired outside (illus.). Stamens 4–5, protruding noticeably from the corolla, filaments pale. Calyx divided almost to the base with narrow-lanceolate lobes, 6–7mm long. In pastures and fallow land; widespread in S Europe. Fl 4–8. *E. asperrimum* is similar to above, differing in its large flesh-coloured corolla, 1.3–1.8cm long, and stamens with red filaments. In the W Mediterranean region. *E. boisseri* is a striking biennial with stems 1–2.5m, inflorescences wand-like; the dead stems remain standing, conspicuous in winter. Flowers small, flesh-coloured, 1.6–1.8cm long, with 5 long projecting stamens and pink-carmine filaments (illus.). Frequent on roadsides and uncultivated slopes in S Portugal and S Spain. Fl 4–7.

Honeywort

Pale Bugloss

Echium boisseri

Purple Viper's-bugloss *Echium plantagineum* Plants annual or biennial, 20–60cm, with branched, erect stems covered with soft, reddish bristles. Basal rosette plantain-like, hence the specific name. Leaves stalked, ovate, 5–14cm long, with prominent midribs and lateral veins. Inflorescences branched, panicle-like; flowers initially blue, later purple-red, with broadly funnel-shaped corollas, 18–30cm long, cut obliquely at the ends, outer surface with hairs only at margins (illus.). Stamens 2, protruding. Calyx divided almost to base with lobes 7–10mm, enlarging to 15mm at fruiting time. On waste ground, waysides and coastal sand-dunes in the Mediterranean region and W Europe. Fl 4–6. **Viper's-bugloss** *E. vulgare* is similar, with branched stems covered with rough hairs; basal leaves lanceolate, narrowed into the stalk, lateral veins not prominent. Corolla only 1–1.9cm, pink turning vivid blue; stamens 4–5, red, protruding. Very widespread. Fl 5–9.

Echium creticum A biennial plant with erect stems 20–90cm, covered with spreading, bristly hairs and an underlayer of shorter, downward-pointing hairs flattened against the stem. Basal leaves lanceolate, 8–18cm long and 1–2.5cm broad, narrowed into a stalk; stem leaves stalkless, narrowed at the base. Inflorescence more or less branched, panicle-like. Corolla remaining red or changing to bluish-purple or blue, 1.5–4cm long, broadly funnel-shaped and cut obliquely at the end; stamens 1 or 2, protruding (illus.). Calyx divided almost to base into narrow, lanceolate lobes, 7–9mm long, expanding to 1.2–1.9cm in fruit. On waste ground, waysides and fallow land in W Mediterranean. Fl 4–7. *E. tuberculatum* is similar to above but leaves greyish-white with flattened bristles; flowers dark blue-purple, 1.6–2.5cm, narrowly funnel-shaped with 2–4 unequal stamens, which are longer than the corolla. In S and central Portugal.

Small-flowered Bugloss *Echium parviflorum* Plants annual or biennial 10–40cm tall with several erect or ascending flowering stems. Leaves 2–8cm long, ovate to lanceolate, hairs short, adpressed. Flowers pale or dark blue, 10–13mm long; stamens do not protrude beyond the corolla. Calyx 6–8mm at flowering time, up to 15mm in fruit, with lobes 3–6mm wide at the base. Widespread in coastal, sandy places and on rocks. Fl 4–7.

Nonea vesicaria A plant, annual or biennial, with ascending or erect stems, 10–50cm, with rough bristles and short glandular hairs. Leaves stalkless, lanceolate, 3–20cm long; upper leaves clasping stem. Flowers maroon, 3–5mm across; corolla with cylindrical tube 8–12mm long, lobes short, blunt, stamens not protruding, attached above the middle of the tube. Calyx 5–7mm, enlarging to 1–1.5cm in fruit. Nutlets have wrinkled surface and collar-like basal ring. In open stony and sandy places on Iberian Peninsula, Balearic Islands, and Sicily. Fl 3–5.

Nonea pulla A plant 20–40cm high, greyish-hairy, and glandular. Leaves oblong-lanceolate, 8–12cm with upper ones stem-clasping. Flowers purplish to brown, 1–1.5cm long; corolla funnel-shaped with cylindrical tube. Calyx much enlarged at fruiting; nutlets almost spherical. In cornfields, fallow land and waysides in central and S Europe. Fl 5–8. *N. lutea* has a yellow corolla, 7–12mm long and 5–7mm wide, with hairy calyx lobes. In waste land and gravel pits from S Europe eastwards.

Large Blue Alkanet *Anchusa azurea* An erect perennial plant with stems 20–150cm, much-branched in the upper part and densely covered with stiff, white hairs. Leaves lanceolate; lower ones 10–30cm long and 1.5–5cm wide, narrowed at base into a stalk; upper leaves stalkless. Inflorescence consists of clusters of bright-blue or violet flowers forming large panicles. Flowers are 1–1.5cm in diameter, with a central white ring of scales with long hairs; corolla tube 6–10mm, with 5 lobes spreading flat. Calyx about as long as corolla tube, divided almost to base into 5 linear, pointed lobes. Bracts shorter than calyx; nutlets oblong, 7–10mm, swollen and densely warted. On waysides, fallow and cultivated land in the Mediterranean region and Canary Islands. Fl 4–8.

Purple Viper's-bugloss (left)

Echium creticum (right)

Purple Viper's-bugloss

Small-flowered Bugloss (left)

Nonea vesicaria (right)

Echium creticum

Large Blue Alkanet (left)

Nonea pulla (right)

Undulate Alkanet *Anchusa undulata* A biennial 10–50cm tall with spreading bristles and flattened, downy hairs. Lower leaves wavy with toothed margins. Corolla blackish-purple, fading to deep blue, 3–8mm across, tube 7–13mm; calyx divided for half of its length into blunt lobes. In sandy and stony fields in Portugal and Mediterranean region. Fl 4–8. *A. calcarea* is similar to above but perennial, with a woody stem base. Bristles sparse but with conspicuously swollen bases – particularly obvious on dead leaves. Inflorescence often suffused with reddish-purple, corolla dark blue with tube 6–8mm long; calyx shorter than corolla, divided for a third of its length. On coastal sands, and calcareous sands inland, in Portugal and S Spain. *A. granatensis* has bristles but few or no short hairs; corolla tube about 6–8mm, calyx as long or slightly shorter with pointed lobes. In richer soils in mountain areas, S and central Portugal and S Spain.

Green Alkanet *Pentaglottis sempervirens* A fairly robust bristly-haired perennial of medium height with ovate-acute leaves; upper leaves stem-clasping. Inflorescence consists of branched leafy clusters of bright-blue long-stalked flowers, each 5–7mm across, with white throat scales forming an 'eye'. In damp and shady places in woods and on hedgebanks in NE Portugal, central and N Spain and S and W France. Fl 4–7.

Lycopsis variegata A delicate hairy annual with erect stems up to 30cm, sparsely branched from the base. Leaves oblong, blunt, with long bristles on slightly toothed margins. Inflorescence with flowers in small, tight, clusters at the end of long, leafy branches. Flowers small, sweet-scented, variegated purple and white, with irregular rounded petals: corolla tube longer than calyx teeth. On cultivated ground, track-sides and rough ground from Italy eastwards. Fl 2–6.

Borage *Borago officinalis* An erect, bristly-haired annual with stout stems 20–70cm. Basal leaves in a rosette, ovate to lanceolate, 5–20cm long, narrowing to a winged stalk; upper leaves stalkless, clasping stem. Inflorescence lax, branched, with short-stalked nodding flowers. Corolla tube very short with 5 lanceolate pointed lobes spreading out flat, 2–3cm across, bright blue (rarely white). Calyx more than half as long as corolla, anthers dark violet. On cultivated and fallow land, waste ground and roadsides, throughout the Mediterranean region; native in the west but widely cultivated as a herb. Fl 4–9. *Once used to purify the blood and treat coughs. B. pygmaea has bell-like flowers; plant resembles a Campanula species. In damp places in Corsica, Sardinia and Capri.*

Blue Hound's-tongu

Lycopsis variegata (lef

*Cynoglossur
cheirifolium* (right

Blue Hound's-tongue *Cynoglossum creticum* Plant 20–80cm biennial, with stems usually branched above, and an even, dense covering of soft hairs. Leaves lanceolate, 5–15cm long; lower ones in a rosette narrowing to a basal stalk, upper leaves stalkless and semi-clasping the stem, lateral veins not prominent. Inflorescences are bractless clusters of flowers on short stalks which become recurved with age. Corolla 7–9mm across, pink at first, later pale blue with dark veins; lobes roundish, hairless, about as long as the tube. Calyx 6–8mm, divided almost to the base into 5 oblong, blunt lobes. Nutlets 5–7mm, rounded and densely covered with hooked spines, margin not thickened (illus.). On fallow land, waysides and garrigue in the Mediterranean region. Fl 4–7.

Cynoglossum cheirifolium A plant with erect, felted stems 10–40cm, branched in the upper part. Leaves oblong-lanceolate to narrowly spoon-shaped, without visible lateral veins, and felted on both surfaces; upper leaves stalkless but not clasping the stem. Inflorescence with bracts; flowers pale red at first, becoming purplish then blue. Corolla about 8mm long with 5 lobes, hairless and shorter than the tube. Calyx lobes ovate, felted, 5–7mm long. Nutlets 5–8mm in diameter, sometimes smooth, usually covered with hooked spines, margins distinctly thickened (illus.). In open rocky places; W Mediterranean eastwards to Italy and Sicily, absent from Corsica. Fl 4–6.

Cynoglossum cheirifoliu

VERBENA FAMILY, VERBENACEAE

Herbs or shrubs with leaves opposite or in whorls, entire or lobed. Flowers 4- to 5-merous, zygomorphic but not obviously, calyx usually small. Fruit often a drupe, rarely a capsule, dividing into 2 or 4 1-seeded nutlets.

Vervain *Verbena officinalis* A hairy square-stemmed perennial, with stems up to 60cm. Leaves 2–7.5cm long, deeply cut into oblong-ovate lobes; upper leaves narrower and less divided, sometimes entire. Inflorescence has tiny lilac-blue flowers in a dense spike, elongating in fruit; corolla 4mm across, 5-lobed, slightly 2-lipped; calyx 2–3mm long, hairy, ribbed. On track-sides, screes and in waste places throughout the Mediterranean region. Fl 5–9. *Considered to be a cure-all by Hippocrates.* **Procumbent Vervain** *V. supina* differs in its trailing stems with leaves twice-cut pinnately into oval segments. Flowering spike unbranched; corolla pale lilac, 3mm across. In sandy places and waysides near the sea, in central Portugal, S, central and E Spain. Fl 5–8.

WATER-STARWORT FAMILY, CALLITRICHACEAE

Herbs with opposite leaves, flowers axillary, perianth absent, 1 stamen. Fruit separating into 2 mericarps.

Common Water-starwort *Callitriche stagnalis* Plants with submerged, narrowly elliptical leaves and floating rosettes, usually with 6 broadly elliptical pale-green leaves. Both sets of leaves 5-veined. Flowers formed from rosette leaves only, solitary or paired; stigmas 2–3mm long becoming recurved. Fruit has all 4 lobes broadly winged. In springs and still slow-moving water, also on mud; widespread in Europe. Fl 5–9. **Blunt-fruited Water-starwort** *C. obtusangula* is similar in form to above but differs in having submerged leaves linear, often notched deeply, and up to 12 rosette leaves together, roughly diamond-shaped. Fruit slightly keeled but not winged, 1.5mm across. In fresh or brackish, usually slow-moving water. S and W-central Europe. Fl 5–9.

Chaste Tree *Vitex agnus-castus* A shrub, 1–3m, with young branches 4-angled and white-felted. Leaves deciduous, stalked, palmate with 5–7 lanceolate leaflets; dark green above, white-felted beneath. Inflorescences are long interrupted spikes of small, sweet-scented, lilac flowers. Corolla 6–9mm long, hairy outside, more or less 2-lipped; stamens project well beyond corolla. Calyx bell-shaped, white-felted, with 5 triangular teeth. Fruit fleshy, black, 2mm in diameter. On stream banks and damp coastal sites, often cultivated as an ornamental shrub, throughout the Mediterranean region. Fl 6–9. *The shrub has been associated with chastity because of its supposed ability to suppress desire; conversely, the fresh seeds have been reputed to have aphrodisiac properties. Also the source of a yellow dye.*

BIGNONIACEAE

An essentially tropical family, comprising several genera of climbing plants and shrubs such as *Tecoma*, *Pandorea* and trees such as *Catalpa*. None are native in Europe but are widely cultivated in parks and gardens. Leaves vary from entire to pinnately divided, flowers are horn- or trumpet-shaped bells.

Indian Bean or Catalpa *Catalpa bignonioides* A wide-spreading deciduous tree, to 20m, with very large, heart-shaped leaves which are long-stalked and oppositely arranged; pale green above and downy below. Flowers white, bell-shaped, in numerous broad pyramidal clusters of 3; corolla 3–4cm across with 2 yellow streaks and purple spots within. Fruit long and narrow, up to 40cm, hanging down in large numbers. A native of the southern states of the USA, often grown in gardens, parks and streets in S Europe as an ornamental tree. Fl 7–8.

Common Water-starwort (left)

Blunt-fruited Water-starwort (centre)

Indian Bean (right)

MINT FAMILY, LAMIACEAE

A distinctive family of shrubs and herbs with 4-angled stems and simple leaves in opposite pairs. Flowers are in whorls, which may be bunched or in an elongated spike. Corolla tubular, often 2-lipped, with a large upper lip and lower lip divided into 3 or more lobes. Calyx 5-toothed. Many species are important as culinary herbs (basil, hyssop, marjoram, rosemary, sage, savory and thyme); and as sources of volatile oils (lavender, mint, patchouli and peppermint).

BUGLES *Ajuga*   A genus characterized by its corolla lips: the upper lip is very short while the lower is conspicuously 3-lobed. Ring of hairs within the corolla tube.

Ground-pine *Ajuga chamaepitys*   A low-growing annual with aromatic pine scent when crushed. Stem spreading, branched at base, with crowded leaves that are narrow, hairy and divided into 3 segments, which are themselves divided into 3 blunt lobes; surface slightly glandular and sticky. Flowers are solitary or in pairs in the leaf axils, with bright-yellow, 2-lipped corolla, 7–15mm long, often with reddish-brown spots. In fields, dry hills, mainly on limestone, throughout the Mediterranean region. Fl 3–10. *Used by Arabs to cure hysteria in horses and paralysis in animals.*

Blue Bugle *Ajuga genevensis*   A plant with hairy, 4-angled stems, 10–30cm, no stolons. Basal leaves long-stalked, upper ones 3-lobed or deeply toothed, often suffused with blue. Flowers dark blue; corolla 1.2–1.8cm long, upper lip very short, 2-lobed, lower lip much longer, 3-lobed; 4 stamens. On sunny slopes, path margins and calcareous grasslands; scattered in S Europe, common in Causses region of France. Fl 4–6. **Pyramidal Bugle** *Ajuga pyramidalis* is similar to above, with hairy stems and oval leaves that are hardly toothed. Flowers pale violet-blue, rarely pink or white, in dense, leafy pyramidal spike; corolla 1–1.8cm long. In meadows and stony places in mountains from 1,300–2,800m, often on acid soils in S Europe. Fl 4–8. **Common Bugle** *Ajuga reptans* is distinguished by rooting runners and stems hairy on two sides only. Flowers blue, 1.4–1.7cm, in leafy spike, with leaf-like bracts, tinged purplish-brown. In damp grassy places and woods. Widespread throughout Europe. Fl 4–7.

GERMANDERS *Teucrium*   This genus is characterized by the flowers: the corolla has no upper lip, and has a 5-lobed lower lip (middle lobe much larger). There is no ring of hairs within the corolla tube.

Tree Germander *Teucrium fruticans*   A handsome evergreen shrub with 4-angled, white-felted stems: the small dark-green, shiny leaves are short-stalked, ovate and white-felted beneath. Flowers stalked, in pairs in the upper leaf axils, forming a long inflorescence. Corolla pale blue to lilac 1.5–2.5cm long: lower lip 5-lobed with an elongated middle lobe: upper lip absent, throat lacks ring of hairs. Stamens and styles project well beyond corolla; calyx bell-shaped, green within, white-felted outside. In evergreen thickets near the coast in the W Mediterranean region; also cultivated as an ornamental shrub. Fl 2–6. *T. brevifolium* is a small shrub to 60cm; differing in its blue, solitary flowers about 1cm long. In E Mediterranean region. *T. marum* has purple flowers about 1cm long, in narrow, spike-like inflorescence. In Balearics, Corsica and Sardinia. (Numerous endemic species in the Mediterranean region.)

Wall Germander *Teucrium chamaedrys*   A spreading, low-growing herbaceous perennial with hairy stem, 10–30cm, and a woody base. Leaves are small oval-oblong 2cm long, 1cm wide, with distinct, rounded teeth; blade hard, shiny above, strangely veined. Flowers reddish-purple, 9–16mm, almost stalkless with 2–6 on 1-sided, elongated head. Corolla with lateral lobes acute, calyx hairy, reddish and bell-shaped. In dry places, hills and open woods, especially on limestone, in the Mediterranean area. Fl 5–6. *Used to reduce fever.*

Ground-pine Germander *Teucrium pseudochamaepitys*   A small, usually hairy perennial with a rather woody base. Stem simple, erect and very leafy. Leaves 2–3cm, deeply divided into 3–5 entire, pointed lobes. Flowers in whorls of 2, stalked, almost all in loose inflorescence facing the same way. Flowers white, pale rose or purple, with corolla 1–1.5cm long, and 5-lobed lower lip; upper lip absent. Throat lacks ring of hairs, filaments protrude and calyx is bell-shaped, much shorter than corolla. In stony pasture, garrigue and grassy pasture, in S France and the Iberian Peninsula. **Fl** 4–7.

Ground-pine
Germander (left)
Prasium majus (right)

Felty Germander *Teucrium polium*   A small, white-felted subshrub with erect or ascending stems. A very variable species with numerous micro-species. Leaves opposite or in tufts, 7–27mm oblong-ovate, very short-stalked and margins recurved with 2–5 rounded teeth on each side. Flowers in dense, simple or compound heads with leaf-like bracts. Corolla white or reddish, 5mm long, a little larger than calyx; lower lip 5-lobed with upper lip absent, hairy or hairless outside, no ring of hairs in throat. In stony pasture and garrigue throughout the Mediterranean region. **Fl** 4–8. *Used in a steam bath for stomach troubles, colds and fevers.*

Yellow Germander *Teucrium flavum*   A shrubby perennial, up to 50cm, with hairy stems and rather leathery, stalked leaves 10–40mm long with rounded, toothed margins, paler above. Flowers 1.5–2cm in 1-sided spike; corolla yellow with blunt calyx teeth, 7–10mm, in clusters of 2–6, 7–10. In rocky places throughout the Mediterranean. **Fl** 5–7.

White Horehound
(left)

Prasium   Flowers have 4 stamens projecting; upper corolla lip arched and convex. Calyx 2-lipped. Leaves oval and toothed.

Prasium majus   A small, irregularly branched shrub, up to 1m, with woody stems, often climbing. Leaves shiny, dark green, ovate, 2–5cm long with stalks 1–1.8cm, heart-shaped at base, margins toothed. Whorls with only 1 or 2 white (pale-lilac) flowers 1.7–2.3cm. long. Corolla has ring of scale-like hairs within tube; upper lip arched, lower lip 3-lobed with broad middle segment. Calyx enlarged at fruiting time; 10-veined, bright green, hairless, with 5 pointed teeth. In garrigue, maquis and evergreen woods near the coast in the Mediterranean area (except France). **Fl** 2–6.

HOREHOUNDS *Marrubium*   Flowers white or yellow; corolla tube shorter than the calyx; stamens 4, not projecting. Calyx has 5–12 hooked, not spiny, teeth. Leaves have network of wrinkles.

White Horehound *Marrubium vulgare*   An unpleasant-smelling perennial, greyish-white, up to 60cm, with stout rhizome, stems sparsely branched. Leaves 1.5–4.5cm long, with white-woolly appearance, paired, rounded with rounded teeth; surface wrinkled, green and hairy above, white and hairy below. Corolla white, about 1.5cm long, 2-lipped, tube shorter than calyx. Calyx with 10 small, hooked, recurved teeth. On dry slopes, waste ground, village paths and fallow land, in the Mediterranean region. **Fl** 4–10. *Used to reduce fever and as a stimulant.*

Marrubium incanum
(left)

Marrubium peregrinum
(right)

Marrubium incanum   A perennial with stems 20–60cm high, woody at the base, usually with short, erect, non-flowering stems. Leaves oblong to ovate, wedge-shaped at base, edges crenate, leaf stalk shorter than blade, surface densely felted; grey-green above, white below. Flowers white, held in dense many-flowered false whorls carried separately along stem with awl-shaped bracteoles curving upwards. Corolla hairy on outside, protruding slightly from calyx with flat upper lip divided for about a third of its length. Lower lip 3-lobed. Calyx tube 6–7mm with ring of hairs in throat. In stony grassland, garrigue, rough pasture and fallow land; in Italy and Sicily, eastwards to Balkans. **Fl** 6–8. *M. peregrinum* has leaves oblong-ovate with leaf stalk shorter than the blade. Flowers very small, white or yellowish in well-spaced false whorls. In S France. **Fl** 6–8.

Sideritis   The corolla tube is shorter than the calyx, white or yellow; calyx has 5 spiny teeth. Leaves not wrinkled.

Sideritis romana   A small annual, soft and densely haired, with stems 10–30cm, simple or branched in lower part. Leaves green, coarsely toothed, oblong-ovate, 1–2.5cm long by 5–12mm broad; lower ones stalked, upper ones sessile. Flowers in false whorls of 6 with no bracteoles in axils, forming an uninterrupted, leafy spike. Flowers whitish (also yellowish or purplish) with 2-lipped corolla 7–10mm long. Upper lip undivided, flat. Calyx 10-veined, about as long as corolla, with 5 teeth; upper tooth 2–3 times broader than the others. All teeth bear a sharp bristle and these spread at fruiting time. In garrigue, maquis and grassy pasture in the Mediterranean. Fl 4–8. Ssp *curvidens* differs in having calyx teeth with long spines curving outwards. *The plants have been used as a tea. S. montana* is also an annual, but differs from *S. romana* in having yellow flowers with or without a brownish lip; calyx teeth more or less equal, ovate, spine-tipped. In derelict fields in S, central and E Spain, and France. Fl 4–8.

Sideritis scorpioides   A greyish or green shrublet with oblong to oblong-ovate, toothed leaves and curled hairs on the stem. Flowers in 3–10 widely separated whorls, surrounded by broad, spiny-lobed bracts. Corolla 8–10mm, yellow, sometimes with purple markings. Calyx 6–9mm, with a ring of hairs inside the tube. On dry hills, mainly limestone, in S, central and E Spain, and France. Fl 4–7. *S. hirsuta* is similar to above but differs in having more or less spreading, straight hairs on the stem. Very variable. In vineyards and dry rocky places, in N, E and S Portugal, and the Mediterranean. Fl 4–7.

Sideritis incana   A slender, woody-based, felted perennial with entire, linear leaves and an elongated spike of 2–10 separated whorls of yellow or pink flowers. On rocks, screes, and in dry sunny places, in S, central and E Spain. Fl 4–8.

JERUSALEM SAGES *Phlomis*   Perennials, often woody, with large flowers; corolla with arched upper lip, calyx with 5 equal teeth. Some species are used to make herbal teas.

Jerusalem Sage *Phlomis fruticosa*   A shrub up to 1m, with much-branched cottony stems. Leaves are large, oval, around 1½–2 times as long as broad, with white-velvety undersides. Flower heads with 1–3 terminal whorls of 20–30 yellow flowers, each 3cm long, with a hairy, curved hood and spreading, darker yellow lip (illus.); there are oval-lanceolate bracts under the flower clusters. Calyx with short, rigid, recurved teeth. In dry, rocky places in the Mediterranean area. Fl 4–6.

Jerusalem Sage

Phlomis lychnitis   A subshrub with narrower leaves than Jerusalem Sage, 5–6 times as long as broad. Bracts beneath whorls are broadened at base, prolonged to a spiny apical point and covered with long silky hairs. Flowers yellow, grouped into 4–8 whorls, each carrying 6–10 flowers (illus.). Calyx teeth 4–5mm, straight, sharp-pointed, silky-hairy. In rocky places, open woods and garrigue, largely on calcareous soils, from Spain to France. Fl 5–7.

Phlomis herba-venti   A perennial with herbaceous stems from 20–60cm, much branched, downy with spreading, not glandular, hairs. Leaves are paired, oval to lanceolate with round-toothed margins and leathery; shiny above, white-woolly below. Flowers in 2–5 whorls, each with 10–12 flowers; 2 sterile bracts at the end of each whorl while bracts below whorls are stiff, curved and somewhat spiny. Flowers purple, 2cm long, with hairy corolla; calyx has very sharp, spreading teeth. In dry places, field-edges, rocks and track-sides, in the Mediterranean. Fl 5–7. *P. purpurea* A dwarf shrub, differing from above in having leaves deeply wrinkled above and white-felted below. Flowers pinkish in whorls of about 8 flowers; bracts soft, spineless, hairy. In hills and rocky places in Spain. Fl 4–6.

Phlomis lychnitis

Melittis   The corolla has upper lip entire; lower lip with 2 rounded lobes. Calyx upper lip 3- to 4-lobed; lower lip 2-lobed.

Bastard Balm *Melittis melissophyllum*   A perennial herb with erect stems 20–70cm. Leaves 2–15cm long, 1–8cm wide, with toothed margins. The large flowers are carried in false whorls of 2–6 spaced along the stem (illus.). Calyx 2-lipped, 1.2–2.5cm. Corolla 2.5–4cm. Upper lip 2-lipped, weakly hooded, lower lip 3-lobed; white, pink or purple, sometimes variegated. In light woodland and bushy places in W, central and S Europe. **Fl** 5–8. Ssp *albida* has a stem that is densely covered with small glandular leaves; largest leaves 6–15cm with 20–30 teeth on either side. Corolla white with pink or purple markings on lower lip. In S Italy and Sicily.

DEAD NETTLES *Lamium*   This genus has rather large flowers; corolla 2-lipped, upper lip hooded, lower lip 3-lobed with 2 lateral tooth-like projections. Calyx funnel-shaped, 10-veined and 5-lobed.

Spotted Dead-nettle *Lamium maculatum*   A very variable, sparsely to densely hairy perennial, 15–80cm tall. Leaves 1–8cm long, 1–7cm wide, with irregularly lobed or toothed margins. Calyx 8–15mm, teeth shorter than tube. Corolla 2–3.5cm, pinkish-purple, rarely white or brownish-purple. Tube 1–1.8cm, curved, longer than calyx. Upper lip 7–14mm, entire; lower lip 4–6mm and heart-shaped. Anthers hairy. In open woods, hedges, ditches and waste places in central and S Europe.

Lamium garganicum   A perennial with stem up to 50cm. Leaves variable, up to 7cm long, with fine, distinctly toothed margins. Stem, leaves and calyx densely hairy. Inflorescence a series of crowded, false whorls. Calyces 7.5–18mm, with 5 veins and 5 more or less equal teeth (shorter than or equal to tube). Corolla 2-lipped; upper lip hooded, 1–1.5cm, bifid; lower lip broadly ovate, heart-shaped, 1–1.5cm (illus.). Anthers hairy. In rocky hills and mountain regions, in S Europe, Corsica and France. **Fl** 4–8. Ssp *laevigatum* has hairless or sparsely-haired stems; upper corolla lip shallowly toothed, not bifid. In the northern part of range. *L. corsicum* closely related to above, but has almost smooth stems; leaves no more than 4cm long. Calyx 1cm; teeth half as long as tube. Corolla 1.5–2cm. On mountain rocks and screes in Corsica and Sardinia.

Ballota   The corolla is 2-lipped with upper lip concave; calyx funnel-shaped, 10-veined and usually 5-lobed.

Black Horehound *Ballota nigra*   A perennial with hairy stems up to 10–20cm. Leaves 3–8cm long. Inflorescence many-flowered in a series of false whorls. Calyx 10-veined, 9–13mm, toothed, with 5 triangular-shaped lobes. Corolla 9–15mm, pink, lilac or white. Corolla tube shorter than calyx with ring of hairs inside; 1.2–1.4cm, lilac. Six subspecies occur in Europe (polymorphic). Naturalized in many places throughout Europe. **Fl** 4–6.

Ballota hirsuta   A perennial with stems 60–80cm, woody at the base. Stem leaves simple and glandular; lower leaves 3–6cm long, 3–5cm wide, heart-shaped at base, ovate with scalloped margin. Inflorescence of many-flowered false whorls. Calyx 1–1.2cm, bell-shaped, with 10 or more lobes which are small, triangular, with stiff points. Corolla 1.4–1.6cm, purple or white. On roadsides and in waste places in central and S Portugal, central, S, and E Spain, and the Balearics. **Fl** 4–5. *B. rupestris* has stems up to 70cm, covered with downy hair, woody at the base. Calyx 8–10mm, cylindrical with 6–10 lobes, triangular-lanceolate in shape. Corolla 1.2–1.4cm, purple and white. In rocky places in central and S Italy, Sicily, and the former W Yugoslavia.

Bastard Balm (le

Black Horehou
(righ

Bastard Bal

Spotted Dead-nettl
(lef

Lamium garganicu

Lamium garganicu
(lef

Ballota hirsuta (righ

CAT-MINTS *Nepeta* Corolla cylindrical or bell-shaped: upper lip 2-lobed, lower 3-lobed with midlobe concave. Calyx 15-veined with 5 teeth.

Cat-mint *Nepeta cataria* An erect perennial with hairy branched stems 40–100cm. Leaves 2–8cm, toothed, grey and woolly-hairy beneath. The inflorescence is spike-like with flowers in false whorls. The calyx is 5–6.5mm, with teeth 1.5–2.5mm. Corolla 7–10mm, extending slightly beyond the calyx (illus.). Flowers white with small purple spots. In rocky places, hedgebanks, waysides. Widely naturalized throughout W, S and central Europe. *Formerly used as a medicinal herb.* **Fl** 6–9. *N. italica* is a plant with grey-haired stems. Inflorescence spike-like, with calyx 7–8mm, slightly curved; teeth 3–3.5mm with upper ones slightly longer than lower ones. Corolla creamy white, 1.1–1.3cm. In E and central Italy.

Cat-mint (le

Stachys recta (rig

Cat-mi

WOUNDWORTS *Stachys* This genus has calyx tubular or bell-shaped, 5- or 10-veined and 5-lobed; corolla 2-lipped, upper lip flat or arched, lower lip 3-lobed, with middle lobe the longest.

Stachys cretica A plant with woolly-hairy stems 20–80 cm. Leaves ovate and at least 3 times as long as wide (e.g. 3–10cm long, 1–3cm wide); grey-green, densely woolly-hairy above, grey or white below. Flowers pink to reddish in false whorls. Calyx toothed, 6–12mm, with bristles no more than 1mm; corolla 1.5–2cm long, with pink segments. In grasslands and garrigue, in S Europe from S France eastwards. **Fl** 5–7. Ssp *salviifolia* has leaves less than 2–3 times as long as wide, with lowest often rounded. Calyx bristles no more than 1mm. Throughout the Mediterranean.

Stachys recta An erect perennial with glabrous or sparsely hairy stems 15–100cm. Lower leaves oblong 1–8cm long, becoming linear higher up the stem. Each false whorl carries 6–16 flowers; these are separate low on the stem, crowded higher up. Calyx is 5–9mm, with teeth shorter than tube; corolla 1.5–2cm, pale yellow and finely hairy with upper lip 4–7mm, lower lip 5–12mm. In dry areas, garrigue and maquis throughout Europe, south of Belgium. **Fl** 5–7.

Downy Woundwort *Stachys germanica* An erect perennial 15–60cm, with downy, greyish-white felted stems and leaves. Leaves oblong to heart-shaped, finely toothed, long-stalked; upper leaves stalkless, green above, greyish-white beneath. Flowers pale pinkish-purple, 1.5–2cm in false whorls. In woodland edges and clearings, on rocky ground and screes, often on limestone to 1,750m. Widespread in mountains of S Europe. **Fl** 6–9. *S. heracleae* has glandular-hairy stem and leaves. Flowers magenta; upper lip of corolla rounded, lower lip 3-lobed with middle lobe extended, pointed, and white basal area has some striping in deep magenta. Calyx glandular-hairy with teeth just shorter than corolla tube. In S Italy.

Downy Woundwo

(le

Stachys heracleae (lef

SELFHEALS *Prunella* All 4 species mentioned are interfertile; thus hybrids occur where 2 or more grow together.

Large Selfheal (righ

Cut-leaved Selfheal *Prunella laciniata* A densely hairy plant with stems up to 30cm. Leaves 4–7cm long, with the upper ones deeply divided or lobed. Inflorescence subtended by leaves. Calyx 1cm with 2 lips; teeth of lower lip 2–2.5mm. Long corolla 1.5–1.7cm, yellowish-white, rarely rose-pink or purplish. In dry grasslands, meadows, roadsides and light woodland in the central, south and west of the region.

Large Selfheal *Prunella grandiflora* A sparsely haired plant with stem up to 60mm. Leaves ovate/ovate-lanceolate, with entire or finely crenate margins. Inflorescence not subtended by leaves; calyx 1.5cm with teeth of lower lip 3–4mm. Corolla 2.5–3cm with whitish tube and lips deep violet. On calcareous soils throughout S Europe. **Fl** 5–8. Ssp *pyrenaica* has inflorescence up to 8cm long. On acid soils.

Selfheal *Prunella vulgaris* A plant with stems up to 50cm, more or less hairy. Leaves ovate 4–5cm long, entire or finely lobed margins. Inflorescence usually subtended by the leaves. Calyx 8–9mm; middle tooth of upper lip wider than lateral teeth, teeth of lower lip 1.5–2mm. Corolla 1.3–1.5cm, deep violet-blue, rarely white. Widespread throughout in meadows, light woodland, roadsides. Fl 5–9.

Prunella hyssopifolia A plant with hairless or sparsely haired stems up to 40cm Leaves 3–6cm long, linear-lanceolate, with entire margins. Inflorescence subtended by leaves; calyx 8–9mm with teeth of lower lip 3–3.5mm. Corolla 1.5–1.7cm; violet, rarely whitish. Meadows and light woodlands. In SW Europe. Fl 4–8.

Balm (left
Cleonia (right

Cleonia *Cleonia lusitanica* An annual with coarsely hairy stems up to 40cm, simple or branched from the base. Leaves 3–9cm long, stalkless, oblong-linear; usually coarsely scalloped to deeply toothed. Calyx 5–7mm, glandular, coarse-haired, 2-lipped: upper lip flat with 3 more-or-less distinct teeth ending in a bristle; lower lip 3-lobed. Corolla 2–3cm, purplish-violet (rarely white); corolla tube protrudes beyond calyx (illus.). In dry, open habitats in central and S Spain and Portugal. Fl 5–7.

Cleonia lusitanica

Balm *Melissa officinalis* A branched, usually hairy perennial with stems up to 1m. Leaves yellowish-green, ovate, pointed, stalked, lemon-scented when crushed, with toothed margin. Inflorescence has flowers in false whorls, white with leaf-like bracts. Corolla 2-lipped; upper lip erect and notched, lower lip 3-lobed. Calyx 13-veined, 2-lipped; upper lip 3-lobed, lower lip 2-lobed. In bushy and shady places throughout the Mediterranean region; an escape from cultivation in many places. Fl 6–9. *Once used to attract bees and make them swarm.*

Winter Savory (left,

SAVORIES *Satureja* This genus has corolla 2-lipped, with upper lip flat or convex, lower lip 3-lobed; calyx 2-lipped.

Winter Savory *Satureja montana* A perennial with a stout woody stock and flowering stems 1–4cm, hairless or with very fine hairs. Leaves linear-lanceolate 5–30mm long. Inflorescence a series of densely crowded false whorls with up to 14 flowers. Calyx 4–6mm, tubular, divided almost to the base, with 5 more or less equal teeth. Corolla 2-lipped, with straight tube 6–12mm, white to pale pink or bright purple. In Spain eastwards. Fl 4–6.

Summer Savory *Satureja hortensis* An annual, 10–25cm, with very fine hairy leaves 1–3cm long, 1–4mm wide, linear or lanceolate. Flowers 2–5 in false whorls, crowded or lax; bracts exceed whorls. Calyx 3–4mm, finely haired, teeth slightly unequal; upper equal to length of tube, lower distinctly longer than tube. Corolla 4–7mm, white, pink or lilac. In fields, waysides, ovoid walls throughout the Mediterranean region; cultivated as a pot herb. Fl 5–7.

Summer Savory (left

Satureja thymbra A much-branched dwarf shrub, 20–35cm, with a covering of fine grey hairs. Leaves 7–20mm long, 2–9mm wide, oblong-ovate, acute. Inflorescence many-flowered, globular, in false whorls; bracts as long as whorls. Calyx 4–7mm with long white hairs and pointed teeth slightly shorter than tube. Corolla 8–12mm, bright pink or reddish-purple. Garrigue, mainly on chalk. On S coast of Sardinia. Fl 4–6.

Micromeria This genus has calyx bell-shaped with 13–15 veins and 5 equal pointed lobes.

Micromeria nervosa A dwarf shrub, 10–40cm, with many erect or ascending stems. Leaves 7–10mm long, ovate to ovate-lanceolate, acute with very short stalk. Flowers 4–20, in fairly dense false whorls. Calyx 3–4mm, with long, dense hairs and teeth two-thirds as long as tube. Corolla 4–6mm, purplish, 2-lipped with straight tube. Stamens shorter than corolla. Stony pastures, garrigue especcially on chalk. In the Mediterranean region. Fl 4–7.

Micromeria graeca   A dwarf shrub, 10–50cm, erect or ascending stems: several subspecies recognized for S Europe with stems varying from finely hairy to coarse or even bristle-haired. Lower leaves ovate-lanceolate, the rest ovate. False whorls with 4–18 short-stalked flowers. Corolla tube 2–4mm longer than calyx tube. Widespread throughout the area. Fl 4–7.

Round-leaved Mint *Mentha suaveolens*   A perennial herb with a creeping rhizome; stems 4–100cm with sickly sweet scent. Stems vary from sparsely haired to a dense white covering. Leaves 3–4.5cm long, sessile or with very short petiole, strangely ridged with serrated margins. Leaves hairy above, with grey- or white-woolly hairs beneath. Many false whorls in inflorescence, usually congested to form a terminal spike. Calyx 1–2mm, hairy, bell-shaped. Corolla whitish or pink. In S and W Europe; also cultivated. Hybridizes with other species. Fl 6–9. *A culinary herb.*

Hyssopus   Flowers have a tubular 15-veined Calyx with 5 equal teeth.

Hyssop *Hyssopus officinalis*   A perennial herb with numerous erect stems 20–60cm. Leaves linear-lanceolate or oblong, 1–5cm long, hairless or fine-hairy. Calyx, 3–5mm, hairless or fine-hairy, tubular, 15-veined with 5 equal teeth (1–3mm). Corolla 7–12mm, blue or violet (rarely white), 2-lipped, upper lip erect, lower one hanging, 3-lobed with middle lobe the largest. Several subspecies occur. On dry hillsides and rocky ground, in S, central and E Europe; locally naturalized elsewhere from gardens. Fl 7–9.

Origanum   This genus has flowers clustered on spreading terminal heads; calyx bell-shaped, hairy within, 13-veined and 5-lobed.

Marjoram *Origanum vulgare*   A woody, rhizomatous perennial with hairy stems up to 90cm or more, usually branched above. Leaves 1–1.4cm long, ovate with smooth or finely toothed margins. Inflorescence in false whorls, which are grouped into small spikes (spicules), 5–30mm long, ovoid in shape. The spikes themselves form a corymb or panicle. Bracts 4–5mm, greenish-purple, with glands on outer surface. Calyx hairy or glabrous. Corolla 4–7mm, 2-lipped; upper lip entire, lower 3-lobed. Dry grassland, scrub rocky slopes on lime. Throughout most of Europe. Fl 6–9.

Origanum compactum   A dwarf shrub with unbranched, hairy stems up to 35cm Leaves 1.8–2cm long, ovate, densely glandular on both surfaces. Spicules 1–2.3cm, arranged in bundles to form a long panicle. Bracts twice as long as calyx; purplish. Corolla 8–10mm, 4 times as long as the calyx tube; pink or white. Rocky places on limestone in SW Spain. Fl 6–9.

Origanum majorana   Annual, biennial or perennial herb with erect or ascending stems 10–20cm with hairless or fine-downy covering. Leaves 5–20mm long with veins raised. Spicules of flowers 5–12mm, globed or ovoid, densely grouped at the end of short branches to form a narrow terminal panicle. Bracts 3–4mm, glandular, spotted. Calyx 2.5mm, single-lipped with a deep slit on 1 side. Corolla 0·4mm, white, pale lilac or pink. Cultivated and locally naturalized on limestone soils in S Europe. *Used as a culinary herb.* Fl 6–9.

Basil Thyme *Acinos arvensis*   A hairy, sprawling annual, 10–30cm, smelling of peppermint. Leaves opposite, ovate-lanceolate, almost stalkless, 1–2cm long, with 1–4 teeth on either side and very prominent veins beneath. Inflorescence rather 1-sided, flowers in whorls of about 6 with short bracts. Corolla 8–10mm long, blue-violet; calyx 2-lipped, 5–7mm long, with dense, spreading hairs, and teeth broadened below to give inflated calyx. On walls, rocks, stony grasslands and arable fields; scattered throughout central and S Europe. Fl 6–9.

Thymus In this genus, the calyx is 2-lipped, upper lip 3-toothed and hairy, lower lip with very narrow lobes.

Thymus capitatus A dwarf shrub, 20–50cm, with ascending to erect woody branches bearing axillary leaf clusters (often only single leaves in the dry season). Leaves of long shoots 6–19mm long, stalkless, and linear. Inflorescence in false whorls crowded to give terminal oblong-concave shape. Calyx 2-lipped, with 5mm upper lip shorter than lower, all teeth fringed. Corolla 2-lipped with straight tube, up to 1cm. Upper lip bifid, purplish-pink. Stamens protrude beyond tube. On dry calcareous soils and garrigue in the Mediterranean and Portugal. Fl 5–9.

Thymus vulgaris A plant 10–30cm, with erect to semi-patent, woody branches. Leaves 3–8mm long, linear to elliptical, margins rolled under. Inflorescence many-flowered. Bracts similar to leaves. Calyx 3–4mm, tube bell-shaped. Corolla whitish to pale purple. Very variable in shape of leaves, bracts and inflorescence. In W Mediterranean; widely cultivated. Fl 4–6. *Used as a culinary herb.*

Thymus zygis A plant 10–30cm, with ascending to erect finely hairy woody stems. Leaves 6–10mm long. Inflorescence up to 10cm, usually interrupted. Bracts similar to leaves. Calyx 3–4mm, greyish-green, downy. Corolla whitish. In maquis and dry fields in Spain and Portugal. Fl 7–8.

Rosmarinus This genus has the corolla 2-lipped, the upper deeply divided, the lower spreading and 3-lobed; stamens 2, projecting; calyx is 2-lipped, lower lip 2-lobed.

Rosemary *Rosmarinus officinalis* An evergreen shrub, up to 2m, with erect or ascending brown branches. Highly aromatic. Leaves 1.5–4cm long, linear, with rolled-under margins, bright green, finely wrinkled and leathery above, white-downy below, stalkless. Calyx 3–4mm, greenish or purplish, sparsely downy when young, later 5–7mm, distinctly veined; upper lip entire, lower lip 2-lobed. Corolla 1–1.2cm, 2 lipped, upper strongly concave, bifid; lower trifid with twisted lower lobe. Stamens 2, exceeding corolla. In dry scrub throughout the Mediterranean, Portugal and NW Spain; also cultivated. Fl 1–12. *R. eriocalyx* is similar to above but usually spreading, not erect, with grey branches. Leaves 5–15mm long, hairless, green or greyish, and downy. On calcareous rocks in SE Spain. Coastal plants are densely downy; mountain plants are glabrous. Fl 3–5.

LAVENDERS *Lavandula* A genus characterized by flowers in a tight blue spiral; corolla tube longer than calyx, stamens not projecting.

French Lavender *Lavandula stoechas* A small shrub 30–100cm tall. Leaves oblong-lanceolate, 1–4cm long with margins rolled under, grey-felted on both sides. Inflorescence a dense, stalked, false spike with 4-angled section. Flowers carried in 6- to 10-flowered whorls and borne in the axils of broad rhombic bracts which are membranous, hairy and purple-veined, 4–8cm long. Terminal bracts conspicuous bright purple, a characteristic of this species. Flowers small, dark purple, 6–8mm long, with 2-lipped corolla. Calyx 4–6mm and 13-veined. In open maquis, garrigue and dry hills, on siliceous soils, in the Mediterranean. Fl 2–6. *L. viridis* is similar to above with stem and leaves with short hairs; bracts light green; corolla white. SW Spain. **Toothed Lavender** *L. dentata* An aromatic subshrub, 30–100cm, with grey-felted stems. Similar to above, but differing in the following aspects: leaves narrow, 1.5–3.5mm long with margins rolled under but deeply cut into small, rounded teeth. Flower spike smaller, 2.5–5cm long with long stalks. Lower bracts ovate, pointed, 5–8mm long; upper bracts again conspicuous, purple, 8–15mm long. Flowers blue-purple; corolla about 8mm long, 2-lipped. Calyx 5–6mm and 13-veined; upper tooth with large appendage at free end. In garrigue, mainly on calcareous soils, in Spain and the Balearics. Fl 4–7.

Toothed Lavende

Common Lavender *Lavandula angustifolia* A subshrub, 20–100cm, with strong scent. Leaves entire, linear-lanceolate, 2–4cm long, hairless and green; young leaves white-felted. Flowers carried in false whorls with 6–10 flowers in a simple long-stalked, spike-like inflorescence. Bracts strongly veined, broadly ovate, pointed and membranous. Corolla blue-purple, 1–1.2cm long, 2-lipped; calyx grey-purple, 4.5–6mm long, 13-veined with an indistinct appendage to end of upper tooth. In garrigue and stony pasture up into mountains in S Europe. Fl 4–7. *Cultivated elsewhere for the aromatic oil used in medicine and perfumery.* **Broad-leaved Lavender** *L. latifolia* is similar to above, but with broader leaves covered with very dense short, white hairs when young; older leaves hairless, grey-green. Corolla 8–10mm, calyx 13-veined. Scent camphor-like. In S Europe.

Cut-leaved Lavender *Lavandula multifida* A subshrub, 20–100cm with sparsely hairy leaves, bipinnately divided; stems grey-felted to long-haired. Inflorescence sometimes branched at base, spike-like, 2–7cm long, long-stalked, composed of 2-flowered false whorls with membranous, ovate bracts. Corolla up to 12mm long, 2-lipped, blue-purple. Calyx about 5mm long, 15-veined; upper tooth without an appendage. Not distinctly aromatic like other lavender species. On stony pasture, garrigue or fallow land, on Iberian Peninsula, and in S Italy and Sicily. Fl 3–6.

Common Lavender (left)

Cut-leaved Lavender (right)

SAGES *Salvia* The calyx is 2-lipped; upper lip with 3 teeth, lower with 2. Stamens 2, each with 2 branches: 1 is long and curved with a single anther; the other branch is sterile.

Sage *Salvia officinalis* An aromatic subshrub with erect or ascending stems 20–60cm, covered with a felt of spreading hairs. Leaves narrowly elliptical to oblong-ovate; usually simple, stalked, opposite, with wrinkled surface, finely toothed margins; white-felted above at first, becoming hairless. Bracts long-pointed, ovate-lanceolate, with false whorls in their axils, one above the other with 5–10 short-stalked flowers in each. Corolla pale purple (rarely white) 2–3.5cm long with a 3-lobed lower lip and straight upper lip. Calyx bell-shaped, 2-lipped, often purple-tinged, 1–1.4cm long with 5 pointed teeth (illus.); lips dotted with glands. In stony pasture and garrigue on limestone. A Balkan native. Fl 7–8.

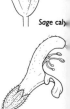

Sage (left)

Clary (right)

Sage calyx

Three-lobed Sage *Salvia triloba* An aromatic shrub, 30–150cm, with felted stems. Leaves grey-green, wrinkled above, grey-felted below, stalked, narrowly ovate; simple or with 2, rarely 4, lobes at the base. Inflorescence spike-like with 2- to 6-flowered false whorls and small bracts. Corolla blue-purple, pink (rarely white) 1.6–2.5cm long. Upper lip more or less straight with 3-lobed lower lip (illus.). Calyx bell-shaped, indistinctly 2-lipped, 5–8mm long, and often purple-tinged with 5 triangular teeth about 2mm long. In garrigue and maquis in E Mediterranean, westwards to S Italy and Sicily. Fl 3–6. *Leaves used as a culinary herb.*

Three-lobed Sage

Wild Clary *Salvia verbenaca* An herbaceous species with stems 10–80cm, in flower for much of the year. Upper part of stems more or less glandular-hairy; basal-rosette leaves oblong-ovate, 5–10cm × 2–4cm, long-stalked, dull green, wrinkled above and coarsely toothed at the edges. Stem leaves sessile, or very short-stalked; bracts ovate, about 6mm long, and pointed. Inflorescence often branched and ranges from a fairly lax to a dense spike, with false whorls of 4–10 stalked flowers. Corolla pale blue-purple, 6–15mm long, and 2-lipped. Calyx bell-shaped with prominent veins and long white hairs (illus.). On cultivated and fallow land and roadsides, largely on limestone and clay; throughout S Europe. Fl 2–7.

Wild Clary (left)

Wild Clary calyx

Clary *Salvia sclarea* A robust, sticky, strong-smelling biennial or perennial, up to 1m. Leaves hairy, ovate- to heart-shaped. Flowers lilac or pale blue (illus.); corolla 2–3cm, with a strongly curved hood distinguished by lilac or white bracts that are longer than the flowers. Calyx with spiny teeth, glandular-hairy. In bushy places and on rocks, in NE Portugal, S, central and E Spain, and S France. Fl 6–8.

Clary

Salvia lavandulifolia   An aromatic subshrub, 30–100cm, with erect or ascending stems. Leaves ovate to elliptical, stalked, with younger ones whitish-grey. Flowers in well-separated false whorls of 6–8 on a hairless stem. Corolla pale blue-purple, 2–2.5cm long with a 3-lobed lower lip and straight upper lip. Calyx tinged purple, 8–12mm long, divided into 5 teeth of equal size for half its length, with simple hairs, and dotted with glands. In stony mountain pasture in Spain and S France. Fl 7–8.

Red-topped Sage *Salvia horminium*   A small annual sage with stems simple or branched at base, up to 40cm. Leaves hairy, pale green, blunt, long-stalked, 1–2.5cm long; margins finely toothed with rounded teeth. Inflorescence an elongated spike of small pink flowers, 1–1.5cm long, in false whorls of 4–6. Bracts orbicular, pointed; terminal bracts conspicuously coloured violet or reddish making a tuft. In dry places, fields and track-sides, always on limestone, in the Mediterranean region. Fl 3–6.

Whorled Clary *Salvia verticillata*   A hairy, rather unpleasant smelling perennial, with purple-tinged stems and leaves. Leaves stalked, toothed, oval- to heart-shaped with one or two basal lobes. Distinguished by lilac-blue or purplish flowers in numerous tight whorls of 15–30: corolla 8–15mm long. In dry grassy and stony places, usually in mountain regions to 2,400m, in S Europe. Fl 5–8.

NIGHTSHADE FAMILY, SOLANACEAE

A family embracing many species of herbs or shrubs of commercial importance which are grown throughout S Europe, such as Tomato, Capsicum, Aubergine, Potato and Tobacco: the stems and leaves of most family members contain toxic alkaloids which are often of medicinal importance. Leaves alternate, often stalked; flowers 5-petalled, joined at base. Fruit a capsule or berry.

Tea Tree *Lycium europaeum*   A spiny, much-branched shrub, 1–4m. Leaves rather fleshy, entire and narrowly spathulate, 2–5cm long, growing in tufts. Flowers are formed in the leaf axils, usually in pairs. Corolla pale purple or white, narrow, funnel-shaped, 1.1–1.3cm long with 5 rounded lobes, 3–4mm long. Calyx 5-toothed, 2–3mm, later 2-lobed. Berries reddish. On waysides, in thickets and hedges throughout the Mediterranean; possibly an introduction in some places. Fl 4–9. **Duke of Argyll's Tea Tree** *L. chinense* is up to 2.5m tall with lanceolate to ovate leaves, 1–14cm long. Corolla tube is narrowly cylindrical at base, with lobes 5–8mm long, purple becoming brownish. Occasionally cultivated for hedges in W, central and S Europe (origin: China). Fl 5–7.

Deadly Nightshade *Atropa bella-donna*   A tall, stout-stemmed, well-branched perennial 50–150cm tall. Leaves ovate, pointed, up to 20cm long, light bluish-green above, paler below. Flowers solitary, drooping, 2.5–3cm long, with a bell-shaped corolla that has 5 spreading, pointed lobes (illus.); base of corolla tube greenish darkening to dull brownish-purple; brown on the upper part and lobes. Calyx 5-pointed, light bluish-green, persisting in fruit. Stamens shorter than the corolla. Fruit a black globular berry, 1.5–2cm in diameter. Widespread in woods, scrub and rocky places on limestone, in S and W Europe. Fl 6–9. *Plant highly poisonous. Contains the alkaloid atropine used in eye-surgery to dilate the pupil. Long used in witchcraft and folk medicine.* A. baetica is similar to above, but has greenish-yellow, erect flowers, solitary, with long stalks. Corolla twice as long as calyx and stamens longer than corolla. On shady rocks and in stony places on limestone mountains in S Spain.

Deadly Nightshade

White Henbane *Hyoscyamus albus* An erect plant, 20–80cm, covered with glandular woolly sticky hairs, with slightly unpleasant odour. Leaves ovate, stalked with wavy, blunt-toothed margins. Inflorescences dense, leafy and spike-like with flowers facing mostly the same way. Corolla yellowish-white with green or purple throat, tubular to bell-shaped, 3cm across, with 5 more or less regular lobes, glandular-hairy outside; anthers protruding only slightly, if at all. Calyx glandular-woolly, 2–2.5cm at fruiting time. In waste ground, on walls usually near villages, ancient sites and other settlements, throughout the Mediterranean and Canary Islands. Fl 3–9. *Poisonous plant.*

Common Henbane *Hyoscyamus niger* An annual, or biennial, medium to tall, sticky-hairy, with unpleasant odour. Leaves oblong, few-toothed, up to 20cm long; upper leaves stalkless, stem-clasping. Flowers in a leafy cluster, bell-shaped, dingy creamy-yellow with a distinctive network of purplish veins. On bare and disturbed ground often near ruins and old buildings; widespread, especially near the coast. Fl 5–9. *Highly poisonous plant.*

Black Nightshade *Solanum nigrum* An annual, 10–60cm, with hairy or hairless stems. Leaves ovate, either entire or with shallowly lobed margin, becoming wedge-shaped at the base. Flower small, white, with starry appearance, 6–8mm across; petals spreading at first then becoming reflexed; anthers yellow, protruding. Fruit a black berry (occasionally green or greenish-yellow) about 8mm in diameter. On cultivated ground, waste places and track-sides, throughout the Mediterranean; a cosmopolitan weed of cultivation. Fl 1–7. *Leaves sometimes boiled and eaten like spinach; berries have been eaten as 'garden huckleberry' in former times.*

Apple of Sodom *Solanum sodomeum* A much-branched shrub, 50–300cm, with star-shaped hairs and stout, straight yellowish spines, up to 1.5cm long, on the stems and along leaf veins. Leaves are oval in outline, 5–13cm long, short-stalked, but divided pinnately into rounded lobes almost to the midrib. Inflorescence few-flowered; flowers have stalks and a blue-purple corolla with 5 irregular lobes spreading to 2.5–3cm. Fruit a berry 2–3cm in diameter, whitish-green turning to bright yellow. On sandy beaches, waysides and waste ground; naturalized in S Europe (native to S Africa). Fl 5–9. *Poisonous. S. bonariense* is a shrub, to 2m, spiny only when young, leaves not divided, ovate-lanceolate with scattered star-shaped hairs. Flowers in a cluster of 2–4, with corolla white or pale blue, 2.5–3.5cm in diameter. In the W Mediterranean; naturalized S American species.

Cape Gooseberry *Physalis alkenkengi* Fruits lantern-shaped with edible berries within (illus.). Sometimes naturalized in S Europe.

Apple of Peru *Nicandra physalodes* A medium-tall 10–100cm high foetid annual, often hairless. Leaves pointed, oval, 4–15cm long toothed or lobed. Flowers bell-shaped, solitary, 30–40cm across; blue or pale violet with a white throat opening for only a few hours. Fruit a brown berry encased in the net-veined, bladder-like swollen sepals. In bare and waste places; widely cultivated for ornament, locally naturalized in central and SE Europe, originally from Peru. Fl 7–10. *Highly poisonous.*

Thorn-apple *Datura stramonium* A stout, branched, hairless annual with leafy stems from 40–100cm. Leaves pointed, ovate, up to 20cm, and coarsely toothed. Flowers are large solitary white trumpets, about 6–10cm long, held erect; corolla tube has narrow, long-pointed lobes, usually white, sometimes purple. Calyx pale green, about 4cm long, and 5-angled with 5 narrow, triangular teeth. Fruits distinctive: 4–5cm long and spiny, resembling Horse Chestnut fruits (illus.). On cultivated ground and waste places throughout the Mediterranean. Fl 4–9. *Highly poisonous and narcotic: contains the alkaloids hyoscine, hyoscyamine and scopolamine formerly used in small quantities as a narcotic and in larger quantities to kill.*

Cape Gooseberry fruit

Thorn-apple fruit

Common Henbane (left)

White Henbane (right)

Black Nightshade (left)

Cape Gooseberry (right)

Apple of Peru (left)

Thorn-apple (right)

Mandrake *Mandragora autumnalis* A low-growing plant, 10–20cm, with a thick, fleshy root sometimes forked like a human torso. Leaves stalked, ovate-oblong, with wavy margins. lying in a rosette, flat on the ground. Inflorescence in the leaf centre with short-stalked flowers; corolla lilac-purple, erect, bell-shaped, 3–4cm long with 5 broadly triangular lobes. Calyx enlarged beyond berry at fruiting time. Fruit an ovoid berry 2.5–3cm, yellow-orange. On waysides, fallow and cultivated land, often near villages, in S Mediterranean. **Fl** 9–11. *Poisonous plant. Long used in folk medicine and witchcraft, in the former for the poisonous alkaloids in the root, in the latter for the 'human' root shape, as much as anything, and the supposed property of shrieking as it is pulled from the ground, causing death to whoever effected the removal.* Many authorities now recognize autumn- and spring-flowering plants as separate species: *M. officinarum* (also *M. vernalis*) but differs in its greenish-white flowers, only 2.5cm long, with narrow triangular lobes. Calyx much shorter than roundish berry. **Fl** 2–5. In N Italy and the former W Yugoslavia.

Shrub Tobacco *Nicotiana glauca* A slightly branched shrub, 2–6m, hairless with blue-green stems and leaves. Leaves entire 5–25cm, ovate and pointed or ovate-lanceolate, alternately arranged; leaf stalks long, not winged. Inflorescence a loose terminal panicle with tubular yellow flowers. Corolla yellow, hairy outside, 2.5–4.5cm long; lobes 5, very short, bluish anthers not protruding. Calyx 1–1.5cm with 5 triangular pointed teeth. Fruit an elliptical capsule, 7–10mm. A S American native; naturalized in the Mediterranean region and Canary Islands on waste ground, waysides and in ruins, gardens and parks. **Fl** 4–10. The following two herbaceous Tobacco species are commercially grown and widespread in the Mediterranean: **Large Tobacco** *N. tabacum* Leaves sessile or slightly stem-clasping; leaf stalks short, winged. Leaves glandular-hairy. Flowers pink or cream. **Small Tobacco** *N. rustica* is similar to Large Tobacco but leaf stalks not winged, flowers greenish-yellow.

Several members of the family are grown commercially throughout southern Europe. They include Aubergine, Capsicum, Potato and Tomato. Because tomato, Lycopersicon esculentum, seeds pass through the human digestive system unscathed, areas near estuaries and along river banks – anywhere that untreated sewage is pumped back into the environment – have become colonized by this species.

BUDDLEJA FAMILY, BUDDLEJACEAE

Shrubs or small trees with stipules often reduced to a ridge; inflorescence a cyme or long panicle, corollas with a nearly cylindrical tube and patent limb.

Butterfly Bush *Buddleja davidii* A deciduous shrub, up to 5m, with arching stems and downy twigs. Leaves 10–25cm long and lanceolate with dark-green upper surfaces and white-felted undersides. Flowers tubular, fragrant, borne in dense clusters, and highly attractive to butterflies. Colour varies from pale lilac to deep violet-purple with an orange ring at the corolla mouth. Of Chinese origin but widely cultivated and a widespread escapee growing in waste places and along river banks. W and central Europe. **Fl** 6–9. Several species cultivated for ornament are occasionally naturalized in France. *B. albiflora* similar but growing to 10m, twigs hairless. Corolla pale lilac with tube 2–3 times as long as the calyx. Naturalized in France; originating in W China. *B. japonica* is a deciduous shrub up to 1.5m. Twigs sharply 4-angled with winged angles and stellate hairs. Flowers in large hanging panicles up to 25cm across; corolla tube lilac with curved tube densely hairy outside. Origin Japan. *B. lindleyana* is similar to *B. japonica* but twigs not winged and flowers in erect panicles; corolla purple, tube with soft hairs in tufts. Origin China.

FIGWORT AND MULLEIN FAMILY, SCROPHULARIACEAE

Herbs, rarely shrubs, that have leaves with no stipules, alternate, opposite some-times basal (*Verbascum*). Flowers either barely zygomorphic – open and more or less flat with 4 or 5 joined petals as in *Verbascum* – or distinctly zygomorphic with 2 lips which can be divided or entire and the corolla tube open or closed as in *Scrophularia, Linaria*.

MULLEINS *Verbascum*   The flowers of this genus are clustered into long, ter-minal spikes; the corolla is a spreading 5-lobed cup with 5 stamens.

Purple Mullein *Verbascum phoeniceum*   A perennial with erect, unbranched stems 30–100cm, densely glandular-hairy in upper part, white-felted towards the base. Most leaves in a basal rosette, oval 4–17cm long, on stalks 5–40mm long, margins lobed, weakly to pronounced. Stem leaves few, small and stalkless. Inflo-rescence long and loose; flowers formed on stalks 1–2.5cm long, each in the axil of a small bract. Corolla dark purple, 2–3.5cm across, with 5 lobes; stamens 4–5 with purple-woolly hairs, anthers attached at their centres to the filaments. In dry pasture and thickets from Italy eastwards into central Asia. Fl 4–7. **Moth Mullein** *V. blattaria* is a biennial species similar in appearance to above – glandular-hairy in upper part and smooth below – but with yellow or whitish flowers. Leaves smooth and coarsely toothed. Flowers solitary with stalks 5–25mm; stamens 5 with white and purple filaments. In damp places on uncultivated ground and roadsides.

Verbascum sinuatum   A woolly-hairy biennial with erect stems 50–100cm. Basal rosette large, with short-stalked, sinuately lobed, coarsely toothed leaves, 15–35cm long, that have wavy margins. Stem leaves spoon-shaped with a broad base, stalkless and slightly clasping the stem. Inflorescence has slender, spreading branches; stalkless flowers in clusters of 2–5 in the axils of small bracts. Corolla 5-lobed, 1.5–3cm in diameter, yellow with reddish markings inside near base. Sta-mens 5 on violet-purple filaments, to which anthers are attached at their centres. On fallow lands and waysides throughout the Mediterranean into SW Asia and the Canary Islands. Fl 4–7.

Round-leaved Mullein *Verbascum rotundifolium*   A perennial with white-woolly hairs 50–150cm tall. Basal leaves rounded to broadly elliptical, 15–25cm long, stalked, entire or shallowly toothed. Inflorescence usually not branched; yel-low flowers 15–40mm across, have stamens with violet filament hairs. In Mediter-ranean Spain. Fl 4–7.

FIGWORTS *Scrophularia*   This genus has corolla dull-coloured with nearly globular tube and 5 small lobes. Fertile stamens 4, with 1 sterile lobe. Stems often 4-angled.

Nettle-leaved Figwort *Scrophularia peregrina*   An annual with hollow, 4-angled, often reddish stems, 30–60cm. Leaves light green, paired, nettle-like, ovate and pointed with unevenly toothed margins. Flowers in long-stemmed clusters of 2–5 in the axils of the leaves; corolla 5–8mm long, dark brown-purple with a cir-cular staminode (a small flap replacing the fifth stamen). Sepals green without a membranous border. On cultivated ground, bushy places, walls and vineyards in the Mediterranean region. Fl 4–6.

Elder-leaved Figwort *Scrophularia sambucifolia*   A robust, almost hairless perennial 50–100cm high with once- or twice-cut leaves 6–15cm long. Flowers green with brownish-red or pinkish-red upper lip (illus.); about twice as large as other species in the area (1.2–2cm) in short-stalked axillary whorls. In wet places in S and central Portugal and S Spain. Fl 4–6.

Elder-leaved Figwort

Scrophularia lucida A biennial with branched stems, 15–50cm. Leaves shiny grey-green; lower ones simply lobed, the upper ones once- or twice-cut into oblong-toothed lobes. Flowers in elongated leafless heads, all stalked, small (4–9mm long), with stamens more or less included in the corolla. Staminode kidney-shaped. In rocky and stony places, on cliffs and walls, from France eastwards. Fl 3–6. *S. canina* is similar to above but is perennial with variable leaves once- or twice-cut. Smaller blackish-purple flowers, about 3mm (illus.); upper petals have white margins and stamens projecting. Staminode, if present, acute and lanceolate. On dry hills, rocks and screes, throughout the Mediterranean. Fl 3–7. *S. frutescens* is stout, robust and woody-stemmed, similar to *S. canina* in having tiny blackish-purple flowers, but leaves are thick, leathery, entire or toothed, and range from oblong to lanceolate. Corolla 4mm; lateral petals have white margins. On coastal sands in Portugal and W Spain. Fl 3–7.

Snapdragon usual pink
colour (left)

Scrophularia canina

SNAPDRAGONS *Antirrhinum* The corolla is strongly 2-lipped with the lower lip 3-lobed, and a boss-like 'palate' closing the throat. Capsule opens by 3 pores.

(a) Leaves and stems hairless (mostly).

Snapdragon *Antirrhinum majus* An erect, short to medium perennial, 30–100cm, with stem woody and hairless below, sometimes downy higher up. Leaves narrow, lanceolate, untoothed, about 2–10 times as long as broad, distinctly wedge-shaped at the base. Inflorescence with stalked flowers in a terminal cluster; flowers 3–4cm long, usually pink or purple, less often pale yellow (illus.). Upper lip 2-lobed, lower 3-lobed. Calyx deeply divided into 5, with blunt lobes 7–9mm long. In stony pasture and on walls; native in W Mediterranean but widely cultivated elsewhere. Fl 5–9. *A. siculum* is similar to above but has leaves 2–6mm wide, linear to narrowly elliptical. Corolla yellow, 1.7–2.5cm. In Sicily and SW Italy.

Snapdragon

Antirrhinum barrelieri An erect, often climbing perennial 50–120cm high, usually hairless in lower part, with slender branches. Leaves narrow, 10–60mm long, hairless, linear to lanceolate. Inflorescence a spike of rosy-purple flowers, 2–3cm long. Flower stalks 1–4mm, calyx 3–6mm, with a white or yellow throat-boss. In hedges and rocky places in S Portugal, and S and E Spain. Fl 4–7.

(b) Leaves and stems hairy.

(i) Glandular-hairy.

Antirrhinum graniticum A tall erect, sometimes climbing, glandular-hairy perennial. Leaves ovate-oblong lanceolate, blunt, opposite below, alternate higher up the stem. Flowers 2.5–3.2cm, with stalks 3–15mm, longer than bracts; pinkish or whitish with an orange boss. Fruit 8–10mm and glandular-hairy. On rocks, walls and stony hillsides in N Portugal and S and central Spain. Fl 5–8. *A. australe* is similar to above but has stout, erect, sparingly branched stems. Leaves ovate, mostly opposite or in whorls of 3. Flowers larger 4–4.5cm, bright pinkish-purple. On calcareous rocks in S and SE Spain.

*Scrophularia
canina* (left)

Antirrhinum barrelieri
(right)

Antirrhinum hispanicum An ascending or spreading dwarf shrub, much-branched and non-climbing, either glandular-hairy or shaggy-hairy. Leaves rounded to lanceolate, opposite below, alternate higher up the stem, or nearly all alternate. Inflorescences are spike-like clusters of medium-sized pink or white flowers: the throat boss is sometimes yellow. Corolla 2–2.5cm, calyx 6–8mm, flower stalks 2–20mm. Fruits 9–15mm and glandular-hairy. On rocks and walls in SE Spain. *A. grosii* is similar to above in having spreading stems and glandular-hairy leaves, but flowers yellow 3–3.5cm. Fruit 8–10mm. On granite cliffs; endemic to Sierra de Gredos in central Spain.

Large Snapdragon *Antirrhinum latifolium* A plant with erect stems, 30–90cm, usually glandular-hairy to the base. Leaves ovate, 1½–2½ times as long as broad, blunt at the tip; lower ones opposite, upper alternate. Flowers in terminal clusters with stalks 3–8mm long. Corolla yellow, 3.3–4.8cm, bag-shaped at base; upper lip 2-lobed, lower 3-lobed with a swelling that closes the throat. Calyx deeply divided into 5 almost equal blunt lobes. Capsule 1.3–1.7cm, oblong-ovate, glandular hairy. On walls and in stony pasture in NW Mediterranean region, from NE Spain to central Italy. **Fl** 5–9.

(ii) Not glandular-hairy.

Antirrhinum pulverulentum A softly hairy, dwarf shrub with oblong-elliptical leaves rounded at the apices, upper ones alternate. Flowers pale yellow, white or buff, with an orange boss and purple lines on the upper lip. Fruit hairy but not glandular-hairy. On calcareous rocks in Jaén to Teruel provinces in SE Spain.

TOADFLAXES *Linaria* With numerous species in the Iberian Peninsula, this is a difficult genus to identify in the field. The corolla is strongly 2-lipped with a spur projecting downwards; the capsule opens by 4–10 apical valves. Detailed analysis begins with a division according to seed shape:
1. more or less globular, but often 4-angled, not winged.
2. flattened disks with a broad or narrow wing and smooth or netted sides.
The grouping of the following species is primarily based on colour and includes the commoner species together with a few endemics.

(a) Flowers predominantly purple or violet.

(i) Glandular-hairy inflorescence.

Linaria aeruginea A perennial, rarely annual, with stems 3–40cm, spreading or ascending leaves linear 4–18mm long. Corolla 1.5–2.7cm, ranging from almost completely purplish-brown or violet to yellowish tinged with purplish-brown. Calyx 3–6mm with linear-lanceolate lobes. Spur 5–11mm; capsule 4–6mm, globose. In Portugal, S and E Spain and the Balearic Islands. **Fl** 4–7.

Linaria clementei An erect, sparsely leafy, grey-green perennial 80–150cm, with linear, fleshy leaves 1–2cm long. Flowers violet, 1.3–1.7cm, in a dense terminal cluster; flower stalks 2–4mm glandular-sticky, just longer than the bracts. Spur 3mm; stigma deeply 2-lobed. In dry, sandy and calcareous places around Malaga (S Spain).

Linaria incarnata A slender annual with linear leaves. Inflorescence short, rather lax, with strongly scented flowers; corolla 2.2cm, mainly violet but conspicuously bicoloured owing to the white throat-boss, which has a yellow spot and gaping lips. Upper lip has diverging lobes. Spur slender, up to 1.1cm, straight or curved. In dry grassland and cultivated ground in Portugal and W Spain.

Linaria elegans A slender erect annual with narrow linear or lanceolate leaves. Inflorescence long, lax and glandular-hairy. Flowers lilac or dark violet with lips strongly diverging; throat-boss whitish and tube mouth more or less open. Spur 1–1.4cm, curved, longer than the rest of the corolla. Stigma club-shaped. On dry open ground in Portugal and W Spain. *L. algarviana* is similar to above but has spreading or ascending stems and an inflorescence with 1–8 flowers. Flowers 2–2.5cm, violet, spotted with white or yellow on the throat-boss. Spur 1.1–1.2cm. In dry sandy places in the Algarve. **Fl** 4–9.

Linaria amethystea   A slender, erect, unbranched annual. Inflorescence with purplish glandular hairs, lax, often interrupted, with few bluish-violet, bright-yellow or cream flowers, each with an orange throat-boss and purple spotting. Corolla 1–2.7cm; spur slender 4–15mm. Fruit 3–5mm, seeds flat with warty projections; the thickened wing of the seeds is a distinguishing feature. In open places and cultivated ground in Portugal and Spain. *L. triornithophora* has oval, lance-shaped leaves in whorls of 3. Readily distinguished by the large flowers (3.5–5.5cm), which are violet-purple, strongly veined and have a yellow throat-boss. The spur is pointed and longer than the rest of the corolla. In hedges and thickets in central and N Portugal and NW and W-central Spain. *L. micrantha* has tiny purple flowers (4–8mm including the spur): the smallest of the Mediterranean toadflaxes. Calyx glandular-hairy; seed has a broad wing. On sandy and cultivated ground, and rocky areas throughout the Mediterranean. Fl 3–5.

Purple Toadflax (left)

Pale Toadflax (right)

(ii) Hairless inflorescence.

Pale Toadflax *Linaria repens*   A plant with numerous leaves, mostly in whorls, linear to lanceolate, 1–3mm wide. Inflorescences are slender, elongated, dense spikes. Flowers small (8–15mm), pale violet with conspicuous darker veins. Spur 3–5mm, conical. In dry places and screes in mountain areas, in E Spain and France. Fl 6–9.

Linaria viscosa (left)

Linaria hirta (right)

Purple Toadflax *Linaria purpurea*   A greyish-green, medium, unbranched perennial with numerous untoothed linear leaves up the stem. Inflorescence is a stalked spike with bright-violet flowers, occasionally pink, 8mm (illus.). Spur, long and curved. Widespread on walls and waste ground in S Europe. Fl 6-9.

Jersey Toadflax *Linaria pelisseriana*   A slender, hairless, grey-green annual with unbranched, erect stems 15–40cm. Stem leaves very narrow, strap-shaped and pointed. Flowers at first in tight cluster which elongates, bright violet with a white throat-boss and slender, intense-violet spur; 1.5–2cm including spur, which is about as long as the rest of the corolla. Calyx hairless with acute, white-margined lobes. Seeds flattened, with hairy, winged margins. Widespread in sandy, stony, grassy places and fields in S Europe. Fl 6–8.

Purple Toadflax

(b) Flowers predominantly white, yellow or tricoloured.

(i) Glandular-hairy inflorescence.

Linaria hirta   A robust, thick-stemmed, erect annual, 15–60cm, with bluish oblong-lanceolate, semi-clasping leaves, 4–15mm broad, in groups of 3. Inflorescence glandular-hairy, a dense terminal spike with pale-yellow flowers; corolla 2–3cm, throat-boss orange, spur 1–1.5cm. Calyx 7–8mm, lobes unequal. Fruit 5–6mm, seeds tetrahedral with slightly winged angles. On cultivated ground in Portugal, and S, central and E Spain. *L. viscosa* is similar to above but inflorescence is densely glandular-hairy. Flowers bright yellow, sometimes violet. Flower stalks 8mm erect; calyx lobes long-pointed. In sandy fields and waste places in S Portugal and S Spain. Fl 4–7.

Prostrate Toadflax

(left)

Prostrate Toadflax *Linaria supina*   A grey-green perennial (or annual). Leaves 5–20mm, linear to oblong-lanceolate, whorled low on the stem. Inflorescence few-flowered, glandular-hairy with pale-yellow flowers usually tinged with violet. Spur 1–1.5cm. Seeds grey or blackish with a broad wing. Widespread in sandy places throughout area. *L. caesia* is similar to above but the flowers are yellow with brown veins; seeds metallic shiny.

(ii) Hairless inflorescence.

Three-leaved Toadflax
(left)

White Toadflax
(centre)

Common Toadflax
(right)

Linaria spartea A slender, erect, sparsely leafy annual with narrow linear leaves. Inflorescence lax with bright-yellow flowers 1.8–3cm; spur 9–18mm, lips closely pressed together. Calyx about 4mm with blunt lobes. Fruit 4mm, seeds tetrahedral, black. Widespread in dry open places.

Three-leaved Toadflax *Linaria triphylla* A robust, hairless annual with thick, erect stems up to 40cm, branched only at the base. Leaves broadly ovate, 3-veined, whorled in groups of 3. Inflorescence a cylindrical, fairly close-packed spike. Flowers pale yellow with orange throat-boss: corolla and spur 1.5–2cm long. Spur 8–10mm, flushed with purple. Calyx hairless with oval lobes. Near the coast in fields, vineyards and on open ground; widespread. Fl 2–6.

White Toadflax *Linaria chalepensis* A slender, erect, hairless annual, usually unbranched, 20–40cm, with linear leaves. Inflorescence slender, lax; distinguished by small, pure white flowers and long slender, curved spur 8–11mm long. Corolla including spur 1.2–1.6cm. Widespread on stony ground and in grassy places throughout the Mediterranean. Fl 4–7.

Common Toadflax *Linaria vulgaris* A short to medium, hairless, grey-green perennial with numerous linear, untoothed leaves up the stem. Flowers 1.5–3cm in spike-like inflorescence, stalked, yellow with an orange spot on the lower lip. Spur long, curved. Widespread in waste places throughout Europe. Fl 6–10.

*Chaenorhinum
origanifolium* (left)

Daisy-leaved Toadflax
(right)

Daisy-leaved Toadflax *Anarrhinum bellidifolium* A medium-tall hairless perennial (biennial) with a basal rosette of ovate to elliptical leaves. Stem leaves linear and deeply cut with narrow palmate lobes. Inflorescence a long, leafless, slender, rather 1-sided spike. Flowers small (corolla 4–5mm), blue or lilac, with a short, slender spur. Calyx lobes narrow, tapering. On waysides and in dry places; widespread in S Europe. Fl 3–8. *A. duriminium* has a glandular-hairy inflorescence with pale-yellow or cream flowers. Stem leaves 3-lobed, with central lobe broader and larger. In hedges, fields, walls and waysides in NW Portugal and NW Spain.

Chaenorhinum The leaves are entire. Corolla is cylindrical, with straight basal spur, 2-lipped with the upper lip 2-lobed and the lower 3-lobed, and a throat-boss that does not close the mouth of the corolla tube.

Chaenorhinum origanifolium A small, spreading or erect perennial with rounded to lanceolate leaves; plants variable in leaf shape and hairiness. Flowers tubular, in rather lax clusters, violet with a yellow throat-boss (illus.). Corolla 1–2cm, spur 2–6mm; calyx lobes narrow oblong-lanceolate. Fruit globular. On limestone rocks and walls; scattered throughout S Europe. Fl 5–9.

Chaenorhinum origanifolium

Small Toadflax (left)

Chaenorhinum macropodum A woolly-hairy perennial, relatively robust, leaves up to 3cm long with sizeable lilac flowers (1.5–2.5cm) in an elongate cluster, each with violet veins and a white or yellow throat-boss. Spur 5–8mm, flowers stalks about 2.5cm; calyx 7–9mm. Fruit ovoid. On dry hills and rocky places in mountains in S Spain. Fl 5–9.

Chaenorhinum villosum A densely shaggy-hairy, sticky perennial with rather thick leaves obovate to rounded; the hairs are yellowish and translucent. Flowers 1–1.8cm long, pale lilac or pale yellow, with violet veins. Spur 2–6mm; flower stalks up to 2.2cm. Fruit globular, about half as long as the calyx. On walls and rocks in mountains in SW France and S Spain.

Small Toadflax *Chaenorhinum minus* A slender, downy annual with greyish untoothed, linear leaves scarcely stalked. Flowers on long stalks arising from the leaf axils, pale purple, 6–8mm, with mouth slightly open; spur short and blunt. Widespread in waste places, a weed of cultivation, in S Europe. Fl 5–10.

Lesser Snapdragon or **Weasel Snout** *Misopates orontium* A plant with erect stem, 20–60cm, with few branches. Leaves short-stalked, narrowly linear or oblong-lanceolate, pointed 2–5cm long, opposite below becoming alternate higher up the stem. Inflorescence a loose terminal cluster: flowers arise singly from axils of bracts on short, glandular-hairy stalks (illus.). Corolla 2-lipped, pink (sometimes whitish), 1–1.5cm long: calyx teeth unequal, up to 1.7cm long. Fruit capsules ovate, glandular-hairy 8–10mm long. Widespread on cultivated and fallow land, and roadsides. Fl 3–9. *M. calycinum* differs from above in having a white corolla which is larger, 1.8–2.2cm. Calyx shorter than the corolla. In the W Mediterranean region.

Ivy-leaved Toadflax *Cymbalaria muralis* A trailing, often purple-tinted, perennial, with palmately lobed, ivy-like leaves 12mm long, exceptionally to 50mm long by 60mm wide, on long stalks. Flowers 8–10mm, solitary on long stalks arising from the leaf axils, lilac with a yellow spot (illus.). Spur short, curved. On walls and rocks; widespread and naturalized. Fl 4–11.

Cymbalaria aequitriloba A delicate, finely hairy creeping plant. Leaves entire or kidney-shaped with 3 (5) rounded, equal lobes, up to 25mm long by 25mm wide, but usually much smaller. Flowers 8–13mm, lilac to violet with a yellow throat-boss; calyx about 3mm. In damp, shady places in the Balearic Islands.

FOXGLOVES *Digitalis* Corolla cylindrical tube, constricted at base, lips 2-upper shorter than lower. Stamens 4.

(a) Flowers orange-brown to brown.

Spanish Rusty Foxglove *Digitalis obscura* A hairless subshrub, 30–120cm, with stem leafless below but with closely set narrow, curved, leathery leaves in the upper part; entire in ssp *obscura* but serrated in ssp *lacinata*. Flowers in a lax, 1-sided inflorescence, with a 2-lipped, bell-shaped corolla 2–3cm long (illus.); colour rusty-brown to orange-yellow, with darker markings inside. Fruit pointed, longer than calyx. In stony pasture in mountain regions in Spain. Fl 4–7. *Poisonous.*

Digitalis ferruginea A plant, 30–120cm, with alternate, lanceolate leaves which are entire, often with light hairs on the underside. Flowers in a dense cluster each 1.5–3.5cm, reddish-brown or yellowish, with dark veins (illus.); lower corolla lip has dense, glandular hairs. Calyx lobes blunt with a broad membranous margin. In bushy places and woodland edges in mountain regions from Italy eastwards. Fl 7–8.

Digitalis parviflora An erect, leafy perennial with numerous leathery, oblong-lanceolate leaves, entire or slightly toothed. Inflorescence white-woolly, a long, dense spike of numerous small dull reddish-brown flowers, each with a purple-brown lower lip. Calyx lobes ovate. On rocks in mountain regions in N and NE Spain. Fl 5–8.

(b) Flowers yellow.

Both species mentioned are predominantly mountain plants but they are met with in woodlands at lower altitudes in the mountain regions of S Europe.

Digitalis grandiflora A medium to tall, hairy perennial with unbranched stems. Leaves ovate-lanceolate, finely toothed, shiny green and hairless above, greyish-hairy below. Flowers in a long slender spike, corolla pale yellow with purple-brown veins, 3–4cm long, tubular, with 2 lips, hairy outside. In woods and stony places in mountain regions; in Massif Central: elsewhere, widespread in the Alps. Fl 6–8. *D. lutea* has leaves that are hairless on both sides. Flowers smaller 1.5–2cm, plain yellow, hairless outside. In woods and stony hillsides mainly on lime in mountain regions; in the Pyrenees (France) and Apennines (Italy). Fl 6–8.

Ivy-leaved Toadflax (left)

Lesser Snapdragon (right)

Lesser Snapdragon

Digitalis parviflora (left)

Spanish Rusty Foxglove (right)

Ivy-leaved Toadflax

Spanish Rusty Foxglove

Digitalis grandiflora (left)

Digitalis ferruginea

(c) Flowers pink or white.

Digitalis thapsi   Similar to widespread Common Foxglove, but the whole plant has a covering of yellowish glandular-sticky hairs. The inflorescence is lax, usually branched at the base. Flowers are large, 4–7cm, pink, finely hairy outside, spotted within. On rocky slopes and in waste places in E Portugal, and W and central Spain.

Yellow Bartsia *Parentucellia viscosa*   An erect, semi-parasitic annual, pale green and sticky-hairy, stems 10–70cm. Leaves stalkless, opposite, ovate-lanceolate, 1–4.5cm long, with toothed margins. Inflorescence spike-like, 4-sided, with yellow flowers in the axils of bracts (illus.). Corolla 1.6–2.4cm with upper lip helmet-shaped, lower lip 3-lobed, longer and much broader. Calyx tubular, 1–1.6cm, with 4 linear-lanceolate lobes about as long as tube. Capsule hairy, oblong. In damp grassy pasture and fallow land in the Mediterranean and W Europe. Fl 4–9.

Southern Red Bartsia *Parentucellia latifolia*   A small, red-tinged, semi-parasite with stems 5–20cm, unbranched with glands. Leaves stalkless, ovate, lobed or fairly deep-toothed. Inflorescence spike-like, leafy, 4-sided, short and dense at first. Corolla reddish-purple with white tube (sometimes completely white), about 1cm long. Upper lip entire, lower longer than upper, 3-lobed. Calyx 6–10mm with 4 teeth half as long as the tube. In grassy pasture in the Mediterranean region and the Canary Islands. Fl 3–6.

Bellardia trixago   An erect, sticky-hairy, semi-parasite with stems 10–80cm, usually unbranched. Leaves unstalked, opposite, oblong-lanceolate to linear with a few blunt teeth. Inflorescence 4-sided, dense, spike-like with white flowers 20–25cm long in the axils of the bracts (illus.). Corolla usually has pinkish, purple or sometimes yellow tinge; upper lip helmet-shaped with a longer, much broader 3-lobed lower lip. Calyx 8–10mm, bell-shaped, with 4 triangular teeth less than a quarter of the tube length. Capsule spherical, pointed, hairy, about as long as calyx; seeds ribbed lengthwise. In pasture, fallow land and garrigue; widespread in the Mediterranean. Fl 4–7.

Crested Cow-wheat *Melampyrum cristatum*   A slightly downy, semi-parasitic annual with erect stems, branched above, 15–40cm. Leaves narrow-lanceolate, unstalked; bracts purple, serrately toothed. Flowers in short, squarish spikes, yellow and purple; corolla 1.2–1.6cm with mouth almost closed. In rocky places and dry grasslands, and woodland margins in mountain regions; widespread. Fl 6–9. **Field Cow-wheat** *Melampyrum arvense* is similar to above but highly variable, with lanceolate leaves, toothed or not, and green, whitish or reddish-pink bracts that are deeply toothed. Flowers in loose spikes, purplish-pink marked with yellow, 2–2.5cm; corolla 2-lipped with mouth closed. In dry grassy and rocky places to 1,500m; widespread (frequent in Massif Central). Fl 6–9.

Foxglove, or **Empress, Tree** *Paulownia tomentosa*   A rounded tree, up to 16m, with thick, spreading branches and woolly-hairy twigs. Leaves large, up to 80cm wide, oval to 5-lobed, deciduous with long stalks; upper surface dark green, greyish-hairy below. Large foxglove-shaped flowers, violet outside and yellow-striped inside, carried in conical sprays which form in autumn and open the following spring. Fruit is an oval, pointed capsule holding winged seeds. Native of China, planted in Mediterranean parks and gardens. Fl 4–5.

Purple Toothwort *Lathraea clandestina*   A low, parasitic perennial with a yellowish, branched, subterranean stem forming tufts at the earth's surface. Scale-leaves stem-clasping, kidney-shaped, alternate or opposite, with bracts similar to scale-leaves. Flowers violet, borne in small clusters, with reddish-purple lower lip 4–5cm long; upper lip hooded. In woodland, coppice and hedgerows in damp shady places on roots of Alder, Poplar and Willow. In W Europe, Spain and Italy; an escape elsewhere. Fl 4–5.

Yellow Bartsia (lef

Southern Red Bartsi
(right

Yellow Barts

Bellardia trixago (lef

Foxglove Tree (right

Bellardia trixag

Field Cow-wheat (lef

Purple Toothwor
(right

GLOBULARIACEAE

Perennial herbs or small shrubs with simple leaves that are alternate or in rosettes. Flowers 5-merous, usually blue, in dense head surrounded by an involucre. Stamens 4 (rarely 2); calyx persistent, enclosing fruit.

Shrubby Globularia *Globularia alypum* An evergreen shrub, 20–100cm, much-branched with leathery, short-stalked, oblong-ovate leaves arranged in clusters on old stems; leaves sometimes pointed or 3-toothed at the ends. Flowers in small globular heads, 1–2.5cm across, blue, surrounded by broadly ovate, overlapping, papery bracts with hairy margins. Individual flowers tubular; upper lip has 2 short teeth, the lower is 3-lobed. Calyx teeth have long-haired margins. In garrigue and stony pasture – sometimes forming the shrub cover – in the Mediterranean region. **Fl** 10–4. *Has been used as a purgative. G. spinosa* An herbaceous perennial, up to 20cm, with a stout stock. Distinguished by its oval or spoon-shaped leaves, which come to a spiny apex with 2 or more spiny teeth on either side; adult leaves have a chalky surface deposit. Flowers 2–2.5cm across; calyx teeth about as long as corolla tube. On limestone rocks in mountains in N and E Spain and the Pyrenees. **Common Globularia** *G. vulgaris* has leaves elliptical to lanceolate with flat margins; apex 3-toothed. Flower heads about 2.5cm in diameter on stems up to 20cm. Bracts lanceolate, long-pointed. On dry hills and in sunny rocky places in Portugal, S Spain and S France.

ACANTHACEAE

Herbs or shrubs with simple opposite leaves, no stipules. Flowers zygomorphic in a spike-like inflorescence, bracts often conspicuous, coloured. Corolla with short tube, 2-lipped; the upper lip more or less entire, the lower 3-lobed. Stamens 2 or 4. Fruit a capsule.

Bear's-breech *Acanthus mollis* An imposing, striking perennial, up to 1m. Leaves very large, dark green, stalked, soft not spiny, and deeply divided almost to the midrib to produce large pointed-toothed lobes (illus.). Inflorescence a long terminal spike up to 60cm long; flowers 3–5cm, set among spiny bracts. Corolla white with purple veins and single 3-lobed lip; flower bracts ovate with purple-tinged spiny teeth. Calyx hairless. On hills, and in cool and rocky places widespread from Spain to Greece. **Fl** 5–7. **Spiny Bear's-breech** *A. spinosus* is a similar, robust species, but with stiff, deeply dissected leaves bearing stiff white spines (illus.). Corolla about 4cm; calyx 4-lobed, the upper lip tinged purple. In open woods and pasture in S Europe from Italy westwards. **Fl** 4–8. *Acanthus leaves are often claimed to be the inspiration behind the leaf motifs on Corinthian columns.*

BROOMRAPE FAMILY, OROBANCHACEAE

A very distinctive family of hairy parasitic perennial (sometimes annual) plants that lack chlorophyll in leaves and stem. Leaves are reduced to bracts; the inflorescence is a dense spike with flowers borne in the axils of bracts. Flowers zygomorphic; corolla 2-lipped, often curved; calyx tubular. Stamens 4, fused to corolla.

Cistanche phelypaea A hairless, yellowish, parasitic species 20–70cm, with a swollen base. Stems stout and erect, bearing numerous ovate-lanceolate scales with papery margins. Inflorescence a dense, oblong-cylindrical spike of large yellow flowers; corolla tubular, 3–5cm long, narrowed at the base – the mouth is wide with five equal lobes (unlike in *Orobanche*). Calyx bell-shaped with rounded, toothed lobes. There are 2 colour forms: deep-yellow flowers, growing in saltmarshes, coastal sands and other saline areas in S Portugal, and S and SE Spain; and pale-yellow flowers which have deep-yellow lower-lip folds – often with violet on the corolla – grey to violet bracts, and a white stigma. In steppe country in Almería province. **Fl** 3–5.

BROOMRAPES *Orobanche* The Broomrapes are a difficult genus: they are annual or perennial root-parasites with a tuberous swelling attached to the root of the host plant. Since flowering spikes can seem to appear some distance from the plant it is often hard to distinguish the host with certainty; but this is often essential for positive identification.

(a) Blue- or purple-flowered.

Hemp Broomrape *Orobanche ramosa* A plant usually distinguished by its erect stems, 5–30cm, 1.5–4mm, branching from the base; single stems occur in some plants. Bracts and bracteoles 6–8mm long: each flower has 2 bracteoles held flat against the 4-toothed calyx. Corolla 1–2.2cm, glandular-hairy, blue or purple (rarely whitish); tube narrowed and whitish above ovary, curved and gradually widening towards the mouth (illus.). Lobes of lip rounded, with prominent, white hairy ridges between the 2 lobes of the lower lip; upper lip has 3 lobes. Filaments and anthers hairless. Parasitic on crops – potato, hemp, tomato and tobacco; widespread in the Mediterranean. Fl 4–9. *O. lavandulacea* is similar to above but has taller stems (15–60cm), flowers 1.6–2.2cm; anthers hairy. Parasitic on Pitch Trefoil in the Mediterranean. **Yarrow Broomrape** *O. purpurea* A rarely branched plant with yellowish stems, 15–60cm x 3–8mm. Flowers bluish-purple veined with deep violet, and larger than Hemp Broomrape's (1.8–3cm), with 3 bracteoles. Lip with pointed lobes (illus.). Anthers hairless. Parasitic on various species of the daisy family, e.g. *Achillea* species; widespread in S Europe, Fl 4–6.

Sand Broomrape *Orobanche arenaria* A glandular-hairy plant with stems 15–60cm x 3–6mm. Whole plant tinted bluish or violet; bracts lanceolate. Flowers 2.5–3.5cm, bluish-violet, with hairy anthers and 3 bracteoles per flower. Parasitic on various species of the daisy family, e.g. *Artemisia* species. On coastal and alluvial sands in N and central Portugal, S, central and E Spain and France. Fl 4–6.

(b) Clove- or carnation-scented.

Bean Broomrape *Orobanche crenata* A plant, often robust, with stems 20–70cm, forming a dense cylindrical spike. Flowers large 2.5–3cm, whitish (rarely yellow) streaked with bluish or violet (also red). Corolla more or less straight-tubed; lower lip has central lobe twice as broad as laterals. Stamens attached near the base of the corolla tube, filaments hairy at base, stigma white. Flowers smell of carnations. A pest on beans, clovers and other species of the legume family in fields and uncultivated ground throughout the Mediterranean. Fl 3–6.

Bedstraw Broomrape *Orobanche caryophyllacea* A short annual with yellowish or purplish stems. Flowers large 2–3.2cm, much longer than the single bracteole (illus.). Corolla regularly curved in profile, pinkish or pale yellow tinged with purple; corolla hairs colourless or pale yellow. Filaments hairy at the base, stigma purple. Flowers strongly clove-scented. Parasitic on bedstraws (*Galium* species) in France and Germany. Fl 6–7.

Thyme Broomrape *Orobanche alba* A glandular-hairy plant, 10–20cm, purplish-red tinted. Scale-leaves lanceolate, flowers 1.5–2.5cm long (illus.); corolla slightly curved, purplish-red (rarely yellowish or whitish), with middle lobe of lower lip larger than lateral lobes. Corolla hairs dark at the base or apex. Flowers clove-scented. Filaments densely hairy, stigma red or purple. Widespread on thymes and other species of the mint family. Fl 4–7.

Hemp Broomrape (le

Yarrow Broomra

(rig

Hemp Broomra

Bedstraw Broomra

(le

Bean Broomrape (rig

Yarrow Broomra

Thyme Broomra

(le

Bedstraw Broomr

Thyme Broomr

(c) Blood-red inside corolla.

Orobanche gracilis   A plant with stems 15–60cm x 2–7mm. Flowers 1.5–2.5cm, yellowish outside, usually with red veins, reddish towards the lips, dark red inside (illus.). Lower lips have rounded lobe, similar to Thyme Broomrape, crenate-edged. Stigma orange, style purple. Parasitic on members of the pea family, rarely *Cistus*; widespread. **Fl** 4–6.

Orobanche sanguinea   A plant with stems 10–40cm x 3–7mm. Flowers 1–1.5cm, dark red or purplish, yellow at the base, dark red inside; lips dark red, lower ones with 3 pointed lobes. Stigma purple. Parasitic on *Lotus* species in Portugal, and S and E Spain. **Fl** 4–5.

(d) Other species.

Greater Broomrape *Orobanche rapum-genistae*   A plant with stems 25–70cm, honey-brown tinged with purple, occasionally yellow. Flowers 2–2.5cm, upper lip hooded not lobed (illus.). Stigma lobes yellow, filaments hairy; 1 bracteole. Often in clumps under shrubby Legumes such as brooms and gorse which it parasitizes. On sandy soils; widespread. **Fl** 6–7. *O. densiflora* is distinguished by its lemon-yellow stems, narrow dark bracts and parchment-coloured flowers in a dense terminal spike. Stigma bright yellow. On dunes in central Portugal and SW Spain. **Fl** 4–5.

Common Broomrape *Orobanche minor*   A very variable species, 15–60cm, with small flowers 1–1.8cm long (illus.). Corolla curved with upper lip forming a continuation to the tube, not at an angle, pale yellow with a violet tinge towards the tip. Stigma purple, rarely yellow. Filaments hairless. Widespread with a number of distinct varieties on various host plants: clovers, daisies and sea-holly. **Fl** 4–7. These are similar species in the *O. minor* group: *O. latisquama* has flowers that are tinged with purple, whitish at base. Calyx teeth fused below, stigma white or yellow. Parasitic on *Cistus* species and Rosemary; in central Portugal, frequent in S, SE and E Spain near the coast. **Ivy Broomrape** *O. hederae* has yellowish flowers, tinged with brownish-purple (illus.); yellow stigma lobes. Widespread on ivy growing on limestone. **Oxtongue Broomrape** *O. loricata* has yellowish-white flowers tinged and veined with violet (illus.); corolla 1.4–2.2cm. Stigma purple, filaments very hairy below. Widespread; parasitic on the daisy and carrot families.

PLANTAIN FAMILY, PLANTAGINACEAE

Annual or perennial herbs with all leaves, usually basal, forming a rosette. Flowering stems leafless, bearing close heads or spikes of small flowers with parts in fours. Petals papery, corolla fused, stamens 4 with long thin stalks and large anthers; calyx fused at base.

Plantago serraria   A plant with numerous flowering stems, 5–20cm, curving upwards. Leaves 6–15cm long, all in a basal rosette; hairless or hairy with serrated margins. Flower spikes dense, cylindrical, 3–13cm long, 4–6mm wide, topping a hairy stem that is longer than the leaves. Flowers inconspicuous; corolla 4-lobed, hairy outside, with a membranous-edged bract as long as or shorter than the hairy calyx. In sandy and waste places, cultivated ground and fallow fields in S and central Portugal and S Spain. **Fl** 4–6.

Buck's-horn Plantain *Plantago coronopus*   A low, downy biennial. Stems barely or not branched at the base, with pinnate lobes usually divided once or twice; occasionally just toothed. Flowers brown with yellow anthers in short, greenish spikes; corolla lobes about 1mm long. In dry, bare, often sandy places, most frequently near the coast, in NW Europe, the Mediterranean and Canary Islands. **Fl** 5–10.

Orobanche gracilis (left)

Orobanche sanguinea (right)

Orobanche gracilis

Common Broomrape

Greater Broomrape (left)

Greater Broomrape

Ivy Broomrape

Common Broomrape (left)

Orobanche latisquama (centre)

Orobanche loricata (right)

Oxtongue Broomrape

Branched Plantain *Plantago arenaria* A short, downy annual sparsely covered in minute glands, with much-branched stems 10–40cm. Leaves linear or barely toothed, not in a rosette; the lowest 2 bracts at 6–10mm long are much larger than the upper ones and have lateral veins at their bases. Flowers pale brown in long-stalked ovate heads up the leafy stem. In waste and sandy places in the Mediterranean region. **Fl** 5–8. *P. afra* is a similar erect or ascending species, densely glandular-hairy in the upper part, and with opposite branched stems 10–40cm. Leaves opposite, sessile, linear-lanceolate. Flowers in long-stalked, ovoid to roundish heads in the upper leaf axils (illus.). In fields, waste ground, waysides and garrigue in the Mediterranean region. **Fl** 4–7.

Plantago af

Plantago subulata A perennial species with small, branched woody stems, 10–40cm, bearing dense rosettes of leaves; often forming cushions in established plants. Leaves dark green, narrowly linear, about 1mm broad with a triangular cross-section and hairless or fringed margins. Inflorescence stalks about as long as the leaves, straight or somewhat curving: flowers inconspicuous in dense cylindrical spikes, 1–5cm long. Corolla 4-lobed, hairy outside. On rocks near the coast in S Europe. **Fl** 4–6.

Hare's-foot Plantain *Plantago lagopus* A plant, usually annual, with stems 10–40cm. Leaves up to 30cm long, lanceolate with a few teeth: usually in a basal rosette; more rarely alternate. Inflorescence stalks grooved, 2–4 times the length of the leaves with inconspicuous flowers in an ovoid to oblong spike. Corolla tube hairless outside but with 4 long-pointed hairy lobes (illus.). Bract and calyces have long silky hairs; whole spike has a hairy appearance. In pasture, fallow fields and waysides in the Mediterranean region and Canary Islands. **Fl** 4–6.

Hare's-foot Planta

Plantago albicans A perennial with branched woody stems and lanceolate leaves 5–15cm, with long silky hairs. Flower spikes much longer than the leaves, silvery-white, long and slender, often interrupted below (illus.). Bracts and sepals oval-blunt, ciliate. In sandy places by the sea, uncultivated ground and on waysides in S Portugal, Spain and S France. **Fl** 4–6.

MYOPORACEAE

Shrubs or small trees with simple alternate leaves, entire or toothed, and no stipules. Flowers 5-merous, corolla with a short tube and 5 lobes; calyx deeply lobed. Fruit a drupe.

Myoporum tenuifolium A shrub or round-topped small tree up to 8m with leaves ovate-lanceolate to narrow-lanceolate, acute or pointed, 4.5–10cm long, bright glossy green above. Flowers in flat-topped clusters arising from the leaf axils; corolla bell-shaped, white with violet spots, 1cm across, hairy within. Fruit ovoid, violet-purple. Native of E Australia, grown for shelter and ornament; naturalized in Portugal and Spain. **Fl** 4–7. *M. tetrandrum* is similar to above but is usually a shrub with leaves dark glossy green above. Planted for shelter near the coast in Portugal.

Plantago albica

HONEYSUCKLE FAMILY, CAPRIFOLIACEAE

Lonicera implex..

Deciduous, rarely evergreen, shrubs or woody climbers, with entire leaves and no stipules. Flowers in axillary pairs, terminal heads or whorls; bracts usually present. Corolla has long tube, 5-lobed or 2-lobed, with 4-lobed lower lip; calyx 5-lobed. Fruit a few-seeded berry.

Laurustinus *Viburnum tinus* An evergreen, much-branched shrub from 1–3m, occasionally larger. Leaves pointed, varying from elliptical through to lanceolate, 3–10cm × 1.5–7cm, entire and leathery; shiny dark green above and lighter, sparsely hairy below. Inflorescences are dense, umbel-like clusters 4–10cm in diameter with flowers 5–9mm across; corolla 5-lobed, pink outside, white within. Fruits 8mm across, dark metallic-blue when ripe. In shady moist places in evergreen woods and maquis in the Mediterranean region and Canary Islands; sometimes cultivated. **Fl** 1–6.

Lonicera implexa An evergreen climbing subshrub with hairless, blue-green stems up to 2m. Leaves opposite, more or less oval, stalkless and leathery with narrow, transparent margins; shiny dark green above, blue-green beneath; upper leaf pairs are fused and encircle the stem. Flowers held in stalkless clusters of 2–6 in the axils of the leaf pairs (illus.). Corolla creamy-yellow, pink outside and 2-lipped; corolla tube 3–4.5cm long, 3–4 times the length of the lobes. In woods, hedges and maquis; widespread in the Mediterranean. **Fl** 4–6. **Etruscan Honeysuckle** *L. etrusca* differs from above in being deciduous with leathery leaves that are usually hairy beneath. The inflorescence consists of clusters in groups of 3, each with 12 or more flowers (illus.); the clusters have stalks 3–4cm long. Fruit ovoid, red. Always on limestone in woods, hedges and thickets throughout the Mediterranean. **Fl** 5–7. *L. biflora* is deciduous with ovate leaves that are hairless and dark green above, finely hairy grey-green beneath. Paired flowers in the axils, crowded at the ends of the twigs. Fruit black. In hedges on salt-rich, clay soils near the sea around Alicante (SE Spain). *L. splendida* is an evergreen climber with stalkless clusters of whitish-yellow flowers. Similar to *L. implexa* but clusters contain more flowers and the corolla is glandular. Endemic to mountains in S Spain.

Fly Honeysuckle *Lonicera xylosteum* A hairy, deciduous shrub, up to 3m. Leaves stalked, grey-green, oval or almost rounded, hairy above and beneath. Flowers in pairs at base of upper leaves (illus.), each 8–12mm long, 2-lipped, yellowish-white and hairy outside. Berry bright red. On limestone in woods, scrub and hedges in mountain areas (Massif Central). **Fl** 5–6.

Lonicera imple..

Laurustinus (le...

Fly Honeysuckle (righ...

Etruscan Honeysuckl...

CORN SALAD FAMILY, VALERIANACEAE

Annual to perennial herbs, sometimes woody at the base, with whorled or basal opposite leaves and no stipules. Flowers often in dense cymes, hermaphrodite or unisexual; corolla tubular with 5 slightly unequal lobes, stamens 1–4, inserted near base of tube and alternating with lobes. The genera are similar, so a brief description of each is given to aid identification.

Fly Honeysuc...

Etruscan Honeysuckl...

Valerianella Annuals with tiny flowers in terminal heads. Corolla funnel-shaped, with 3 stamens; calyx a funnel-shaped rim or tooth.

Corn Salad *Valerianella echinata* A small annual, 5–20cm, with few branches and light-green, oblong-ovate, toothed leaves. Inflorescences are small, rounded terminal heads of pink or lilac flowers. Fruiting heads in pairs, with stems thickened beneath and clusters of spines; each fruit has 3 spines with one much stouter and longer than the others. In fields throughout the Mediterranean. **Fl** 4–5.

Fedia   Annuals with long-tubed flowers and 2-lipped petals. Stamens 2 or 3.

Fedia cornucopiae   A hairless annual, 10–30cm, with thick hollow stems branching dichotomously. Leaves ovate-elliptical, sparsely toothed at the base. Inflorescences are thick-stalked, paired terminal clusters with stalkless, rose-coloured flowers with long tubular 2-lipped corolla pouched at base (illus.); petals 5 with lobes unequal. Stamens 2 or 3. Fruit of 2 kinds: central fertile, outer sterile. In pasture and other cultivated areas, on rocks and sands from Italy eastwards. Fl 3–6.

VALERIAN *Centranthus*   Perennials with calyx inrolled during flowering, expanding to form a pappus in fruit. Corolla tube with spur or sack at base; 1 stamen.

Red Valerian *Centranthus ruber*   A hairless, blue-green plant, with erect or ascending stems 30–80cm. Leaves opposite ovate-lanceolate, 3–8cm long; the upper ones sessile with a heart-shaped base. Flowers in clusters, pink, occasionally white (illus.); corolla has 5 unequal lobes, a tube 7–10mm long, a thin spur 5–10mm long and 1 protruding stamen. Fruits have a tuft of feathery hairs (illus.). On walls, cliffs, rock crevices and scree in the Mediterranean region; also cultivated as ornamental plants. Fl 4–9.

Narrow-leaved Valerian *Centranthus angustifolius*   A grey-green plant with very narrow leaves 3–10cm long. Flowers pinkish-red in dense, rounded, flat-topped clusters; corolla tube 6–9mm, with spur 2–4mm long. On calcareous rocks and pasture in mountains, in N, E, and SE Spain, and SW France. *C. calcitrapae* is an annual species with upper leaves deeply divided. Corolla tube small (1–3mm) with bag-shaped swelling instead of a spur at the base. On cultivated ground and in sandy places; scattered throughout.

SCABIOUS FAMILY, DIPSACACEAE

Annual to perennial herbs, rarely shrubs, with leaves opposite or whorled, no stipules. Florets in a dense head subtended by involucral bracts; corolla 4- to 5-lobed, more or less unequal or 2-lipped.

Cephalaria   The scales of the receptacle to which flowers are attached are membranous; calyx has bristles; corolla is 4-lobed.

Cephalaria leucantha   Plant up to 100cm tall with slender, erect stems, much-branched from the base. Leaves opposite, 5–20cm long, usually hairless, and sometimes pinnately divided. Lower leaves long-stalked, upper ones sessile with uniform narrow, lanceolate or linear segments with widely separated teeth. Flowers white, in conspicuously long-stalked globular heads, 2–3cm across with numerous blunt, papery involucral bracts. Corolla 4-lobed, 1–1.5cm long, calyx small and cup-shaped. In stony and grassy pastures, and roadsides in S Portugal, Spain and Massif Central. Fl 7–9.

Knautia   The receptacle is hemispherical, and hairy without bracts; calyx has 8 teeth or bristles; corolla tube is short, unequally 4-lobed.

Knautia integrifolia   A hairy annual with stems 3–60cm, and a basal rosette of leaves, deeply cut into ovoid segments. Stem leaves cut into narrow, linear segments, or uncut and narrowly lance-shaped. Flower heads almost flat, with outer florets spreading, pale pink or lilac, surrounded by 8–12 hairy, lanceolate, long-pointed bracts shorter than the flowers. Fruit has numerous white hairs and is surmounted by 2 sets of teeth. In fields, hills and rocky places throughout the Mediterranean. Fl 4–6.

Fedia cornucopiae (left)

Red Valerian (right)

Fedia cornucopiae

Red Valerian

Narrow-leaved Valerian (left)

Centranthus calcitrapae (right)

Scabiosa   The receptacle is elongated, not hairy, but with lanceolate bracts; calyx has bristles or teeth; corolla is 5-lobed.

Sweet Scabious *Scabiosa atropurpurea*   A branched annual or perennial, with stems 20–60cm high. Leaves toothed or cut into narrow segments. Inflorescence with flattened pink or lilac flower heads 20–30mm across; outer florets spreading with 5 unequal lobes; calyx long-stalked with 5 long spines. Fruiting head distinctive: greatly elongated, ovoid or cylindrical, with numerous long, russet-coloured spines formed from the calyx; fruit hairy, with 8 ribs. On sand and uncultivated ground, often coastal, throughout the Mediterranean. Fl 6–10.

Scabiosa stellata   A rough-hairy annual, 10–40cm. Basal leaves toothed or deeply cut; stem leaves divided into narrow, long-pointed segments. Flowering head blue, 2–3.5cm across; calyx has 5 long bristles. Fruiting head distinctive: globular and entirely covered with papery yellowish frills, 1cm or more across. On hills and uncultivated ground in Spain, France and Sardinia. Fl 4–7.

BELLFLOWER FAMILY, CAMPANULACEAE

Herbs or, very rarely, small shrubs, usually with latex in the stems. Leaves alternate without stipules. Corolla more or less deeply 5-lobed, calyx 3- to 5-lobed. Fruit a capsule with numerous seeds.

Rampion Bellflower *Campanula rapunculus*   A biennial with slender, rough-hairy stems up to 80cm, sparsely branched and containing a milky juice. Leaves few: lower ones oblong and bluntly lobed, broadening towards the apex and narrowing to a stalk at the base. Upper leaves stalkless and lanceolate. Inflorescence consists of numerous short-stalked flowers in a narrow, elongated spike; flowers blue-lilac, 2–2.5cm long, erect, broadly funnel-shaped and narrowed at the base with triangular lobes that are a third of the tube's length. Calyx teeth narrow, lanceolate, shorter than the corolla. In fields, grassy and bushy places, vineyards and waysides throughout the Mediterranean. Fl 5–7.

Creeping Bellflower *Campanula rapunculoides*   A slender species with creeping rootstock, erect, unbranched stems and evenly toothed leaves. Lower leaves on long stalks, heart-shaped, the upper ones small and ovate-lanceolate. Flowers 2–3cm in a 1-sided, leafless, spike-like cluster; corolla lobes about as long as the tube, spreading with spreading hairs. Calyx hairy, reflexed after flowering. In open woodland; widespread in central and S Europe. Fl 6–7.

Sheep's-bit *Jasione crispa*   A more or less hairy perennial with a stout woody stock, short non-flowering shoots and flowering stems 2–10cm, erect or ascending. Leaves rather leathery, with thickened margins, linear-oblong to linear-lanceolate, usually flat, entire to remotely toothed. Corolla blue, 5-lobed to its base, with 5 stamens and 2 stigmas; calyx 5-toothed, often purplish, hairless to densely woolly-hairy, outer involucral bracts lanceolate to ovate, entire to sharply toothed. On mountain rocks and screes, rarely on maritime sands, in SW Europe. Fl 5–8.

Venus's-looking-glass *Legousia speculum-veneris*   A slender, erect annual, up to 40cm, with sparsely branched stems. Leaves oblong, stalkless, hairless or sparsely hairy, with shallowly wavy margins. Flowers bright violet-blue, opening wide to 2cm with a central white 'eye'; stalkless, some in clusters of 3–5 forming a lax spike, others solitary. Corolla 1–1.2cm long with petals as long as the calyx teeth which are linear, long-pointed and spreading. Fruit 1–1.5cm long, contracted at the apex. On cultivated ground, in fields and waste places, in the Mediterranean. Fl 4–7. *L. pentagonia* is a rough-hairy plant with larger flowers (2–3cm across); corolla 1.5–1.8cm long, spreading wide to form a pentagonal star. Calyx teeth 2–3 times shorter than the tube, covered with long white hairs; teeth spreading in fruit. Fruit not narrowed at apex. In the Mediterranean. Fl 4–7.

Scabiosa stellat
fruit (left)

Rampion Bellflower
(right)

Creeping Bellflower
(left)

Venus's-looking-glass
(right)

DAISY AND THISTLE FAMILY, COMPOSITAE

The largest and most widespread of all the families of flowering plants, character-ized by the tiny flowers (florets) packed into a compound head and surrounded by sepal-like bracts. Florets are of 2 kinds, both with petals that are joined in a tube: disc florets, where the corolla ends in short teeth; and ray florets, where it ends in a conspicuous flat flap. The flower heads fall with a few exceptions conve-niently into 3 types: rayed, which have disc florets at the centre and ray florets round the outside, e.g. daisies and asters; rayless, which have disc florets only, e.g. thistles; and dandelion-like, which have ray florets only. The fruits are very small, often surmounted by a feathery pappus to facilitate wind dispersal.

(a) Flower heads with disc and ray florets.

Southern Daisy *Bellis sylvestris* A plant, 10–30cm, with all leaves in a basal rosette. Leaves oblong to narrowly obovate, the blade narrowing to a broad-winged leaf stalk towards the base, either entire or with widespread serrations, 3–18cm long; young leaves have flattened hairs. Flower heads 2–4cm in diameter, solitary on stout stalks. Involucral bracts 7–12mm long, more or less pointed in 2 rows; ray florets white, often tinged with purple-red on both sides. Fruit com-pressed, hairy with bristles (illus.). In woods, pasture and thickets in the Mediter-ranean region. Fl 9–5. **Common Daisy** *B. perennis* is distinguished by its leaves which have 1 distinct vein, and blades abruptly narrowing to a stalk; flower heads generally smaller (1.5–3cm across) with blunt involucral bracts. Very widely dis-tributed into S Europe and Mediterranean. Fl virtually all year.

Southern Dai

Annual Daisy *Bellis annua* A plant 3–12cm, with leafy stems branched below. Leaves are not in an obvious rosette. Leaves spoon-shaped to tongue-shaped, entire or serrated, up to 2–5cm long. Flower heads 5–10mm in diameter on thin stalks. Involucral bracts in 2 rows, florets white, tinged red below. Fruit com-pressed, hairy, without a pappus (illus.). In grassy, often damp places, from Mediter-ranean region to Canary Islands. Fl 2–6.

Alpine Aster *Aster alpina* A perennial plant, low, hairy with leafy stems. Leaves elliptical to spoon-shaped, with margins entire; upper leaves narrower than lower ones, and stalkless. Flowers violet-blue or mauve, solitary, 3.5–4.5cm in diameter. In dry meadows, rocky and stony places to 3,200m. Widespread in Alpine regions of S European and Mediterranean mountains; abundant on lime-stone in Causses (France) at lower levels. Fl (5) 6–9.

Annual Dais

Sea Aster *Aster tripolium* A plant with short to medium stems, well-branched, hairless and rather fleshy. Lowest leaves bluntly oval with stem leaves narrow-lanceolate, dark green, usually not toothed. Flowers with yellow disc florets and pale-purple to whitish rays; involucral bracts blunt. In coastal salt-marshes in W and S W Europe. Fl 6–10.

Goldilocks Aster *Aster linosyris* A hairless perennial with unbranched, leafy stem and numerous linear leaves up the stem. Flower heads yellow, without rays, in a flat-topped, umbel-like cluster. In woods and grassy places on rocks, often coastal, always on limestone; in S Europe extending into W Europe. Fl 9–11.

Evax pygmaea A very low species, 1–4cm, with stems branched at base, leafy, ascending. Leaves grey-felted, oblong-ovate to spoon-shaped, 5–16mm long, spreading and clustered into a rosette in the upper part of the stem. Flower heads almost sessile in a cluster nestling in the rosette centre and barely a third the length of the leaves; flowers minute, yellow, tubular. Involucral bracts yellowish, 3–4mm long, bristle-tipped. In garrigue and open grassy pasture, often coastal, in S Europe eastwards into Asia Minor. Fl 4–6.

Helichrysum stoechas An everlasting shrubby perennial, 15–60cm, with white-felted stems and linear leaves, 2cm or more long, which are recurved at the margins and tend to become hairless up the stem. When crushed, leaves smell of curry. Flower heads globular, 4–6mm across, in dense clusters 1.5–3cm in diameter; flowers tubular, bright yellow, external florets female only. Involucral bracts in several rows, loosely overlapping without glands, and forming a 'globe'. In stony, rocky and sandy places, from Spain to Italy. Fl 4–6. Ssp *barrieleri* has smaller, often spoon-shaped leaves and the curry smell is much less apparent. From Sicily westwards to Turkey. *H. rupestre* has leaves 3–8cm long; plant scentless, with inflorescence 3–7mm in diameter and the involucre 4–7mm across. In W and central Mediterranean.

Helichrysum foetidum A robust, strong perennial, up to 1m, with oblong clasping stem and leaves, white beneath. Distinguished by flower heads, which are relatively large (1.5–2cm across) with involucral bracts spreading; glistening white or yellow, papery. A S African native (Cape of Good Hope), naturalized in Portugal and Spain. Fl 4–6.

Helichrysum italicum An aromatic subshrub, 20–60cm, grey-white felted when young. Leaves narrowly linear, with recurved margins, thinly felted above. Flower heads in dense clusters; flowers yellow, tubular with bell-shaped involucre, 2–3mm across, comprising bracts in several closely overlapping rows. In garrigue and stony pasture in S Europe. Fl 5–8.

Golden Samphire *Inula crithmoides* A plant with erect or ascending leafy stems, 10–90cm, woody at the base, sparsely branched. Leaves linear 2–4.5cm × 2–4mm, fleshy, hairless, entire or 3-toothed at tip. Flower heads about 2.5cm across, with orange-yellow disc florets and yellow ray florets 1.4–2.5cm long. Involucre hemispherical, much shorter than florets, with linear bracts; inner ones 5–10mm long, outer ones 3–4mm long. Fruit 2–3mm, pappus not joined at base. Coastal; on rocks, sands and marshes, in the Mediterranean and W Europe. Fl 8–10. *I. montana* has densely white-woolly stems and leaves, with upper stem leaves stalkless. Flower head solitary, bright yellow, 4.5–5cm across. Involucral bracts woolly-hairy, unequal (illus.). On rocky slopes in central and N Portugal, S, central and E Spain. *I. ensifolia* is a brittle-stemmed, almost hairless species, with linear or lanceolate leaves which are parallel-veined with hairy margins. Flowers large 2.5–5.5cm across. In S Europe. *I. verbascifolia* has stems 30–50cm, woody at the base and covered with white-woolly felt. Basal leaves long-stalked, ovate-lanceolate, pointed, entire or crenate, with prominent veins beneath. Flower heads have tubular florets and yellow ray florets. Involucre 7–12mm, with spoon-shaped bracts at base (illus.). In rock-crevices on limestone around Gargano (Italy).

Aromatic Inula *Dittrichia viscosa* A plant with erect simple or branched stems, woody at the base, 50–130cm, glandular-sticky and densely leafy. Lower leaves oblong-lanceolate, 3–7cm long, entire or with wide-spaced teeth; upper leaves partially stem-clasping. Inflorescence a panicle, leafy, narrowly pyramidal (illus.), flower heads about 1.5cm across, with orange-yellow disc florets and yellow ray florets 1–1.2cm long. Involucral bracts shorter than ray florets. Plant aromatic but not pleasantly. On waysides, fallow land and roadsides, often over large areas in the Mediterranean region. Fl 7–11.

Jasonia tuberosa Plants 10–45cm tall with simple or branched stems. Leaves to 5cm long, patent, linear-lanceolate. Florets yellow, ligulate with involucral bracts glandular near the apices. Pappus hairs in two rows: the outer short, the inner long. In rock crevices and river gravels in SW Europe. Fl 7–9.

Helichrysum stoechas (left)

Helichrysum italicum (right)

Inula montana

Golden Samphire (left)

Inula ensifolia (right)

Inula verbascifolia

Aromatic Inula (left)

Jasonia tuberosa (right)

Aromatic Inula

Common Fleabane *Pulicaria dysenterica* A plant with stem 20–100cm high, branched in the upper part. Leaves hairy, oblong-lanceolate, margins wavy and with wide-spaced teeth: upper leaves stem-clasping, lower leaves with short stalks, withering at flowering time. Flower heads yellow, numerous, in loose flat-topped clusters; ray florets about 5mm longer than involucre in which the bracts are linear-lanceolate and hairy. Fruit has bristly pappus hairs about 4mm long (illus.); the fruit's base has a small ring of scales which the similar *Inulas* do not have. Wide-spread in damp places – marshes, by streams and rivers – from the Mediterranean northwards and eastwards. Fl 7–10. *P. odora* is similar to above, with flowers the same size, but basal leaves are green at flowering time. In the Mediterranean.

Small Fleabane *Pulicaria vulgaris* A short annual with much-branched stems. Leaves downy, oblong, alternate, wavy-edged. Flowers yellow, solitary, in loose clusters; ray florets short, no longer than sepal-like involucral bracts. In damp, bare places; widespread in S Europe. Fl 8–9.

Pallenis spinosa A plant with stems 10–60cm, branched in the upper part, with spreading hairs. Leaves entire with flattened hairs; the lower ones ovate-oblong narrowing to a stalk at the base, the upper ones pointed and partially stem-clasping. Flowers yellow, about 2cm across, in long-stalked heads where the middle flower stalks are considerably shorter than the laterals. Ray florets 3-toothed in 2 rows; outer involucral bracts much longer than florets, leaf-like, 1.5–3.5cm long, with rigid spine-tips and parallel veins; inner bracts ovate, hairy, papery. Fruit 2–2.5mm long, flat, winged. In rocky places, olive-orchards, fields and roadsides. Throughout the Mediterranean. Fl 4–6.

Astericus maritimus A rough-hairy dwarf shrub with stems erect or ascending, 5–25cm, or prostrate and capable of covering a substantial area. Leaves narrowing gradually to the base, entire; upper stem leaves spoon-shaped. Flower heads bright yellow, 3–4cm across, terminal, solitary; disc florets cylindrical, ray florets have 3-toothed tips. Outer involucral bracts almost as long as ray florets with blunt spoon-shaped tip. Fruit wingless, 1.5mm, 3-sided (illus.). In coastal, stony places in S Europe, Canary Islands and N Africa. Fl 4–7.

Astericus aquaticus A plant 10–40cm, with erect stems, simple or branched in upper part. Leaves oblong, spoon-shaped and hairy, lower leaves stalked, upper ones stalkless and partly stem-clasping. Flower heads sulphur yellow, 1.5–3cm across, terminal, solitary; disc florets tubular, ray florets fairly short, 3-toothed at tips. Outer involucral bracts a distinguishing feature: 2–3 times the length of ray florets, with blunt leaf-like tip. Involucral bracts leathery, ovate, with a short green tip. Fruit wingless, 1.5–2mm, with fringed pappus scales (illus.); silky-hairy, more or less triangular. Coastal; in sandy damp places in the Mediterranean and Canary Islands. Fl 4–8.

Rough Cocklebur *Xanthium strumarium* A plant with erect stems, 20–100cm, often much-branched from the base. Leaves with short hairs, green on both sides, entire to 5-lobed and long-stalked; leaf blades ovate to broadly triangular, becoming heart-shaped at the base, with coarsely toothed margins. Flower heads in terminal clusters or in leaf axils; unisexual, with male flowers above the female; female flower heads have 2 flowers buried in a spiny, ovoid involucre. On waste ground, especially in sandy coastal areas, river banks and roadsides; widespread in Europe. Fl 7–9. Ssp *italicum* has aromatic flowers and stems often suffused with violet. From the N Mediterranean. Fl 7–9.

Spiny Cocklebur *Xanthium spinosum* A plant with erect stems, 10–100cm, much-branched from the base. Plant spiny: hooked spines on involucre and where the leaf stalk meets the stem. Fruiting heads 1–1.2cm, spiny, with 2 'beaks' of different length at the end (illus.). On waysides and waste ground; a S American native but naturalized throughout the Mediterranean. Fl 7–9.

Common Fleabane

Astericus maritimus

Astericus aquaticus

Spiny Cocklebur

Lavender Cotton *Santolina chamaecyparissus* An aromatic, dwarf, ever-green subshrub, with a silvery, downy appearance and branched stems growing up to 50cm. Leaves linear, with pinnate lobing no more than 2mm long or teeth, and more or less cylindrical in section. Flower heads deep yellow, 1–1.5cm across, solitary, globular and rayless. Involucral bracts white-downy. On dry rocky ground and banks to 1,200m, in W and C Mediterranean. Fl 7–9. *S. rosmarinifolia* is very similar to above having greyish-green leaves with remote teeth or lobes, but has broader flowerheads (1.5–1.8cm across), bright yellow, with all bracts of involucre having a papery apex cut into narrow segments. In sandy, stony places from lowlands into mountains; widespread in S Europe. Fl 6–8. *S. obtusifolia* has broad flower heads, 1.5–1.8cm, but leaves of non-flowering shoots are oblong spoon-shaped with comb-like lobing. In W central Spain.

Yellow Milfoil *Achillea tomentosa* A plant with a covering of long, thin hairs; non-flowering shoots spreading, flowering stems unbranched, 5–20cm. Leaves lanceolate in outline but divided pinnately several times up to the midrib, giving a 'fern-like' appearance. Flower heads tiny, yellow, grouped in dense umbellate panicles; ray florets 4–6 in number with white-woolly bracts with pale-brown borders. In dry grassland and rocky steppes from S Europe into the Alps. Fl 5–7. *A. ageratum* has erect, branched stems, 10–50cm. Differs from above in being only sparsely haired, with leaves oblong in outline, tapering to the stem and with toothed margins (illus.); many of the teeth are divided at the tip. Flower heads yellow, almost globular, in dense clusters. In W Mediterranean from Portugal to Italy. Fl 4–10.

Achillea ageratu

Woolly Chamomile *Anthemis tomentosa* A white-woolly plant, varying from spreading with branched prostrate stems, to more or less erect, 5–30cm. Leaves ovate-oblong in outline, pinnate or twice-cut, with blunt segments oval to wedge-shaped. Flower heads solitary, 1.5–3.7cm broad, on stalks that later thicken; disc florets yellow and tubular, ray florets white, 5–10mm long. Involucral bracts very hairy with a membranous margin to the inner ones. On sandy coasts and fallow land from S Europe westwards to Italy and Sicily. Fl 4–6.

Anthemis maritima A long-lasting, aromatic plant with prostrate to erect stems, 12–30cm, woody at the base, hairless to finely hairy. Leaves mostly in lower part of stem, alternate, rather fleshy, 1–4cm × 2cm, cut once or twice into lance-olate lobes up to 5mm × 2.5mm (illus.). Flower heads 1.5–3cm across, terminal in groups, on reddish stems 3.5–10cm long, with white blunt oval ray florets and yellow disc florets in a tight hemisphere (illus.). Coastal, on dunes and sandy beaches and rocks, in W Mediterranean – S Portugal to Italy. Fl 4–8.

Yellow Chamomile *Anthemis tinctoria* An erect branched perennial, 30–60cm. Leaves dark green, compound, divided into narrow lanceolate segments which have saw-toothed margins. Flowers unusual in being golden yellow, 2.5–4cm across; outer ray florets narrow, 6–10mm × 2mm. On sunny slopes in rocky areas, on walls and railway tracks, largely on limestone, in the Mediterranean. Fl 5–8. *A yellow dye can be obtained from the flowers*

Corn Marigold *Chrysanthemum segetum* A hairless blue-green annual, with rather waxy, fleshy appearance and erect unbranched stems up to 50cm. Leaves oblong to obovate, with margins deeply cut or toothed; lower leaves narrowing to a stalk, upper ones almost uncut and partly stem-clasping. Flower heads solitary, 2.5–4.5cm across, on stalks slightly thickened below the flowers; all florets orange-yellow. Involucral bracts broadly ovate, pale green, with broad pale-brown margins. Fruit without pappus. On cultivated and fallow land, largely on siliceous soils; native to E Mediterranean and Asia Minor but widely introduced as a weed of cultivation throughout Europe. Fl 4–8. *Colostephus myconis* (formerly *Chrysanthemum myconis*) has similar flowers, but leaves are finely toothed and fruit has a pappus with a membranous crown.

Crown Daisy *Chrysanthemum coronarium*   A stout, hairless annual, with very leafy, much-branched stems 30–80cm. Leaves finely twice-divided with pointed lanceolate lobes, feathery, stalkless and partially stem-clasping. Flower heads solitary, 3–6cm across, with yellow disc and ray florets (illus.). Var. *discolor* has pale-yellow ray florets which become deep yellow towards the base (both colour forms often grow together). Involucral bracts ovate with translucent membranous margins. Fruit without pappus; those from ray florets triangular in section with winged angles. On cultivated and fallow land and waste ground, often spreading to cover large areas, in the Mediterranean. Fl 3–9.

Cottonweed *Otanthus maritimus*   An aromatic stout-stemmed perennial, with a dense white felting. Stems erect, branched and rather woody, 10–45cm. Leaves numerous, clustered, oblong or spoon-shaped, stalkless, 5–17mm long, with entire or finely toothed margins. Flower heads grouped at the ends of stem branches in short, flattened clusters; individual heads almost globose, 8–10mm across, composed of small tubular disc florets (no ray florets). Involucral bracts oval and white-woolly. Fruit about 4mm, curved, without a pappus. Coastal, on sandy beaches on Mediterranean and Atlantic coasts in S Europe. Fl 6–9.

Cladanthus arabicus   An annual with unbranched stems up to about 15cm. Leaves very finely divided, once- or twice-cut into thread-like segments about 1cm long – like a French Marigold in appearance; upper leaves encircle the flower heads. Flower heads solitary, bright yellow, about 3cm across; ray florets broad with notched ends, disc small with radiating branches arising directly below the heads and curving upwards. Involucral bracts woolly-hairy and papery. In dry pasture and cultivated ground in S Spain and N Africa. Fl 3–6.

Doronicum orientale   A plant 20–60cm, arising from a rhizome covered with tufts of white hairs. Basal leaves long-stalked, rounded, ovate, with heart-shaped base; stem leaves 1 or 2, stalkless, stem-clasping. Flower heads yellow, long-stalked, solitary, 2.5–6cm across with narrow ray florets: involucral bracts linear-lanceolate, half to three-quarters the length of the ray florets. In deciduous woods and rocks in mountain areas, and as a garden plant, in Sicily and Italy eastwards into Asia Minor. Fl 4–6.

Silver Ragwort *Senecio bicolor*   A shrubby species, 25–60cm, much branched, with white-felted stems and leaves. Leaves tend to be clustered in the lower part of the stem, ovate in outline, pinnately divided to the midrib, with segments further cut into blunt oblong lobes (illus.). Flower heads 1.2–1.5cm across, short-stalked in clusters; disc florets orange-yellow with pale-yellow ray florets, 3–6mm long; involucral bracts white-felted, 3–6mm long. On coastal rocks and in sandy places, in W and central Mediterranean; widely grown throughout Europe as an ornamental species. Fl 5–8. *S. leucanthemifolius* An often prostrate species, with spreading stems 5–40cm. Leaves dark green, almost hairless, broadly oval to linear in outline, narrowing towards the base, entire to pinnately lobed with fine teeth. Flower heads yellow, 2–5cm across, terminal, giving plants the appearance of being ringed by flower heads. Coastal, in sandy places in W and central Mediterranean from Portugal to Yugoslavia. Fl 5–8.

Field Marigold *Calendula arvensis*   A prostrate to ascending plant, 10–30cm, with branched downy-hairy stems. Leaves oblong-lanceolate, with margins slightly wavy, entire to few-toothed, stalkless with upper leaves stem-clasping. Flower heads solitary, terminal, 1–2cm across; ray florets golden yellow to orange; involucral bracts just over half the length of the ray florets (illus.). When ripened, there are 3 distinct kinds of fruit in the head: in the centre are the slender curled fruits (illus.); then those with lateral wings to facilitate wind dispersal; outside are those with spines, which are easily dispersed on animal coats. On waysides, cultivated and fallow land from the Mediterranean region eastwards. Fl 4–10.

Crown Daisy (le
Cottonweed (righ

Crown Dai

Cladanthus arabicu
(lef
Silver Ragwort (righ

Silver Ragwor

*Senecio
leucanthemifolius* (left
Field Marigold (right

Calendula arvensis
floret and curled fru

Garden Marigold *Calendula officinalis* A much more robust; flowers larger with ray florets 2cm long, at least twice as long as the involucral bracts. Probably of garden origin and widespread as an escapee in S Europe. *C. suffruticosa* has woody stems at the base and flowers similar to those of above, with ray florets more than twice the bract length. From S Europe (extreme south) into N Africa and Asia Minor.

(b) Flowers with disc florets only.

Carlina corymbosa A very variable biennial, with stiffly erect, much-branched stems 20–70cm, hairless or with fine 'cobweb' hairs. Leaves thistle-like, oblong-lanceolate in outline, up to 9cm long, with margins toothed to pinnately divided with spined lobes; upper leaves stem-clasping. Flower heads yellow, 1.5–2cm across. Involucral bracts differ: outer ones leaf-like, dissected and very spiny, green and spreading; whereas the inner ones are lanceolate, shorter and golden yellow spreading like ray florets in dry weather. On fallow land, pasture and rocky coastal places in the Mediterranean region. Fl 6–9.

Carlina acanthifolia A distinctive, stemless species 5–10cm, with all the leaves clustered into a basal rosette, 20–50cm in diameter. Leaves pinnately divided just over half-way to the midrib into spine-toothed segments, hairy-felted beneath. Flower heads solitary, 3–7cm in diameter, with yellowish to reddish disc florets (no ray florets). The involucral bracts are shiny whitish-yellow, up to 6cm long, and in dry conditions spread like ray florets. In stony pasture and dry grassland; widespread in S Europe. Fl 7–9. *Flowers persist in the dry state for a long time and are often used in dried-flower arrangements or, in the Massif Central, as door ornaments*

Calendula suffruticosa (left)

Carlina acaulis (right)

Carlina lanata An erect plant with branched or unbranched flowering stems 10–50cm. Leaves white-woolly, lanceolate in outline, cut into spiny lobes; upper leaves stem-clasping. Flower heads white-woolly, 1.5–3cm across, often solitary; disc florets yellow, involucral bracts purple (distinguishing this from other species). In rocky, dry, uncultivated places throughout the Mediterranean. Fl 6–8.

Carlina macrocephala A plant almost hairless or with 'cobweb' hairs, with stiff, erect stems 15–40cm, unbranched or slightly branched. Leaves 7–11cm long, wavy, pinnately divided with spiny teeth to the lobes. Flower heads 1.5–3cm across; inner involucral bracts whitish above, purple beneath, 1.3–1.8cm × 1.5–2mm, spreading in dry conditions like ray florets. In open woodland in mountain areas of Sicily, Sardinia, central Italy and Corsica. Fl 7–8. *C. sicula* is a similar perennial species with broader inner involucral bracts, 2.5–3mm across. *C. acaulis* has hairless leaves, all stalked, with narrow segments, flower heads 1–1.4cm across. In the Massif Central and Pyrenees.

Carlina racemosa

Carlina racemosa A plant with stems forked from the base, 10–40cm. Leaves stiff with remote spiny teeth; lower ones stalked, upper stalkless. Flower heads 8–15mm across, with yellow disc florets. Inner involucral bracts sulphur yellow, like ray florets in dry weather, 1–1.2cm × 1–2mm; outer involucral bracts leaf-like, exceeding the flower heads. In pasture land in large numbers, in S Spain, Portugal and Sardinia. Fl 8–10.

Carlina acanthifolia

Atractylis humilis A plant with unbranched erect stems, 5–30cm, hairless or woolly-hairy. Basal leaves 2.5–5cm long, short-stalked; stem leaves numerous, stalkless, pinnately divided into spiny segments. Flower heads terminal, purple, solitary, 1.5–2.5cm across. Florets tubular: outer involucral bracts leaf-like, bipinnately divided at the base; inner bracts entire, cut squarely or notched at the end, and tipped with a narrow spine. Fruit silky-hairy, with pappus of white hairs. In garrigue and stony pasture on limestone, in Spain, the Balearic Islands and France. Fl 7–9.

Atractylis cancellata   An annual, sparingly branched, 5–20cm, with rather soft, white-woolly leaves. Leaves stalkless, narrow-lanceolate, entire, with spiny hairs at the margins. Flower heads small, purple, 1.5cm across; involucre has green outer bracts that are leaf-like, cut into long comb-like spiny segments spreading on each side from a spiny midrib and enclosing the flower head. In dry rocky places, track-sides and hills throughout the Mediterranean. Fl 4–7.

Atractylis gummifera   A stalkless species with compound thistle-like leaves in a low rosette. Flower heads purple, large (3–7cm across) in the rosette centre. Involucral bracts spreading and spiny, surrounding the Flower head; innermost bracts tipped with red. On roadsides and verges in central and E Mediterranean; Corsica eastwards to Asia Minor. Fl 7–9.

Globe Thistle *Echinops ritro*   A plant with erect, often branched stems, 20–100cm, almost hairless or white-felted. Leaves leathery, shiny green above and white-felted beneath; elliptical in outline but irregularly cut into broad lobes with very sharp spines, 3–15mm long, and recurved margins. Inflorescences blue, terminal, 3.5–4.5cm across, consisting of dense, almost spherical clusters of 1-flowered heads. Individual flower heads (headlets) have surrounding ring of bristles a third to a half the length of the involucre (illus.). Involucral bracts 1.2–1.7cm long, hairless but fringed with bristles in several overlapping rows. Pappus hairs bristle-like. In dry stony pasture, grassland, and as a garden species, in S and E Europe (not Balearics, Corsica and Sardinia). Fl 6–9. *E. sphaerocephalus* has leaves with a dense covering of woolly and glandular hairs, leaf lobes scarcely bristled: upper leaf surfaces have scattered bristles. Inflorescences spherical, 4–8cm across, pale blue to whitish. In S and E Europe and Asia Minor, naturalized in central Europe.

Echinops spinosissimus   A very robust, spiny species, 50–150cm, with branched stems densely covered in woolly and glandular hairs. Leaves often directed downwards, twice-cut, with spiny segments glandular-hairy above, white-felted below with glandular hairs on the veins. Inflorescences greyish or greenish-blue 3.5–7cm across; outer involucral bracts spoon-shaped, finely toothed and pointed. In stony pasture and fallow land from Sicily eastwards. Fl 6–9.

Cirsium echinatum   A biennial, with stems to over 1m. Leaves green and hairy above, white-woolly below, very spiny and with long spiny tip. Flower head ovoid-conical, solitary, with purple flowers overtopped for 2–3cm by the upper leaves; outer involucral bracts curved outwards and downwards. Pappus bristles have feathery hairs (illus.) – a feature that distinguishes *Cirsium* from *Carduus*. In arid places, verges of fields, in S and E Spain, the Pyrenees and S France. Fl 5–8.

Plymouth Thistle *Carduus pycnocephalus*   An annual thistle with sparsely branched stems to 1m. Leaves green above, white-woolly below, lanceolate in outline, spiny and toothed, with the blades running down the stem to form spiny 'wings'. Flower heads rose-purple, 2–5 at the tips of branches, cylindrical, 1–1.5cm long, and not overtopped by upper leaves; middle involucral bracts lanceolate, 2–3mm broad (illus.). In rough waste places, track-sides and cultivated ground, throughout the Mediterranean. Fl 4–7.

Ptilostemon hispanicus   A plant with stems 60–100cm, woody at the base and white-felted. Leaves leathery, in groups of 2–4, dark green above, white-felted below, ovate lanceolate in outline, lobed or with wide-spaced teeth and stout yellow spines 1–2cm in length. Flower heads 2.5–4cm across, stalked and grouped to form a terminal cluster; florets purple, tubular. Involucral bracts have a long, sharp, spreading spine (illus.). On waysides in S Spain. Fl 7–9. *P. casabonae* has leaf margins with spines in groups of 2–4, arising from the same point. Flower heads almost stalkless and arranged in a spike-like inflorescence rather than a cluster. In the central Mediterranean region. Fl 7–9.

Atractylis gummifera

Globe Thistle floret

Echinops sphaerocephalus (left)

Globe Thistle (right)

Cirsium echinatum achene

Plymouth Thistle achene
Ptilostemon casabonae (left)

Ptilostemon hispanicus achene

Syrian Thistle *Notobasis syriaca*   An annual, 30–60cm. Basal leaves in a large rosette, green, with contrasting silvery-white mottling or streaking, oblong-lanceolate in outline with wavy, shallowly lobed margins and numerous spiny teeth; stem leaves clasping with 2 rounded wings. The species is easily recognized by the uppermost leaves beneath the flower heads, which are cut into narrow, spreading, pointed segments that are purple-tinged and exceed and surround the flower heads. Flower heads egg-shaped, 2.5cm long, grouped singly or severally; florets purple, tubular. Involucral bracts short, spiny and woolly-hairy (illus.). Fruit 5–6mm, dark brown, hairless, with numerous pappus hairs, feathery. In fallow and cultivated land and on waysides, from the Mediterranean region eastwards. Fl 4–6.

Galactites tomentosa   An annual, or biennial, with erect stems, 10–100cm, usually branched in the upper part only. Basal leaves in a rosette, almost hairless above, flecked with white, and white-felted below, pinnately divided with spines 1.5–5mm long, and bases that extend a short distance down the stem. Flower heads pink, pale purple or white, 1–1.5mm in diameter. All florets tubular (illus.); outer ones infertile and for display are much longer, spreading and more brightly coloured. Involucral bracts ovate and woolly-hairy (illus.), narrowing into a grooved, greenish tip 5–10mm long. Fruit 3–5mm with feathery white pappus 1.2–2cm long. On fallow land, pasture and waysides in S Europe, NW Africa, Canary Islands. Fl 4–8.

Cotton, or Scotch, Thistle *Onopordum acanthium*   A spiny biennial, 50–150cm or more, with broadly winged stems. Leaves oblong in outline, pinnately lobed, with broadly triangular spiny toothed segments. Flower heads solitary, 3–6cm across with tubular purple florets 2cm long; no ray florets. Involucral bracts sepal-like, narrow-lanceolate, ending in long stiff yellow spines, and woolly-hairy at the base. On dry ground and hillsides, often on sandy soils; widespread in W, central and S Europe. Fl 7–9.

Onopordum nervosum   A very robust plant, up to 3m, with broadly winged, stout, spiny stems. Leaves large with shallow lobes, spiny margins and a network of conspicuous white veins beneath. Flower heads pink, oval-conical, 4cm long, spiny, with numerous stiff, erect, spine-tipped, almost hairless involucral bracts which are shorter than the florets. On arid, stony ground, abandoned cultivation, in central Portugal and S, central and E Spain. Fl 6–8. *O. illyricum* is similar to above but is a white-woolly biennial with glandular-hairy involucral bracts, which are narrowly oval and end abruptly in a short, recurved spine; inner bracts erect, purplish. In dry, arid places and on waysides in S, central and E Spain, and S France.

Globe Artichoke *Cynara scolymus*   A robust plant, 50–250cm. Leaves pinnately divided, sometimes simple, up to 80cm long, becoming hairless above, grey felted below, soft; segments have a short spiny tip or none at all; lower leaves stalked, upper ones stalkless. Flower heads very large with bluish-purple, tubular florets. Involucral bracts ovate with a blunt or notched tip; and fleshy base and receptacle. Widespread in S Europe as a vegetable. Fl 4–8. *Fleshy base and receptacle eaten as part of the vegetable. Heads are picked for eating just before flowering time. The leaves contain cynarin which makes anything eaten after it taste sweet; it is used in baby foods and to treat gall-bladder problems.* **Cardoon** *C. cardunculus* Probably the forerunner of the Globe Artichoke; a stout species with firm leaves divided 1–2 times into segments with yellow spines, 15–35mm long. Flower heads smaller than in above; involucral bracts have an erect or spreading spine 1–5cm long (illus.). In W Mediterranean; cultivated elsewhere and naturalized. *Leaf stalks are eaten as a vegetable after blanching.*

Cotton Thistle (left

Galactites tomentosa
(right

Syrian Thistle

Cardoon (right

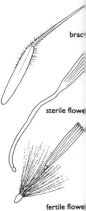

bract

sterile flower

fertile flower

Globe Artichoke

Globe Artichoke (left

Cardoon

Milk Thistle *Silybum marianum*   An erect, branched species, with stems 20–150cm. Leaves in a large rosette which overwinters, shiny dark green, almost hairless above, netted and veined in white, white-hairy below; leaves divided deeply into triangular lobes with wavy margins and spines up to 8mm long, the upper leaf bases encircle the stem. Flower heads 4–8cm across, long-stalked, solitary; flowers reddish-purple, all tubular; outer involucral bracts broadly ovate ending in a stout, yellow recurved spine 2–5cm long. Fruit 6–8mm, shiny black marked with grey; pappus 1.5–2cm long. On waste ground and waysides, often in considerable numbers, in the Mediterranean region. Fl 4–8. *Young leaves are eaten as a salad plant in Arab countries. The seeds contain silymarin which can be used to treat gallbladder and liver disorders.*

Leuzea conifera   A plant with erect, felted, usually unbranched stems 5–30cm. Leaves ovate-lanceolate in outline, pinnately divided or not, with short-spined margins; upper leaves stalkless, lower ones stalked. Flower heads solitary, terminal, with reddish-purple or whitish florets (illus.). The involucre is the distinguishing feature with the overlapping bracts producing a 'pine cone' 4–5cm in diameter, often borne close to the ground. Fruits purple or whitish, 4mm long, with feathery white pappus hairs 2–2.5cm long. In garrigue, pasture and open woodlands from W Mediterranean to Italy and Sicily. Fl 5–8.

Centaurea   A very confusing genus, containing numerous species and their subspecies. For positive identification of many species the involucral bracts are important: their shape, colouring, length of terminal spines and other appendages. The species described here are grouped by colour.

(i) Flowers reddish-purple.

Red Star-thistle *Centaurea calcitrapa*   A biennial, 20–60cm. Stem has diverging branches arising just below older flower heads. Leaves rough but spineless with bristly pointed teeth; lower leaves deeply cut into narrow lobes, upper ones irregularly toothed to almost entire. flower heads, 8–10mm across, reddish-purple, very spiny, with new heads overtopping older heads. Involucral bracts have a long, spreading spine, 2–2.5cm, with shorter spines at the base (illus.). In dry fields and track-sides throughout the Mediterranean. Fl 5–7.

Centaurea sphaerocephala   A plant with prostrate to erect stems, 5–70cm long, simple or branched, leafy up to the flower head. Leaves coarse to felted, hairy with spined tips; lower ones stalked, pinnately divided, upper ones entire or toothed, stem-clasping. Flower heads solitary with purple florets, the outer ones spreading. Involucre 1.2–3.5cm across; bracts have recurved appendage and 5–9 yellow spines, 3–6mm long (illus.), arranged in 1 plane (the middle one longer than the rest). On sandy beaches and pasture land in W Mediterranean. Fl 4–6.

Centaurea pullata   A biennial, very variable in height, 1–30cm, with single or sparsely branched stems. Leaves stalked, cut into widely spaced triangular lobes. Flower heads often solitary, 5–6cm across, pale rose-purple, bluish or white, with narrow leaves below head spreading beyond the florets. Involucral bracts green with narrow black margin ending in a branched spiny comb of 4–11 bristles (illus.). In fields, on roadsides and hillsides from Spain to France. Fl 4–6.

Greater Knapweed *Centaurea scabiosa*   A branched perennial, 30–150cm high. Leaves divided 1–2 times pinnately, dark green, oblong-lanceolate in outline. Flower heads 2–3cm across with tubula florets, the largest spreading at the margins: involucral bracts green with black triangular appendages and margins fringed like combs. Common and widespread throughout the whole of Europe on calcareous grassland, woodland margins. Fl 6–9.

Leuzea conifera (le[ft])

Milk Thistle (righ[t])

Leuzea conifera flower an[d] bra[ct]

Centaure[a]
sphaerocephala (lef[t])

Red Star-thistle brac[t]

Centaurea sphaerocephal[a] brac[t]

Centaurea pullata (lef[t])

Greater Knapwee[d]
(right[)]

Centaurea pullata brac[t]

(ii) Flowers yellow.

St Barnaby's Thistle *Centaurea solstitialis* A plant with much-branched, winged stems, 20–100cm, grey-green, woolly-hairy or densely felted. Lower leaves pinnately divided, often withered at flowering time; upper leaves linear-lanceolate, entire with spine-tip, base extending down to stem to form wing. Flower heads solitary, yellow, at the ends of branches, not glandular; marginal florets not spreading. Involucre spherical to ovoid, 7–12mm across; bracts tipped with a 1–1.5cm- long yellowish spine which has 1–3 lateral spines at the base (illus.). On cultivated and fallow land in the Mediterranean. Fl 7–9. *C. melitensis* is similar to above but florets are densely glandular and middle spine of bract (illus.) is shorter (5–8mm long).

Centaurea nicaensis A rather robust biennial or perennial, with entire, clasping upper leaves and pinnately lobed lower leaves. Flower heads bright yellow, 1.5–2cm across, with uppermost leaf just below. Involucral bracts oval, green, hairless, with a long, spreading terminal spine and smaller brown spiny bristles at the base (illus.). In fields in SE and E Spain. Fl 4–6.

Centaurea sulphurea A pale-green annual with winged stem branches, narrow leaves, all lanceolate, the lower ones pinnately lobed. Flower heads yellow, terminal and conical, with glandular florets; involucral bracts oval, closely appressed, ending in a fan of 7–9 spines (illus.); the middle spine longest (up to 2cm) and dark-purplish, the lateral spines whitish. On rocky ground in S Spain. Fl 4–6.

Centaurea stenolepsis A perennial with stems up to 100cm, densely leafy and branched above. Leaves sparsely cobweb-hairy, undivided, ovate to lanceolate; lower leaves with short stalks. Flower heads terminal, yellow to pinkish-orange. Involucral bracts form a short cylinder 12–14mm in diameter with bracts green, leathery with a pale yellowish or yellowish spine at the tip with a comb-like appendage at the base. Central and S Italy north to Czechoslovakia and E Europe. Fl 6–9.

(iii) Flowers blue.

Cornflower *Centaurea cyanus* A plant, 40–80cm, with greyish-green, downy stems. Lower leaves pinnately lobed or toothed, and stalked: upper leaves lanceolate, entire, and not stalked. Flower heads solitary, 1.5–3cm across, apparently rayed; outer florets sterile, spreading, bright blue, larger than inner florets which are purplish-blue. In cornfields and still occurring in large numbers in fields in S Europe as a weed of cultivation (but only in 'undeveloped' areas). Fl 5–7.

Perennial Cornflower *Centaurea montana* A plant with stems spreading to more or less erect, downy-hairy, with broad wings provided by leaf blades running down stem. Leaves greyish-green, oblong or lanceolate, entire or very slightly toothed. Flower heads 6–8cm across, with blue outer florets and violet inner ones. Involucre 1–1.5cm across; bracts have short dark-brown comb-like appendage (illus.). In meadows and open woods, usually on limestone, in hill and mountain regions; also a garden escape. Fl 5–7. *C. triumfetti* has narrowly winged stems and cottony-hairy, green, linear-lanceolate leaves; leaf blades do not run down stem. Flower heads 5–6cm across, bluish-violet or purple, becoming pinker towards the centre. Involucral bracts have a broad blackish-brown papery margin and fringe of whitish bristles (illus.). In grassy and rocky places, in mountain pasture in NE Portugal and S, central and E Spain. Fl 5–8.

St Barnaby's Thistle br

Cornflower (le

Centaurea melitensis br

Centaurea nicaensis bra

Perennial Cornflow

Centaurea sulphurea bra

Perennial
Cornflower
bract

bracts of *C. triumfetti* (left)
and Cornflower
(right)

Blessed Thistle *Cnicus benedictus*   A plant with erect stems 10–60cm, which are grooved, angular and covered with woolly and glandular hairs. Leaves similarly haired, pale green, with prominent white veins on the undersides, pinnately divided, with wide, irregular, spine-tipped teeth; upper leaves stalkless and semi-stem-clasping. Flower heads yellow, 3–3.5cm across, terminal, solitary, surrounded by uppermost leaves; florets tubular and yellow. Outer involucral bracts short-spined (illus.); inner ones have a divided spine. Pappus has yellow bristles: 10 outer ones about 1cm long, and 10 inner ones that are shorter. On cultivated and fallow land. Mediterranean and SW Asia. Fl 4–7.

Carthamus lanatus   A plant with straw-coloured stems 15–80cm, usually branched above, covered at first with glandular hairs. Leaves leathery, ovate-lanceolate in outline with broadened bases, pinnately divided with triangular segments and sharp points; upper leaves stalkless and semi-stem-clasping. Flower heads orange-yellow, solitary, and surrounded by the upper leaves; florets all tubular. Outer involucral bracts have a spine-toothed apex, the inner ones are much shorter, oblong, with membranous appendage. Fruit ovoid, 4-angled, with pappus hairs in several rows. In pasture and fallow land in the Mediterranean eastwards. Fl 6–9. *C. arborescens* is a much taller species (up to 2.5m) with stems that are much-branched, glandular-hairy and smelling of goats. Leaves bright green with conspicuous veins, netted on the underside, ovate in outline with wavy margins, very spiny irregular teeth and sharp-pointed apex; upper leaves ovate and semi-clasping the stem. Flower heads yellow, up to 5cm across. Outer involucral bracts like the leaves and spreading to twice the width of the heads; inner bracts yellow, as long as the florets, spiny but lacking the membranous appendage. Pappus fragile, lilac. Coastal; on sands and hills in S and SE Spain. Fl 4–8. **Safflower** *C. tinctorius* has entire leaves, oblong to elliptical, with marginal bristles. Flower heads large, orange-yellow. An Asian native, sometimes naturalized in S Europe.

Carduncellus caeruleus   A plant with erect, usually unbranched, ridged stems, 20–60cm, white-woolly. Leaves variable; lower ones stalked, pinnately divided and coarsely toothed, with sharp white bristle-tips; upper ones stalkless, semi-stem-clasping and ovate-lanceolate in outline. Flower heads solitary with bluish-purple tubular florets. Outer involucral bracts leaf-like, with spiny teeth about 3cm broad; inner ones glandular-hairy with rounded, fringed membranous appendage. Fruit 6mm (illus.), wrinkled above with whitish pappus scales. In garrigue, fallow land and arable pasture in S Europe and N Africa. Fl 5–7. *C. monspelliensis* has lower leaves pinnately cut into 6–9 pairs of linear or oblong segments with spiny teeth; no more than 6 stem leaves. Flower heads solitary, bluish-violet, often stalkless, 2–4cm across, on stems 2–20cm. Outer involucral bracts leaf-like, spiny, green and spreading. Pappus about 4 times the fruit length. On calcareous soils in hills and mountain regions in S, central and E Spain and Mediterranean France.

(c) Flowers with ray florets only.

Spanish Oyster Plant *Scolymus hispanicus*   A spreading, biennial plant, 20–80cm; stems usually branched and hairy with interrupted spine-toothed wings. Stem leaves rigid, pinnately divided, with spine-toothed segments whose bases extend a short way down the stem so that the wings are not continuous. Flower heads golden-yellow, solitary, terminal, and in leaf axils; ray florets exceeded by 3 spine-toothed bracts. Involucral bracts lanceolate, narrowing to a point, sparsely haired. Outer fruit appear winged, being enclosed by receptacle scales (illus.). On fallow ground and roadsides in the Mediterranean region and Canary Islands. Fl 6–9. *S. maculatus* is similar but stems have continuous wings; leaves, bracts and wings have thick white horny margins. Flower heads grouped at the end of branches: involucral bracts have black hairs outside; anthers dark. Pappus absent. In the Mediterranean region and Canary Islands. Fl 6–9.

Safflower

Carduncellus caeruleus (right)

Blessed Thistle seed outer b...

Carduncellus monspelliensium (...)

Carthamus arborescens s...

Carduncellus caeru... outer b...

Spanish Oyster Pl...

Scolymus maculatus (right)

Spanish Oyster Plant s...

Cupidone *Catananche caerulea*   A plant with tall, stiffly erect stems, 30–90cm, slightly branched and with short, flattened hairs. Leaves linear, 3-veined, 20–30cm long, almost all basal, entire or with few teeth. Flower heads on long stalks with blue spreading ray florets only; involucral bracts silvery, papery, inflated, overlapping, carrying a single brown vein and narrowing to a sharp point. Fruit 5-angled with a pappus of 5–7 narrow scales. In open woodlands and garrigue, especially on limestone, in W Mediterranean to NW Italy (not Corsica and Sardinia). Fl 5–9.

Yellow Cupidone *Catananche lutea*   A bluish-green annual with stems 8–40cm, little branched, with rough-hairy lanceolate leaves. Flower heads about 2.5cm across, with yellow ray florets which are shorter than the long, pointed, papery inner involucral bracts; outer bracts shiny pale brown. On cultivated ground in the Mediterranean region. Fl 5–9.

Hyoseris radiata   A dandelion-like perennial, 10–35cm. Leaves all basal in a rosette, often long-stalked, 5–25cm long, and deeply cut into backward-pointing triangular toothed lobes. Flower heads yellow, 3cm across, solitary, borne on leafless, hairless erect stalks. Outer involucral bracts narrowly ovate, 4–5mm long; inner ones lanceolate and about half the length of the ray florets, spreading at fruiting. Fruits 8–10mm, brown, with stiff yellowish pappus (illus.). In grassy and stony pasture in the Mediterranean region. Fl 1–12.

Salsify *Tragopogon porrifolius*   A hairless to woolly-hairy biennial with cylindrical tap-root and stems 30–110cm, simple or sparingly branched. Leaves blue-green, narrow-lanceolate with parallel veins, and sometimes wavy margins, broadening at the base and semi-clasping the stem. Flowers solitary, lilac to reddish-purple, terminal, with stem beneath distinctly swollen and club-shaped; ray florets numerous, involucral bracts 8, length 3–5cm (as long as florets in ssp *porrifolius*, about half as long in ssp *australis*). Fruits scaly and narrowed vertically into a long 'beak' carrying a pappus of feathery hairs; when ripened this forms a large spherical dandelion-like 'clock' (illus.). In meadows fields, dry places and stony hillsides throughout the Mediterranean. Fl 4–6. *The tap-roots can be cooked and eaten, for which various forms are cultivated.*

Tragopogon hybridus   An annual with stems 20–60cm, simple or branched. Leaves linear, long-pointed. Flowers pinkish or rosy-violet with 8 conspicuous outer ray florets much shorter than the narrow, acute involucral bracts. Outer fruits have 5 unbranched hairs; inner fruits have feathery pappus. On uncultivated and cultivated ground in S and central Portugal, S Spain and S France. Fl 4–6. *T. crocifolius* has stems that are not swollen below the flower heads, and slender leaves 2–4mm wide. Flowers brownish to purple, with ray florets much shorter than the involucral bracts, and distinctive yellow central florets. In NE Portugal, the Mediterranean and Massif Central. Fl 5–6.

Purple Viper's-grass *Scorzonera purpurea*   A hairless perennial with unbranched or sparingly-branched stems, up to 45cm. Leaves narrow and keeled. Similar to Salsify in having solitary pale-purple to lilac flowers, but ray florets are much longer than the involucral bracts, which are numerous, sepal-like and arranged in overlapping rows. In grassy and rocky places in the Massif Central. Fl 5–7.

Black Salsify *Scorzonera hispanica*   A plant with much-branched stems up to 1m. Leaves very variable, narrowly oval or linear, 4–6mm wide. Flowers yellow; ray florets longer than involucral bracts. Widespread in grassy and rocky places. C and S Europe into Southern Russia. Fl 5–9. *Long cultivated for the black, edible tap-root; also used in folk medicine.*

Yellow Cupidone (le

Cupidone (rig

Hyoseris radiata se

Hyoseris radiata (lef

Salsify se

Salsify (le

Tragopogon crocifoli (righ

seeds of *Tragopog hybridus* (upper) and *crocifolius* (low

Chicory *Cichorium intybus* A perennial, sometimes hairy, with tough well-branched green stems 30–120cm. Leaves variable: basal ones short-stalked, lanceolate, entire and deeply lobed or toothed; the upper ones undivided and stem-clasping. Flowers clear bright blue, 2–3 carried in the axils of upper leaves; flower heads 2.5–4cm across, all florets are ray florets. Pappus of scales one-tenth to one-sixth the length of the fruit. On uncultivated ground and waysides, usually on limestone, throughout the Mediterranean. Fl 5–9. *The dried roots can be ground and used as a coffee substitute; the roots are supposed to have aphrodisiac properties.*

Spiny Chicory *Cichorium spinosum* A much-branched spiny perennial shrub up to 30cm. Leaves narrow, blue-green. Flowers carried singly and comprising 5 (exceptionally 6) florets in the flower head. On arid coastal sites in Almeria (SE Spain), otherwise in the E Mediterranean. **Endive** *C. endivia* is often cultivated in S Europe where the young leaves are eaten in salads. Naturalized.

Tolpis barbata A plant with widely divergent, almost leafless, branches up to 40cm. Leaves narrowly lanceolate and toothed. Flower heads solitary, terminal, 2–3cm across, with yellow ray florets and black, brown or reddish central florets giving a dark 'eye' to the flower heads. Flower stems swollen beneath the heads; involucral bracts numerous, thread-like, spreading beyond the ray florets. Outer fruits have a scaly crown. In arid sandy places in the S Mediterranean. Fl 4–7. *T. umbellata* is a slender hairless annual, which has smaller flower heads (1–1.8cm across), without the dark 'eye', and borne in a much-branched, flat-topped inflorescence. In pasture, uncultivated ground and sandy places. In Portugal and Spain. Fl 4–7.

Blue Lettuce *Lactuca perennis* A plant with stems 30–80cm, branched only in the upper part. Leaves blue-green, hairless, deeply pinnately cut into narrow lobes; upper leaves lanceolate in outline, partly stem-clasping, uppermost bract-like. Flower heads 3–4cm across, lilac or blue, borne on rather long stalks in a loose, spreading branched cluster. Ray florets 12–20; involucre 1.2–2cm long at flowering. Fruit black, with long 'beak'; pappus white. In hills and mountains, in grassy places and rocks, in S, central and E Spain and S France. *L. tenerrima* is similar, but stems have numerous slender branches forming a 'tufted' growth; leaves mostly basal. Flower heads smaller, 1.5–2cm across, violet. Fruit brown, pappus yellowish. In similar habitats in S, central and E Spain, and Mediterranean France.

Pliant Lettuce *Lactuca viminea* A plant with erect stems 30–140cm, bearing numerous rod-like branches. Leaves blue-green, hairless; lower ones pinnately divided (shallowly or deeply), with toothed segments, upper leaves lanceolate, with 2 characteristic linear lobes that extend downwards at the base and unite with the stem. Flower heads pale yellow with 5 ray florets arranged in a spike-like inflorescence. Fruit ribbed and blackish; pappus white. Dry, rocky or stony places in S and central Europe, extending to C France. Fl 7–9.

Pink Hawksbeard *Crepis rubra* A plant with stems simple or once-branched, 5–40cm, solitary or several together. Leaves mostly basal in rosette, hairy, oblong-lanceolate, 2–15cm long, deeply toothed to divided, with backward-pointing lobes. flowering stems have a few bract-like leaves and 1–2 flower heads, (3–4cm across) with characteristic pink (occasionally white) ray florets. Involucre 1.1–1.5cm long, with outer bracts pale or papery, usually hairless; inner bracts twice as long and glandular-hairy. Fruit dark brown, outer ones short-beaked, inner ones long-beaked In bushy or grassy places in the E Mediterranean westwards to S Italy. Fl 4–6.

Pyrenean Hawksbeard *Crepis albida* A variable, low to short-stemmed species. Leaves mostly basal, lanceolate to oblong, 215cm long, toothed to pinnately lobed. Flower heads yellow, solitary or paired, 25–45cm across. Involucral bracts white or yellowish and hairy. In grassy and stony places, usually on limestone, up to 2,000m; in the Pyrenees and Maritime Alps. Fl 6–8.

Chicory (
Tolpis barbata (rig

Tolpis barb

Blue Lettuce (le
Blue Lettuce (rig

seeds of Blue Lett
(upper) and Pliant Lett
(low

Pink Hawksbea

seeds of Pink Hawksbe
(upper) and Pyren
Hawksbeard (low

YUCCA FAMILY, AGAVACEAE

Rosetted perennial succulents with sword-shaped, sharp-toothed leaves. Introduced into Europe.

Century Plant *Agave americana* A plant with a 1–2m-tall basal rosette of
thick, fleshy, grey-green leaves that are 15–25cm wide with wide-spaced spines
along the margin, and a terminal spine 2–3cm long. A single flowering stem, up to
8m tall, is produced after 10–15 years of growth. Flowers fragrant, 7–9cm long,
borne in a panicle and clustered at the ends of the panicle's horizontal branches.
Plant dies after the fruit ripen although the stems persist visibly, looking like tele-
graph poles from a distance. Propagation is mostly vegetative by means of suckers. Some varieties have yellow-edged leaves. A Mexican native that has been
widely cultivated in the Mediterranean region since the sixteenth century and is
often used as a natural, impenetrable hedge. Often found near the coast around
the Mediterranean. **Fl** 6–8. *In Mexico, the sap produced when an incipient flower spike
is cut is fermented to produce Pulque, a national drink. A. atrovirens is similar in
general appearance but has dark–green leaves up to 40cm wide with a terminal
spine 10cm long.*

Yucca Yuccas that are naturalized in Europe originated as garden escapes and
are usually from native stock of the SE and E States of America. Flowers are infertile in Europe and reproduction is via the leafy bulbils which replace some of the
flowers.

Yucca filamentosa A plant with tufts of slightly grey-green leaves, 45–60cm ×
4–5cm, with whitish margins from which whitish fibrous filaments are constantly
separating. Inflorescence a panicle around 1m long with flexuous branches and
creamy–white flowers. Naturalized in SE France and NW Italy. *Y. gloriosa* is a shrub,
often with branched stems and rigid, dark-green leaves, 50–100cm × 5–8cm, which
have reddish–brown margins. The panicle is 1–1.5m long, often with ascending
branches and white flowers tinged with purplish–red. On sand-dunes and waste
ground in N and central Italy.

Dragon Tree *Dracaena draco* A tree with a distinctive and very peculiar
appearance derived from its silvery-grey trunk with its multi-branched stems ending in tight rosettes of leathery sword-shaped leaves up to 1m long, reddish at the
base. Inflorescences terminal, branched, with greenish–white flowers. Fruit a globose, red-orange berry up to 1.5cm across. Trees said to be very long-lived but
most ancient wild trees have been cut down; in 1867 one died that was claimed
to be over 6,000 years old. Commonly cultivated in parks throughout the Mediterranean region but very rare in the wild (Canary Islands and Madeira). *When scarred
the trunk exudes a red gum, 'Dragon's blood', which was once in great demand for its
reputed magical and medicinal properties, and was used in potions.*

DAFFODIL FAMILY, AMARYLLIDACEAE

Usually herbaceous plants with bulbs and narrow, basal leaves. Flowers solitary or in umbels enclosed in papery bracts before flowering. Flower parts in threes with 2 whorls of petal-like segments (tepals) and sometimes with an additional inner ring (corona) in the throat of the corolla tube. Stamens 6. Fruit a capsule.

Sternbergia   The corolla is funnel-shaped with 6 perianth segments; flowers erect and crocus-like.

Sternbergia lutea   A plant with strap-like leaves, 4–10cm long, which grow from a bulb 1–2cm long and appear before or during flowering. Flowers crocus-like, golden-yellow and held erect on a stem 4–10cm long. They have a short tube and 6 ovate-elliptical perianth segments, 3–4cm long, with a membranous spathe at the base of the corolla funnel. Stamens 6, with filaments much longer than the anthers. In garrigue and rocky pasture; sometimes cultivated for its autumn colour. Fl 9–10. Ssp *sicula* has leaves 3–5mm wide, with distinct tiny teeth on the margin, and more obviously pointed perianth segments. In S Italy and Sicily. *S. colchiciflora* has narrower leaves (2–5mm), which appear after flowering. Flower stems only 1–2cm long, concealed by the bulb tunics and mostly below ground. Perianth tube almost as long as the segments. On dry, stony ground in hills and mountains from Spain eastwards to Asia Minor. Fl 9–10.

SNOWFLAKES *Leucojum*   The inflorescence is an umbel of 1–5 flowers, each with a bell-shaped corolla; 6 similar segments, white or pink. Filaments are much shorter than the anthers.

Summer Snowflake *Leucojum aestivum*   A plant with stems up to 70cm, with light-green, strap-shaped basal leaves. The flowering stem is stout with 2–8 bell-shaped flowers 15mm across carried in a terminal cluster; the perianth segments are white with green tips 15–20mm long. In damp low-lying fields, river banks and other wet places, throughout S Europe. Fl 4–6.

Autumn Snowflake *Leucojum autumnale*   The slender stems are 10–25cm, with very narrow basal leaves appearing after the flowers. Inflorescence carries 1–3 bell-shaped flowers, 8–12mm long, which are white tinged with pink. On stony and rocky hillsides in Portugal, W and central Spain, Sicily and Sardinia. Fl 10. *L. roseum* A small plant with narrow leaves 2–2.5cm long, which appear after flowering. Flowers are solitary (rarely 2 or 3) with pink perianth segments 5–9mm long. On rocky ground and dry pasture in Sardinia and Corsica. Fl 10. There are 3 spring-flowering species occuring within our area: *L. longifolium* has narrow leaves 12–25cm × 1–2.5mm, well-developed at flowering time. Flowers 1–4, with white, blunted perianth segments 8–11mm long; style thread-like and shorter than the stamens. On rocky ground and dry slopes in Corsica. Fl 4–5. *L. trichophyllum* has narrow leaves 4–12cm long, developed before flowering. Flowers 2–4 with perianth segments 12–20mm, white sometimes tinged with pink; the outer 3 with pointed apex. Style thread-like, slightly longer than stamens. On dry, sandy ground in SW and S-central Spain and Portugal. *L. nicaense* A similar species with narrow leaves 10–30cm × 1.5–2.5mm developed before flowering. Flowers usually solitary (rarely 2 or 3) with white perianth segments 8–12mm long; the outer 3 are pointed at the apex. Style thread-like, slightly longer than the stamens. In SE France (from Nice to the Italian frontier). Fl. 4–5. The very similar *L. valentinum* has leaves appearing after flowering in late summer or autumn. In E Spain (north of Valencia).

Snowdrop *Galanthus nivalis*   Low plants, often tuft-forming, no more than 12cm. Leaves grey-green or bluish-green, linear-strap-shaped, partly developed at flowering time. Spathe as long as flower stalk. Flowers white, 12–25cm long; the inner perianth segments have a green patch only at the free, 'notch' end. In deciduous woods, streamsides, banks and shady places to 2,200m; widespread in central and S Europe, often naturalized. Fl 1–4.

Narcissus   The flowers are solitary or several in a long-stalked umbel. Corolla has a cylindrical tube and spreading or reflexed perianth segments; there is a corona at the throat which can vary from a shallow ring, through cup-like, to a trumpet shape.

(a) Flowers with a white or green perianth.

(i) Autumn-flowering species.

Narcissus serotinus   A delicate bluish-green plant with thin flower stems 10–30cm, bearing a single flower (rarely 2). Leaves rush-like, solitary or in pairs, 1mm across, cylindrical, usually absent at flowering time. Flower fragrant, 2–3cm across, with a narrow green tube 1.2–1.7cm long, with short white spreading lanceolate petals, 9–12mm long, and a narrow orange corona only 1–2mm long. Spathe 1.5–3.5mm, membranous. In garrigue, pasture and dry hills in the Mediterranean region (not France). Fl 9–11. *N. elegans* has linear leaves 2–4.5mm wide, channelled, appearing before or with the flowers. Flowers fragrant in clusters of 3–7, bicolored, 2.2–3.8cm across. Corona shallow, yellow or orange-brown. In dry and rocky places at low altitudes in Italy, Sicily and Balearic Islands. Fl 9–11. *N. viridiflorus* has hollow, rush-like leaves. A species easily recognized by the small flowers with narrow, dull olive-green perianth segments; corona 1mm long. Scent rather fetid. In damp sandy places at low altitudes in S Spain (Algeciras to San Roque) and Gibraltar. Fl 9–10.

Tapeinanthus *Narcissus humilis*   A short plant with rush-like leaves to 1mm wide. Flowers yellow 18–22mm across often solitary with narrow oblong pointed sepals: cup very shallow consisting of 6 small scales. Grassy places and open woods in SW Spain. Fl 9–10.

(ii) Spring-flowering species.

Bunch-flowered Daffodil *Narcissus tazetta*   A plant with flowering stems 20–60cm, stout, compressed 2-edged. Leaves blue-green, 3–6, linear, 5–20mm broad with a blunt keel. Flowers in an umbel of 3–15, scented, on stalks of unequal length; corolla tube greenish, 1.5–2cm long, with 6 white, cream or yellow perianth segments broadly ovate 1.2–2.5cm long, usually touching or overlapping and spreading or slightly reflexed. Corona cup-shaped, yellow or orange, 3–6mm long. Spathe at the base of inflorescence membranous 3–5mm long. In meadows, pasture and cultivated land to 500m, in the Mediterranean region and Canary Islands. Fl 2–5. *N. papyraceus* is similar, sometimes regarded as a subspecies of above, but with pure-white flowers. *N aureus* has yellow perianth.

Pheasant's-eye Daffodil *Narcissus poeticus*   A plant with flower stems 2–6cm, 2-edged, with 3–5 linear flat leaves, 5–14mm broad, about as long as the stem. Flowers usually solitary, nodding, scented, with corolla tube greenish, 2–3 cm long; segments 6, white, widely spreading, ovate to roundish, 1.5–3cm long, with overlapping margins. Corona cup-shaped, 1–3mm long, yellow, with a red curly rim; 3 stamens protruding. A variable species sometimes present in numbers large enough to cover fields in white. In mountain meadows and deciduous woods in S Europe; absent from the islands. Fl 4–6.

(b) Flowers with a yellow perianth.

Wild Daffodil *Narcissus pseudonarcissus*   A plant with flowers that have perianth segments spreading, pale yellow, oval-lanceolate; corona deep yellow, trumpet widening towards the mouth, 2–3.5cm long, margin with irregular rounded lobes. In meadows and hillsides; widespread in mountain regions except in S and SW Spain. **Spanish Daffodil** *N. hispanicus* is similar but leaves are grey-green, spirally twisted and 8–12mm broad, flowers large, 1-coloured, 4–6.5cm long, with twisted perianth segments. In S and N Spain, the Pyrenees and the Cévennes.

Hoop Petticoat Narcissus *Narcissus bulbocodium*   A short, often tufted species with deep-green, more or less upright leaves 1–1.5mm wide, 2–4 from each bulb. Flowers held horizontally, widely cone-shaped. 7–25mm long, with short, narrow, spreading tepals. Colour varies from pale to deep orange-yellow; stamens do not protrude beyond the trumpet. In mountain pasture, rocky places and scrub, 200–1,800m, in Portugal, Spain and W France. **Fl** 2–4. *N. cantabricus* is a similar, dainty species with white flowers, held horizontally; tepals lanceolate, pointed, cup quite large, 1.2–1.8cm long, cone-shaped, with a rather flared and toothed rim. In scrubby places to 1,250m in Spain. **Fl** 2–4.

Angel's Tears *Narcissus triandrus*   A low to short species up to 30cm, with dark-green leaves, flattish or half–round in section, 1.5–3mm wide, keeled beneath. Flowers distinctive: drooping in clusters of 2–6, white or very pale creamy-yellow, each with a large cup-shaped corona; tepals lanceolate and strongly reflexed. On scrub-covered hillsides in central Portugal, central and N Spain, and the Pyrenees. **Fl** 3–5.

Jonquil *Narcissus jonquilla*   A dainty species, very sweetly scented with rush-like leaves, 2–4mm wide, slightly channelled. Flowers in clusters of 2–5, rich golden-yellow, 2.2–3.2cm across, corolla tube 2–3cm long, cup 3–4mm deep. In meadows and damp places in S Portugal, and S and central Spain; introduced elsewhere. **Fl** 3–4.

Cyclamen-flowered Narcissus *Narcissus cyclamineus*   A short, slender plant with bright-green, narrow, strap-shaped leaves 3–5mm broad. Flowers solitary, pendulous, rich bright yellow with the tepals narrow and bent back against the ovary; corona noticeably broadened towards the mouth, same length as tepals. In damp mountain pasture and streambanks, to 1,000m, in NW Portugal and NW Spain. **Fl** 2–3.

Pancratium   The flowers are in a long-stemmed terminal umbel. Corolla is funnel-shaped and widening, with 6 long narrow petals and a corona with 12 teeth.

Sea Daffodil or **Sea-lily** *Pancratium maritimum*   A plant with stems 20–60cm, arising from a large, deeply buried bulb, 5–7cm across, with 5 or 6 grey-green, linear, twisted leaves 5–14mm broad, which appear in spring long before the flowers. Inflorescence carried on a stout stem, with 3–15 flowers 10–15cm long, on stalks 5–10mm long, clustered into an umbel. Flowers large, white and highly scented; corolla tube 6–9cm long; segments linear-lanceolate, 3–5cm long, and spreading. Corona funnel-shaped, about 1.5–2.5cm long, and 12-toothed, with all stamens projecting beyond it. Capsule has pitch-black seeds. On coastal dunes in the Mediterranean. **Fl** 7–9.

Illyrian Sea-lily *Pancratium illyricum*   A plant with stems up to 45cm, and leaves 15–30cm wide. Flowers fragrant, 6–9cm long, with a short, stout corolla tube about a quarter the length of the flower; corona deeply divided into 6 lobes each with 2 teeth. In rocky places generally near the sea, in Corsica, Sardinia and Capri. **Fl** 5–6.

YAM FAMILY, DIOSCOREACEAE

Tuberous perennials, twining climbers, some succulent and herbaceous, others evergreen.

Black Bryony *Tamus communis*   A plant with grooved, clockwise-twining stems 1–4m long, and a large underground tuber. Leaves deeply heart-shaped, shiny dark green, alternate, each with 3–9 curved and branched veins and 2 small stipules at the leaf base. Inflorescence on male plant has small, yellowish-green flowers with 6-lobed perianth in many-flowered panicles. Female plant has few-flowered racemes formed in the leaf axils. Fruit a fleshy red berry, 1–1.5cm, green at first. In woods, hedges and undergrowth; widespread in W Europe and the Mediterranean. **Fl 4–6.** *Plants poisonous, with juice a skin-irritant.*

IRIS FAMILY, IRIDACEAE

Hairless perennial plants with bulbs or conspicuous rhizomes, flowers often large and showy with 2 whorls of perianth segments joined at base to form a short tube: stamens 3, style 3-lobed with lobes sometimes large and petal-like. Ovary inferior with 3 compartments.

Iris   Outer falls have a broad 'blade' and narrow basal 'haft'; some species are 'bearded' with tufts of hairs on the upper surface. The inner 'standards' are narrow and erect. Styles broad, petal-like.

(a) Bearded irises.

Iris lutescens (I. chamaeris)   A long to medium species, 5–25cm, with a thick rhizome and stems not branched. Leaves greyish-green, more or less straight, 5–25cm × 5–25mm, not dying away in winter. Flowers 1 or 2, variable in colour from mid-violet to yellowish, whitish or bicoloured, with a yellow beard in the centre of the falls; flower tube usually 2–3cm long. In rocky and grassy places 400-1,000m, NE Spain, S France and Italy. **Fl 5–6.** *I. pseudopumila* is a similar species, sometimes not regarded as distinct. Differs in having a single flower, rounded spathes, without a keel, tightly sheathing the flower tube which is 5–7cm long. Flower colour very variable. In rocky places to 300m in Gargano (SE Italy), Sicily, Malta and Gozo. **Fl 2–4.**

Flag iris *Iris germanica*   A very robust species with branched stem up to 1m arising from a thick rhizome, with broad sword-shaped leaves 1.5–3cm across, shorter than flower stem; bracts below each flower group swollen, green at base, dry and rusty-coloured in the upper part. Flowers large, 10cm across, blue-violet with a yellow beard, in groups of 2–3; 4–5cm petals nearly as long as broad. Widely planted, with many cultivated varieties, but naturalized in many places; a characteristic plant of Moslem cemeteries; throughout the Mediterranean. **Fl 4–6.**

Iris florentina   A robust plant, 40-60cm, with branched, many-flowered stem. Leaves shorter than flowering stem, 1.5–2.5cm broad, sword-shaped. Bracts below flowers boat–shaped, green, keeled with dry papery margins. Flowers large, white, sweet-scented, with a very faint tinge of blue or lilac; petals longer than broad. Naturalized in rocky areas, often cultivated in the Mediterranean region; probably of hybrid origin. **Fl 3–4.** *The source of Orris Root, used for perfumery in Italy. Probably the model for the heraldic 'Fleur-de-Lys'.*

(b) Beardless irises.

Spanish Iris (le

Snake's-head Iris (rig

Blue Iris *Iris spuria*   A tall plant, usually 40–80cm, with a thick brown rootstock covered in old leaf bases and a flower stem with short branches. Leaves grey-green, erect and rather tough; 50–70cm × 0.8–12mm. Flowers 2–4, falls rounded, greyish-blue or lilac with darker veins and a yellow strip in the centre of the fall blade; hafts yellow, crests violet. A variable species with a number of named varieties. In damp places, usually in saltmarshes or near the sea; widespread in Europe through to the Himalayas. **Fl** 5–7.

Spanish Iris *Iris xiphium*   A bulbous plant with flowering stems 30–60cm, longer than the narrow–channelled leaves (3–5mm wide). Flowers large, solitary, with slightly swollen bract, violet-purple or blue, with a yellow ridge in the centre of the falls. Flower tube only 1–3mm long, falls with haft only 1cm or less wide. In sandy or rocky places, scrub and dunes to 1,500m, in Spain, France, Corsica and Sardinia. **Fl** 4–5. *I. filifolia* is similar but with thread-like leaves less than 3mm wide. Flowers deep reddish-purple with a bright-orange ridge in the centre of the falls. Flower tube longer, 1–3cm. In dry rocky places in SW Spain and Gibraltar. **Fl** 4–5.

(c) Iris-like species.

Snake's-head, or **Widow, Iris** *Hermodactylus tuberosus*   Perennial with several spreading fleshy finger-shaped tubers, differing from *Iris* species in having tuberous roots. Leaves 1.5–3mm broad, rush-like, 4-angled, longer than flowering stem which is 20–40cm high. Flowers solitary, on a stem that bears a broad, leafy sheath up to 20cm long; outer perianth segments have a brown-purple blade, recurved, 4–5cm long, inner segments erect, 2–2.5cm long, narrow and with a long point. The 3 broadened and petal-like style branches are 2-lobed. On fallow land, stony pasture and garrigue in the European Mediterranean from SE France eastwards. **Fl** 2–4.

Barbary Nut *Gynandriris sisyrinchium*   The only member of a mainly S African genus in Europe, differing from *Iris* in its deep-seated corm with fibrous-netted coat. Stems slender, flexuous, up to 45cm. Stem leaves 2, 3–8mm broad, linear and channelled. Flowers pale blue, in groups of 2–5 in axils of papery, swollen bracts. Corolla variable in size, falls have a white patch at the centre, standards erect and lanceolate. Stamens and style-branches adhering and forming a column. Each flower opens for only half a day. In garrigue, grassy pasture and sandy places near the coast in the Mediterranean region. **Fl** 3–5.

Barbary Nut (le

White Crocus (rig

Crocus   This genus has a corm covered with usually fibrous bases of old leaves; leaves have a white midrib. Flowers stalkless at first with ovary below ground; corolla a long slender tube with 6 perianth segments. Many species are superficially similar and a detailed analysis depends on factors such as the structure of the corm tunic. The species below can be identified on floral characteristics alone.

(a) Spring-flowering species.

White Crocus *Crocus albiflorus*   A plant with a corm that has slightly netted fibres. Leaves green, partly developed at flowering time. Flowers pure white, but often feathered with violet or purple towards the base of the perianth segments. Tepals 1.5–3.5cm × 40–12mm. In woods and meadows, often abundant, 600–3,000m in S Europe and the Alps. **Fl** 2–6. **Riviera Crocus** *C. versicolor* has a corm tunic with parallel fibres only. Leaves grey-green, partly developed at flowering time. Flowers white or pale lilac; outer 3 tepals striped with purple. In meadows and stony places in Provence and Dauphine Alps. **Fl** 2–3.

Crocus nevadensis   A plant with leaves that have 2 lateral grooves on the undersides. The corm has a soft brown tunic of parallel fibres. Flowers pinkish-white with pale-lilac veining; throat greenish-yellow and stigmas white. On stony mountain slopes; endemic to S Spain (Sierra Nevada to S Bermeja). Fl 2–6. *C. corsicus* has a corm with fibrous tunic, finely netted in the upper part. Leaves narrow, linear, 0.5–1.5mm broad. Flowers 1–3, purple with dark veins; perianth segments usually 2–3.5cm. Anthers orange, stigmas scarlet. Bract undivided, membranous with brown markings. In garrigue and stony pasture, 300–2,600m in Corsica and Sardinia. Fl 2–6, depending on altitude. *C. minimus* is closely related and restricted to the same islands. Distinguished by its perianth segments 1.7–2.7cm long. Anthers pale yellow, stigmas yellow. Flowering earlier and at a lower altitude; up to 600m. In scrub in S Corsica and Sardinia. Fl 1–4.

Crocus corsicus (le◼
Crocus sativus (rig◼

(b) Autumn-flowering species.

Saffron Crocus *Crocus sativus*   A plant with lilac-purple flowers, strongly veined darker or pure white with purple veins becoming purple at the base of the tepals. Stigma divided into 3 branches, each 2.5–3.2cm long; these cannot support themselves and flop sideways out of the flower. Probably a Turkish native. Fl 9–10. *Cultivated in Europe for centuries for saffron, the yellow dye produced from its stigmas; it takes more than 3,000 plants to yield 25g of dye.*

Crocus longiflorus (lef◼
Romule◼
bulbocodium (righ◼

Autumn Crocus *Crocus nudiflorus*   A plant with corms that produce offsets at the ends of stolons forming patches of plants. Leaves, 2–4mm wide, 3–4 from each corm, absent at flowering time, appearing late winter to spring. Flowers deep lilac-purple or purple, with little or no veining; corolla tube unusually long (10–22cm). Throat white or lilac, tepals 3–6cm long by 9–20mm wide, blunt. Stamens with yellow anthers and white filaments; stigma divided into numerous orange branches. In meadows, to 2,000m, in SW France and N and central Spain. Fl 9–10. *C. longiflorus* has leaves which normally show at flowering time. Flowers lilac to purple with darker veining, throat deep yellow; stamens with yellow anthers and filaments; stigma divided into 3 orange-red branches. In SW Italy, Sicily and Malta. Fl 10–11.

SAND CROCUSES *Romulea*   These are similar to *Crocus*, but flowers are long-stalked on simple or branched stems; corolla with a short tube. Flowers produced singly from a bract and bracteole.

Romulea bulbocodium   A plant with narrow, rush-like leaves. Flower stems 2–3cm long, rising from a corm with leathery scales, and carrying 1–5 flowers 2–3.5cm long with a pair of ensheathing bracts, 1–2cm long, below the flowers. Corolla funnel-shaped with lanceolate tepals, purple or lilac with a hairy orange throat and greenish or violet-striped exterior. Stamens about half the length of tepals; 3 stigmas, each 2-lobed, divided to the base and longer than stamens. In dunes and sandy places near the sea throughout the Mediterranean. Fl 2–5. *R. ramiflora* has flowers 1–2cm long, pointed, pale to deep bluish purple; flower tube 2–6mm long. On grassy or bare places near the sea, in Spain, Balearics, S France, Italy, Sardinia and Sicily. Fl 2–3. *R. revelierei* has flowers that are 1–1.5cm long with rounded to rather pointed tepals, purple-blue with darker veins; no yellow in the throat. Corolla tube 3–5mm long. Bract 8–14mm long, green with papery margin. Bracteole papery, with rust-coloured flecking and central green band. In moist places near the sea, in Corsica, Italy and Capri. Fl 2–3.

Romulea ramiflora ss◼
ramiflora (lef◼
Romulea revelierei
(right◼

Sand Crocus *Romulea columnae*   A plant with small flowers (1–1.2cm) with pointed tepals; corolla tube 2–5mm long. Flowers very pale lilac or purplish with darker veins; sometimes greenish on the outside. Bracteole papery, rusty-spotted. In grassy, or damp sandy places – mainly coastal in central Portugal and the Mediterranean region. Fl 2–4.

Gladiolus   The flowers are carried in a long spike, showy, inclined or horizontal, with a very short curved corolla tube; leafy bracts on flower stems.

Gladiolus italicus (l

Wild Gladiolus (rig

Gladiolus italicus (G. segetum)   A plant with stems 40–80cm, arising from a globular corm covered in a mesh of thick fibres. Leaves 3–5, 1–1.6cm broad, borne towards the stem base. Inflorescence has 6–10 flowers in a 1-sided terminal spike, each with a bract; in the lower flowers this is leafy and as long as the flowers. Flowers rose-purple, 4–5cm long, with noticeably unequal perianth segments; the upper ones longer and nearly twice as broad as the laterals. Anthers longer than filaments; seeds not winged. In cornfields and on cultivated ground, often in large numbers, throughout the Mediterranean. **Fl** 4–6. *G. communis* is similar to above, but the bracts are shorter than the flowers they subtend; perianth segments of almost equal size, the upper ones barely longer than the laterals. Anthers shorter than filaments. In meadows and waste ground from Spain to Greece. **Fl** 4–6. *G. byzantinus* has large rosy-purple flowers, 4–5cm long, with segments not clearly separated (unlike in *G. italicus*). Anthers equal to filaments in length; seeds compressed and winged. In fields and on uncultivated ground in Italy, Corsica, Sardinia and Sicily, eastwards to Israel. **Fl** 4–5.

Wild Gladiolus *Gladiolus illyricus*   A rather delicate species with narrow, lanceolate leaves 10–40cm × 5–9mm. Inflorescence a fairly lax 3- to 10-flowered, 1-sided spike; flowers each with 2 bracts. Flowers 3.5–4cm long, with perianth segments united below into a short, slightly curved tube; upper 3 segments unequal, the middle broadly oblong-elliptical and longer than the lateral oblong-ovate petals. Anthers spear-shaped at the base, shorter than the filaments; stigmas narrow at the base and broadening into an oval blade. Seeds winged. In stony pasture, open woods and maquis in S and W Europe and Asia Minor. **Fl** 4–6.

POSIDONIACEAE

A family of rhizomatous marine or estuarine plants.

Posidonia oceanica   An aquatic plant, with a stout rhizome densely covered by the fibrous brown remains of dead leaves. At the end of each rhizome branch are 5–10 ribbon-like dark-green leaves, which are rounded at the ends with 13–17 veins, and up to 55cm × 6–10mm. Inflorescence, rarely produced, is a series of spikes carrying 3–5 flowers. On fine sandy ground in shallow water around the Mediteranean and the SW Atlantic coasts (leaves torn off and worn by the surf are found as brown balls). **Fl** 10–5.

Common Eel Grass *Zostera marina*   A submerged, perennial marine herb, with thin, non-fibrous, creeping rhizomes. Leaves on non-flowering shoots 20–50cm or longer; flowering stems much-branched, up to 80cm long. Inflorescence enclosed in the sheathing base of a spathe; stigma twice as long as the style. On fine gravel, sand or mud, from low water down to 10m; widespread on coasts of N hemisphere.

Posidonia oceanica 'se
balls' (le

Common Eel Gra
(righ

LILY FAMILY, LILIACEAE

Flower parts in 2 whorls of 3; inner and outer perianth segments often the same colour with flowers appearing 6-petalled. Stamens 6, opposite each perianth segment; ovary within perianth, 3-compartmented with numerous ovules on a central axis.

ASPHODELS *Asphodelus* A genus that has leafless stems, and leaves all basal. Perianth segments all similar; flowers on simple or branched stems. Tuberous. *Asphodeline* has many-leaved, many flowered stems. Lowest perianth segment narrower and slightly separated from the others. Rhizomatous.

Hollow-stemmed Asphodel *Asphodelus fistulosus* An annual or short-lived perennial, with numerous slender fibrous roots and stems 20–60cm. Leaves slender (4mm wide), basal, semi-cylindrical in section and hollow, up to 35cm long; edges are slightly rough. Flowers (10–15) are carried in a lax raceme on a long smooth hollow stalk with membranous whitish bracts. The 6 perianth segments (5–12mm) spread like a star; petals white or pinkish with a reddish or greenish vein on each. Fruit capsules spherical or ovoid, 5–7mm. On cultivated ground, dry sandy and rocky places, roadsides and garrigue throughout the Mediterranean region. Fl 3–6. *A. tenuifolius* is an annual closely related to the above. It differs in having leaves 2.5mm broad, rough on all veins. Inflorescence stalks rough below; perianth segments 5–12mm long, capsules 3–5mm. In S Italy and Sicily (to N Africa and the Canaries).

White Asphodel *Asphodelus albus* A perennial, 50–120cm, with rather fleshy, swollen roots. Leaves basal, narrow, up to 60cm × 1–2.5cm with a keel. Inflorescence a raceme, sometimes branched at the base; perianth segments 1.5–2cm long, narrowly elliptical, white with a green or red-brown mid-vein. Ssp *albus* has dark-brown bracts and capsule 8–15mm × 6–13mm: ssp *villarsii* has whitish bracts and capsule 1.6–2cm × 1.8–2.5cm; In meadows, heaths, open woods and mountain pastures: ssp *albus* occurs thoughout S Europe; ssp *villarsii* occurs only in SW Europe. Fl 4–6.

Asphodel *Asphodelus aestivus* (*A. microcarpus*) A perennial with thickened, spindle-shaped roots. All leaves basal, 25–45cm long, 1–2(4)cm wide, flat with slight keel. Inflorescence carried on a stout stalk, much-branched to form a pyramidal shape. Bracts membranous to pale green, 1–1.5cm long. White perianth segments spreading; 1–1.6cm long, on stalks 5–7mm long, vein red-brown. Capsule ovate to spherical, 5–8mm × 6–10mm, with 2–7 transverse grooves. In garrigue and rough pasture throughout the Mediterranean; frequently one of the few species to survive goats' grazing. Fl 3–6. *A. ramosus* is similar to above, with less-branched or simple inflorescence. Perianth segments 1.5–2cm long; capsules 1.5–2cm × 1.6–2.2cm with 7–8 transverse grooves. SW Europe.

Yellow Asphodel *Asphodeline lutea* A medium, hairless, perennial herb with short yellow fleshy roots. Stems stout, 40–120cm. Leaves linear, 2–3mm wide, and carried along the whole stem length. Flowers golden-yellow, 3–4cm across, in a densely packed raceme 15–30cm long; each tepal has a median green stripe; flowers open fully towards evening. Capsules almost spherical with black, triangular seeds. In rocky places, generally in hilly or mountainous areas, to 2,000m. In E Mediterranean westward to Italy. Fl 4–6.

Antherium   This genus has flowers on simple or branched stems. Perianth segments spreading with 3–5, white on both sides.

St Bernard's Lily *Anthericum liliago*   A semi-erect perennial with short root-stock and rather fleshy roots. Leaves usually as long as the flowering stem, 5–7mm wide. Flowers white, flattish, 3–5mm across, 6–10 in a loose raceme, tepals 3-veined and style curved. In grassy and stony scrub, roadsides and open woodland in mountains, in France, NE Portugal, NE Spain, SE Spain and S Italy. **Fl** (5) 6–7. *A. ramosum* is similar to above but distinguished by its branched inflorescence, its smaller flowers (2.5cm across) and its almost reflexed tepals when first open. Leaves much shorter than the flowering stem; 4–5mm wide. In dry sunny places in open scrub, in France, SW, central and E Spain. *A. baeticum* is a smaller plant with unbranched inflorescence carrying 1–10 flowers, 1.2–2.4mm across; stamens equal to perianth in length. Leaves much shorter than inflorescence, very slender, 2–4mm wide. In damp places in mountains in Sierra Nevada.

Aphyllanthes   This genus has blue, terminal flowers and leafless, rush-like stems.

Aphyllanthes monspeliensis   The single species in this distinctive genus. It grows in tufts with numerous blue-green, ribbed, rush-like stems about 1mm thick. Reddish-brown sheaths, remains of modified leaves, are found at the base of each stem. Flowers, 1–3, terminal, pale blue with a single dark vein, each surrounded by 1–3 bristle-tipped bracts, 8–10mm long, below which lie 5 blunt sepal-like bracts united at the base. In garrigue, also in open woods, throughout the W Mediterranean region, eastwards to NW Italy and Sardinia. **Fl** 4–5.

AUTUMN CROCUSES *Colchicum*   These are perennials with corms, occasionally with stolons enclosed by tunics which often extend into a neck above the corm. Flowers have petals united into a tube, styles are separated from the base into 3 thread-like arms. Autumn-flowering species do not produce leaves until late winter or spring. *Colchicum* species yield colchicine, an important substance used in plant breeding, which when applied to seeds or meristems can cause chromosome numbers to double, and allow creation of useful plant variants. Autumn Crocus was regarded by the ancients as a dangerous poison.

Meadow Saffron *Colchicum autumnale*   Corm 3–5cm long, with a dark brown, membranous or leathery tunic with a long neck. Leaves produced in the spring in a group of 4 or more, 4–5cm long. Flowers solitary, or in groups of 2–5, 10–25cm tall with very long stalk-like tubes and orange stigmas, each curved into a hook; stamens attached to petals at 2 different levels, anthers pollen-yellow. In damp meadows throughout S Europe from Spain to Greece. **Fl** 8–10. There are several closely related autumn-flowering species forming a poorly understood group scattered throughout our region. Two of them are detailed here: *C. lusitanicum* has perianth segments 4–6cm long with anthers blackish-purple to pale purplish-pink or yellow. SW Europe into S Italy. **Fl** 9–11. *C. neapolitanum* has perianth segments 3–4.5cm, with yellow anthers. Flowers pinker, with veins more or less wavy, stigmas less curved and shallowly arched with stamens attached to petals at 1 level. In dry sandy places in the Mediterranean region and Portugal. **Fl** 8–9.

Colchicum bivonae   With 1–6 flowers, pale to dark rose, distinctly chequered; perianth segments oblong-broadly lanceolate, with free portions 5.5–6.5mm long. Styles 3, recurved at their tips, with stigmas extending along them. In pasture and open woods into the mountain zone, in the E Mediterranean, westwards to Sardinia. **Fl** 8–9.

St Bernard's Lily (le

Aphyllanth
monspeliensis (rig

Colchicum bivona
(righ

Meadow Saffron (lef

Colchicum triphyllum   A low plant, to 8cm, with oblong, membranous corm; tunic reddish-brown. Leaves, usually 3, normally 3–5cm × 4–6mm, dull green, present at flowering time with later expansion to 15cm × 1cm. Flowers, 1–4, 2–3cm in diameter, pinkish-violet, not chequered. Tepals 1.5–3cm long, anthers blackish or purplish. In stony places to 1,500m in central and S Spain to SE Greece. **Fl** (12–) 2–3 (–5).

Colchicum cupanii   A very variable species, to 8cm, with 2 bright shiny-green or dull dark-green leaves; shape varies from narrow to broad as does state of development at flowering time. Flowers, 1–5, 1–2cm in diameter, pinkish-purple or pale pink. Tepals 1–2.5cm long; anthers deep brownish purple. In rocky places, to 1,300m, in the Mediterranean region from SE France eastwards to Italy and Greece. **Fl** 9–12.

Androcymbium europaeum   Low *Colchicum*-like plants with glossy green leaves about 1cm wide. Flowers 1 to several, pinkish or white with mauve striping, 2–2.5cm across. On open sandy or rocky places in the Capo de Gata (Spain). **Fl** 12–2.

FRITILLARIES *Fritillaria*   These are bulbous perennials with comparatively large, solitary flowers (rarely in few-flowered racemes). Corolla nodding, bell-shaped, often marked with alternating squares of dark and light colour (tessellations) and a longitudinal stripe of clear green down the middle. Nectaries conspicuous and glistening at the base of the perianth segments.

Fritillaria lusitanica   A plant, very variable in height, with stems 10–50cm, and 7–9 glaucous leaves. Lower leaves linear-lanceolate, usually 5–10mm wide, and opposite; upper leaves narrower. Flowers solitary (sometimes 2–3), 2–4cm long, bell-shaped, yellowish within and green outside, through dull brick red or sometimes purplish outside, becoming sparingly brown-chequered. In stony and bushy places in SW Spain, central.and S Portugal. **Fl** 3–4. *F. hispanica* is sometimes considered a separate species, and has 7–13 scattered leaves, lower ones linear-lanceolate, upper ones linear. Flowers bell-shaped, red-brown, with a yellow-green median band outside but not chequered; brown chequering with yellow median band inside. In thickets from lowlands to mountains, in S central and E Spain.

Fritillaria messanensis   A plant, 15–40cm, with 7–10 linear leaves. Lower leaves 4–9cm long, often opposite; others alternate, uppermost ones in whorl of 3. Flowers broadly bell-shaped, nodding, with perianth segments 2.2–3.2cm long, expanded at the mouth; indistinct yellowish-, brownish- or purple-chequered pattern with a green margin on the back. Nectar grove at the base of the segments 6–10mm. In open woods, grassy pasture and thickets, in Sicily, S Italy. **Fl** 4.

Fritillaria involucrata   A low plant, 15–45cm. Leaves grey-green, linear or very narrowly lanceolate, with lowest pair more or less opposite; upper 3 in a whorl, intermediate opposite or alternate. Flowers pale green, but distinctly chequered with purplish brown (rarely appearing uniform mahogany). In clearings in light woodland and rocky places in scrub, 500–1,500m, in SE France and NW Italy. **Fl** 4–6.

Fritillary *Fritillaria meleagris*   A low to medium plant, 10–30cm, with (3)4–6(8) narrowly linear, grey-green, alternate leaves. Flowers solitary, nodding, and widely bell-shaped, about 2.5–4cm in diameter and 3–5cm long. Colour can vary from pale to deep pinkish-purple, chequered darker or white. In damp meadows to 1,000m in mountain regions; *en masse* it makes one of the sights of the European plant world. **Fl** 4–5.

Colchicum cupanii (le?

Androcymbiu
europaeum (righ?

Fritillaria messanensi
(lef?

Fritillary (righ?

Fritillaria involucrat
(left

Merendera pyrenaica A plant with leaves all basal, linear, 4–8mm broad and up to 22cm long, folded; usually appearing after the flowers and arising from a corm with a thick black membranous tunic. Flowers solitary or in pairs formed at ground level in autumn, rose-purple, with 6 lanceolate perianth segments 3–4.5cm long (unlike *Colchicum*, they are not united). Anthers yellow, 8–12mm, attached at the base. In pasture in the mountain zone; Pyrenees and Iberian peninsula. Fl 8–9. Similar species include: *M. filifolia*, which is an autumn-flowering species with leaves appearing at or just after flowering time; no more than 3mm broad. Anthers yellow, usually 6–8mm. On sandy soils in SW Europe (W Mediterranean). *M. androcymboides* is a spring-flowering species with leaves 6–12mm wide. In dry places in Serranía de Ronda (SW Spain).

Gagea Flowers are solitary or in clusters, yellow, with leafy bracts below the flowers.

Gagea arvensis A plant with hairy stems and stalks, rarely more than 15cm, with a lily-like appearance and 2 tiny bulbs enclosed in a papery sheath. There are 2 channelled basal leaves, each with a rounded keel, 2mm broad; and 2–3 leaves below the flowers. Flowers yellow, with a greenish exterior, 1–1.5cm long, held in a loose umbel-like cluster of 5–12. In vineyards, stony fields and on road-verges throughout the Mediterranean from Spain to the Middle East. Fl 4–5. *G. foliosa* has hairless stems, 5–12cm. Basal leaves 2 (rarely 1), narrowly lanceolate, about 3–4mm wide. Flowers 1–4, yellow with a green exterior, 1.5–2.5cm in diameter, on hairy stalks. In sparse woodland or scrub in the Mediterranean mountain region from S France to SE Italy. Fl 4-7.

Early Star-of-Bethlehem *Gagea bohemica* A tiny, inconspicuous plant, 2–6cm, with 2 thread-like basal leaves, often curled and lying on the ground. Flowers 1–4, yellow with a greenish exterior, about 1–2cm in diameter, on hairy or hairless stalks. On dry grassland in central and S Europe. Fl 2–3. Two subspecies occur in the range of this book: ssp *nebrodensis* has flowers, stem and basal leaves hairless; in N Sicily. Ssp *gallica* has a velvety stem and whitish-hairy basal leaves; in W France.

Tulipa The flowers are terminal, erect, large; corolla bell-shaped without nectaries. Stems leafy at the base.

Wild Tulip *Tulipa sylvestris* A plant with stems 8–45cm and bulbs with tough tunics, often with stolons enabling it to form clumps. Leaves, 2–3, are strap-shaped, channelled and rather straggling. Flowers nodding in bud and solitary (rarely 2), often fragrant. Perianth segments 3.5–7cm long, elliptical to oblong, pointed and clear yellow (occasionally pale yellow, whitish): the outer 3 segments have a yellowish-green (more rarely reddish) flush on the outside. Filaments 9–14mm; anthers 4–9mm. In meadows, grassy and rocky places and open woodland to 2,000m; in Italy, Sicily and Sardinia. Fl 4–5. Ssp *australis* is a more slender plant with stems no more than 2mm in diameter; lowest leaf less than 1.2cm wide. Outer perianth segments tinged with pink or crimson on the outside; filaments 5–8mm, anthers 2.5–4mm. Throughout the native range of the species.

Merendera pyrenaica

(le

Gagea arvensis (rig

Wild Tulip (righ

Gagea foliosa (lef

Wild Tuli
ssp *australis* (right

Tulipa agenensis (T. oculis-solis) A large-flowered species with stems 18–65cm; hairless or slightly hairy, with more or less flat green leaves. Flowers reddish-orange, tepals 4.8–8.5cm long, pointed, elliptical to oblong-elliptical; inner 3 shorter than outer. Basal blotch black edged with yellow (hence the former name *T. oculis-solis* meaning eye of the sun). Seed is seldom set; plants proliferate by stolons. From Asia Minor, naturalized in S France and Italy. Fl 4–5. *T. praecox* is similar to above but differs in having blue-green leaves, orange flowers flushed with green outside, tepals 3.6–8cm long with a brownish-green basal blotch, yellow-bordered; inner tepals shorter with a pronounced yellowish median stripe. Originating from SW or S-central Asia, but naturalized in France and Italy on cultivated land and in waste places. Fl 4–5.

Tulipa agenensis (left

Ornithogalu
narbonense (right

STAR-OF-BETHLEHEM *Ornithogalum* The flowers are in umbels; perianth segments are white with a green line. Leaves basal.

Ornithogalum narbonense A plant 20–50cm, with 4–6 leaves that are 8–16mm wide and persist until after flowering. Inflorescence a long raceme with erect flowers, all on stalks of around the same length; bracts as long as flower stalks. Perianth segments wide, spreading, 1.2–1.6cm long, milky-white inside with a prominent green stripe along the length of the back. Anthers yellow; ovary 3.5–5mm with flattened top; thin style as long as or longer than ovary. Flowers scentless. In pasture, cultivated fields and on roadsides throughout S Europe. Fl 4–6.

Spiked Star-of-Bethlehem *Ornithogalum pyrenaicum* A plant with stems 30–80cm, and 4–5 leaves (often withered by flowering time); bracts shorter than flower stalks. Inflorescence long and cylindrical, flower stalks 1–2cm; perianth segments pale yellowish inside, greenish outside with a darker-green median stripe. Outer segments 1.1–1.3cm × 2.5–3mm, flat at first becoming inrolled at margins to give flowers a starry appearance. Anthers pale yellow. In meadows and scrub in W Europe and Mediterranean region. Fl 5–6. *The young shoots of this species can be cooked and eaten like Asparagus.*

Ornithogalu
montanum (left

Ornithogalum arabicum A medium to tall plant, 30–80cm, with a bulb that forms numerous offsets. Leaves 6–8, hairless, green, some 1–3cm wide, in a basal rosette long-tapering at the apex. Flowers carried in a very dense, flat-topped raceme; perianth segments 1.5–3.2cm, creamy-white inside, slightly greenish outside but no green stripe; segments spread to form saucer shape 3–4cm in diameter. The blackish ovary and young fruit give a central 'dark eye'. On rocky ground to 300m in the Mediterranean region; naturalized in some places and cultivated in gardens. Fl 4–5.

Ornithogalum montanum A plant with a dwarf habit, 6–20cm, with 3–6 green leaves in a basal rosette which tapers gradually to the apex from a base width of 1–2cm. Flowers (5–15) carried in a wide, often rather flat-topped raceme, with stalks 3–8cm long, horizontal or semi-erect in the fruiting stage. Flowers white, 2–3cm in diameter with a broad green stripe on the exterior of each tepal. On rocky ground and mountain pasture 1,000–1,500m in central and S Italy and Sicily; also eastwards to Balkans and Asia Minor. Fl 4–5.

Drooping Star-of-Bethlehem *Ornithogalum nutans* A short to medium species with stems 20–60cm; bulb forms numerous offsets. Leaves (4–6) hairless, green, 1–1.5cm wide, and linear. Flowers carried on short stalks in a dense raceme which is more or less 1-sided. Flowers (5–10) almost bell-shaped, with tepals flaring outwards, white or rather silvery with a broad green stripe on the outside of each tepal. In scrub, woods and damp fields to 1,000m; probably a Balkan native but widely naturalized as an escape from cultivation. Fl 3–5.

Star-of-Bethlehem *Ornithogalum umbellatum* A short plant, 15–30cm, from a bulb which forms numerous offsets, each producing a single narrow leaf, giving leafy clumps at flowering time. Leaves 2–5mm wide, each bears a white central stripe on the upper surface making the species readily recognizable. Flowers (5–20), produced in a wide, flat-topped raceme with flower stalks horizontal at flowering time. Flowers white, 1.5–2cm across, with a bright-green stripe on the outer surface of each tepal. Fruits have 6 equal lobes. In woods and grassy places, to 2,000m, throughout Europe; widely naturalized. Fl 4–5.

Urginea The numerous flowers are borne in a long terminal spike; perianth segments are spreading. Bulbs very large.

Sea Squill *Urginea maritima* A plant with large red or white bulbs up to 18cm in diameter, often partly protruding from soil. Leaves shiny, 30–100cm long, strap-like, lanceolate, leathery and more or less flat; appearing with rains in autumn and drying by flowering time. Flower stems robust, 1–1.5m, arising from dry ground; inflorescence a long, dense terminal raceme of 50 or more white flowers. Flower stalks 1–3cm long; perianth segments spreading, star-like, white with a green or purple mid-vein. Anthers greenish. In pasture, stony places, garrigue and on stony beaches, throughout the Mediterranean. Fl 8–10. *U. undulata* is generally smaller and more delicate. Leaves 8–15cm × 3–10mm, with strongly wavy margins; flowers pink in a loose raceme. In E Spain, Corsica and Sardinia. *U. fugax* has leaves that are 2mm or less wide; flowers white or pink. In Corsica, Sardinia and Apulia (Italy).

Scilla The blue flowers, few or many, are borne in clusters or spikes; perianth segments bell-shaped or spreading in a star. Petals have a darker mid-vein and leaves are all basal.

Scilla peruviana A handsome plant growing from a large bulb up to 8cm in diameter; flower stems 20–50cm. Leaves longer than stem (40–60cm long), lanceolate, all basal, often with short hairs on the margins. Inflorescence a broadly pyramidal raceme of 50–100 flowers, carried on a short, stout stalk. Perianth segments blue to purple, sometimes whitish, 5–14mm long. Anthers yellowish; bracts 5–8cm long. In damp grassy pasture and open woods in the Iberian Peninsula, Sardinia, S Italy and Sicily.

Scilla hyacinthoides A robust plant with stout leafless stems to 1m, and bulb up to 10cm. Leaves numerous, very long, flat, rough, 2cm broad; leaf margins have spreading hairs. Inflorescence long, conical, with 40–150 blue-violet flowers on long stalks of the same colour. Bracts only 1.5mm. In hedges, rocky places and fields in the European Mediterranean eastwards. Fl 4–5.

Pyrenean Squill *Scilla lilio-hyacinthus* A low plant with stems up to 15cm. The bulb is distinctive, consisting of a series of yellowish lily-like scales. Leaves 5–10, shiny green, strap-like, 1–3cm wide, with an abruptly narrowed tip. Flowers 5–15 in a loose ovoid raceme, blue, starry, 1–1.5cm wide. Bracts 1–2cm long, papery, white and long-tapering. In woods and meadow-margins, 500–2,000m, in France and N Spain. Fl 4–6.

Autumn Squill *Scilla autumnalis* A low to short species, with stems 2–25cm, and 3–12 hairless, linear leaves that are 0.5–3mm wide and absent at flowering time. Flowers up to 35, starry, in a spike-like raceme, pale to deep lilac, blue or pinkish-purple, 5–7mm across. Bracts absent. In rocky, grassy or sandy places, usually near the coast; widespread around the Mediterranean. Fl 8–10.

Alpine Squill *Scilla bifolia*   A plant with stems up to 15cm. Leaves, usually 2, linear or widening towards the tip, 5–10mm wide. Inflorescence a rather loose, 1-sided raceme; flowers 1–7, blue, starry, 1–1.5cm wide; lower flower stalks slender, 1–3cm long, bracts absent. In short grass or light woodland, to 2,700m, often after melting snow; widespread in mountain regions. **Fl** 1–5.

Alpine Squill (le

Spanish Bluebell (righ

Spanish Bluebell *Hyacinthoides hispanicus*   A plant with stems up to 40cm, and 3–6 bright-green strap-like leaves up to 2.5cm wide. Inflorescence a loose, erect raceme (not 1-sided); flowers pale to mid-blue, pink or white, unscented, bell-shaped; corolla as long as broad, 1.2–2cm, anthers blue. In meadows, in slight shade, and in rocky scrub and mountain areas, 1,000–1,500m, in SW Europe; cultivated and widely naturalized. **Fl** 4–5.

Bellevalia   The flowers are borne in a lax terminal inflorescence; corolla has 6 deeply divided teeth, bell-shaped or tubular but not constricted into a throat.

Bellevalia romana   A plant with stems 15–35cm. Leaves 3–6 exceeding the raceme in length, long, linear-lanceolate, 5–15mm broad with smooth margins. Flowers 20–30, in a cylindrical raceme on spreading to erect stalks 8–20mm long; perianth dirty-white becoming brown later, 7–10mm long, lobes united to about half-way flaring outwards towards tips. Fruits triangular with 3 prominent ribs. In damp meadows and cultivated land from SE France westwards around the Mediterranean. **Fl** 4–5. *B. ciliata* is similar but has flowers pale purple turning greenish brown, 8–10mm long, bell-shaped and pendulous in a very broad cone-shaped raceme; flower stalks 3–4cm or longer. In fields and meadows from Italy westwards; naturalized in S France. **Fl** 3–4.

Muscari neglectum (le

Dipcadi serotinum   A plant 10–40cm with all leaves shorter than the flowering stem, basal, linear and grooved. Inflorescence a loose, erect raceme with 3–10 narrowly bell-shaped flowers, yellowish, brownish or greenish, facing more or less one way (illus.): perianth segments 1.2–1.5cm, quarter to half joined with 3 outer curving outwards and the inner straight at first. Bracts longer than flower stalks, lanceolate. In sunny pasture and sandy places in the W Mediterranean. **Fl** 3–7. *D. fulvum* name given to autumn-flowering plants. Spain, Canary Islands, Morocco.

Dipcadi serotinu

Muscari   Differs from *Bellevalia*: corolla with 6 short teeth, bell-shaped, flowers in dense terminal clusters on leafless stems. Upper flowers usually small, sterile.

Tassel Hyacinth *Muscari comosum*   A plant with flowering stems 15–80cm with linear, grooved leaves 7–40cm, all basal narrowing towards the tip and curved downwards. Inflorescence a loose raceme 4–10cm long; sterile flowers held erect form a striking blue 'tuft' at the apex, fertile flowers brownish-green, 5–10mm long with short, tubular bell-shaped corollas with 6 teeth directed outwards. In fields and cultivated ground, olive groves, rocky places; around the Mediterranean. **Fl** 4–6.

Bellevalia romana (le

Dipcadi serotinu
(cent

Tassel Hyacinth (righ

Muscari neglectum   Plants 10–35cm with 3-6 leaves, all basal, linear to linear-lanceolate, grooved. Inflorescence a short, dense raceme with ovoid flowers on spreading or recurved stalks up to 5mm long. The upper flowers are sterile, small and pale; the lower flowers fertile (illus.), larger, 3.5–7.5mm and blackish-blue with 6 white, recurved 'teeth'. In fields, on hillsides and in vineyards around the Mediterranean. **Fl** 3–4. *M. racemosum* is the name given to plants with semi-cylindrical leaves only 1–3mm across, narrowly grooved on the upper surface. *M. commutatum* is a similar but corolla deep black-purple with teeth the same colour. Very few or no sterile flowers at the apex: if present these are pale blue. From Sicily and Italy eastwards to Greece and the Levant. **Fl** 2–6.

Muscari neglect

Nectaroscordum siculum A hairless, bulbous perennial to 50–150cm with leaves strongly keeled on the underside up to 5cm wide; inner leaf sheathes the stem for about one-third of its length. Leaves smell like *Allium* when crushed and are partly withered by flowering time. Inflorescence a loose umbel with each flower on long, arching stalks which become erect in fruit. Flowers greenish-white or greenish-maroon, bell-shaped, 14–16mm long. Woods or scrub in mountain areas below 1,000m. Widely cultivated. In France, and from Italy eastwards to the Balkans. Fl 4–6.

Allium Plants smelling of onion or garlic; flowers in terminal umbels, generally with 2 encircling bracts.

Wild Leek *Allium ampeloprasum* A robust species with stout flowering stem up to 1m; bulb with numerous small bulbils. Leaves very rough at edges, flattened, 12–35mm broad with keeled midrib beneath. Flower head large, globular, 7–10cm across: flowers numerous, rose-lilac, on long stalks with yellow anthers and two lateral projections from the stalk of the stamen. Hedges, banks and arid places around the Mediterranean. Fl 5–7.

Naples Garlic *Allium neapolitanum* Plants to 20–45cm with triangular-sectioned stem (2 sharp and 1 blunt edge, illus.) and rounded bulb. Leaves only 2–3, linear about 1–2cm wide sheathing the lower part of the stem. Umbels 5–9cm in diameter, with 20–40 flowers, hemispherical or spreading with large glistening white flowers up to 2cm across, starry or cup-shaped (illus.): perianth segments 7–12mm long, bluntly elliptical, the outer somewhat broader than the inner. In dry grassy and stony places, and olive groves around the Mediterranean. Fl 3–6.

Allium nigrum A plant 55–80cm tall with 2–3 basal leaves. Inflorescence 6–8cm across, hemispherical, many-flowered, white or pale pink with green mid-vein on each tepal. Ovary very dark green or blackish. On cultivated land in Spain, Portugal, Italy and France. Fl 4–6.

Rosy Garlic *Allium roseum* A plant 10–65cm with cylindrical stem (illus.): bulb with small bulblets and outer tunic dotted with small holes. Leaves 2–6, linear, basal, flat with blade 4–10mm broad and fine teeth along margins. Inflorescence a hemispherical umbel up to 7cm across with 5–30 erect, pink or white spreading bell-shaped flowers 7–12mm long (illus.), often with bulbils amongst them. Flower bract 2–4 lobed, shorter than the flower stalks. Cultivated and fallow land, often abundant. Around the Mediterranean. Fl 3–6. *A. confertum* is another rose-coloured species with stems only 10–15cm high, umbel 2–3cm across and flowers 5–7mm long. Restricted to Sicily and Sardinia.

Round-headed Leek *Allium sphaerocephalum* A plant with flowering stems 30–80cm leafy on the lower half with leaves 1–1.5mm broad, hollow, cylindrical, grooved. Flower heads dense, spherical, 2–2.5cm across without bulbils. Flowers about 5mm long, bell-shaped, reddish-purple: stamens protruding, the inner with 3-points, the centre longer than the laterals. Bracts below head shorter than flowers. In dry places, cultivated and uncultivated ground around Mediterranean. Fl 6–8.

Three-cornered Leek *Allium triquetrum* A plant with rather thick stems, sharp-angled triangular in section, 10–40cm high. Leaves 2 or 3, hairless, keeled forming a short sheath above the ground. Inflorescence a terminal umbel with 4–12 flowers first hanging to one side, later erect. Flowers bell-shaped, not opening wide: perianth segments white with a green line. Cool shady places by streams. Spain to Italy. Sometimes cultivated for its long-lasting flowers. Fl 2–5. *A. pendulinum* is similar with triangular inflorescence stalk, 2–9 flowers in umbel, flowers at first erect later all drooping; perianth segments with 3 green veins. Corsica, Sardinia, Italy and Sicily. Fl 2–4.

Wild Leek (le

Naples Garlic (rig

Naples Garlic flower
stem sect

Allium nigrum (le

Rosy Garlic (rig

Rosy Garlic flower
stem sect

Round-headed Le
(le

Three-cornered Le
(rig

Allium subhirsutum   A rather delicate species, 20–50cm with cylindrical stem and leaves 2–3, almost basal, soft, flat, 5–10mm broad, 5–45cm long with spreading hairs on the margins. Inflorescence a loose, erect, hemispherical umbel about 7cm across with flower stalks 4cm, without bulbils. Flowers 1cm in diameter, white or with a pinkish stripe spreading like a star. Stamens two-thirds the length of perianth segments, anthers brownish-pink. Bracts below flower head shorter than flower stalks. On fallow and cultivated land on stony, rocky or sandy soils around the Mediterranean. **Fl** 3–6. *A. trifoliatum* is a closely related species with umbels 2.5–4cm across, flower stalks up to 2cm: flowers pink or pink-keeled with narrow, pointed stamens half as long as petals. Flower bract equal to flower stalk. Fields and hills in France eastwards. **Fl** 4–5.

Asparagus   Woody or herbaceous with leaves reduced to scales: branchlets needle-like, green often in clusters. Flowers with bell-shaped corolla; single-sexed.

Asparagus albus   A plant with woody, whitish stems 50–100cm tall, flexuous with smooth or shallowly grooved surface. Stems have spines 5–12mm long which are modified leaves; these broaden toward the base with 10–20 short shoots 5–20mm long in their axils. Flowers carried in groups of 6–15 on stalks 3–5mm long: perianth white, 6-lobed, spreading 2–3mm long. Fruit a berry 4–7mm in diameter red becoming black. **Fl** 8–10.

Asparagus acutifolius   A climbing subshrub with much-branched woody stems 0.4–2mm long with whitish or greyish surface. Leaves small, scale-like: in their axils are 5–30 or more stiff, sharp-pointed shoots 2–8mm long. Flowers solitary or in clusters of up to 4 with stalks 3–7mm long. Perianth 3–4mm long, bell-shaped, 6-lobed, yellowish-green. Berries red becoming black. Woods, garrigue, maquis in the Mediterranean region. **Fl** 7–10. *A. aphyllus* is similar but non-climbing with rough, hairless, angular stems which are much-branched: the branchlets are spiny in clusters of 2–6. Stony sandy places, thickets in Spain, Sardinia, Italy, Sicily and eastwards. **Fl** 7–10. *A. stipularis* has solitary branches which are very stiff. Plants bushy 50–100cm tall, with finely grooved, grey-green stems and no obvious leaves. There are stout, short shoots 1–5cm long modified into spines: at their bases are small leaves which are little more than membranous, with 2–8 flowers on stalks 1–3mm long. Perianth 4mm long, yellowish to purple, 6-lobed. Berries 5–8mm, bluish-black. In S Mediterranean, Corsica, Canary Islands. **Fl** 3–5 and 7–10.

Ruscus   Woody evergreen plants: stems flattened to leaf-like blades. Flowers and fruits borne on one surface of stem.

Butcher's Broom *Ruscus aculeatus*   An evergreen shrub with ribbed stems: spiny and bushy with branches flattened into ovate, leaf-like blades 1–4cm long, arranged in two rows each ending in a spiny tip: these are situated in the axils of tiny scale-leaves. Flowers single-sexed on separate plants: inconspicuous, greenish-white, 1–2 in the axil of a papery bract – apparently growing from the 'leaf' surface. Fruit: a red berry 1.5cm in diameter. In undergrowth of maquis and other woodland into montane zone on limestone. In the W European Mediterranean region and the Canary Islands. **Fl** 10 and 2–4. *Young shoots edible like asparagus.*

Smilax   Climbing plants with heart-shaped leaves, hooked spines and paired tendrils at the leaf bases.

Smilax aspera   An evergreen climbing shrub up to 15m tall: stems, leaf margins and veins have hooked spines. Leaves leathery, shining, hairless, heart-shaped up to 11cm long (illus.). Flowers in clusters of 5–30 produced on branches: terminally and from the axils. Perianth segments greenish or pinkish, 2–4mm long, flowers fragrant. Berries green, turning red then black. In maquis and woods and on walls, from the Mediterranean region eastwards. **Fl** 8–11.

Asparagus stipul

(

Butcher's Broom

flower (rig

Smilax aspera (le

Butcher's Broom

fruit (rig

Smilax as

PALM FAMILY, PALMAE

Mainly plants of tropical or sub-tropical rain forest: leaves more or less fan-like or stiffly fern-like in a terminal crown. Flowers numerous, often small, greenish or yellowish, with male and female separate in a plume or cascade-like cluster, forming the spadix and springing from a large bract (spathe).

Dwarf Fan-palm *Chamaerops humilis* A bushy, often dwarf palm, stemless in the wild because of grazing; in cultivation or inaccessible places, a trunk covered with grey or whitish fibres develops, and plants reach 4m or more; suckers develop from the base. Leaves clustered at the top, fan-like, spreading not drooping, with 12–15 blades (illus.); lanceolate, sharp, untoothed. Leaf stalks slender with straight spines on the margins. Flowers among the leaves in dense yellow panicles with sheathing bracts. Fruits inedible, 1–3cm, yellow, becoming reddish-brown. In garrigue, stony pasture and sandy places, also grown ornamentally, from W Mediterranean eastwards to Italy. Fl 4–6.

Dwarf Fan-palm

Chusan Palm *Trachycarpus fortunei* A tree 4-12m, with trunk densely covered with dark-brown fibres. Leaves bright green, with stalks 40–100cm long, and fan-like blade 50–60cm in diameter, divided almost to the base to give numerous long, stiff segments (illus.). Male and female flowers on the same tree carried in panicles 30–60cm long. Fruits blue-black, grape-like, 1.2–1.4cm in diameter. Native of SE Asia; grown ornamentally in the Mediterranean. Fl 4–6. Several other 'Fan-palms' are seen along the Mediterranean coast in gardens, parks and as street trees: *Livistona australis* is an Australian native with slender, tall trunk with ringed bark. *Washingtonia filifera* is a Californian native; leaves have hanging white threads. *W. robusta* has a smooth trunk with diagonal furrows; upper part covered by dried leaves.

Washingtonia robusta (left)

Arum pictum (right)

Date Palm *Phoenix dactylifera* A tall palm, up to 30m, with slender trunk; pattern on surface caused by scars of fallen leaves. Leaves clustered at the top of the tree; spreading, curved, 3–5m long, pinnately divided, grey-green. Leaflets linear-lanceolate, long-pointed, keeled and arranged in a 'V'; middle ones 30–40cm long. Inflorescences much-branched, at first in sheath-like bracts. Fruits 2.5–7.5cm, fleshy, dark, but variable in form (illus.). Ornamental in much of the Mediterranean; plantations in S Spain. Fl 2–6. **Canary Palm** *P. canariensis* is similar to above but has solitary trunks, is generally stouter and has a leafier crown with fronds 5–6m long, more graceful and less leafy (illus.); middle leaflets 40–50cm long. Fruits inedible 1.5–2.5cm, oblong, orange becoming dark brown. Native to the Canary Islands, but widely planted throughout the Mediterranean because it is both more tolerant to cold and faster-growing than above. Fl 2–6.

Chusan Palm

Date Palm

ARUM FAMILY, ARACEAE

Italian Lords-and-Ladies (left)

Tuberous perennials with the inflorescence comprising separate male and female flowers in dense whorls, the male above the female on a single axis at the base of the spadix. A leafy bract (spathe) encloses the flowers at its base.

Italian Lords-and-Ladies *Arum italicum* A perennial, 20–60cm, with large oblong tuber and long-stalked leaves. Leaves appearing in autumn are arrow-shaped, 15–35cm long, with pointed lobes; those appearing in winter are larger with rounded, overlapping lobes at the base. The inflorescence is surrounded by a large yellowish-green bract (spathe) up to 40cm long (illus. overleaf), whitish inside, and has flowers on a single axis (spadix), the visible part of which is yellow, flowerless and about a third the length of the spathe. Berries red. In hedges, banks, woods and bushy places; widespread in S Europe from Spain to Turkey. Fl 4–5. Ssp *italicum* has dark leaves with white veins, whereas ssp *neglectum* has leaves of one colour. *A. pictum* is autumn-flowering with a dark-purple spathe. In Corsica, Sardinia, and the Balearic Islands.

Canary Palm

Friar's Cowl *Arisarum vulgare* A perennial with short underground tuber and stems 20–40cm. Basal leaves long-stalked, rounded, with basal lobes ranging from heart- to arrow-shaped. Flower stem about equal to the leaf stalks, spotted, and ends in a curious green, cylindrical spathe, striped with purple and ending in a 'flap' and a long, curved, greenish spadix just protruding from it; the whole has been likened to a friar's cowl or old-fashioned pulpit (illus.). Flowers 1-sexed, arranged at the base of the spadix. In rocky places, shady valleys and on uncultivated ground throughout the Mediterranean. Fl 3–5 or 10–11. *A. proboscideum* is similar to above but has arrow-shaped leaves where the basal lobes are angled out away from the stalk. Under Cork Oaks in Cadiz (Spain).

Biarum tenuifolium A plant 10–20cm, with linear-lanceolate leaves 5–20cm long, with flat or undulate margins appearing after flowering time. Spathe brownish-purple, long, tongue-like, often appearing straight from the soil with no stalk; spadix often longer than spathe, purple and cylindrical. Flowers unisexual with sterile flowers above and male flowers below. In garrigue, stony and grassy pasture in central, S and E Mediterranean. Fl 10–3. *B. arundanum* has a blackish-purple spathe but with a short stalk 1.5–1.8cm and leaves oblong-ovate narrowing to a short stalk and appearing after summer flowering. In mountains in Sierra de Ronda (S Spain). *B. carratracense* has a purple spathe, 10–13cm with a short tube, a short stalk and flat, spreading limb. Spadix incurved with anther zone separated from ovary zone by awl-shaped swellings. Leaves lanceolate, appearing after flowering, and broadly sheathing the base. In fields and on roadsides in S Spain.

Dragon Arum *Dracunculus vulgaris* A dramatic, almost sinister-looking species with large globular tuber and stems 60–120cm. Leaves long-stalked with purple-brown mottled sheaths which encircle the flower stem; leaf blades are deeply divided into finger-like, lanceolate segments often mottled in white. Spathe very large, up to 35cm, with wavy purple margin; green outside but deep chocolate-purple within. Spadix thick, fleshy, often as long as the spathe and dark purple-brown; male and female flowers separated by only a few sterile flowers. Flowers have fetid carrion smell. In woods, bushy places, uncultivated ground and rocky gullies, from Corsica and Sardinia to E Mediterranean; probably introduced elsewhere. Fl 4–6. *D. muscivorus* is a similar species with spathe that is hairy on inner surface and spadix completely covered with thread-like structures. In Balearics, Corsica and Sardinia.

RUSH FAMILY, JUNCACEAE

Erect perennials with stems often filled with white pith. The very narrow sheathing leaves can be rigid or hollow with internal cross-partitions. Differs from superficially similar grasses and sedges in having regularly formed flowers with 6 similar perianth segments and 6 stamens.

Sea Rush *Juncus maritimus* A tuft-forming rush with stems 30–100cm high, 1.5–2mm in diameter, and a short, creeping rhizome. Leaves 2–4, sharp-pointed, cylindrical, the same length as stem. Inflorescence branched, loose, elongated, with 2–3 flower heads; flowers 6-segmented, straw yellow, without bracteoles. Outer perianth segments longer and more pointed than inner ones. Capsule triangular, ovoid, pointed, 2.5–3.5mm. In saltmarshes and coastal meadows in the Mediterranean region, and on coasts of W and N Europe. Fl 6–9.

Sharp Rush *Juncus acutus* A rush with stems 30–150cm, forming dense tufts. Leaves stiff, sharp-pointed and cylindrical. Flowering stem 2–4mm across. Perianth segments 6, about equal in length; inner 3 broader with membranous appendages at the tips. Capsule 5–6mm short-pointed. On sandy beaches and in saltmarshes on the Mediterranean and Atlantic coasts. Fl 4–7.

Italian Aru

Dragon Arum (lef

Friar's Cov

Sea Rush (left

Sharp Rush (right

GRASS FAMILY, GRAMINEAE

A vast family, dominating areas of the world with low rainfall, and providing numerous fodder and cereal crops. The leaves have a sheathing base and narrow blade; at the junction of sheath and blade is a flap called the ligule. Flowers are clustered into spikelets with 2 scale-like bracts at the base (glumes) and 1 or more tiny flowers, each with an outer bract (lemma) and inner bract (palea). Spikelets are either stalked in loose clusters (panicle), or stalkless in a spike.

Aegilops *Aegilops ovata*   A low-growing, tufted annual, 10–30cm, with few short, narrow, broad-based, triangular-bladed leaves that are much shorter than the leaf sheaths. Inflorescence easily recognized by the compact flowering heads; narrowly ovate, of 2–5 spikelets (illus.) with tough, strongly ribbed outer glumes ending in 3 (2–4) stiff awns up to 5cm long. In arid, grassy places throughout the Mediterranean. Fl 4–6.

Aegilops

Marram *Ammophila arenaria* ssp *arundinacea*   A common coastal grass with stems 50–120cm, and stout, branched, creeping rhizomes which form dense tufts and stabilize dunes close to the sea. Leaves with stiff green blade, up to 6mm broad; upper part curls inwards, closing in dry weather. Inflorescence an erect panicle but condensed, spike-like, 7–25cm long. Spikelets 1–1.6cm, 1-flowered, glumes lanceolate, about as long as lemma, which has fine white hairs 4–5mm long. On sandy beaches and dunes on the Mediterranean coasts and Atlantic coasts of Portugal. Fl 5–8. Ssp *arenaria*, from N and W Europe, extends to NW Spain.

Giant Reed *Arundo donax*   The largest European grass, often planted for wind breaks. Stems 2–6m, woody and overwintering; rhizomes vigorous and far-creeping. Leaf blade flat, grey-green, with rough margins up to 60cm. Flowers in second year produce dense panicles 30–60cm long with spikelets 1.2–1.8cm (illus.); florets purple-tinged, glumes hairless, membranous; lemma with 2 tips and shiny silvery hairs on the back. In ditches, river banks and damp places; widespread in the Mediterranean. Fl 8–12. *Used for making baskets, mats and awnings, etc.*

Giant Reed

Great Quaking-grass *Briza maxima*   A slender annual with stems 10–60cm and flat, hairless leaves. Recognized by the large, pendulous, egg-shaped spikelets on fine branches with glumes overlapping like scales (illus.).

Fern Grass *Desmazaria rigida (Catapodium rigidum)*   A many-stemmed annual, 5–20cm, with fine leaves. Flowering heads erect, stiff, 1-sided, linear or somewhat branched. Spikelets mostly stalked (illus.), very small, 2–4mm long, linear-lanceolate, several-flowered. Glumes with fine tips, not awned; lemmas blunt. On walls, track-sides, and in dry places throughout the Mediterranean. Fl 4–7.

Great Quaking-grass

Bermuda-grass *Cynodon dactylon*   A low, perennial, greyish-green, creeping, mat-forming grass. Leaves 2–15cm × 2–4mm with row of short hairs where blade meets sheath. Flowering stems slender with 3–6 terminal spikes 3–4cm long; narrow purple or pale green, spreading. Spikelets 2–2.5mm long, 1-flowered, in 2 overlapping rows, ovate, flattened (illus. overleaf). On uncultivated ground, track-sides, and in dry places throughout the Mediterranean, but widely introduced as a lawn grass for dry climates worldwide. Fl 5–8.

Rough Dog's-tail *Cynosurus echinatus*   A plant with stems thin, smooth, 10–100cm, growing singly or clump-forming. Leaf blades 3–10mm broad, flat and rough above. Panicle dense, ovoid, 1-sided and condensed into an awnless spike, 1–4cm × 1.5cm across. Spikelets of 2 kinds: fertile with 1–5 flowers, membranous, pointed glumes and rough lemma (illus. overleaf); sterile with narrow, awned scales arranged in 2 distinct rows.

Fern Grass

Hare's-tail *Lagurus ovatus*   A delicate hairy annual, 5–50cm. Grey-green leaves, shorter than the inflated, ribbed sheaths, covered with woolly hairs. Inflorescence distinctive: softly hairy, erect, spherical or oval, up to 6cm × 2cm, from which awns protrude. Spikelets barely stalked, 1-flowered, 7–9mm long; glumes have spreading hairs and a slender bristle, and lemma has a bent awn, narrowing into 2 bristles. On sandy soils near the coast, fallow land and waysides in the Mediterranean. Fl 4–6. *Used in dried-flower arrangements.*

Albardine *Lygeum sparteum*   A tuft-forming species with stems 20–80cm, often covering large areas. Leaves rush-like, curled inwards, up to 1.5mm broad, touching and arching over at the ends; ligule about 7mm. Spikelet 2-flowered, but enclosed in characteristic sheath-like bract which is white, ovate, pointed and 3–5cm long (illus.); spikelets fall when ripe. Glumes absent, lemmas 2cm with long silky hairs, united into tube below. In grassy steppes, especially on clay and saline soils, from the S Mediterranean northwards to Spain, Sardinia and S Italy. Fl 3–5. *Used for rope-making and in paper manufacture.*

Esparto Grass *Stipa tenacissima*   A species with stems 60–100cm, which can form large tufts and cover large areas. Leaves very tough, green and flat only in growing season, otherwise grey, curled inwards, with strongly ribbed upper surface covered with dense, fine hairs. Inflorescence a dense panicle 25–35cm long with 1-flowered spikelets; glumes membranous, long-pointed 2.5–3cm long, lemma 1cm, membranous and deeply divided at tip with an awn 4–6cm long. In steppes, pasture and open pinewoods in S Spain, S Portugal and Balearics to NW Africa. Fl 4–7. *Used for high-quality paper-making and for rope.* **Feather Grass** *S. pennata* has bluish-green, bristle-like leaves; and few spikelets, 1.5–2cm long and slender. Awns long, feathery, up to 35cm, trailing in the wind. In dry steppe-like areas in Causses (France). Fl 5–7.

Golden Dog's Tail *Lamarkia aurea*   Low growing in tufts or as individual plants 5–20cm high. Panicle spike-like up to 60cm long, first green then yellow: spikelets spreading on one side. Fallow land, waysides in Mediterranean. Fl 3–7.

SEDGE FAMILY, CYPERACEAE

Unbranched, usually hairless perennials with grass-like leaves usually keeled beneath and channelled above. Sedges differ from grasses in having all flowers arranged around their stalk instead of in opposite rows. Male and female flowers are always distinct, often in separate spikes but on same plant.

Cyperus rotundus   A plant with stems 10–60cm, triangular, with keeled leaves at the base, 2–6mm broad; underground rhizomes about 1mm thick. Inflorescence has 4–10 unequal rays and 2–6 bracts. Spikelets 1–2cm × 1–2mm, with winged axes at ends of rays in groups of 3–12, each with 32 florets arranged in 2 rows (illus.). Scales ovate, red-brown with a green keel, overlapping. Stigmas 3. Fruit triangular. In damp sandy places, often coastal, in the Mediterranean. Fl 8–10. **Papyrus** *Cyperus papyrus* has inflorescence up to 50cm broad with over 100 rays. In Syracuse, the only European location. *Stem-pith used in manufacture of paper by Ancient Egyptians.*

Feather Grass

Hare's-tail (right)

Bermuda-gra

Rough Dog's Ta

Golden Dog's Ta
(lef

Albardin

Papyru

Papyru

ORCHID FAMILY, ORCHIDACEAE

Lady's-slipper (l●
White Hellebori
(rig●

After Compositae, this is the largest family of flowering plants, with greatest numbers in tropical and sub-tropical rainforests. All European species are terrestrial but most tropical species are epiphytes. Flowers with 3 similar outer perianth segments (sepals) and 3 inner (petals), with the median petal modified to form the 'lip'. Male and female reproductive structures are fused in a single 'column': at or near its top are the anthers with pollen grains grouped in masses to form club-shaped pollinia.

Lady's-slipper *Cypripedium calceolus* A plant with creeping rhizomes forming clumps, with stems to 60cm. Leaves 3–5, broadly elliptical, furrowed, arranged alternately up the stem: tips pointed, base sheathing stem. Often single-flowered; sometimes 2–3. Flower bract large, leaf-like. Flowers unmistakable: all perianth segments the same shade of deep maroon-red to purple-brown; median sepal broad, erect or curved forward, lateral sepals fused to point downwards as 'single' tepal with forked tip. Petals strap-like, spreading, twisted. Lip bright yellow, inflated, clog-shaped with edges folded over, and a hairy basal region and white staminode with red spotting near opening. In shady, deciduous and mixed woodland, and stone-strewn slopes on base-rich soils to 1,700m; widespread but rare in montane regions of Europe; in S Europe, confined to mountain woodlands in France and N Italy. Fl 5–7.

White Helleborine *Cephalanthera damasonium* This plant is often the commonest of the family. Stems grow 15–60cm, from a short rhizome. Foliage leaves (2–5) pointed; broadly ovate low down, elliptical higher up; basal leaves (2–3) scale-like. Flowers 3–12, rather dingy, creamy–white; they hardly open, and resemble small hard-boiled eggs of about 1.5–2cm in length. The epichile has 3–5 orange stripes on its surface. Plants flower only after some 10 years of growth, but they can form clumps of up to 15 or more stems. In woods up to 1,800m mostly but not always in shade, preferring base-rich soils; in mountain woodlands around much of the region. Fl 5–7. **Sword-leaved Helleborine** *C. longifolia* is similar to above in some respects, but differs in the following: stem has 4–12 foliage leaves which are long (up to 18cm) and lanceolate, bracts small. Inflorescence lax, with up to 20 flowers, which are pure white, half-opening, with pointed sepals 1.4–1.8cm long. The epichile has 4–7 orange stripes. In open woodland, in grass along woodland edges, occasionally on dune-land, up to 2,000m, generally in semi-shade on base-rich soils; widely distributed in our region, extending through Iran to the Himalayas. Fl 4–7.

Sword-leave●
Helleborine (le●
Red Helleborine (rig●

Red Helleborine *Cephalanthera rubra* A plant with slender and flexuous stems 20–60cm, upper part with glandular hairs; rhizome elongated. Leaves (2–6) rather short and lanceolate, giving this species a delicate appearance. Inflorescence lax with bright magenta-pink flowers, which open widely and are reminiscent of some exquisite miniature *Cattleya*. The epichile is intensely coloured towards the tip but lightens at the base. If overhead light levels fall, plants can revert to a vegetative state. In semi-shaded and shaded woods, up to 2,000m, on base-rich soils, mainly on limestone; widespread and frequent in Massif Central. Fl 5–7.

Broad-leaved Helleborine *Epipactis helleborine* A very variable species, 35–100cm, with 4–10 broadly ovate leaves spiralling up the stem. Inflorescence dense, many-flowered and 1-sided: flowers open wide with perianth incurved and are held horizontally or slightly drooping. Sepals and petals ovate, 8–12mm long, greenish, usually lightly to heavily tinted with reddish or violet. Lip 7–11mm long: hypochile cup-shaped with inner surface dull olive-purplish-brown, outer surface green; epichile wide, triangular, with its apex strongly recurved and 2 bosses near its base, colour variable from greenish-white through pink to purplish. Cross-pollinated. In woodland and scrub, usually in semi-shade; also in dune grassland to 1,800m. Widespread in S Europe but not in the Mediterranean. Fl 6–8. Ssp *tremolsii* has leaves widely ovate to circular with wavy edges. Flowers with sepals and petals spreading, barely incurved; inner surface of hypochile green. In open pinewoods and oakwoods to 1,500m, on calcareous soils in the W Mediterranean: Algarve, Spain and France (departments of Var and Drôme). Fl 4–7.

Small-leaved Helleborine *Epipactis microphylla* A slender species with stems 15–40cm, and 3–12 foliage leaves often sheathing the stem. Leaves narrow-lanceolate above, to wide-ovate lower down the stem, the largest less than 4cm long. Inflorescence lax, 4–20cm long with 4-25 flowers; outer surface of perianth segments and ovary thickly covered with short hairs. Flowers nodding, scented; sepals and petals ovate, 6–8mm × 3–4mm, incurved, whitish-green inside, reddish-tinged outside. Lip about 6mm long: hypochile no more than shallow cup-shaped, pinched sharply at front, inner surface whitish-green to pale pink, outer surface green; epichile greenish to reddish-white, heart-shaped, 3–4mm long, with 2 crinkled bosses near the base as in Dark-red Helleborine. In shady, broad-leaved and coniferous woodland, to 1,700m, usually on limestone. In S Europe. Fl 5–8.

Dark-red Helleborine *Epipactis atrorubens* A plant with stems 20–80cm, with 5–11 oval foliage leaves, usually more than 5cm long and well separated into 2 rows. Inflorescence elongated, 1-sided, with upper stem and flowers thickly covered with short hairs. Flowers purplish to brownish-red, nodding, vanilla-scented, with pointed perianth segments; sepals roughly triangular and petals ovate. The lip is 5–6.5mm long, the same colour or slightly lighter: hypochile cup-shaped, reddish inside and out, epichile broader than long with recurved tip, bosses and central ridge pale to dark violet. Cross-pollinated. In open woodland and on stony slopes in mountain areas to 2,200m, on calcareous soils, throughout Europe. Fl 5–8. **Small-flowered Helleborine** *Epipactis parviflora* is similar to above, but more delicate with stems 15–50cm. Stalks and leaves shading to violet, not red. Flowers small, with sepals and petals about 5mm long, greenish to pale brown, and strongly incurved. Cross-pollinated. In open pinewoods and oakwoods in mountain regions, 1,200–1,500m, on calcareous soils, in E Spain. Fl 5–6.

Violet Limodore *Limodorum abortivum* A species with no green leaves; stout stems 30–90cm, dingy purple with only sheathing scale-leaves. Inflorescence lax, 10–30cm long, with 4–25 flowers; bracts longer than ovaries. Flowers pale or reddish-violet with darker veins (rarely white): perianth segments about 2cm long with sepals rather broad and petals much narrower and a little shorter. Lip yellowish and violet, margin wavy; large, triangular epichile, constricted hypochile, spur slender, 1.5–2.5cm, as long as ovary. In bushy grassland, shady banks in pinewoods and mixed woodland, invariably near growing pines on calcareous soils; in the Mediterranean, northwards into warmer parts of S Europe. Fl 4–7. Ssp *trabutianum* is a more slender species with stems to 50cm, violet flowers hardly opening, lip spoon-shaped and not constricted near base; spur short (only 1–4mm long). In open pinewoods and oakwoods, and in scrub often growing with Violet Limodore; in S Spain, SW France and the west of N Africa.

Broad-leave
Helleborine (le

Small-leave
Helleborine (rig

Dark-red Helleborin
(le

Violet Limodore (righ

Ghost Orchid *Epipogium aphyllum* A plant seldom more than 25cm, with no green leaves; only 2–5 brownish scales sheath a pink stem. Rhizome covered in scale-leaves with many short-lobed branches and 1–2 narrow stolons. Inflorescence lax with 1–6 flowers, comparatively large for the plant's size. Flowers short-stalked, ovary not twisted; lip uppermost. Perianth segments yellowish to pale reddish, curving downwards, of about equal length (8–15cm). Lip whitish or pinkish with reddish-violet spots, 3-lobed with upward-pointing middle lobe. Spur thick, 3–5mm, often bent. Sometimes flowering below ground. In shady beechwoods and pinewoods in montane zone, especially in the south; known from a large part of Europe but very rare. Fl 7–8.

Bird's-nest Orchid *Neottia nidus-avis* A honey-brown plant with stems 20–45cm, sheathing scale-leaves and no green leaves: below ground is a tangled creeping rhizome like a bird's nest. Inflorescence many-flowered, less dense towards the base. Flowers-yellowish brown, short-stalked; sepals and petals similar, 4–6mm long. Lip 12mm long, convex near the base and deeply divided at the tip into 2 rounded, spreading lobes. In shady beechwoods, and mixed pinewoods to 2,000m on nutrient- and base-rich soils; widespread in Europe, in montane woods in the south. Fl 5–7.

Twayblade *Listera ovata* A plant with very hairy stems, 20–60cm, usually with 2 (1 or 3) ovate foliage leaves, 4–13cm × 3–8cm, almost opposite, low on stem. Inflorescence lax with 20–80 flowers and short bracts. Flowers yellowish-green, perianth segments of about equal length, curved forwards: sepals about twice the width of petals. Lip 7–15mm with blunt lobes. In woodland scrub, meadows, poor grasslands and fenland, to 2,000m, on damp, base-rich soils; widespread and relatively common in Europe, rare in the Mediterranean. Fl 5–7.

Autumn Lady's-tresses *Spiranthes spiralis* A very short species with stems 5–20cm, (exceptionally more). The rosette of ovate-elliptical leaves for the following season's flowering stem grows alongside the current stem and overwinters, withering before flowering. Inflorescence fairly dense, lax, with 6–30 scented, greenish-white flowers held horizontally in 1 spiral row. Perianth segments 4–7mm long, sepals glandular outside; lateral sepals spread slightly while the middle one forms a tube with the petals. Lip 4–7mm long, greenish with a white edge. In poor meadows and pasture, often in short turf, and in pinewoods in the Mediterranean on base-rich and acidic soils; widespread. Fl 8–10.

Summer Lady's-tresses *Spiranthes aestivalis* A plant with stems 10-40cm, slightly glandular in upper part; 3–6 basal foliage leaves, upright, linear-lanceolate, up to 12cm long. Inflorescence fairly lax, 3–10cm long with 6–20 flowers, horizontal in 1 spiral row. Flowers differ from those of Autumn Lady's-tresses in being pure white, with all perianth segments forming a tube which opens slightly at the end. Lip 6–7mm long, tongue-shaped, yellowish towards the base; front edge notched and turned downwards. In fenland, to 1,400m, often associated with limestone tufa and decreasing because of habitat loss. In W and central Mediterranean areas, northwards into W and central Europe. Fl 6–8.

Two-leaved Gennaria *Gennaria diphylla* A plant with a single tuber and stems 10–50cm, often in clumps because new tubers form at tips of runners. Foliage leaves 2, arranged alternately; the lower wide, heart-shaped, 4–12cm × 2.5–8cm, clasping the stem, the upper similar but smaller. Inflorescence dense, 1-sided, up to 13cm long, carrying 10–45 flowers. Perianth segments of similar length 3.5–4mm; sepals green pointing forwards, petals yellow-green with tips curved backwards. Lip yellow-green with 3 lobes: lateral lobes shorter and thinner than middle lobe. Spur pouched, grooved, 1.5mm long. In broad-leaved, evergreen or coniferous woods, garrigue and shady gullies; in Sardinia, Corsica and near the coast in the W Mediterranean to Madeira and the Canary Islands. Fl 1–4.

Greater Butterfly-orchid *Platanthera chlorantha*   A plant with 2 tubers; stems 20–80cm, with 2 (3) large, elliptical to ovate foliage leaves near the ground and 1–4 small leaves higher up. Inflorescence fairly lax, many-flowered, up to 25cm long. Flowers scented, white, often with a pale-greenish or yellowish tinge; central sepal broad, heart-shaped, 6.5–10mm long, forming a 'helmet' with the 2 petals, lateral sepals spreading, generally twisted with a wavy edge, 9–12mm long. Lip tongue-shaped, 9–18mm long, bent downwards or backwards, intensely coloured near the tip. Spur 1.8–4cm long, flattened at the sides but broadening towards the tip. Anthers held at an angle to one another, further apart at base than at free ends. In damp open woodland and meadows, often on limestone; widespread, mainly in mountains in S Europe and the Mediterranean region. Fl 5–8. **Lesser Butterfly-orchid** *P. bifolia* is similar but more slender in appearance. Flowers smaller, more sweetly scented, lateral sepals flatter and less twisted. Stamens parallel and close together, spur not widened towards the tip. In open woodland, poor meadows and heaths up to 2,300m, often in acidic conditions; widespread in mountains in S Europe. Fl 5–8.

Frog Orchid *Coeloglossum viride*, Small White Orchid *Leuchorchis albida*, Fragrant Orchid *Gymnadenia conopsea* and Creeping Lady's-tresses *Goodyera repens* are all widespread in Europe. They grow in the northern part of the region covered by this book but only in montane areas.

Barton's Orchid *Dactylorhiza insularis*   A plant with 2 ovate tubers, slightly forked at the tip, stem 20–50cm, with 6–8 light-green foliage leaves spread out up the stem not in a rosette. Inflorescence fairly lax, with up to 20 flowers, cylindrical in shape; bracts about as long as or shorter than the flowers. Flowers lemon yellow, lateral sepals spread horizontally or held upwards at an angle, 7–10mm long, central sepal slightly shorter and curving over lateral petals. Lip 5–9mm long, almost flat, 3-lobed with middle lobe almost as large as the laterals and reddish-brown spots or blotches towards its base. Spur cylindrical, 1.5–2mm thick, straight, held horizontally. In pinewoods and sweet-chestnut woods in Italy, Sardinia, Corsica and Spain, and the W Mediterranean basin. Fl 4–6.

Roman Orchid *Dactylorhiza romana*   A plant with 2 ovate-spherical tubers, forked to at most a third of their length; stem 15–35cm. Foliage leaves (3–7) in a basal rosette with 1–3 smaller stem leaves. Inflorescence dense, many-flowered, ovate-cylindrical in shape; bracts somewhat longer than the flowers. Lateral sepals erect and turned outwards, 6–10mm long, central sepal slightly shorter, curving over lateral petals which are wider. Lip 7.5–12mm × 1–1.8cm wide, fairly flat, 3-lobed with raised middle lobe. Spur cylindrical, 1–1.5mm thick, bent to point vertically up. Flowers can be entirely yellow or magenta with flesh- and cream- coloured intermediates or mixed colour forms, such as magenta with yellow on the lip, in the same population. In open woodland and maquis, up to 2,000m on base-rich or weakly acid soils, in E and central Mediterranean region. Fl 3–6. **Sicilian Orchid** *D. markusii* is similar to above, but differs in flowers, which occur only in yellow; spur shorter (7–15mm), held up at an angle, not erect. In Siciliy, Sardinia and Italy. Fl 3–6.

Elder-flowered Orchid *Dactylorhiza sambucina*   A plant with 2 ovate tubers forked to not more than half-way; stems 10–30cm and hollow. Foliage leaves 4–7, arranged along the stem or forming a loose rosette. Inflorescence ovate, dense and many-flowered. Flowers elder-scented, yellow, magenta, intermediate or a mixture. Lateral sepals upright or protruding at an angle, central sepal inclined over the petals. Lip 8–11mm × 1.1–1.7cm wide, elliptical, folded, barely 3-lobed (lips of yellow flowers spotted with orange in horseshoe pattern). Spur cylindrical–tapering, 1–1.5cm long, and curving downwards. In open woodland, poor pasture and meadows, to 2,000m; widespread in high mountain regions of S Europe and the Mediterranean. Fl 3–7.

Robust Marsh Orchid *Dactylorhiza elata* A stately species with hollow stems 30–125cm. Foliage leaves (5–10), ovate-lanceolate, unspotted, up to 25cm long, along the lower half of the stem. Inflorescence long and many-flowered, bracts longer than flowers; flowers lilac-pink to dark purplish-red with lateral sepals 9–18mm long, turned up and twisted, often spotted. Lip 3-lobed, with small middle lobe and lateral lobes usually turned down with horseshoe pattern of dots and markings. In wet meadows and hillside flushes on base-rich soils, to 2,500m, in W Mediterranean. Fl 4–7.

Dense-flowered Orchid *Neotinea intacta* A small plant, 10–30cm, with 4–6 foliage leaves, bluish-green, spotted or unspotted; 1–4 form a rosette, the others sheath the stem. Inflorescence 2–8cm long, dense, many-flowered; bracts shorter than the ovaries. Flowers small, scented and various shades of greenish-white through pinkish to brownish-white; sepals, 3–4mm long, form a hood with the petals. Lip mostly red-marked, 3-lobed: middle lobe downward-pointing, rectangular, 3-toothed at apex, lateral lobes shorter, narrow, linear and spreading. Spur conical, 1–2mm long. In coniferous woods, garrigue and scrubby grassland to 1,600m, on limestone, in the Mediterranean region; also Atlantic islands. Fl 3–5.

Man Orchid *Aceras anthropophorum* A plant 10–40cm, with 4–9 foliage leaves. Lower leaves close together rosette-like; upper ones sheath the stem. Inflorescence narrow, cylindrical, many-flowered and dense with bracts shorter than the ovaries. Flowers have greenish-yellow tint, to varying intensity, with brownish-red. Sepals and petals make a hood with sepal-edges tinted reddish. Lip 1.2–1.5cm, deeply 3-lobed, pendent with 2 swellings near the base. Lateral lobes form 'arms': middle lobe divided to form 'legs'. No spur. Mainly in W and central Mediterranean, spreading in W and central Europe. Fl 3–6.

Bug Orchid *Orchis coriophora* A plant with stems 15–40cm, often in clumps of 2–3. Leaves 4–10, narrowly lanceolate and folded. Inflorescence 5–15cm, oblong, dense, many–flowered, bracts with 1 vein. Flowers brown, red, pink or greenish, with sickly scent (bed bugs). Perianth segments grow together to form a beaked hood. Lateral sepals 6.5–10mm long, the middle one slightly shorter; petals 4–6mm long. Lip dark purple-red with greenish streaks, or greenish; lighter-spotted area near base, 3-lobed, 5–7mm long; lateral lobes slightly toothed and shorter than the middle lobe. Spur conical, downward-pointing, half the length of the ovary. In damp meadows, on slightly acid soils, up to 2,500m; in Cévennes (S France), and N Spain. Fl 5–6. Ssp *fragrans* is more common than above, more substantial; central lobe of lip noticeably longer than lateral lobes, spur about as long as ovary. On hillsides and garrigue, on calcareous soils, from the Mediterranean eastwards. Fl 4–6, after other *Orchis* species. Ssp *matrinii* is a robust plant with thick stems. In W and central Spain, Portugal, and Apulia (S Italy).

Loose-flowered Orchid *Orchis laxiflora* A plant with stems 20–100cm, with 3–8 lanceolate, channelled, unspotted leaves. Inflorescence lax, with 6–20 flowers; bracts have a reddish tinge and are shorter than the ovary. Flowers purplish-red (occasionally white); sepals 7–10mm, outward-spreading, petals 6–9mm, incurved to form a loose hood. Lip 7–9mm long, 3-lobed with the central lobe shorter than the laterals and forming a 'tooth' between them; laterals turned down to give the lip a folded appearance. Centre of lip white, unspotted, contrasting with reddish-purple of lateral lobes. Spur half to two-thirds the ovary's length, thickening to apex. In swamp, meadows and fens, on base-rich soils to 1,500m, often in abundance; from the Mediterranean into W Europe. Fl 4–6. *O. palustris* is similar in appearance to above, but differs most obviously in lip details: central lobe longer than the laterals which are hardly turned down, giving the lip a flatter appearance. Lip centre a lighter shade of purplish-red but not usually white-spotted. Spur tapers to apex. In similar habitats but flowering about 2 weeks later. Rare in the Mediterranean (occurs in Majorca). Fl 4–7.

Robust Marsh Orch
(le

Dense-flower
Orchid (cent

Man Orchid (rig

Bug Orchid s
fragrans (le

Loose-flower
Orchid (rig

Orchis palustris (le

Early-purple Orchid *Orchis mascula*   A species with a number of very distinct races, some of which are now regarded as separate species. A plant 20–50cm, with 3–5 leaves in the lower part and sheaths above; leaves broadly lanceolate, shiny green with dark purplish-brown spots. Bracts lanceolate, with 1–3 veins, shorter than the ovary. Inflorescence fairly dense, cylindrical, with 6–20 flowers smelling of cat's urine. Perianth segments mauve or reddish-purple; middle sepal curves with petals to form a hood with lateral sepals spreading or slightly reflexed. Lip 3-lobed: middle lobe notched at the apex and white with spots towards base; lateral lobes slightly deflexed if at all. Spur as long as ovary, slightly thickened at the end, horizontal or upward-pointing. In open woodlands, hillsides and cliff-tops; locally common in much of central, S and W Europe. **Fl** 4–6.

Orchis olbiensis   A slender species with unspotted leaves which more or less replaces above in the W Mediterranean. Stems 10–25cm, inflorescence lax with 5–12 flowers. Perianth segments pale pink or reddish; lateral sepals turned outwards. Middle lobe of lip 1½ times the length of lateral lobes, pale with fine purple spots at the centre. Spur longer than ovary, upward-pointing. Flowers lack cat's-urine odour. In W Mediterranean: Spain, Balearics, S France, Corsica and Italy (Liguria). **Fl** 3–6. Ssp *ichnusae* is similar to O. *olbiensis*, but spur is short and straight. Sardinian endemic. **Fl** 4–5. *O langei* (also known as O. *mascula ssp hispanica*) has a lax, many-flowered inflorescence. Sepals and petals blunt-ended, purple; middle lobe of lip only slightly longer than laterals. Lip without markings or with fine dots only near base. In open oakwoods and pinewoods, up to 1,500m, on fairly dry, acid soils, in W Mediterranean region from the Pyrenees down through the Iberian Peninsula. **Fl** 4–6.

Pale-flowered Orchid *Orchis pallens*   A robust plant, 15–35cm, with 3–4 broadly oblong, unspotted leaves below with 1–2 sheathing leaves higher up the stem. Inflorescence dense and many-flowered; bracts about as long as ovaries. Flowers yellow with dorsal sepal and laterals curving to form a loose helmet; lateral sepals 6–9mm long, held erect. Lip distinctly 3-lobed, unmarked, bright yellow, almost flat or slightly folded. Spur 7–14mm, cylindrical, horizontal or curving upwards. Flowers strongly scented of elder. In woods in mountain region of S Europe: Spain, French maritime Alps, into E Europe. **Fl** 4–6.

Provence Orchid *Orchis provincialis*   A slender plant with stems 15–35cm; 3–7 heavily spotted basal leaves and 2–3 sheathing above. Bracts narrow with 1–3 veins, longer or as long as ovaries. Inflorescence fairly lax, cylindrical, with 5–20 light-yellow flowers. Dorsal sepal more or less erect, laterals 9–14mm long, spreading, with petals curved to form partial hood. Lip 3-lobed, with middle lobe bent downwards in centre, lateral lobes folded downwards slightly; centre a brighter yellow than other perianth segments and flecked with red. Spur upward-curving, 1.3–1.9cm, with swollen, blunt end. In deciduous and coniferous woods and maquis to 1,700m, in the Mediterranean. **Fl** 4–6.

Sparse-flowered Orchid *Orchis pauciflora*   A plant with stems 10–30cm. Basal leaves (4–9) unspotted and channelled. Inflorescence lax with 3–7 flowers and bracts that are shorter than the ovary. Perianth segments pale yellow; lateral sepals, 10–14.5mm long, held vertically and turned outwards, central sepal inclined over the shorter petals. Lip darker yellow than the other segments with a few brownish-red spots, weakly 3-lobed with middle lobe indented. In poor grassland and garrigue, up to 1,700m, on dry, stony calcareous soils; in Gargano (Italy), Sardinia and the E Mediterranean. **Fl** 3–4.

Pale-flowered Orchi
(lef

Provence Orchi
(centre

Sparse-flowere
Orchid (righ

Fan-lipped Orchid *Orchis collina (O. saccata)* A rather thick-set, almost fleshy species, with stems 10-30cm, and a basal rosette of 2–6 oblong, ovate leaves with up to 4 sheathing the stem. Inflorescence lax, narrow-cylindrical, often few-flowered (4–15); bracts broadly lanceolate, tinged purple. Flowers pinkish to deep purplish-red, variously tinged with olive green and with a white basal area on the lip. Sepals elongated-lanceolate, 9–12mm × 3–4mm; the central one forms a hood with the petals while the laterals point vertically and turn outwards. Lip entire, fan-shaped, with wavy margin coloured brownish-red, lilac, pink, greenish or whitish. Spur short (5–7mm), conical, pointing downwards at an angle. In open woodland, garrigue and poor grassland in the S Mediterranean: Spain, Majorca, Italy (Mt Gargano), Sicily, Sardinia; rare in France. **Fl** 2–4.

Spitzel's Orchid *Orchis spitzellii* A plant 20–50cm, with basal rosette or cluster of 2–7 ovate-lanceolate leaves; stems erect or slightly flexuous. Inflorescence usually dense with 10–35 flowers. Dorsal sepals and petals slightly curved to form a hood; lateral sepals erect or incurving, ovate, 7–11mm long. Sepals tinted olive on inner surface with reddish tinge and spotting. Lip pink and spotted red, without white basal area, 3-lobed; middle lobe indented with a wavy margin and lateral lobes sometimes turned under it. Spur conical, 6–10mm (only just shorter than ovary), 3–4mm thick, curving downwards. Lip base curved to spur mouth to produce broad opening. In mountain grasslands, pine- and beech-woodlands up to 1,800m, always on calcareous soils; wide but discontinuous distribution in Mediterranean and N Africa: Spain and the French and Italian Alps. **Fl** 4–7.

Green-spotted Orchid *Orchis patens* A stately species with stems 25–45cm. Basal leaves (3–5) in a rosette and 1–3 leaves sheathing the stem. Inflorescence lax, with 5–20 flowers; bracts about as long as ovaries. Sepals ovate, 9–11mm, with a green-spotted centre and coloured rim; dorsal sepal curved forwards, laterals held upwards at a steep angle. Lip pale to intense purplish-pink with paler, spotted central region; deeply 3-lobed with divided middle lobe folded lengthwise. Spur 6–8mm × 4–4.6mm, conical, rounded, held horizontal or downwards. Lip base cut with 'V' notch near spur mouth; which has 'stepped sides'. In open woods of sweet chestnut, oak and cedar (N Africa) and poor grassland. Distribution limited to 2 centres: Liguria (Italy), Algeria and Tunisia. **Fl** 3–6.

Pink Butterfly-orchid *Orchis papilionacea* A plant 15–40cm, with 3–8 leaves in a basal rosette and 2–5 sheathing the stem. Inflorescence dense to fairly lax with 4–10 flowers; flower bracts reddish-tinged, longer than the ovary. Perianth segments deep reddish with darker veins, forward-pointing, not forming enclosed hood. Lip not divided, broadening from a narrow claw to a broad limb with crenate margin, often upturned at sides. Colour and size of lip varies with race: (a) average-sized flowers, with lip 1.2–1.7cm long, wedge-shaped limb with reddish-violet surface, whitish near the claw; occasionally called var. *rubra*. In the central Mediterranean region. (b) Large flowers, with lip 1.5–2.6cm long, with a broad fan-shaped limb, heart-shaped near the base, pink with markings radiating to the margin like fan segments: var. *grandiflora*. In W and S-central Mediterranean: Spain, S France, S Italy, Sicily; also in N Africa. In poor grassland, garrigue and open woodland, on fairly dry, base-rich soils, to 1,800m. **Fl** 2–5.

Fan-lipped Orchid (le

Spitzel's Orchid (rig

Green-spotted Orchi
(righ

Pink Butterfly-orchi
(left

Four-spotted Orchid *Orchis quadripunctata* A slender species, 10–30cm, with 2–6 foliage leaves in a rosette and 1–2 long sheathing leaves up the stem. Inflorescence dense to lax, cylindrical, with 8–30 pink or purplish-red flowers; bracts shorter to as long as ovaries. Sepals ovate, 4–7mm long, spreading in same plane. Petals 2–5mm long, curved inwards to form a hood. Lip very variable, 4–7.5mm × 6–11mm, deeply 3-lobed to almost entire; basal area white with 2 or more spots in front and 2 at the spur entrance. Spur 8–14mm, very narrow, turned downwards. In poor grassland, maquis and garrigue, up to 1,500m, on dry, stony soils on limestone; in S Italy eastwards to Turkey and Cyprus. Fl 3–6. **Branciforti's Orchid** *O. brancifortii*, formerly regarded as a variety of above, has shorter stems, 10–25cm, and smaller flowers. Sepals spread widely; laterals 3–5mm long. Lip 3.5–5.5mm long, with a rectangular middle lobe about twice as long as broad, and thin spreading lateral lobes. Spur more or less horizontal, bent into a shallow 'S'. In similar habitats to above, endemic to N Sicily and E Sardinia. Fl 4–6.

Green-winged Orchid *Orchis morio* A variable species with stems 10–50cm, and 5–9 broadly lanceolate leaves in the basal rosette and several as sheaths crowding the stem. Inflorescence lax with 5–25 flowers. Perianth segments converge to form a hood: the lip is rather broad, 3-lobed and almost folded in 2. Flower colour very variable from white through greenish to reddish-pink or purplish-violet. Lateral sepals usually suffused with green and prominently veined. Spur cylindrical with a stub tip about half the ovary's length, horizontal or slightly upward-pointing. Usually but not exclusively, on calcareous soils in open woodland, meadow and on dunes; widespread throughout Europe. Fl 3–6. Ssp *picta* is the name sometimes given to Mediterranean races where plants have smaller tepals than described above (6–8mm compared with 8–10mm) and a lip that is not as folded; the spur tapers gently to the apex. Flowers generally pale but darkflowered races with these characteristics exist. **Champagne Orchid** *O. chapagneuxii* grows in clumps where each plant (10–25cm) produces 2 new tubers on stolons. Sepals 6–8mm in length. Lip has pink to purplish–pink folded lateral lobes but the middle is white and unspotted. The spur is longer and more slender than in Green-winged Orchid. (1–1.5cm long), slightly curved and directed upwards. In open woodland, scrub and poor meadows in the Balearics, Spain and S France. Fl 4–6. **Long-spurred Orchid** *O. longicornu* is 10–35cm, with 6–8 oblong-lanceolate leaves in a basal rosette and upper leaves in a series of sheaths that crowd the stem. Very similar to above but differs in lip details: lateral lobes are mostly dark, purplish-red (although pink or red plants are known); central part of the lip is clearly spotted in the colour of the lateral lobes. Plants produce only a single new tuber each year. Both species have a long upturned spur with a thickened tip. In similar habitats in Sicily, Sardinia, S Corsica, Balearics and Calabria (S Italy). Fl 4–6.

Milky Orchid *Orchis lactea* A plant 10–20cm, with 3–8 light-green foliage leaves in a rosette and 1–3 leaves sheathing the stem. Inflorescence dense, ovoid to elongated with a whiskered appearance owed to the long fine points on the tepals; bracts about as long as the ovaries. Perianth segments whitish or pink with prominent dark-red veining, always with a green centre, curving to form a hood. The lip is 3-lobed, 8–11mm long, with a divided mid-lobe, and white or cream centre with fine red or purplish spots and more intensely coloured lobes. Spur 5–8mm long, cylindrical, curving downwards. In open woodland, garrigue and poor grassland, up to 1,200m, on dry calcareous soils, in central Mediterranean (absent from Iberian Peninsula), eastwards to Turkey. Fl 2–4. *O. conica* is the name given to plants from Spain, and the Balearics, differing in a longer, cylindrical inflorescence, shorter lip and sepals without a green centre drawn into longer, finer points. In similar habitats in the W Mediterranean. Fl 2–4.

Four-spotted Orch
(le

Green-winged Orch
(rig

Branciforti's Orchi
(lef

Champagne Orchi
(lef

Long-spurred Orchi
(centre

Milky Orchid (righ

Toothed Orchid *Orchis tridentata*   A plant with stems 15–45cm, with 3–5 bluish-green, unspotted foliage leaves in a rosette, and 1–2 leaves sheathing the stem. Inflorescence usually spherical with perianth segments curving to form a hood; sepals purplish-pink with darker veins, ovate, 8–13mm long with a short point; petals narrow, tongue-shaped, 5–8mm long. Lip pink, heavily red-spotted, deeply 3-lobed with lateral lobes spreading outwards. Middle lobe more or less triangular, divided into 2 lobules with serrated edges and a 'tooth' between them. In poor meadows, open woodland and garrigue, to 1,500m, on base-rich soils in S, SE and central Europe. **Fl 3–6.**

Monkey Orchid *Orchis simia*   A plant with stems 20–45cm, with 2–5 foliage leaves and 1–2 stem-sheathing leaves. Inflorescence dense and many-flowered, ovate to cylindrical, flowers opening from top downwards: bracts 1–4mm long. Perianth segments curve to form a hood with turned-up points: whitish to pale-lilac outside, spotted and veined lilac inside. Lip deeply 3-lobed with a narrow rectangular pale-coloured central part dotted with red. Lateral lobes and middle-lobe tongues narrow (about 1mm wide) with rounded ends and intense purple or carmine. Spur 4–8mm long, cylindrical, downward-pointing. In poor grassland, open woods and garrigue, to 1,200m, on dry calcareous soils, throughout the Mediterranean and into W, central, and E Europe. **Fl 3–6.**

Military Orchid *Orchis militaris*   A plant with stems 25–45cm, with 3–5 foliage leaves in a rosette and 1–2 leaves sheathing the stem. Inflorescence dense, becoming more lax, with 10–40 flowers; perianth segments curve to form a hood, lilac-red on the outside, purplish-red veins and pale spots inside. Lip pink to purplish-red with pale centre and groups of dark hairs; deeply 3-lobed with lateral lobes, linear turned inwards, middle lobe narrow, dividing into 'legs' at the apex. Ground colour varies from white through to deep pink. In undisturbed calcareous grassland, open woodlands and thickets; widespread in S Europe. **Fl 4–6.**

Naked-man Orchid *Orchis italica*   A plant with stems 20–50cm, with 5–10 foliage leaves in a rosette and 2–4 leaves sheathing the stem. Inflorescence dense and many-flowered, spherical to shortly cylindrical. Flowers whitish-pink with darker veining on the perianth and more intense colouring on the tips of the lip. Perianth segments form a loose hood; lip 1.2–1.9cm long, deeply 3-lobed with lateral lobes and tongues of middle lobe long-pointed. In poor grassland, open woods and garrigue, to 1,200m, on dry to damp base-rich soils; throughout the Mediterranean. **Fl 3–5.**

Lady Orchid *Orchis purpurea*   A plant with stems 30–90cm tall with 3–6 unspotted, shiny foliage leaves near the ground and 1–2 leaves sheathing the stem. Inflorescence dense and many flowered, bracts 1.5–3mm long. Perianth segments curve to form a brownish-red hood. Lip paler with numerous tufts of brownish-red hairs. Lip 3-lobed and very variable: lateral lobes curved with blunt ends forming arms; the middle lobe can be divided to form broad 'legs', or almost entire with an apical 'notch' to form a skirt. In woods and woodland edges, garrigue and poor grassland; widespread in S Europe but rare in the Mediterranean. **Fl 4–6.**

Burnt Orchid *Orchis ustulata*   A plant with stems 10–30cm, with 5–9 foliage leaves which increase in size up the stem; the lower ones tend to form a rosette and the upper ones sheath the stem. Inflorescence many-flowered, long to short, cylindrical, dense at the top, opening below. Perianth segments curve to form a hood that is blackish-brown outside; unopened buds form the 'burnt tip'. Lip 5–8mm long, white with red dots, deeply 3-lobed, with spreading linear lateral lobes and a divided, rectangular central lobe. In poor grassland and meadows up to 2,000m, on dry to moist base-rich or neutral soils; widespread in S Europe but rare in the Mediterranean. **Fl 4–7 (8).**

Toothed Orchid (le

Military Orchid (rig

Monkey Orchid (lef

Naked-man Orchi
(lef

Lady Orchid (centre

Burnt Orchid (right

Pyramidal Orchid *Anacamptis pyramidalis*   A plant 20–80cm, with 4–10 foliage leaves, the lower ones narrow-lanceolate, the upper ones scale-like. Inflorescence pyramidal, becoming spherical to ovoid as flowers open. Flowers light pink to dark purplish-red (some E Mediterranean populations of var. *brachystachis* white). Dorsal sepal and petals curve inwards to form a hood; lateral sepals spread widely. Lip deeply 3-lobed with 2 longitudinal ridges at its base: lateral lobes shorter or as long as middle lobe. Spur 1–1.5cm × 0.5mm thick. In open woodland, scrub and limestone grassland to 2,000m; widespread in Europe. Fl 3–7.

Giant Orchid *Barlia robertiana*   A robust species with 2 large, ovoid tubers, stems 25–85cm. Foliage leaves (5–10) light shiny green, up to 30cm × 10cm. Inflorescence iris-scented, dense, many-flowered, 6–23cm long; lower bracts prominent, longer than flowers. Lateral sepals concave, slightly spreading, forming a hood with petals. Lip 1.3–2cm long, distinctly 3-lobed: lateral lobes have wavy outer edges forming scythe-shaped 'arms', middle lobe divided bearing 2 longitudinal ridges. Flower varying from greenish through to purplish-brown with the lobes coloured and a whitish basal area. Spur cone-shaped, 4–6mm long, with a nectary near the tip. In open woodland, maquis, garrigue and poor grassland on base-rich soils, to 1,700m, in the Mediterranean. Fl 1–5.

Lizard Orchid *Himantoglossum hircinum*   A plant with stems 20-100cm, and numerous foliage leaves decreasing in size up the stem. Inflorescence dense, smelling of goats; with 40–100 flowers, appearing straggling because of spreading flower lips. Perianth segments curve to form a hood, greenish to brownish-white, with brownish-red veins inside; sepals ovate, petals linear. Lip 3-lobed with wavy border at the base, lobes yellowish-green to brownish-lilac: basal area white with reddish spots made up from tiny hairs. Lateral lobes 5–15mm, linear, pointed; middle lobe coiled in bud, twisting as it opens, 3–6cm long, with tip divided for 4–7mm. Spur cone-shaped, 3–7mm long. In poor grassland, scrub and on roadsides on calcareous soils in the W and central Mediterranean, northwards into W and central Europe. Fl 5–7. **Adriatic Lizard Orchid** *H. adriaticum* is similar to above, but inflorescence is more lax and fewer-flowered, scent faint. There are detailed lip differences: lateral lobes 1–2.5cm long, middle lobe has more pronounced division at tip up to 1.8cm. Spur shorter (2–3mm), conical. In impoverished grasslands in mountain regions, to 1,300m, in central and N Italy. Fl 5–6.

TONGUE-ORCHIDS *Serapias*   These plants have 2–5 ovoid tubers and narrow, channelled, usually shiny, leaves. Flowers are arranged in a spike with petals and sepals forming a tubular hood; the lip is in 2 parts with a lobed hypochile near the base and an epichile forming the 'tongue', which gives the plants their common name.

Scarce Serapias *Serapias neglecta*   A plant with 2 spherical tubers and a stem 10–30cm, unspotted. Basal leaves (1–2) scale-like, with 4–7 lanceolate foliage leaves 5.5–11cm long, often bent and folded. Inflorescence short and dense, with 2–8 flowers that look large for the plant's size. Bracts usually shorter than the hood, which is dull grey-violet to greenish on the outside; the visible part of the lip is broad (1.5–1.9cm), directed downwards or at an angle, and yellowish through salmon to pinkish-brown. In open pinewoods, garrigue, damp meadows and olive groves, often on fairly acid soils, up to 600m; along Ligurian sea-coast from Provence (Var) to Elba, Corsica and Sardinia. Fl 3–5.

Pyramidal Orchid (le

Adriatic Lizard Orch

(rig

Lizard Orchid (le

Giant Orchid (righ

Scarce Serapias (le

Heart-flowered Serapias *Serapias cordigera* A plant with stem 15–50cm, unspotted, with 1–2 basal scale-leaves. Foliage leaves 5–9, lanceolate, 7–16cm long. Inflorescence dense with 3–10 flowers (sometimes more) and bracts about as long as the sepal hood, which is grey-lilac with purple-red veins, and held upwards at an angle. Lip broad: epichile heart-shaped, 1.6–2.6cm at widest, and brownish-red to blackish-purple; hypochile has lateral lobes that protrude just beyond the sepal hood and 2 blackish 'humps' (callosities) at the point of attachment. In open woodland, maquis, garrigue and damp meadows up to 1,000m, on base-rich (also lime-free) soils. In the Mediterranean region, east to Crete and W Anatolia. Fl 4–5.

Hybrid Serapias *Serapias olbia* A plant with 3 (4) spherical tubers; those of the current year with long stalks. Propagates vegetatively to produce flower stalks in groups with stems 10–20cm, often spotted on lower part. Foliage leaves 5–7, narrow, lanceolate with 2 scale-like basal leaves. Inflorescence lax, with 2–5 flowers; bracts much shorter than the vertically angled sepal hood, which is grey-lilac outside and darker within. Lip 2.3–3.1cm long, with 2 nearly parallel, purple callosities at the point of attachment; pointed tip bent strongly backwards, densely hairy, blackish-purple to brownish-red. In damp meadows, dune-hollows and slate slopes, near coast on acid soils; in S France (Var and Alpes-Maritimes). Fl 4–5.

Plough-share Serapias *Serapias vomeracea* A plant with 2 spherical tubers and stems 20–60cm, sometimes spotted. Foliage leaves 4–7, narrow, lanceolate, with 2 basal scale-leaves. Inflorescence lax, with 3–10 flowers; sepal hood grey-lilac, pointing steeply upward. The lip has a lanceolate epichile (the 'plough-share'), 2–2.8cm long, ranging from 5–8mm at the base to 8–13mm across the centre. The hypochile has 2 purple callosities at its base and lateral lobes that barely emerge from the hood. Lip points downwards or curves back, is densely hairy towards its centre and rust-red to brownish-violet (rarely ochre). In open pine and chestnut woodland, garrigue, poor grassland, damp meadows and olive groves to 1,000m, on basic or weakly acid soils; in the Mediterranean region to southern foot of the Alps. Fl 3–6. Ssp *laxiflora* (*S. bergonii*) has lax, often curved inflorescence with 4–12 flowers. Bracts often longer than upward-angled sepal hood, which is greyish-lilac outside. Lip has lanceolate epichile, bent backwards, not hairy, and ranging from 3.5–5mm wide at the base to 4–7.5mm at the middle. Colour dull brownish-red to dull ochre. Mainly eastern with isolated populations in Sicily (Ragusa province) and N Italy (Parma Siena and Grossete). Fl 3–6. **Eastern Serapias**, *Serapias orientalis* is similar to Plough-share Serapias but usually shorter with a broader lip. Stems 10–30cm. The lip has an epichile 1.8–2.6cm × 1–1.4(–2)cm across the middle, variable in colour from pale yellow through ochre to brick red and purplish. In garrigue, poor grassland and damp meadows to 1,000m, with preference for calcareous soils; in Gargano (Apulia) and Palermo (Sicily), then east to Asia Minor. Fl 3–7. **Sardinian Serapias** *Serapias nurrica* is closely related to Plough-share Serapias ssp *laxiflora* with similar flower dimensions. Endemic, recently discovered (1974) on the islands of Sardinia (Sassari province) and Corsica (Porto Vecchio). Inflorescence short and dense with 5–8 flowers. Lip distinctively 2-coloured, with a brownish-red centre and narrow, dull-lilac border. In garrigue near coast on various rock types (not limestone). Fl 4–6.

Small-flowered Serapias *Serapias parviflora* A small plant with stems 10–30cm, spotted below. Foliage leaves 4–5, narrow, lanceolate and channelled. Inflorescence lax, with 3–5 flowers; bracts about as long as the upwardly angled sepal hood. Lip 1.4–1.9cm long: hypochile 8–10mm long; epichile lanceolate, 7–11mm × 2.5–3mm at the outset, to 3.5–4.5mm across the middle. Lip directed downwards or backwards, sparsely hairy, dull red to yellowish in colour. In open pinewoods, garrigue, damp meadows up to 1,000m, on basic to weakly acid soils; throughout the Mediterranean region and along the French Atlantic coast to the department of Morbihan. Fl 4–6.

Tongue-orchid *Serapias lingua*   A plant with 2 or 3 spherical tubers; current ones are stalked, enabling clumps to form by vegetative propagation. Stems 10–35cm, sometimes spotted below, with 1 or 2 basal scale-leaves and 4–8 lanceolate foliage leaves. Inflorescence lax, with 2–8 flowers; bracts shorter than the sepal hood which is pale to intense greyish-lilac outside. At the base of the lip is a single purple 'hump' (all other *Serapias* have 2). The purplish-red lateral lobes of the hypochile extend beyond the sepal hood; epichile broad (7–12mm at the widest), pointing downwards, surface sparsely hairy and coloured from yellow through lilac to deep brick red. In open woodland, garrigue and wet meadows, often, but not exclusively, on base-rich soils, from the Mediterranean region into Dordogne (central France). Fl 3–6.

Tongue-orchid (left

Tongue-orchid (right

BEE ORCHIDS *Ophrys*   A genus that is highly adapted for insect pollination, both in its appearance and in its production of scents which mimic the sexual attractants (pheromones) of small female bees. Faithfulness of pollinators to 1 or a few species with separate distributions has meant insect and plant have evolved together. The genus is in a state of active evolution and the taxonomy is often confusing. Here groups of closely related species are considered.

All *Ophrys* are characterized by their paired tubers, one being used to produce the current leaves and flowering stem, the other in the process of formation of the next year's growth. Most leaves are in a basal rosette with a few sheathing the stem; they vary from ovate through to broadly lanceolate. Flowers are comparatively few but the dominant feature is a rather fleshy, spurless lip. This can be 3-lobed or entire, is usually hairy, and often carries a pattern of varying complexity even within members of the same species. The pattern often encloses a mirror or speculum in shiny blue, purple or brown, which is thought to resemble the reflections from the closed wings of female bees.

In leaf, *Ophrys* are remarkably similar to each other, though close assocation with plants in the field eventually enables the botanist to tell species apart when flowers are not present. Thus descriptions given below rely heavily on relative dimensions of inner lateral tepals (called petals below as distinct from third petal or lip); outer tepals (sepals); and the lip, together with lip division and patterning.

Dull Ophrys (left)

Rainbow Ophrys (right)

THE *FUSCA* GROUP

Dull Ophrys *Ophrys fusca*   A plant with stem 10–35cm tall and 2–9 flowers. Sepals green petals yellowish to olive, two-thirds to four-fifths the sepal's length. Lip dark brown to blackish-violet with a longitudinal groove at the base; border smooth, same colour as lip or yellow in some populations. In open pinewoods, garigue and poor grassland to 1,400m, on calcareous soils; widespread in the Mediterranean, northwards to Massif Central in France. Fl 12–6 (depending on latitude). Ssp *vasconica* has blackish-purple lip with brown pattern sometimes with paler marbling. In S France (Gers).

Rainbow Ophrys *Ophrys iricolor*   A plant with stem 10–35cm and 1–5 flowers. Flowers comparatively large; sepals green, 1.1–1.8cm long, petals 8–12mm long. Lip velvety blackish-violet, 1.5–2.3cm, slightly arched with basal longitudinal groove; underside reddish. Pattern 2 ovate intense iris-blue areas with faint blackish or purplish marking, usually borderless. In open pinewoods and garrigue, on calcareous marls; widespread in E Mediterranean from Italy eastwards. Fl 2–4.

Atlas Ophrys *Ophrys atlantica* is similar in size and colouring to above, but lip is narrowly pinched at the base and strongly convex (arching forwards). Sepals yellowish-green, ovate, 1.1–1.5cm × 5–8mm, middle sepal bent forward; petals greenish, tongue-shaped, 8.5–8.8mm long, hairless, bent backwards and with wavy edges. Lip 1.5–2cm long, blackish-purple, velvety with short hairs. Pattern plain grey to bluish-violet. In coniferous woodland, bushy grassland and garrigue up to 1,500m, on base-rich (not necessarily calcareous) soils in Malaga province (S Spain) and N Africa. **Fl** 3–6.

Pale Ophrys *Ophrys pallida* A small plant with stem 10–30cm. Sepals whitish to greenish, broadly ovate to elliptical 7.5–10mm 4.5–6.5mm broad – central strongly curved forward, lateral pointing sideways but slightly curving forwards at the ends. Petals greenish yellow to brownish, tongue-shaped, 5–7mm long. Lip brownish purple with greyish brown to violet area and marked central groove near base: distinctive feature – lip has two tiny side lobes and just where these are attached the lip bends sharply downwards at right angles. Pinewoods, garrigue up to 900m on calcareous soils, in W Sicily; also in Tunisia and E Algeria.

Omega Ophrys *Ophrys omegaifera dyris* This is now divided into 3 sub-species occupying different parts of the Mediterranean area. Spanish plants correspond to ssp *dyris*. Sepals green with central one curving forward strongly, 11.5–17mm long; petals half to four-fifths the sepal's length, yellowish-green or brownish with wavy edge. Lip 3-lobed with lateral-lobes curled under, surface brownish-red separated from the brownish-lilac area near its base by a whitish or lilac 'W' (the Greek 'omega'). In woodland, garrigue and poor grassland to 1,800m, in W Mediterranean: Spain from the south, northwards to Catalonia. **Fl** 12–5.

Yellow Ophrys *Ophrys lutea* A plant with stems 10–25cm with 1–4 flowers. Sepals 1.1–1.3cm long, greenish, with central sepal curved forwards; petals greenish-yellow, 7–8mm long, sticking out sideways at right angles, often with wavy edge. Lip 3-lobed with flattened, bright shiny yellow hairless edges up to 6mm wide; centre dark brown to brownish-violet, not spreading into border, with shiny-brown to dark violet basal area. In open woodland, garrigue on base-rich, usually calcareous, soils; widespread in the W central and Mediterranean region. **Fl** 2–5. Ssp *galilea (var. minor)* is one of a number of subspecies. Plants have smaller flowers: sepals 7–10mm long, petals 4.5–7.5mm long. Border shiny yellow or yellowish-green, 2–3mm broad. The dark colouring in the central lip lobe spreads at the apex to form an inverted 'V'. In the Mediterranean, from Italy eastwards. **Fl** 1–6. Ssp *melena* is similar to ssp *galilea*, but dark colouring spreads over lip surface leaving only a fine yellow margin if any. In Italy (Gargano) and E Mediterranean. **Fl** 3–4.

Sawfly Ophrys *Ophrys tenthredinifera* A plant 10–30cm, with 2 basal scale-leaves, 3–5 leaves in a basal rosette and 1–4 sheathing the stem. Flowers 1–10; sepals red to pink, upright or directed backwards, ovate to elliptical, 1.1–1.3cm × 6.5–10mm; petals similarly coloured, small, triangular, 4-5mm long. Lip yellow to light brown with a reddish to deep-brown centre, trapezoid in shape, 1.1–1.3cm × 12–20mm; surface densely hairy, convex, with edges more or less spreading. Pattern small near basal area, and grey-lilac to bluish, with a whitish border. Basal protuberances 2, apical appendage pointing forwards with tuft of coarse hairs above. In open pinewoods, maquis and garrigue, on basic or slightly acid soils, throughout the Mediterranean. **Fl** 3–5.

Bee Ophrys *Ophrys apifera* The best known of all *Ophrys* species with remarkable bee-like flowers (ironically the only species that has evolved to depend on self-fertilization). Stems 20–50cm tall with 3–10 flowers. Flowers have sepals whitish through pink to red, reflexed, ovate-lanceolate, 1.1–1.7cm × 5–9mm. Petals pinkish to greenish, triangular, 2.5–7mm long. Lip rounded, deeply 3-lobed with chestnut-brown central lobe and a strongly reflexed apex which gives it a blunt appearance. Lateral lobes turned down, densely hairy. Pattern surrounding the basal area often extended, sometimes irregularly to give yellowish streaks on the lip; column with 2–3mm 'beak'. In open woodland, broad-leaved and coniferous, and in dry grasslands on base-rich soils; widespread throughout Europe and the Mediterranean. Fl 4–7. Several distinct varieties exist throughout the range of the species. Var. *bicolor* has yellowish or greyish lip in basal half and chestnut in the apical half. Most frequent in the Mediterranean region. Var. *chlorantha* also called var *flavescens*, has white sepals and a yellow lip on which a faint pattern is still visible. Var. *trollii* is sometimes called the Wasp Orchid because of its narrow, pointed lip with a distinctive yellowish and reddish-brown mottled and striped surface; the apex is not recurved. Occasional throughout W and S Europe. Var. *friburgensis* is a variant with much larger petals, coloured like the sepals and from two-thirds to equal their length. Lip smaller with reduced pattern; appendage points downwards and lateral-lobes smaller; slight variations on this theme have been named as var. *botteroni* and ssp *jurana*.

Fly Ophrys *Ophrys insectifera* A slender species, often difficult to see at first, with stems 15–40cm and 2–5 foliage leaves rather than a rosette. The flowers are remarkably insect-like. Sepals green, ovate, 6–9mm × 3–4mm concave and held erect or slightly forwards. Petals are purple-black, 4–6.5mm long and very narrow (forming the antennae to the 'fly'). The lip is dark brown with purplish tinge, 9–12mm × 6–10mm and deeply 3-lobed; the middle lobe is divided at the apex. The pattern is plain in the centre of the lip, varying from bluish-white through shiny blue to bluish-brown. There are 2 small black callosities near the lip base. In open pine- and beechwoods and poor grassland mostly on calcareous soils; throughout W and S Europe and northwards into Scandinavia. Fl 5–7. **Aymonin's Ophrys** *O. aymoninii* is closely enough related to above to be regarded often as ssp *aymoninii*. It differs principally in the shape and colouring of the flowers. Lateral lobes are spreading, triangular, making the lip as broad as it is long (9.5–12mm × 8.5–12mm). Lip dark brown but lacking the purplish hue; the distinctive feature is a bright-yellow border to the middle lobe, 1.5–2mm wide, and yellow tips to the lateral lobes. Open pinewoods and mixed beech and pine; endemic to S France (restricted to the woods of the Causses). Fl 5–6.

Mirror Ophrys *Ophrys vernixia* (*O. speculum, O. ciliata*) A plant with remarkable flowers, often overlooked because of its small stature: stems 5–25cm. Sepals 7–10mm long, green, often striped with reddish-brown; petals reddish-brown 4–6mm long. Lip 3-lobed, 1.2–1.5cm long and slightly arched to form a concave surface. Lateral lobes broadly lanceolate to ovate, fringed like central lobe with long brown hairs. Lip surface gives the orchid its name (*vernixia* meaning varnished, *speculum* meaning mirror) and is shiny dark blue to deep violet (blackish in some Balearic populations), often with a fine yellow border. In open woodland, garrigue, old vineyards and olive groves on dry calcareous soils. In the Mediterranean but with gaps in its distribution, presumably caused by absence of the pollinator. Fl 2–4. **Iberian Ophrys** *O. vernixia* ssp *lusitanica* A taller species with faint striping, if any, on the sepals and orange-yellow petals. The lip is longer in proportion to the width than with above, arched lengthwise and across, and lacks the dense brown hairs; the border is yellow and hairless. In garrigue, poor grassland up to 500m, Estremadura and Algarve (central and S Portugal) and Cordoba (S Spain). Fl 3–5.

Bumble-bee Ophrys *Ophrys bombyliflora*   A small species, 5–20cm high, and the only one to produce new tubers from runners. Sepals green, upright or directed backwards, 9–12mm × 6–8mm; the middle one shorter and narrower than the laterals. Petals yellowish-green, hairy and triangular, 3–4mm long. Lip dark brown, deeply 3-lobed: middle lobe has globular appearance because of the turned-down margins; lateral-lobes hairy, downward-curving. Pattern faint. In open woodland, poor grassland and garrigue on base-rich soils; widespread in the W and central Mediterranean and east to Greece and W Turkey. Fl 2–5.

Woodcock Ophrys *Ophrys scolopax*   A variable species with stems 10–65cm tall and 2–12 flowers in an elongated inflorescence. Sepals narrowly elliptical to ovate, 7–15mm × 3–7mm from green through whitish to pink and brownish-red, petals pink to red, 3–7mm long, hairy. Lip chestnut brown, 6–15mm long, deeply 3-lobed with arched, rounded middle lobe, ellipsoidal in appearance with obvious forward-pointing appendage; lateral lobes densely hairy, turned downwards. The brownish-violet pattern surrounds the basal area, with a pale border extending to the lateral lobes and apex, sometimes forming enclosed loops. In open woodland, scrub, garrigue and poor grasslands on base-rich soils, in the W Mediterranean north into Massif Central and Dordogne. Fl 3–6. Ssp *apiformis* has very small, rounded lip 6–9mm long. In S Spain, Sicily and N Africa. Ssp *cornuta* differs mainly in having sepals that are directed backwards, especially the middle one; a smaller lip and remarkable lateral lobes extended into 'horns', 6–12mm long. In Gargano (Italy), otherwise mainly E Mediterranean.

THE *HOLOSERICA* GROUP

A convenient way to deal with these closely related species is to treat them as a group. *Ophrys holoserica* (formerly *O. fuciflora*) is the best known of these; the others often have very restricted distributions in the Mediterranean region.

Late Spider-orchid *Ophrys holoserica*   A very variable species, showing considerable differences in pattern even within the same population. Stems 10–50cm, sepals broad, 1–1.4cm × 6–9mm, pink or whitish, recurved or spreading; petals pink to red, 3–6mm long, hairy. Lip almost square, 9–16mm long with noticeable protuberances (about 3mm high) near the base and an upturned yellowish apex. Central lip area velvety dark brown or purplish-brown with longer marginal hairs; yellow-lipped forms known. Basal patch shiny violet to purple-brown, enclosed by yellowish border which extends to form an 'H' or more complicated pattern. In open woodland, poor grassland up to 1,400m, on calcareous soils; in W and central Europe, and the Mediterranean region. Fl 3–5. **Apulian Ophrys** *O. holoserica* ssp *apulica* differs from above in having lip 1.4–1.9cm long, which is strongly arched with edges turned down, giving a narrower appearance. Petals 6–8mm long and pattern extensive with several branches. In scrub, open pinewoods and grasslands to 600m; in S Italy (Mt Gargano southwards), and Sicily (rare). Fl 4–5. **Small Patterned Ophrys** *O. holoserica* ssp *parvimaculata* has sepals and petals usually yellowish-green, occasionally pale pink. Lip appears roundish, protuberances greenish on inner sides. Appendage 3-toothed, pattern simple 'H'-shaped extending towards the base. In scrub, grasslands and woods of Downy Oak; in S Italy: Apulia (Foggia, Lecce) and Basilicata. Fl 4–5.

Woodcock Ophr (le

Late Spider-orch (righ

Late Spider-orchi ssp *apulica* (left

Bumble-bee Ophry (left

Woodcock Ophrys ss *cornuta* (right

Spectacle Ophrys *Ophrys biscutella*   A plant with pink sepals, often strongly reflexed 1.3–1.8cm long; petals 7–9mm long. Lip trapeziform, widest in front, 1.25–1.5cm × 1.5–2cm, with a broad reddish-brown basal area surrounded by a pattern of 2 purplish spots with whitish outline joined with cross band. Stigma head 3–4mm across at the base. In open woodland and poor grassland, on limestone, to 1300m; in S Italy: in the west from Mt Pollino to Salerno; in the east, on Mt Gargano. Fl 4–5. **Tall Ophrys** *O. crabronifera* is similar to above but sepals and petals are greenish through whitish to deep pink. Lip broadly rounded, 1.1–1.5cm × 1.3–1.9cm, and reddish-brown with a lighter, more yellowish area near the base; the pattern is no more than a pair of purplish, white-bordered eyes, not enclosing the basal area. Stigma head 4–6mm across at the base. In open pinewoods and garrigue near the coast to 600m; on W coast of Italy, and in Corsica. Fl 4–5. **Kandia's Ophrys** *O. candica* is distinguished by its very small triangular petals (3–4mm long) and a lip with a squarish appearance. A broad white border surrounds the small brownish-violet basal area; the latter sometimes has lighter marbling. In pinewoods, garrigue and poor grassland up to 900m; southern Apulia (S Italy), S Sicily and E Mediterranean. Fl 5, later than Late Spider-orchid or Beaked Ophrys in the same area. **Beaked Ophrys** *O. oxyrrhynchos* has green (usually) or sometimes brownish sepals, 1.15–1.5cm long, petals hairy, triangular, 2.5–5mm. Lip 9.5–12mm × 1.4–1.8cm when spread; central brownish-red hairy ridge which carries an extended violet pattern with a white border. Towards the edges, lip colour lightens and surface becomes hairless. Appendage large (up to 4mm long), upright. In open oakwoods, garrigue up to 600m. In Sicily, and Apulia (S Italy). Fl 3–5. **Lacaita's Ophrys** *O. lacaitae* is closely related to Beaked Ophrys. Sepals green, petals tiny, less than a quarter of the sepal's length. Lip edges flared out giving it a triangular appearance, 1.45–1.85cm broad. Wide hairless yellow border occupies most of the surface, with a strong dark brown ridge at the centre and an 'H'-shaped pattern, brownish-violet with a white border. Appendage large, upright. In open scrub and grassland, sometimes on fairly acid soils, in Potenza, Salerno, Latina, Isernia provinces (S Italy), and N and SE Sicily, near the coast. Fl 4–6. **Bianca's Ophrys** *O. discors* (*O. biancae*) A small-flowered species related to Beaked Ophrys. Sepals whitish to pink, sometimes greenish, 1–1.4cm × 5–7mm; petals triangular, 2–3mm long. Lip 8–10.5mm × 1–1.4cm, with sides turned down; yellowish-hairy perimeter and brownish-red, and a ridged central area, with 'H'-shaped brownish-violet pattern narrowly bordered in white. Appendage up to 4mm. In open pinewoods and garrigue in Sicily (endemic to the south-east – Siracuse, Ragusa, Catania), Fl 3–4, 2–3 weeks before Beaked Ophrys.

THE *SPHEGODES* GROUP   The Sphegodes group shows a great variety in appearance which makes it difficult to classify: plants closer to *Ophrys sphegodes* than others are listed here as subspecies, but the separation is far from distinct.

Early Spider-orchid *Ophrys sphegodes*   A plant with variable flower dimensions. Sepals yellowish-green or whitish, with middle one erect or curved forward. Petals yellowish-green to brownish-red, often wavy-edged. Lip brown or reddish-brown, roundish to ovate, 6–16mm long, entire or slightly 3-lobed with basal protuberances and a greyish-blue pattern with a lighter border; occasional apochromic plants are found where the pattern extends to form a 'mirror' over the lip surface. In open woodland, maquis, garrigue, poor meadows, vineyards and olive groves to 1,300m, on base-rich soils; widespread in S Europe. Fl (1) 2–5 (6). Ssp *sicula* has greenish-white or pinkish sepals and short, slightly darker petals. Lip reddish-brown, entire, with bluish, white-bordered 'H' and hairy margins. In Sicily and S Italy. Fl 2–4. Ssp *panormitana* is very similar but generally has longer petals and a lip that is deeply 3-lobed. In Sicily and S Italy. Fl 2–4.

Tall Ophrys (le

Kandia's Ophrys (rig

Spectacle Ophrys (le

Beaked Ophr

(centr

Lacaita's Ophr

(righ

Bianca's Ophrys (le

Early Spider-orch

(centr

Early Spider-orch

ssp *sicula* (righ

Small Spider-orchid *Ophrys araneola*   A plant that is variously called ssp *litigosa* or ssp *tommasinii*. It is characterized by the small flowers with a yellow lip margin. Sepals green, 8–12mm × 4–6mm; petals strap-like, 5–8mm long, hairless. Lip reddish to blackish-brown, 6.5–9mm × 7.5–11.5mm with yellow hairless margin and grey-violet 'H'-shaped pattern. Protuberances and appendage usually absent. In France, Catalonia, and Italy into S Germany. Fl 2–5.

Gargano Ophrys *Ophrys garganica*   A plant that looks like a large version of Early spider-orchid ssp *provincialis* (a name sometimes given to variants from S France). Sepals green 10.5–13.5mm × 4–7mm; petals large, at least two-thirds the sepal's length, olive green to brown with a wavy edge. Lip roundish, entire or weakly 3-lobed, slightly convex with sides turned down and margins hairless; protuberances absent. Pattern 'H'-shaped with rear branches, violet-blue, with or without a whitish margin. In garrigue, poor grassland, and open pinewoods and oakwoods to 500m in Italy and Sicily. Fl 4–5.

Dark Ophrys *Ophrys incubacea*   This plant has green sepals, occasionally pinkish, 1–1.5cm long; petals strap-like, 6.5–9mm long, green or with reddish tinge and wavy margins. Lip has protuberances up to 3mm high; surface dark reddish to blackish-brown, with long, dark shaggy-hairy margins and a greyish-blue 'H'-shaped pattern, with a whitish border extending to the base of the protuberances. In open wood and scrub, garrigue and poor grassland to 1,000m; in W and central Mediterranean. Fl 4–6. *O. tarentina* is similar but the lip is fringed with yellowish hairs; protuberances absent or very small. In Taranto province, Italy. Fl 3–4.

Crescent Ophrys *Ophrys lunulata*   A plant with slender stems, 15–35cm, with sepals pink to reddish, occasionally whtish with middle one curving forward; the laterals down-pointed at an angle, 12.5–16mm × 5.5–7mm. Petals pink, linear-lanceolate, 8–11mm long, with hairs on margins or hairless. Lip reddish to dark brown with pale-yellowish margin, deeply 3-lobed, but with sides turned down so that it appears long and narrow: middle lobe hairy on margins with tooth-like appendage; lateral lobes densely hairy, turned backwards. Pattern bluish to brownish, often crescent-shaped with 'cup' downwards, sometimes extended towards base. In poor grassland, garrigue, open woodland, old vineyards and olive groves to 800m; in Sicily. Fl 3–4.

THE *ARACHNITIFORMIS* GROUP

Plants that have close links to the *Ophrys sphegodes* group, but with pink perianth segments, have been recorded as '*O. arachnitiformis*'. They do not really form a coherent unit but share characteristics, apart from colouring, with *O. sphegodes*, *O. araneola* and *O. incubacea*. Recent work has shown that, in terms of morphology and distribution, several distinct 'species' can be tentatively identified. Further work will inevitably increase their number.

Moris's Ophrys *Ophrys morisii*   A plant with sepals whitish to lilac-pink (occasionally green), slightly reflexed; petals orange to dark brownish-red, 6.5–10mm long, hairy with wavy margin. Lip dark brown and weakly 3-lobed; the lobes are more like 'haunches' than obviously separate. Pattern variable: essentially an 'H'-shape but much branched and extended; brownish-violet with a pale border. Protuberances usually absent; appendage triangular or 3-toothed. In open maquis, garrigue and poor grassland to 900m; in Sardinia. Fl 3–4. **Tyrrhenian Ophrys** *O. tyrrhena* is similar: some authorities amalgamate this species with the above. There are slight differences from above: petals lilac-pink or brown, sometimes with a dark edge, not wavy. Lip dark brown, undivided or weakly 3-lobed, but generally broader in appearance than in Moris's Ophrys, pattern 'H'-shaped but more restricted. On W Italian coast; endemic around Genoa, Livorno and Siena. Fl 3–5.

Splendid Ophrys *Ophrys splendida*   A plant that has whitish to lilac-pink sepals, 10.5–14.5mm × 5.5–8mm. Petals bicoloured; white to pink but with a hairless, wavy, yellowish or orange edge. Lip entire, convex, dark brown with a yellow edge; protuberances and appendage often absent. Pattern 'H'-shaped but 'arms' often in-filled to form a bluish shield with narrow pale border. In open woodland, poor grassland and garrigue up to 400m; in S France and coastal hills from the Rhône to Cannes. **Fl** 4–5.

Aveyron Ophrys *Ophrys aveyronensis*   A plant with pink-lilac to pink sepals, 1.2–1.6cm × 6–8mm; petals pink with an orange-red edge, 7–10mm long. Lip brown, entire or weakly 3-lobed, with short hairs around the margin, but usually lacking protuberances at the base. Pattern very variable from branched with a border to a broken grey-lilac marbling that covers the lip surface. Appendage small. In poor meadows and on roadsides; in S France, restricted to a few locations close to Causse du Larzac where it occurs in good numbers. **Fl** 5–6.

Siponto Ophrys *Ophrys sipontensis*   A striking species with sepals whitish to pink. Petals pink to brownish-red, broad, strap-shaped, with wavy edge like those of Dark Ophrys, to which this species bears a close relationship. Other similarities include a dark-brown lip with marginal fringe of coarse hairs; differences other than colour include larger flower size, pattern more strongly branched and protuberances absent or very small. In poor meadows, pasture and old quarries on fairly dry limestone soils; in S Italy, endemic to Gargano region around Manfredonia. **Fl** 4.

THE *BERTOLONII* GROUP

Bertoloni's Ophrys *Ophrys bertolonii*   A beautiful species, with stems 10–35cm and 2–8 flowers. Sepals erect to recurved, usually pink, occasionally green, 1.3–1.8cm × 6–8mm. Petals pink to red, narrow, pointed with fine hairs. Lip blackish-purple, hairy, with turned-down sides which give it a narrow appearance; the middle of the lip surface arches forwards with a shiny-blue (sometimes red) borderless shield-shape. In open wood and scrub, garrigue and poor grassland to 1,200m, on base-rich soils; in Balearics, SE France, S Italy, Sicily, and Corsica into the Balkan peninsula. **Fl** 3–6. Large stabilized populations have evolved in W and central Mediterranean regions from crosses between the above and members of the *Sphegodes* group; they are now even partly outside the present range of *O. bertolonii*. Although tepal colour is variable, they have in general retained from the *Sphegodes* ancestry the broad, strap-shaped petals and flattened, rather than forward-curving, lip surface. *O. bertoloniiformis* has sepals that are generally green; petals larger, and green with darker edge. Lip surface flattened, entire; pattern shield-shaped or ringed with or without a pale margin. In Italy on Mt Gargano. **Fl** 4–5. *O. promontorii* is similar to *O. bertoloniformis*, but has large, broad bluntended petals in olive green-brown. Protuberances are like those of Dark Ophrys. In S Italy from Foggia to Gargano. *O. catalaunica* has whitish to pink perianth segments and a small lip 1–1.4cm long, which is entire to 3-lobed. Pattern bluish to reddish, often with a white border. In Catalonia, although similar types occur in S France, Sicily and Dalmatia; some records for Bertoloni's Ophrys can be attributed to this 'species'. **Fl** 4–5. *O. benacensis* has pink tepals and a larger lip (1.2–1.6cm) with flattened surface that is entire or weakly 3-lobed. On the southern edge of the Alps (Como to Treviso); similar plants occur in France (Var). **Fl** 4–5.

Splendid Ophrys (le

Aveyron Ophr

(centr

Ophrys bertoloniforn

(righ

Siponto Ophrys (le

Bertoloni's Ophry

(righ

Ophrys promonto

(le

Ophrys catalaun

(rig

GLOSSARY

STEMS

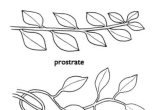

prostrate

with runners/stolons

erect and branched

ascending

twining

LEAVES

alternate – arranged
singly on the stem

basal – in a rosette

distichous – in two
distinct rows up
the stem

opposite – in pairs at
each node, one on
either side of stem

whorled – arising
from the stem at
the same level

decussate – each leaf
pair at right angles
to the pairs immediately
above and below

LEAF ATTACHMENTS

clasping – partly
enclosing stem

perfoliate – surrounding
stem which appears
to pass through it

connate – leaves joined at
base to surround stem

sessile – stalkless

peltate – stalk attached
to leaf 'centre'

long-stalked – joined
by a petiole to the stem

stipules – basal appendages
of a leaf or petiole

BLADE SHAPE

Leaf outline conforms, broadly to a range of geometric shapes all of which have botanical names: in the case of ovoid or elliptical leaves there are even terms which describe various ratios of length to breadth. Using 'ob' in front of a word, such as obcordate, means attached at the narrow end.

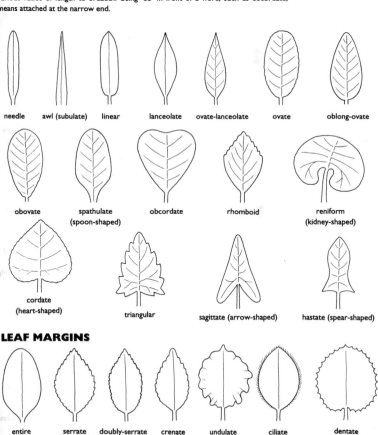

needle   awl (subulate)   linear   lanceolate   ovate-lanceolate   ovate   oblong-ovate

obovate   spathulate   obcordate   rhomboid   reniform
           (spoon-shaped)   (kidney-shaped)

cordate   triangular   sagittate (arrow-shaped)   hastate (spear-shaped)
(heart-shaped)

LEAF MARGINS

entire   serrate   doubly-serrate   crenate   undulate   ciliate   dentate
                                                                          (toothed)

LEAF DIVISION: INCISIONS AND LOBES

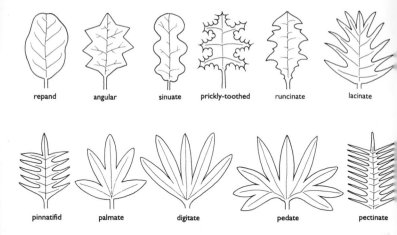

repand   angular   sinuate   prickly-toothed   runcinate   lacinate

pinnatifid   palmate   digitate   pedate   pectinate

DIVIDED INTO 'COMPLETE' LEAVES: LEAFLETS

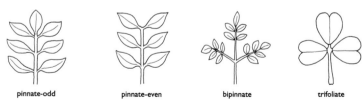

pinnate-odd   pinnate-even   bipinnate   trifoliate

LEAF APICES

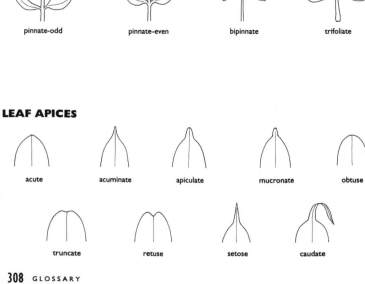

acute   acuminate   apiculate   mucronate   obtuse

truncate   retuse   setose   caudate

LEAF SURFACE-MAGNIFIED

glabrous

pilose

hirsute

woolly

farinose

verrucose

rugulose

papillose

INFLORESCENCE

spike – elongated flower cluster with stalkless (or nearly so) flowers

spadix – spike with a fleshy axis enclosed in a large bract (spathe)

secund-raceme – a one-sided raceme

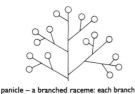

panicle – a branched raceme: each branch bears a raceme of flowers

umbel – a raceme where the axis has not elongated: flower stalks of different lengths arising at the same point

raceme – elongated flower cluster with stalked flowers arranged singly along stem

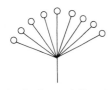

fascicle – like an umbel but with flower stalks of equal length

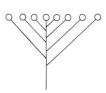

corymb – a raceme with lower flower stalks longer than those above which bring flower to the same level

CALYCES

separate sepals

fused sepals

urn-shaped

inflated

veined

two-lipped

FLOWERS IN HEADS

involucral bracts (involucre)

ligulate florets

tubular florets

ray florets (ligulate)
disc florets (tubular)

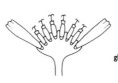

receptacle with receptacular bracts

lemma

palea

glume

flowers in spikelets (grasses)

ORCHID FLOWER STRUCTURES

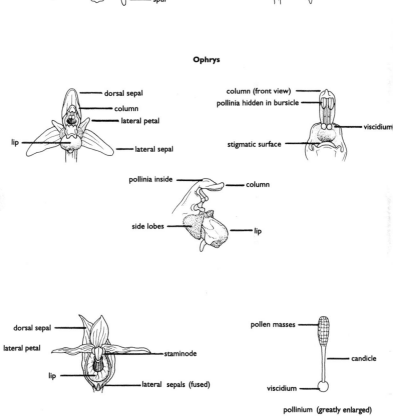

Orchis

dorsal sepal and lateral
petals form a 'hood'

lateral sepal

ovary

lip

spur

Serapias

sepals and lateral
petal form hood

hypochile

lip

epichile

ovary

Ophrys

dorsal sepal

column

lateral petal

lip

lateral sepal

column (front view)

pollinia hidden in bursicle

viscidium

stigmatic surface

pollinia inside

column

side lobes

lip

dorsal sepal

lateral petal

staminode

lip

lateral sepals (fused)

pollen masses

candicle

viscidium

pollinium (greatly enlarged)

INDEX